# Adobe
# Photoshop CS
## one-on-one™

# Adobe
# Photoshop CS
## one-on-one™

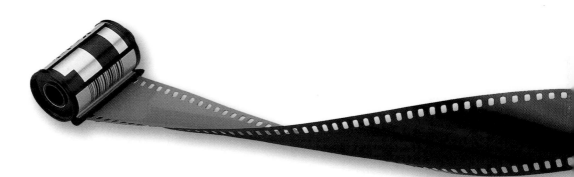

DEKE McCLELLAND

deke™
PRESS
O'REILLY®

BEIJING · CAMBRIDGE · FARNHAM · KÖLN · PARIS · SEBASTOPOL · TAIPEI · TOKYO

# Adobe Photoshop CS One-on-One

by Deke McClelland

Copyright © 2004 Type & Graphics, Inc. All rights reserved.
Printed in the United States of America.

This title is published by Deke Press in association with O'Reilly Media, Inc., 1005 Gravenstein Highway North, Sebastopol, CA 95472.

O'Reilly Media, Inc. books may be purchased for educational, business, or sales promotional use. Online editions are also available for most titles (*safari.oreilly.com*). For more information, contact O'Reilly's corporate/institutional sales department: 800-998-9938 or *corporate@oreilly.com*.

| | | | |
|---|---|---|---|
| **Managing Editor:** | Amy Thomas Buscaglia | **Interior Designer:** | David Futato |
| **Development Editors:** | Brett Johnson and Robert Luhn | **Video Director:** | Brian Maffitt |
| **Copyeditor:** | Susan Pink | **Video Editor:** | Denise Maffitt |
| **Indexer:** | Julie Hawks | **CD Management & Oversight:** | Barbara Ross |
| **Technical Editor:** | Robert Hinde | **CD Graphic Designers:** | Barbara Driscoll and Ellie Volckhausen |
| **Production Manager:** | Claire Cloutier | | |
| **Cover Designer:** | Emma Colby | **Video Compression:** | Carey Brady |
| | | **Video Interface Programmer:** | Marc Johnson |

**Print History:**

February 2004:   First edition.

Special thanks to Val Gelineau, John Bell, Dave Murcott, Laura Perrotta, Steve Holmes, Richard Lainhart, David Rogelberg, Stacey Barone, Laurie Petrycki, Mark Brokering, and Tim O'Reilly.

Deke Press, the Deke Press logo, the One-on-One logo, the *One-on-One* series designations, *Adobe Photoshop CS One-on-One*, and related trade dress are trademarks of Type & Graphics, Inc. The O'Reilly logo is a registered trademark of O'Reilly Media, Inc.

Adobe, Photoshop, Illustrator, and InDesign are either registered trademarks or trademarks of Adobe Systems Incorporated in the United States and other countries.

Many of the designations used by manufacturers and sellers to distinguish their products are claimed as trademarks. Where those designations appear in this book, and Deke Press was aware of a trademark claim, the designations have been printed in caps or initial caps.

While every precaution has been taken in the preparation of this book, the publisher and author assume no responsibility for errors or omissions, or for damages resulting from the use of the information contained herein.

This book was typeset using Adobe InDesign CS and the Adobe Futura, Adobe Rotis, and Linotype Birka typefaces.

0-596-00618-7
[C]     [1/05]

RepKover™
This book uses RepKover™, a durable and flexible lay-flat binding.

*To my sweet Elle, without whom I never could have done this.*

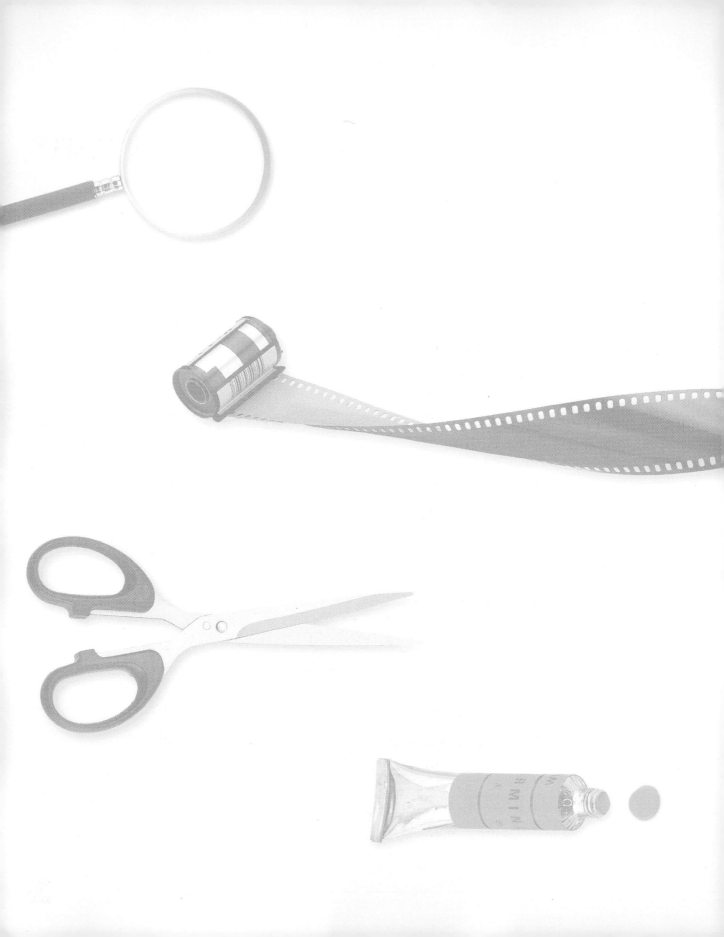

# CONTENTS

# PREFACE

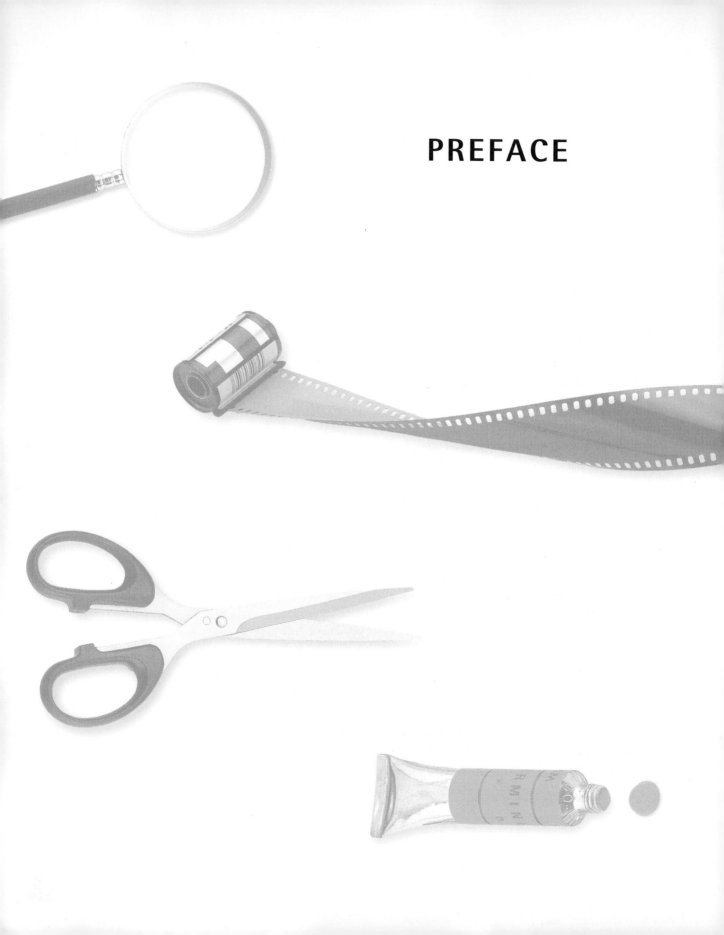

# HOW ONE-ON-ONE WORKS

Welcome to *Adobe Photoshop CS One-on-One*, the first in a series of highly visual, full-color titles that combine step-by-step lessons with two hours of video instruction. As the name *One-on-One* implies, I walk you through Photoshop just as if I were teaching you in a classroom or corporate consulting environment. Except that instead of getting lost in a crowd of students, you receive my individualized attention. It's just you and me.

I created *One-on-One* with three audiences in mind. If you're an independent graphic artist, designer, or photographer—professional or amateur—you'll appreciate the hands-on approach and the ability to set your own pace. If you're a student working in a classroom or vocational setting, you'll enjoy the personalized attention, structured exercises, and end-of-lesson quizzes. If you're an instructor in a college or vocational setting, you'll find the topic-driven lessons helpful in building curricula and creating homework assignments. *Adobe Photoshop CS One-on-One* is designed to suit the needs of beginners and intermediate users. But I've *seen* to it that each lesson contains a few techniques that even experienced users don't know.

## Read, Watch, Do

*Adobe Photoshop CS One-on-One* is your chance to master Photoshop under the direction of a professional trainer with nearly 20 years of computer design and imaging experience. Read the book, watch the videos, do the exercises. Proceed at your own pace and experiment as you *see* fit. It's the best way to learn.

Figure 1.

*Adobe Photoshop CS One-on-One* contains twelve lessons, each made up of three to six step-by-step exercises. Every book-based lesson includes a corresponding video lesson (*see* Figure 1), in which I introduce the key concepts you'll need to know to complete the exercises. Best of all, every exercise is project-based, culminating in a real-world project that you'll be proud to show others (*see* Figure 2). The exercises include insights and context throughout, so that you'll know not only what to do, but just as important, why you're doing it. My sincere hope is that you'll find the experience entertaining, informative, and empowering.

All the sample files required to perform the exercises are included on the CD-ROM at the back of this book. The CD also contains the video lessons. (This is a data CD, not a music CD or DVD. It won't work in a set-top device; it works only with a computer.) Don't lose or destroy this CD. It is as integral a part of your learning experience as the pages in this book. Together, the book, sample files, and videos form a single comprehensive training experience.

Figure 2.

# One-on-One Requirements

The main prerequisite to using *Adobe Photoshop CS One-on-One* is having Adobe Photoshop CS (also known as Photoshop 8) installed on your system. You may have purchased Photoshop CS as a stand-alone package (*see* Figure 3) or as part of Adobe's full Creative Suite. (Photoshop CS is included in both the Standard and Premium editions of the Creative Suite.) You *can* work through many of the exercises using Photoshop 7 and earlier versions, but some steps and some entire exercises will not work. All exercises have been fully tested with Adobe Photoshop CS but not with older versions.

*Adobe Photoshop CS One-on-One* is cross-platform, meaning that it works equally well whether you're using Photoshop installed on a Microsoft Windows-based PC or an Apple Macintosh. Any computer that meets the minimum requirements for Photoshop CS also meets the requirements for using *Adobe Photoshop CS One-on-One*. Specifically, if you own a PC, you will need an Intel Pentium III or 4 processor running Windows XP, or Windows 2000 with Service Pack 3. If you own a Mac, you need a PowerPC G3 processor or faster running Mac OS X version 10.2.4 or higher.

Figure 3.

Regardless of platform, your computer must meet the following minimum requirements:

- 256MB of RAM
- 650MB of free hard disk space (300MB for Photoshop and 350MB for the *One-on-One* project and video application files)
- Color monitor with 16-bit color video card
- 1,024 by 768-pixel monitor resolution
- CD-ROM drive

If your computer is better equipped—say, with a 1,600 by 1,200-pixel monitor and a DVD drive—all the better.

To play the videos, you will need Apple's QuickTime Player software version 5.0.2 or later. Many PCs and all Macintosh computers come equipped with QuickTime; if yours does not, you will need to install QuickTime using the link provided on the CD included with this book.

Finally, you will need to install the *One-on-One* sample files and video software from the CD that accompanies this book, as explained in the next section.

# One-on-One Installation and Setup

*Adobe Photoshop CS One-on-One* is designed to function as an integrated training environment. Therefore, before embarking on the lessons and exercises that await you, you must first install a handful of files onto your computer's hard drive. These are:

- QuickTime Player software (if it is not already installed)

- All sample files used in the exercises (270MB in all)

- Total Training video training software

- *One-on-One* Photoshop preference settings, color settings, and keyboard shortcuts (optional, but recommended)

All of these files are provided on the CD that accompanies this book. To install the files, follow these steps:

1. **Quit Photoshop.** If Photoshop is running on your computer, you must exit the program before you install the *One-on-One* files. On the PC, choose the **Exit** command from the **File** menu or press Ctrl+Q or Alt+F4. On the Mac, choose **Quit Photoshop** from the **Photoshop** menu or press ⌘-Q.

2. **Insert the One-on-One CD.** Remove the CD from the book and place it in your computer's CD or DVD drive.

3. **Open the Adobe Photoshop CS One-on-One Launchpad.** On the PC, the Launchpad window (*see* Figure 4) should open automatically. If it doesn't, choose **My Computer** from the **Start** menu and double-click the *AP1ON1* CD icon.

   On the Mac, double-click the *AP1ON1* CD icon on your computer's desktop. (The CD icon sports the blue-and-white Total Training logo, shown in Figure 5 on the facing page.) Then double-click the *AP1ON1 Installer* file icon to display the Launchpad window.

   ---

   The Launchpad includes everything you need to install files and play the videos. You perform these operations by clicking the buttons in the horizontal strip, just above the scissors.

   ---

Figure 4.

4. *If necessary, get QuickTime.* If your computer does not include the QuickTime Player software, make sure you're connected to the Internet, and then click the **Get QuickTime** button in the **Launchpad**. This takes you to Apple's QuickTime download page, *www.apple.com/quicktime/download*. Under **Download the free player**, select your operating system. Then scroll down to the bottom of the page, click the **Download QuickTime** button, and follow the installation instructions. (This site is subject to change; therefore, the specific installation process may change by the time you read this.)

5. *Install the Lesson files.* Back inside the **Launchpad** window, click the **Install Lesson Files** button to copy the sample files required to complete the exercises to your hard drive. Then click the **Desktop** button to install the files inside a folder on your computer's desktop, which is generally the easiest place to find them. (If you prefer to put the files elsewhere, click **Other Location** and specify where.) The copy operation may take a minute or two. When it completes, you'll find a new folder called *Lesson Files-PScs 1on1* on your desktop.

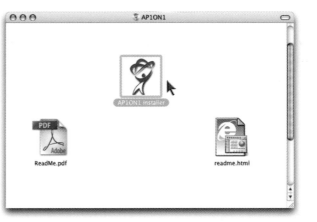

Figure 5.

6. *Install the video training software.* To watch the video lessons, you must install a small piece of software from the good folks who produced the videos, Total Training. To do so, click the **Install Training** button. A *Total Training* folder is added to the *Program Files* folder on the PC or the *Applications* folder on the Mac.

7. *Install the preference, color, and shortcuts settings.* *Preference settings* govern the way Photoshop behaves under certain circumstances. To ensure that you and I are on the same page during the exercises, it's necessary for our settings to match. Therefore, click the gray **Install Deke's Preferences** button located directly below the Install Training button. These files are very small, so the operation completes almost immediately.

If you're an experienced Photoshop user or an instructor using this book as a teaching resource, you may be perfectly happy with the Photoshop preferences you've established already. With this in mind, the Install Deke's Preferences button automatically backs up your preferences before it installs new ones. If, after completing the exercises in this book, you want to restore your original preferences, just click the **Restore Your Preferences** button.

8. *Close the Launchpad (or don't).* We're done with the Launchpad for now. If you like to keep your on-screen world tidy, close the Launchpad by clicking the **Exit** button in the top-left corner of the screen. But bear in mind, the Launchpad is your gateway to the videos. If you plan on watching them in the near future (as explained in "Playing the Videos" on page xviii), then feel free to leave the Lanchpad open.

9. *Start Photoshop.* On the PC, go to the **Start** menu and choose **Adobe Photoshop CS**. (The program may be located in the **Programs** or **All Programs** submenu, possibly inside an **Adobe** submenu.) On the Mac, go to the desktop level and choose **Go→Applications**. Then double-click the *Adobe Photoshop CS* folder and double-click the *Adobe Photoshop CS* application icon.

10. *Close the Welcome Screen.* After Photoshop launches, click the **Close** button in the **Welcome Screen** window to make it go away.

To make the Welcome Screen go away for good, turn off the **Show this dialog at startup** check box before clicking **Close**.

11. *Change the color settings to Best Workflow.* The color settings and keyboard shortcuts files will be installed, but you have to activate them manually to use them. On the PC, choose **Edit→Color Settings**; on the Mac, choose **Photoshop→Color Settings**. Inside the **Color Settings** dialog box, click the **Settings** pop-up menu and choose **Best Workflow** (*see* Figure 6). Then click the **OK** button. Now the colors of your images will match (or very nearly match) those shown in the pages of this book.

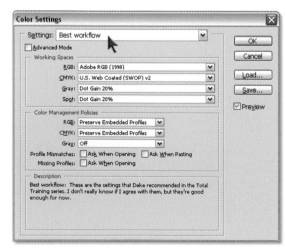

Figure 6.

12. ***Load the Deke Keys shortcuts.*** Choose **Edit→Keyboard Shortcuts**. Inside the **Keyboard Shortcuts** dialog box, click the **Set** pop-up menu and choose **Deke Keys** (*see* Figure 7). Then click **OK**. This loads keyboard shortcuts for some of Photoshop's most essential commands, including Image Size and Unsharp Mask.

13. ***Quit Photoshop.*** You've come full circle. On the PC, choose **File→Exit**; on the Mac, choose **Photoshop→Quit Photoshop**. Quitting Photoshop not only closes the program, it also saves the changes you made to the color settings and keyboard shortcuts.

Congratulations, you and I are now in sync. Just one more thing: If you use a Macintosh computer equipped with Mac OS X 10.3 (AKA, Panther), an important Photoshop keyboard shortcut gets interrupted by a system-level shortcut. To fix this problem, read the following important message. If you use a PC or another version of the Mac OS, feel free to skip this message and move along to the next section.

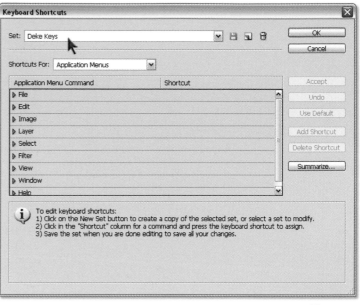

Figure 7.

Normally when using Photoshop for the Mac, pressing ⌘-Option-D chooses the Feather command (which softens selection outlines, as you'll learn in Lesson 4). But in OS X 10.3 (Panther), it hides the row of application icons at the bottom of the screen known as the "dock." To rectify this conflict, go to the desktop level and choose **System Preferences** from the  menu. Click **Show All**, then click the **Keyboard & Mouse** icon. Next, click the **Keyboard Shortcuts** button and scroll down the list of shortcuts until you find the one called **Automatically hide and show the Dock**. Click the existing shortcut, which reads ⌘⌥D, to highlight it. Then press Control-D (which appears as ^D, as in Figure 8). From now on, pressing Control-D will hide and show the dock, and ⌘-Option-D will choose Photoshop's Feather command.

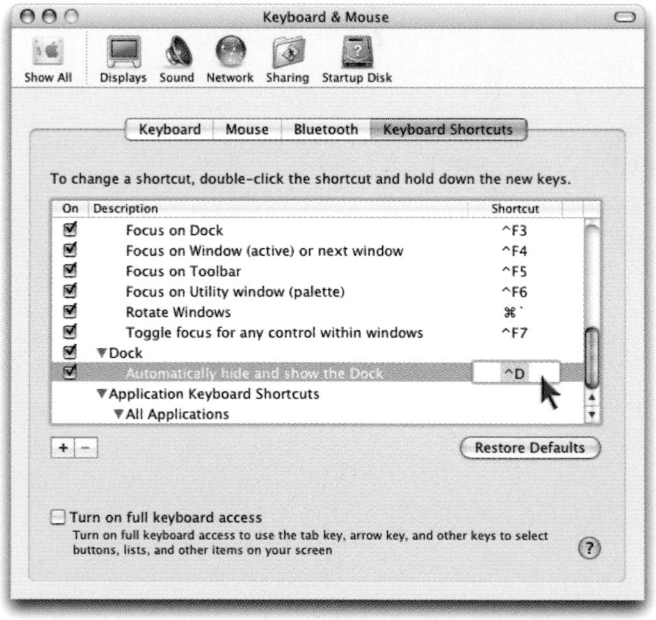

Figure 8.

## Playing the Videos

At the outset of each book-based lesson, I ask you to play the companion video lesson from the CD. Ranging from 8 to 12 minutes apiece, these video lessons introduce key concepts that make more sense when first *seen* in action.

The fact that we provide these videos on CD may lead you to question their playback quality. But you're in for a surprise. Produced by the computer training pioneers at Total Training, each video is rendered at a resolution of 640 by 480 pixels, roughly the equivalent of broadcast television. (If the video looks smaller on your computer monitor, bear in mind that your monitor packs in way more pixels than a TV.) Total Training employs state-of-the-art capture technology and gold-standard Sorenson compression to pack these vivid, legible videos onto the relatively small space available to a CD. This is video training at its finest.

To watch a video, do the following:

1. ***Insert the One-on-One CD.*** You must have the CD in your computer's CD drive to watch a video.

2. ***Open the Adobe Photoshop CS One-on-One Launchpad.*** Again, the Launchpad window opens automatically on the PC. On the Mac, double-click the *AP1ON1* icon and then double-click the *AP1ON1 Installer* file.

3. ***Click the Start Training button.*** Click the button on the far right side of the Launchpad, which is highlighted in Figure 9. Assuming that you've installed the Total Training video training software (*see* Step 6, page xv), you'll be treated to a startup screen (*see* Figure 10 on the facing page) followed by a welcoming message from your genial host, me.

Figure 9.

4. ***Switch to the video lesson you want to watch.*** The twelve videos are divided into four sets of three lessons each. To switch between sets and lessons, click the buttons in the upper-right corner of the player window (*see* Figure 11). Set 1 contains Lessons 1 through 3, Set 2 contains Lessons 4 through 6, and so on. You can watch any video lesson in any order you like. However, the video lessons make the most sense and provide the most benefit when watched at the outset of the corresponding book-based lesson.

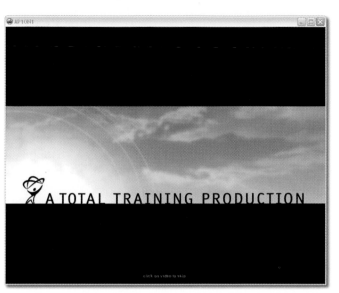

Figure 10.

---

The video is surrounded by an interface of navigational buttons and play controls. To hide the interface and view only the video, move your cursor inside the video image so it changes into a magnifying glass and then click. If you prefer to magnify the video so it fills your entire screen, press the Alt key (or Option on the Mac) and click. To restore the video to its normal state, with interface and all, click anywhere inside the video.

---

Use the play controls in the lower-left corner of the screen (*see* Figure 12) to play, pause, and fast-forward the video. You can also take advantage of the following keyboard shortcuts:

Figure 11.

- To pause the video, press the spacebar. Press the spacebar again to resume playing.

- To skip to the next lesson, press the ⇢ key. This is also a great way to play the next lesson after the current one ends. For example, after viewing the initial personal introduction, press the ⇢ key to play Video Lesson 1.

- To return to the previous lesson, press the ⇠ key. This can be a useful way to revisit one of my personal introductions after watching a lesson.

- Adjust the volume by pressing the + and – keys.

Finally, for help on any element of the interface, click the yellow-on-blue ❓ icon in the lower-right portion of the screen.

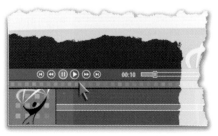

Figure 12.

## Structure and Organization

Each of the dozen lessons conforms to a consistent structure designed to impart skills and understanding through a regimen of practice and dialog. As you build your projects, I explain why you're performing the steps and why Photoshop works the way it does.

Each lesson begins with a broad topic overview. Turn the page, and you'll find a section called "About This Lesson," which lists the skills you'll learn and directs you to the video-based introduction.

Next come the step-by-step exercises, in which I walk you through some of Photoshop's most powerful and essential image-manipulation functions. A CD icon appears whenever I ask you to open a file from the *Lesson Files-PScs 1on1* folder that you installed on your computer's hard drive. To make my directions crystal clear, command and option names appear in bold type (as in, "choose the **Open** command"). Figure references appear in colored type. More than 600 full-color, generously sized figures diagram key steps in your journey so you're never left scratching your head, puzzling over what to do next. And when I refer you to another step or section, I tell you the exact page number to go to. (Shouldn't every book?)

### PEARL OF WISDOM

Along the way, you'll encounter the occasional "Pearl of Wisdom," which provides insights into how Photoshop and the larger world of digital imaging work. While this information is not essential to performing a given step or completing an exercise, it may help you understand how a function works or provide you with valuable context.

More detailed background discussions appear in independent sidebars. These sidebars shed light on the mysteries of color, bit depth, resolution, and other high-level topics that are key to understanding Photoshop.

A colored paragraph of text with a rule above and below it calls attention to a special tip or technique that will help you make Photoshop work faster and more smoothly.

Each lesson ends with a section titled "What Did You Learn?" which features a multiple-choice quiz. Your job is to choose the best description for each of 12 key concepts outlined in the lesson. Answers are printed upside-down at the bottom of the page.

## The Scope of This Book

No one book can teach you everything there is to know about Photoshop, and this one is no exception. If you're looking for information on a specific aspect of Photoshop, here's a quick list of the topics and features discussed in this book:

- Lesson 1: File management and navigation, including the File Browser, as well as the Contact Sheet II and PDF Presentation commands

- Lesson 2: Brightness and contrast adjustments, including the Levels, Curves, and Shadow/Highlight commands, as well as the Histogram palette

- Lesson 3: Color balance adjustments, including the Variations and Hue/Saturation commands, as well as Photoshop's support for Camera Raw

- Lesson 4: Selection tools, including the lasso, magic wand, and pen tools, as well as the Select menu and Paths palette

- Lesson 5: Ways to crop and transform an image, including the crop tool, as well as the Image Size, and Canvas Size commands

- Lesson 6: Painting and retouching, including the paintbrush, healing brush, and color replacement tools, as well as the Brushes and History palettes

- Lesson 7: Masking functions, including the Color Range and Extract commands, quick mask mode, and Channels palette

- Lesson 8: Focus adjustments, including the Unsharp Mask, Gaussian Blur, Median, and High Pass filters

- Lesson 9: Layer functions, including the Layers and Layer Comps palettes, the Layer menu, the Free Transform command, and Blending Options

- Lesson 10: Text and shape layers, including the type and shape tools, the Character and Paragraph palettes, and Warp Text

- Lesson 11: Layer styles and adjustment layers, including Drop Shadow, Bevel and Emboss, and the Styles palette

- Lesson 12: Print functions, including the Print with Preview, Color Settings, and Picture Package commands

To find out where I discuss a specific feature, please consult the Index, which begins on page 455.

---

This book does not cover the following: the Actions palette; the Filter Gallery, Liquify, Photomerge, Pixel Aspect Ratio, Online Services, and Save for Web commands; and Photoshop's companion product, ImageReady. If these topics are important to you, please consult one of my forthcoming *One-on-One* titles or a different training resource.

---

I now invite you to turn your attention to Lesson 1, "Open and Organize." I hope you'll agree with me that *Adobe Photoshop CS One-on-One*'s combination of step-by-step lessons and video introductions provides the best learning experience of any Photoshop training resource on the market.

LESSON

1

# OPEN AND ORGANIZE

FEAR IS a great motivator. And the good folks at Adobe must agree. Otherwise, why would they have created Photoshop, a vast and complicated program with scores of redundant functions and even a few deliberately misleading commands, all devoted to the seemingly prosaic task of changing the color of a few pixels? And why is Photoshop so intent upon revealing the complexities of color corrections and brushstrokes (as symbolically illustrated in Figure 1-1) instead of hiding them, the way other computer applications do?

The answers are as numerous as Photoshop's functions. In fact, as much as I like Photoshop, I'm the first to admit, virtually every feature requires a separate defense. But the fact is, the pain of learning this vast and at times ungainly behemoth is its own reward. Mastering a powerful tool like Photoshop focuses the mind. It toughens the spirit. And finally, it transforms you into an image warrior.

This book is here to take you on that journey of pain and reward. Sure, there may be occasional times when you'll wonder if Photoshop is Adobe's idea of the Nine Circles of Hell. But just as Dante emerged from the lowest circle by climbing down the very Devil himself, we'll conquer Photoshop by descending directly into it and coming out the other side. We will make peace with Photoshop through understanding, the understanding borne by knowledge, the knowledge wrought by experience. Take heart, kindred spirit: mastery will be yours.

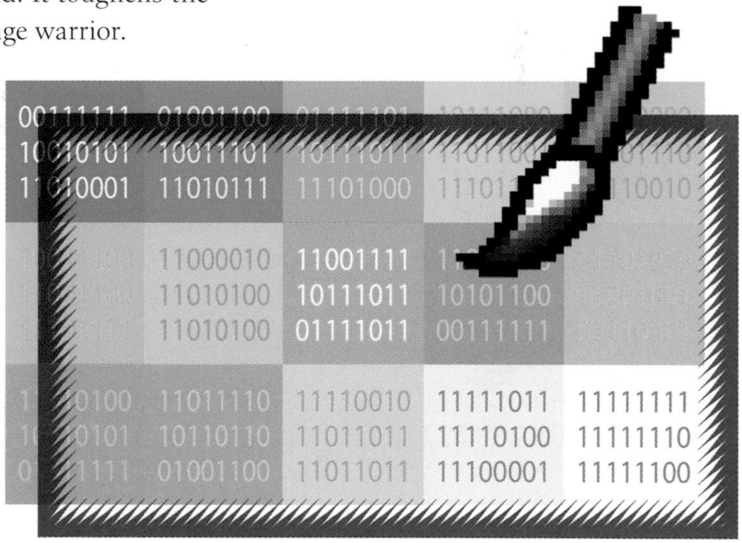

Figure 1-1.

# ABOUT THIS LESSON

## Project Files

Before beginning the exercises, make sure that you've installed the lesson files from the CD. You do this from the **Launchpad** by clicking the **Install Lesson Files** button, as explained in Step 5 on page xv of the Preface. This should result in a folder called *Lesson Files-PScs 1on1*, which contains a subfolder for each lesson in this book. We'll be working with the files and folders in the *Lesson 01* subfolder.

Before you can use the vast array of tools and functions inside Photoshop, you must know how to open an image, move around inside it, and organize your image files on disk. As glad fortune would have it, that's precisely what this lesson is about. In the following exercises, you'll learn how to:

- Open an image on screen . . . . . . . . . . . . . . . . page 5
- Use Photoshop's File Browser to organize your ever-expanding library of digital images . . . . . . . page 10
- Determine how a photograph was captured; add copyright information and keywords . . . . . . page 17
- Rename multiple images in one fell swoop. . . . . . page 23
- Print a contact sheet of thumbnails of all images in a folder . . . . . . . . . . . . . . . . . . . . . . page 26
- Create a slideshow for others to view . . . . . . . . page 30

## Video Lesson 1: Navigation

Another topic you should get under your belt right away is navigation. Not *doing* anything to an image, mind you, just moving around inside it: magnifying a portion of an image so you can do detail work, panning to the part of the image you want to modify, or stepping back to take in the whole thing.

Navigation is the subject of the first video lesson included on the CD. To view this video, insert the CD, click the **Start Training** button, and then select **1, Navigation** from the Lessons list on the right side of the screen. The movie lasts 8 minutes and 57 seconds, during which time you'll learn about the tools and keyboard shortcuts listed below:

| Operation | Windows shortcut | Macintosh shortcut |
| --- | --- | --- |
| Zoom in or out | Ctrl+plus, Ctrl+minus | ⌘-plus, ⌘-minus |
| Zoom in with magnifying glass | Ctrl+spacebar-click in image | ⌘-spacebar-click in image |
| Zoom out with magnifying glass | Alt+spacebar-click in image | Option-spacebar-click in image |
| Magnify a region | Ctrl+spacebar-drag around region | ⌘-spacebar-drag around region |
| Scroll up or down | Page Up, Page Down | Page Up, Page Down |
| Scroll to the right or left | Ctrl+Page Up, Ctrl+Page Down | ⌘-Page Up, ⌘-Page Down |
| Scroll with the hand tool | spacebar-drag in image window | spacebar-drag in image window |
| Fill the screen with the image | F | F |
| Hide or show toolbox and palettes | Tab | Tab |
| Hide or show right-hand palettes | Shift+Tab | Shift-Tab |
| Show the menu bar in full-screen mode | Shift+F | Shift-F |

# What Is Photoshop?

Photoshop, as the fellow says, is an *image editor.* That is to say, it lets you open an image—whether captured with a scanner or a digital camera or downloaded from the Web—and change it. You can change the brightness and contrast, adjust the colors, move things around, sharpen the focus, retouch a few details, and scads more. When you're finished, you can save your changes, print the result, attach it to an email, whatever. If you can imagine doing a thing to an image, Photoshop can do it. It's that capable.

But it doesn't end there. You can also use Photoshop to enhance artwork that you've scanned from a hand drawing or created with another graphics program. If you're artistically inclined, you can start with a blank document and create a piece of artwork from scratch. If that's not enough, Photoshop offers a wide variety of illustration tools, special effects, and text formatting options, from placing type on a path to checking your spelling.

# Opening an Image

Like every other major application on the face of the planet, Photoshop offers an Open command under the File menu. Not surprisingly, you can use this command to open an image saved on your hard disk or some other media. But that's the sucker's route. Photoshop offers a much better way to open files using its File Browser. Here's how to use it.

1.  *Choose File→Browse.* The command appears in Figure 1-2. You can also press Ctrl+Shift+O (⌘-Shift-O on the Mac). Either way, you get the immense **File Browser** window.

2.  *Navigate to the Sault Locks folder.* The File Browser is divided into four main panels, three on the left and the large *thumbnail browser* on the right, each labeled black in Figure 1-3 on the following page. (Blue-green labels show ancillary options.) The top-left panel is the *folder tree,* which lets you navigate to the folder on your hard disk or other media that contains the image or images you want to open. Scroll up and down the tree (so-called because it branches off into folders and subfolders) until you see the *Lesson Files-PScs 1on1* folder. On the PC, click the plus sign (⊞) in front of the folder to expand it; on the Mac, click the "twirly" triangle (▶).

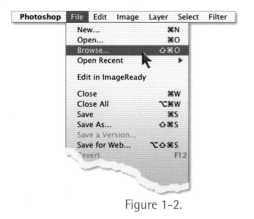

Figure 1-2.

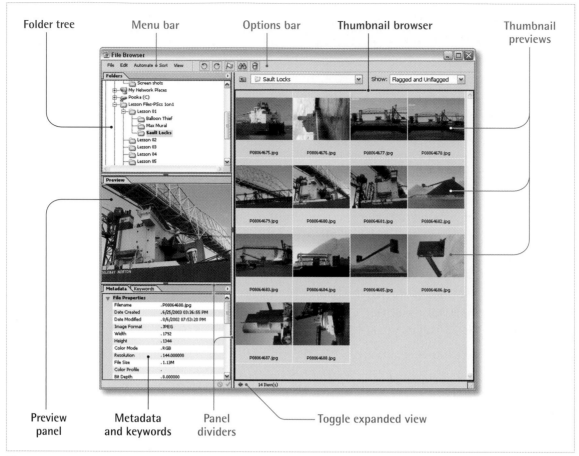

Folder tree    Menu bar    Options bar    Thumbnail browser    Thumbnail previews

Preview panel    Metadata and keywords    Panel dividers    Toggle expanded view

Figure 1-3.

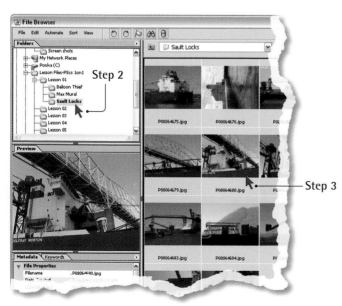

Figure 1-4.

Then click the ⊞ or ▶ in front of the *Lesson 01* folder. Finally you'll find a folder called *Sault Locks*. Click that folder to fill the thumbnail browser with a collection of 14 tiny industrial photos, as in Figure 1-3.

3. *Click a thumbnail.* Locate and click the image called *P08064680.jpg* in the thumbnail browser, highlighted in Figure 1-4. (These images were captured and automatically named by a digital camera, an Olympus E02N, hence the cryptic names.) This activates the image and displays a larger **Preview** panel on the left side of the File Browser window.

To view more details, enlarge the Preview panel by dragging the vertical and horizontal panel dividers that separate the four panels.

4. ***Double-click the image preview.*** Alternatively, you can double-click the selected thumbnail or choose **File ›Open** (Ctrl+O on the PC, ⌘-O on the Mac). Photoshop opens the image in a separate window.

---

When you open an image, Photoshop leaves the File Browser window open in the background. To close the File Browser as you open an image, press the Alt key (Option on the Mac) while performing any of the operations described above.

---

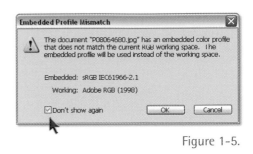

Figure 1-5.

5. ***Disable the color warning.*** Assuming you selected the Color Settings options I suggested in Step 11 of the Preface (see page xvi), Photoshop greets you with a warning that you are about to open an image in the sRGB color space—widely employed by midrange digital cameras and inkjet printers—as opposed to Photoshop's preferred working space, Adobe RGB. Not to worry. Just check **Don't Show Again** (see Figure 1-5) so Photoshop will stop bugging you in the future. Then click **OK**.

Photoshop loads the photograph and displays it in a new image window (see Figure 1-6), ready for your edits.

Asterisk means Photoshop is displaying image in sRGB color space

Figure 1-6.

The title bar in Figure 1-6 lists the name of the image and magnification level followed by a color notation, **RGB/8***. These six characters convey three pieces of information. **RGB** tells you that you're working with the three primary colors of light—red, green, and blue—the standard for scanners, digital cameras, and the Web. The next item, **/8**, lets you know the image contains 8 bits (one byte) of data for each of the red, green, and blue color channels. I'll spare you the math, but that means the photo can contain as many as 16.8 million colors, the same number a typical state-of-the-art computer screen can display. Finally, the asterisk (*) alerts you that you're working in a color environment other than the one you specified in the Color Settings dialog box (sRGB instead of Adobe RGB, as you approved in Step 5). The upshot: Photoshop is aware of this image's special color conditions and has bent like a reed in the wind to accommodate them. In other words, rejoice, for Photoshop is doing everything in its power to deliver brilliant and accurate color.

# Interface and Image Window

As with any modern computer application, bossing around Photoshop is a matter of clicking and dragging inside the program's interface. Labeled in the figure below, the key elements of the Photoshop CS interface are listed as follows in alphabetical order:

- **Cursor:** The cursor (sometimes called the *pointer*) is your mouse's on-screen representative. It moves as your mouse moves and changes to reflect the active tool or operation. Keep an eye on it and you'll have a better sense of where you are and what you're doing.

- **Docking well:** That gray bar in the upper-right corner of the screen is the docking well. Drag a palette tab and drop it into the well to move it out of view. Click a tab inside the well to temporarily display the palette. Drag a tab out of the well to restore a freestanding palette.

- **Image window:** Each open image appears inside a separate window, thus permitting you to open multiple images at once. In Photoshop, the image window is your canvas. This is where you paint and edit with tools, apply commands, and generally wreak havoc on an image.

- **Menu bar:** Click a name in the menu bar to display a list of commands. Choose a command by clicking on it. A command followed by three dots (such as New...) displays a window of options called a *dialog box*. Otherwise, the command works right away.

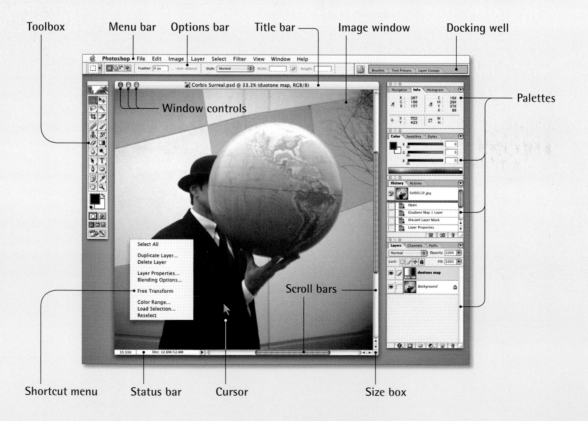

Toolbox  Menu bar  Options bar  Title bar  Image window  Docking well

Window controls

Palettes

Shortcut menu  Status bar  Cursor  Size box

Scroll bars

- **Options bar:** The settings here modify the behavior of the active tool. The options bar is *context sensitive*, so you see a different set of options each time you switch to a different tool. If the options bar somehow disappears, you can restore it by pressing the Enter key (Return on the Mac).

- **Palettes:** A palette is a floating window of options that remains visible on screen regardless of what you're doing. Move a palette by dragging the title bar at the top of the palette. Many palettes contain multiple panels. To switch between panels, click one of the wedge-shaped tabs below the title bar.

---

You can customize the arrangement of panels by dragging a tab from one palette and dropping it into another. Drag a tab onto the bottom of a palette to attach one palette to the bottom of another, a technique Adobe calls *docking* (even though it has nothing to do with the docking well).

---

- **Scroll bars:** Only so much of an image can fit inside the image window at once. The scroll bars let you pan the image horizontally or vertically to display hidden areas. If a scroll bar is empty, you are zoomed out far enough to see the entire width or height of the image. For more information on zooming and scrolling, watch Video Lesson 1, "Navigation," on the CD (see page 4).

- **Shortcut menu:** Under Windows, right-click the mouse to display a shortcut menu of options for the active tool. If your Macintosh mouse doesn't have a right mouse button (Apple's mice don't), press the Control key and click. Photoshop provides shortcut menus in the image window and inside many palettes. When in doubt, right-click.

- **Size box:** Drag the bottom-right corner of the image window to make it bigger or smaller.

---

If you own a Mac and you're using an Apple mouse, drop everything and shell out the $30 for a two-button mouse. It makes life way easier. You'll never look back.

---

- **Status bar:** At the bottom of the screen (or at the bottom of each image window on the Mac) is a status bar that sports a zoom value, the file size, a preview box, and a pop-up menu of various preview options. (If you can't find the status bar, choose **Window→ Status Bar**.) Under Windows, you also see a line of text telling you how to use the active tool.

- **Title bar:** Each open image is topped off by a title bar that lists the name of the last-saved version of the image. If you haven't saved the image, it may appear as *Untitled*. Click the title bar to make an image window active so you can edit its contents; double-click to display the image full screen; drag the title bar to move an image out of the way.

- **Toolbox:** The toolbox provides access to Photoshop's drawing, editing, and selection tools, as well as common screen and color controls. Click an icon to select a tool; then use the tool in the image window. A small triangle shows that multiple tools share a single box, or *slot*. Click and hold a slot to display a flyout menu of alternate tools. Or press the Alt key (Option on the Mac) and click a slot to cycle between tools.

---

Press the Tab key to hide the toolbox, options bar, and all palettes. Press Tab again to bring them back. (If Tab does not summon the toolbox, choose **Window→ Tools**.) To hide or show the palettes independently of the toolbox and options bar, press Shift+Tab.

---

- **Window controls:** Whether you're working on a Mac or PC, you'll see three controls in the title bar that let you hide, size, and close an image window. The Mac controls are on the left, the Windows controls are on the right.

## Organizing Your Photos

As fortune would have it, the File Browser lets you do more than just open image files. In many regards, it's a full-blown image manager, letting you review images, change their display order, rotate them, move them to different folders, and flag them for later consideration or follow-up. If you just have a few dozen images lying around your hard drive, this may seem like overkill. But if you have a few hundred, thousand, or hundred thousand, it's an absolute necessity.

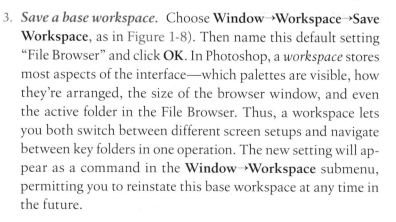

PEARL OF WISDOM

That said, the File Browser does have its limitations. It is not a cataloging utility, so you can't use it to generate independent indexes of vast image libraries archived to a CD or other external media. The File Browser is best suited to managing folders of images on local hard drives or servers, as well as gathering images into folders for later archiving.

To get a sense of what the File Browser can do, including resizing and prioritizing thumbnails, try the following steps:

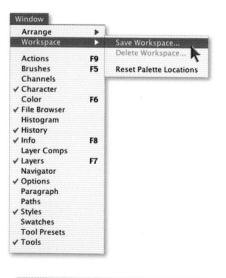

Figure 1-7.

1. *Open the File Browser.* As before, you can choose **File→Browse**. Or for quicker access, click the folder-and-magnifying-glass button just to the left of the docking well in the options bar (see Figure 1-7).

---

The File Browser button is a *toggle*, meaning that it alternatively opens the File Browser and closes it. If the File Browser window is in front, you can close it from the keyboard by pressing Ctrl+W (⌘-W on the Mac), the same keystroke combination used to close image windows.

---

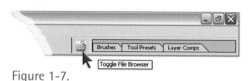

2. *Navigate to the Sault Locks folder.* It's inside the *Lesson 01* folder inside the *Lesson Files-PScs 1on1* folder.

3. *Save a base workspace.* Choose **Window→Workspace→Save Workspace**, as in Figure 1-8). Then name this default setting "File Browser" and click **OK**. In Photoshop, a *workspace* stores most aspects of the interface—which palettes are visible, how they're arranged, the size of the browser window, and even the active folder in the File Browser. Thus, a workspace lets you both switch between different screen setups and navigate between key folders in one operation. The new setting will appear as a command in the **Window→Workspace** submenu, permitting you to reinstate this base workspace at any time in the future.

Figure 1-8.

4. *Enlarge the thumbnails.* The File Browser lets you change the size of thumbnails. By default, they're set to Large, which permits a maximum height or width of 128 pixels. The problem is, with screen resolutions on the rise, 128 pixels just ain't what they used to be. In fact, by modern standards, Large is quite small. To make the thumbnails larger, so that you can truly make sense of an image without opening it, choose **View→Custom Thumbnail Size** in the File Browser, as shown in Figure 1-9.

---

If Custom Thumbnail Size isn't quite the right size, choose **Edit→Preferences**, again in the File Browser. Then enter a new **Custom Thumbnail Size** value (by default, 256 pixels) and click **OK**. I recommend that you experiment with the value to find a size that lets you see three or four images across.

---

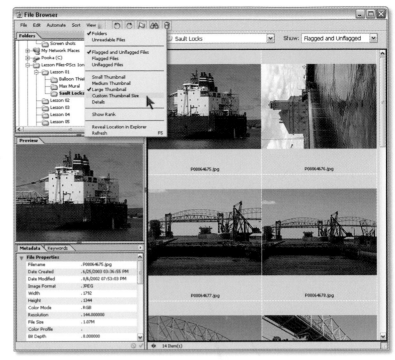

Figure 1-9.

5. *Increase the thumbnail space.* One of the downsides of larger thumbnails is that you can see fewer of them at a time. The solution? Increase the size of the File Browser. Here's how:

   - First, free up some screen space by pressing Shift+Tab to temporarily hide the palettes along the right side of the screen. (If you later need the palettes, press Shift+Tab again to bring them back.)

   - Next, drag the size box in the lower-right corner of the File Browser window to expand the window so it fills the screen. (On the Mac, clicking the green plus button in the upper-left corner of the window does much the same thing.)

---

If you need still more room, you can turn over the entire File Browser to the thumbnails by clicking the double-arrow button at the bottom of the File Browser window (see **Figure 1-10**). Photoshop calls this the *expanded view*. Click the button again when you want to bring back the left-hand panels.

---

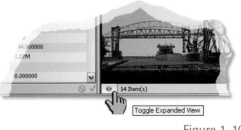

Figure 1-10.

6. *Save this special workspace.* Again, choose **Window→Workspace→Save Workspace**. Name this setting "Big Thumbnails" and click **OK**. Now you can return to this expanded thumbnail view anytime you like.

7. *Select all sideways images.* Four of the images in the *Sault Locks* folder are lying on their sides. Few digital cameras are smart enough to know when you rotate the camera to take a vertical shot, so as a rule, all images come in horizontally. No problem, the File Browser can turn them upright. To select the four images, do the following in the order indicated in Figure 1-11:

- Click the last thumbnail (labeled ❶ in the figure).

- Press the Shift key and click the third-from-last thumbnail (labeled ❷ below). This selects the range of thumbnails.

- The remaining sideways thumbnail is separated from the other three. So press the Ctrl key (⌘ on the Mac) and click it (❸ below).

Another way to select multiple thumbnails is to press Shift while pressing one of the arrow keys (↑, ↓, ←, →). With each press, the File Browser adds a single thumbnail to the selection.

❸ And finally, Ctrl-click (⌘-click) here

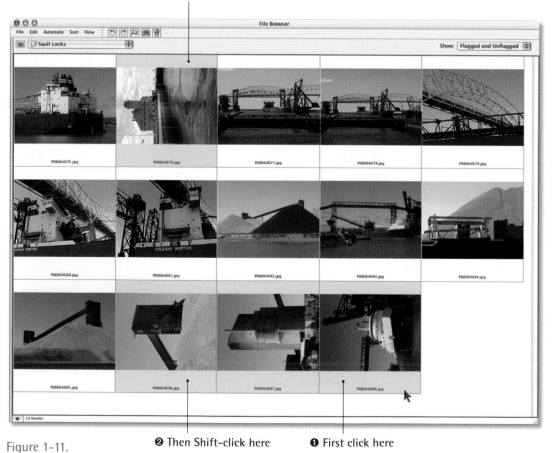

Figure 1-11.　❷ Then Shift-click here　❶ First click here

8. ***Stand the thumbnails upright.*** Just to the right of the File Browser's menu bar is a group of five buttons. The second button in (see Figure 1-12) rotates thumbnails 90 degrees clockwise. Click it and all the selected images snap upright.

9. ***Address the rotation warning.*** If this is the first time you've rotated a thumbnail in the File Browser, you'll see an alert message (see Figure 1-13) that tells you that the rotation is applied not to the source image, but only to the thumbnail. (This rotation information is saved to a special file that only Photoshop knows about. See the sidebar "The File Browser and Its Slippery Cache" on page 15 for more info.) That's a good thing because it means Photoshop is protecting your original images from unnecessary or inadvertent alterations. For now, check **Don't Show Again** and click **OK**. Tiny rotation icons (↻) accompany each rotated thumbnail.

Figure 1-12.

---

To rotate a selected thumbnail clockwise from the keyboard, press the Ctrl or ⌘ key with the right bracket, ]. Press Ctrl+[ or ⌘-[ to rotate the thumbnail counterclockwise. To apply a rotation permanently to an image, choose **Edit→Apply Rotation** in the File Browser. Photoshop will alert you that this action requires resaving the file.

---

Figure 1-13.

10. ***Prioritize thumbnails by dragging them.*** You can sort thumbnails by filename, creation date, and other attributes by choosing commands from the File Browser's Sort menu. But new to Photoshop CS, you can also create custom sorts by dragging selected thumbnails in the browser window. Try dragging the rotated thumbnails to the beginning of the list, as shown in Figure 1-14 on the next page. A thick vertical line shows where the thumbnails will land.

PEARL OF ⦿ WISDOM

Note that the File Browser does not have its own Undo command. If you want to reverse an operation, such as rotating or sorting thumbnails, you have to do it manually.

---

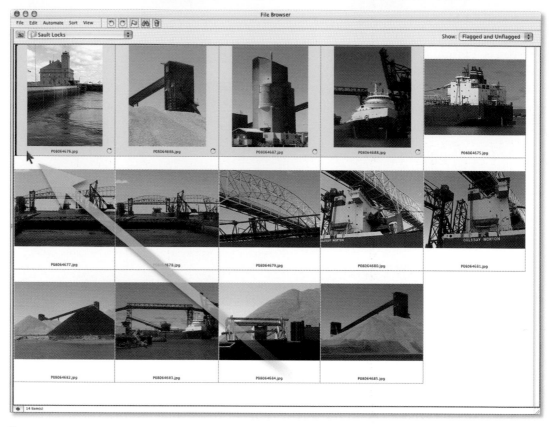

Figure 1-14.

Okay, so that's not such good news, but this is: Photoshop automatically saves your manual thumbnail reorganization as a custom sort state. That means you can choose **Sort→Filename** to alphabetize the thumbnails, and then restore your manual sort state by choosing **Sort→Custom**. I must say, this is one smart program.

11. *Flag important images.* The next step is to decide which images you like best and flag them for later development. I selected the five images highlighted in Figure 1-15 on page 16, but you can select any you like. (Please don't say you don't like any of them. That would hurt my feelings.) Then click the flag icon to the right of the rotate buttons at the top of the File Browser, or press Ctrl+' (⌘-' on the Mac). Tiny ⚑ icons appear in the bottom-right corner of each thumbnail.

To view just the flagged thumbnails, choose **Flagged Files** from the **Show** pop-up menu in the upper-right corner of the File Browser. From here, you can also view just the unflagged thumbnails by choosing the **Unflagged Files** command. The active command reverts to **Flagged and Unflagged** whenever you switch folders.

In many ways, the File Browser behaves like your operating system's file manager (called Windows Explorer on the PC and the Finder on the Mac). For example, if you click a thumbnail's filename, such as *P08064683.jpg* below, the File Browser invites you to enter a new name. Right-click in the thumbnail browser to display a shortcut menu that, among other things, lets you create a new folder. Press the Delete key to dump a selected image in the trash. Through it all, Photoshop magically tracks your changes, never once asking you to save your work.

This may lead you to believe that every change you make is permanent and will be recognized outside Photoshop by the operating system and other programs. But in fact, some actions are recorded in ways that only Photoshop can recognize and even it sometimes ignores. Worse, Photoshop can lose track of your changes, requiring you to redo your work from scratch.

For the record, here are some permanent changes you can make in the File Browser that all applications will recognize:

- Renaming or deleting a file.

- Creating or renaming a folder.

- Dragging a file from one folder to another.

Temporary changes that Photoshop saves to its proprietary (and sometimes unreliable) cache files include:

- Generating a thumbnail preview. This happens whenever you view a folder full of images for the first time or enlarge the thumbnails to Custom size.

- Rotating a photograph.

- Assigning a flag to an image.

- Modifying the sort order.

Permanent changes are 100-percent safe. Temporary changes are maintained only if you move and rename files and folders exclusively inside the File Browser. Photoshop tracks temporary changes based on the *path*, or specific location, of a file. If that path changes even slightly without Photoshop knowing about it—say, if you rename or move files from the desktop—Photoshop loses track of the file and the temporary change is lost.

For example, suppose you copy a folder of images to a CD or other media outside Photoshop. The copied folder is on a different disk, therefore its path is different, therefore Photoshop can't see your temporary changes. It can still read the files, but it can't tell whether they're rotated, flagged, and so on. Your work is gone, you have to start over, 15 minutes of your life must be relived inside the File Browser.

What's a savvy user to do? What Photoshop ought to be doing on its own—export the cache to the same folder as the images, as documented in Step 14 on page 17. This ensures that Photoshop can find the cache no matter what you name a folder or where you move it. But here's the trick: You must export the cache for every single folder you work on. And you must repeat the operation every time you perform a transient change.

Net result: **File→Export Cache** is your Save command inside the File Browser. Get in the habit of using it and you'll never have to redo another thumbnail, rotation, flag, or sort. The part of you that doesn't want to spend all day in the File Browser will thank you.

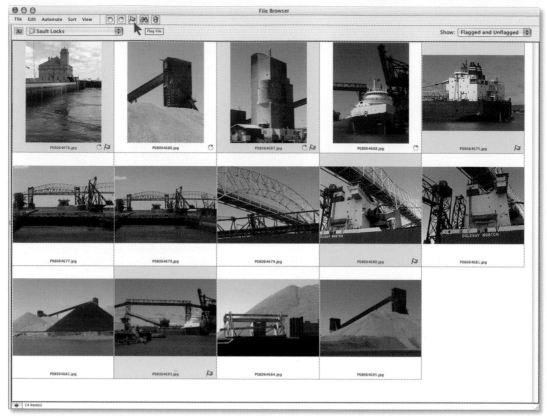

Figure 1-15.

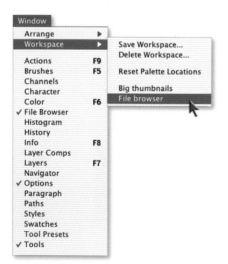

Figure 1-16.

12. ***Restore the base workspace.*** In the next step, you'll need to access the folder tree. You could click the expanded view button (Step 5) to summon this and other panels. But if you also want to restore the thumbnail sizes, palettes, and File Browser configuration you had way back in Step 3, choose **Window→ Workspace→File browser** from the Photoshop menu bar (see Figure 1-16). Just like that, the File Browser screen is restored to the nice, clean setup you saved in Step 3.

13. ***Add a folder to favorites.*** If you want to view the images in a specific folder on a regular basis, save the folder as a favorite. Right-click on the **Sault Locks** folder in the folder tree (press Control and click on the Mac) and choose **Add Folder to Favorites**, as shown in Figure 1-17 on the facing page.

---

It's all very well and good to collect favorite folders. But where does Photoshop keep them? Press the End key or scroll all the way to the bottom of the folder tree. There you'll find a yellow star labeled **Favorite Folders**. Click the ⊞ or twirly ▶ to open it up and you should find an alias to the **Sault Locks** folder inside. Any other favorites you add will appear here as well.

---

14. ***Export the cache to the local folder.*** If you spend any amount of time working in the File Browser, it's a good idea to back up your work. By default, Photoshop automatically stores File Browser data—rotations, sort order, flagged thumbnails, and so on—to secret *cache files* buried deep in your hard drive. To back up these files in the same folder that contains your images, choose **File→Export Cache** in the File Browser (see Figure 1-18). A second or two later, Photoshop tells you that the cache exported successfully. There are actually three cache files in all. The one named *AdobeP8M.md0* contains numerical *metadata*, such as rotation and flag information; the others, *AdobeP8P.tb0* and *AdobeP8T.tb0*, contain all generated sizes of the thumbnail previews.

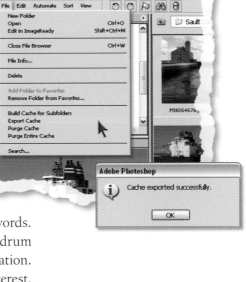

Figure 1-17.

## Using Metadata

The prefix *meta* comes from the ancient Greek preposition meaning (among other things) *after*. Nowadays, based in part on English critic Samuel Johnson's derisive characterization of fanciful 17th-century poets as "metaphysical" (by which he meant contrived), it has come to mean *beyond*. And so it is, *metadata* is data beyond the realm of the image.

In sum, metadata is extra information heaped on top of the core image that most applications don't pay any attention to. True to Johnson's vision, metadata is whatever the poet decides to make of it.

Fortunately, despite its otherworldly timbre, metadata has very practical applications. Digital cameras use metadata to record focal length, exposure time, F-stop, and other illuminating information. Search engines use it to retrieve topics and keywords. And designers and photographers can use it to store—drum roll please—copyright statements and contact information. If that doesn't stoke the fires of your pecuniary self interest, then perhaps the following steps will:

AdobeP8M.md0

AdobeP8P.tb0

AdobeP8T.tb0

Figure 1-18.

1. ***Open the File Browser.*** Choose **File→Browse** or press Ctrl+Shift+O (⌘-Shift-O on the Mac). If the File Browser is already open, this will bring the window to the front.

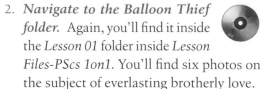

2. ***Navigate to the Balloon Thief folder.*** Again, you'll find it inside the *Lesson 01* folder inside *Lesson Files-PScs 1on1*. You'll find six photos on the subject of everlasting brotherly love.

3. ***Select all the photos and rotate them upright.*** Currently, the photos are on their sides. Choose **Edit→Select All** in the File Browser or press Ctrl+A (⌘-A on the Mac) to select all six thumbnails. Then click the rotate clockwise button or press Ctrl+] (⌘-]) to stand the images upright. Figure 1-19 shows the result at the large Custom thumbnail size.

4. ***Make more room for Metadata.*** You'll be working inside the **Metadata** panel in the bottom-left portion of the File Browser, so you might as well make more room for it. Drag the **Preview** tab up and drop it into the **Folders** panel. This combines the two panels and leaves the middle one empty. Now collapse the middle panel by dragging its horizontal divider upward, as illustrated in Figure 1-20. This expands the Metadata and Keywords panels to about twice their previous size.

Figure 1-19.

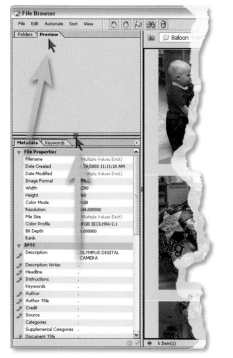

Figure 1-20.

5. *Save your workspace.* It may seem compulsive, but there's no time like the present to develop good habits. And saving workspaces is about the best habit I know of that doesn't involve a toothbrush. Choose **Window→Workspace→Save Workspace** from the Photoshop menu bar, name the setting "Metadata," and click **OK**. Now you have a special metadata view that will serve you well into your dotage.

6. *Select a single thumbnail.* Each image contains different metadata, so you'll generally want to review one image at a time. In the File Browser, choose **Edit→Deselect All** or press Ctrl+D (⌘-D on the Mac) to deselect all the thumbnails. Then click the last picture, titled *P5196922.jpg.* This is the climax to the series, where one brother expresses displeasure with the habitual aggravated burglary of the other. (Note that I expanded the Preview panel a bit in Figure 1-21 for a better view.)

Figure 1-21.

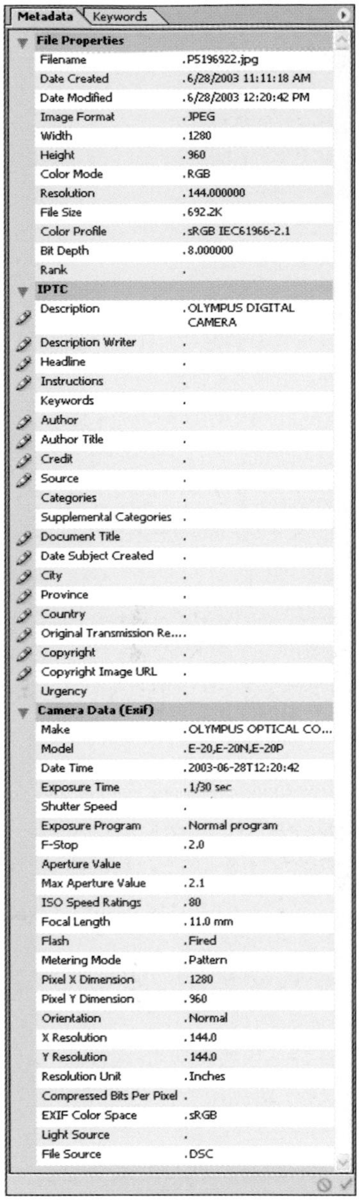

Figure 1-22.

7. **Review the metadata.** If you scroll around inside the Metadata panel, you'll see a total of six metadata categories that you can open or close. Pictured in the elongated Figure 1-22, the three most useful categories are as follows:

- **File Properties** houses the most elemental image specifications, such as the name of the file, the date it was last modified, the height and width in pixels, and other attributes that have been listed in the header of digital images for years.

- **IPTC** stands for International Press Telecommunications Council, a group in charge of standardizing the inclusion of credits and instructions in the field of photo journalism. The tiny pencils next to the IPTC items indicate that you can edit them, as we shall in Step 9.

- **EXIF** stands for Exchangeable Image File, supported by virtually all digital cameras sold today. So not surprisingly, Camera Data (EXIF) describes the inception of your photograph as witnessed by a digital camera. Here we find out that this particular photograph was shot with an Olympus E-20N using a ¹/₃₀-second exposure and a focal length of 11 millimeters, just shy of the widest zoom setting available in this particular camera. I can even confirm that the flash fired.

There's certainly a lot of information here, but the thing I want to know most—when exactly the photo was taken—is not listed. Instead, I see the date when I copied the file to this disk, which doesn't help me much. Fortunately, we can remedy this.

8. *Set the Metadata Display Options.* Click the ⊙ arrow in the upper-right corner of the **Metadata** panel to display the panel menu. Then choose the **Metadata Display Options** command. Inside the Metadata Display Options dialog box, scroll to the **Camera Data (Exif)** options and check the **Date Time Original** and **Date Time Digitized** items, highlighted in Figure 1-23. (If they're already checked, leave them checked.) I also recommend that you turn off the **Date Time** item, since this information is already included with the File Properties data.

Turn on the **Hide Empty Fields** check box at the bottom of the dialog box. This frees up room in the panel that would otherwise be wasted on blank attributes that the camera did not record. Click **OK** to return to the File Browser. We now see that the photograph was shot on May 19, 2003 at 10:22 AM. My, how time flies.

Naturally, the accuracy of the metadata hinges on the accuracy of the information recorded by your camera. So if you use a digital camera, make sure you set its time and date properly. A few months from now—when you haven't the vaguest idea of what you did when—you'll be glad you did.

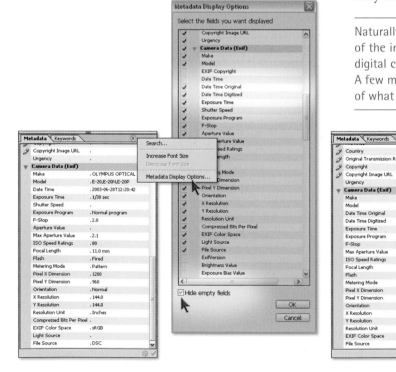

Figure 1-23.

9. *Modify the IPTC information.* Scroll up to the **IPTC** heading and click on the text to the right of **Description**. The text becomes highlighted, permitting you to edit it. In this example, I changed the entry to "A brotherly battle," but you can enter anything you want. Then press Tab to advance to the next editable item. My entries appear in Figure 1-24—if you want to follow them, fine; if not, feel free to go your own way. I was never much of a stickler for metadata decorum. When you finish, press the Enter key.

---

If you want to enter the copyright symbol © in the **Copyright** field under Windows, press and hold the Alt key, then type 0-1-6-9 on the numeric keypad. On the Mac, just press Option-G.

---

10. *Switch to the Keywords panel.* Click the **Keywords** tab to the right of the Metadata tab. *Keywords* allow you to identify specific items in a photograph and then later search for them. The most obvious concepts for keywords are who, what, and where, represented by the default categories People, Event, and Place. You can create more categories (which Photoshop calls *keyword sets*) and keywords, as we'll see.

11. *Assign a predefined keyword.* Check the **Birthday** item under **Event**. This is, after all, Sammy's Happy Birthday balloon.

12. *Make your own keywords.* Unless all your photographs are of people named Michael and Julius, you'll need to create your own keywords. To identify the kids in this domestic squabble, right-click (on the Mac, Control-click) the **People** item and choose **New Keyword**. Make one keyword for Sammy and another for the aggressor, Max, and then turn on their check boxes. I also added a couple of keywords under **Place**, namely Home and Living Room (see Figure 1-25). If you're feeling ambitious, you can add your own categories, such as Furniture, Action, or Underlying Psychological Motivation, by right-clicking in the panel and choosing **New Keyword Set**.

13. *Mark the image as copyrighted.* Not all metadata info is available from the File Browser. For example, to mark an image as copyrighted—so that Photoshop displays a copyright symbol in the title bar when you open it—you have to dig a little deeper. Go to the File Browser's **File** menu and choose **File Info**. The ensuing dialog box repeats much of the IPTC data you already entered, including keywords. But there is one notable addition, **Copyright Status**. Set it to **Copyrighted**.

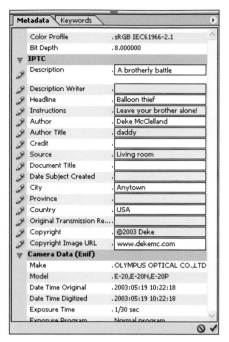

Figure 1-24.

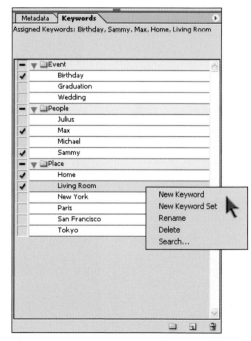

Figure 1-25.

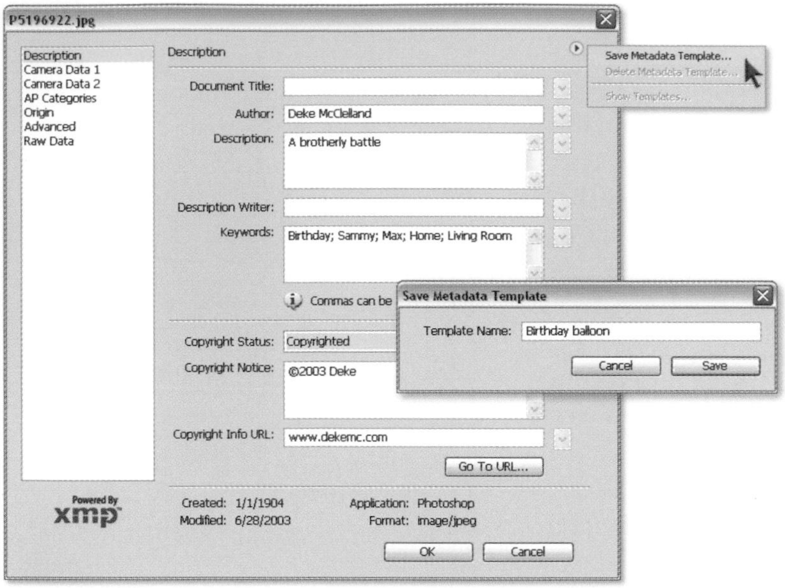

Figure 1-26.

At this point, you're basically finished. The only problem is that it took thirteen steps to annotate a single image. Wouldn't it be great if you could annotate the others without repeating all these steps again? Fortunately, there is a way, as the remaining three steps explain.

14. *Save a metadata template.* To do so, click the ⊙ arrow in the upper-right corner of the file info dialog box and choose **Save Metadata Template**, as illustrated in Figure 1-26. Then name the template "Birthday Balloon," or words to that effect, and click **Save**. Click **OK** to exit the dialog box and return to the File Browser.

15. *Select the other images.* Once inside the File Browser, press Ctrl+A (or ⌘-A on the Mac) to select all the thumbnails. Then Ctrl-click (⌘-click) the last image to deselect it. You should now have the first five thumbnails selected.

16. *Apply the metadata template.* In the File Browser, choose **Edit→Append Metadata→Birthday balloon**. Photoshop warns that you can't undo this action and asks whether you are sure (see Figure 1-27). Click **Yes**, you are.

Figure 1-27.

Photoshop has now applied your IPTC information, keywords, and copyright status to all the images inside the *Balloon Thief* folder. And unlike rotations, flags, and thumbnails (see "The File Browser and Its Slippery Cache," page 15), metadata and keywords are permanently appended to the image file. To confirm this, press Ctrl+D to deselect the thumbnails, and then click any one of them. Scroll to the top of the **Metadata** panel and look at the **Date Modified** item in the **File Properties** section. The date should be today; the time just a few minutes ago. You can copy these files anywhere you want and your changes to the metadata go with them.

## Batch Renaming

All these exercises, and we have yet to name a single image. Well, that's about to change. Not only will you name a single image, you'll name lots of images, and all at the same time.

1. *Restore the base workspace.* Choose **Window→Workspace→File Browser**. This not only loads the workspace settings you saved back in Step 3 on page 10, but it also opens the File Browser. So no need to choose File→Browse this time. Aren't you glad you've been saving workspaces? Me too.

2. *Navigate to the Max Mural folder.* Find the *Lesson 01* folder inside the *Lesson Files-PScs 1on1* folder that you copied from the CD to your hard drive, and open the *Max Mural* folder (see Figure 1-28). Inside are a dozen photos shot over the course of several weeks showing the progress of a mural I painted on a wall in my son's bedroom, inspired by what was for a fleeting moment my son's favorite book (and I believe maintains a firm spot in his top ten), Maurice Sendak's *Where the Wild Things Are.*

3. *Rename the first image.* Click on the name of the first image, which happens to be *P3226430.jpg*. Photoshop highlights the *P3226430* so you can rename it without changing the *.jpg* extension.

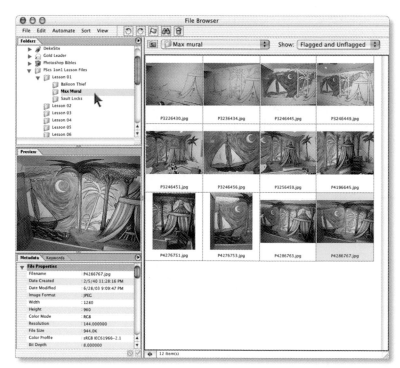

Figure 1-28.

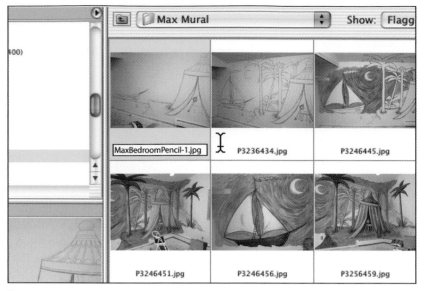

Figure 1-29.

Figure 1-30.

Enter the new filename "MaxBedroomPencil-1" (see Figure 1-29) and press the Tab key.

4. **Rename the second image.** By pressing Tab, you advance to the second image and highlight its name. Enter "MaxBedroomPencil-2" and press Tab again.

5. **Select the remaining thumbnails.** The Tab key makes it convenient to jump from one filename to the next. But manually renaming images is a chore. Thankfully, Photoshop gives you a way to rename multiple images in one operation. Start by clicking the first painted version of the mural, *P3246445.jpg*, then Shift-click the last image, *P4286767.jpg*. This selects the entire range of ten images.

6. **Initiate Batch Rename.** Choose **Automate→Batch Rename** in the File Browser. Photoshop opens the **Batch Rename** dialog box, shown in Figure 1-30.

7. **Enter a base name.** Press the Tab key four times (or just once on the Mac) to highlight the **Document Name** field, and change it to "MaxBedroomMural" (one word). This becomes the base name for all selected images.

8. **Assign a two-digit serial number.** Click the ⬍ arrow to the right of the **Extension** item in the top row to display a pop-up menu of predefined naming options, as shown in Figure 1-31. Choose **2 Digit Serial Number** to sequentially number the selected images from 01 to 10.

As it turns out, you don't have to start the numbering at 01; you can start it anywhere. Just enter the desired starting number in the **Starting Serial#** option box. Better yet, kill two birds with one stone by entering the starting value surrounded by pound signs (#) in one of the six **File Naming** fields. For example, if you replace **Extension** with *#06#*, Photoshop automatically assigns a two-digit serial number beginning with 06. This handy technique works regardless of the Starting Serial# value.

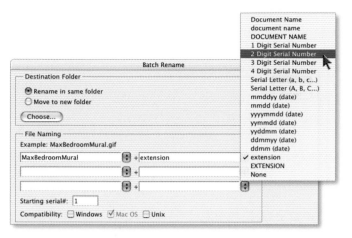

Figure 1-31.

9. *Set the third field to Extension.* This time, click the ⬍ arrow for the third field—the one directly below the base filename—and choose **Extension** from the pop-up menu. This adds to the end of the filename the proper three-character extension that identifies the file type, whether it be JPEG (.jpg), TIFF (.tif), native Photoshop (.psd), or something else.

### PEARL OF WISDOM

It is imperative that you add an extension to the end of a filename so that Photoshop and other programs can recognize the file as an image. This is even true on the Mac, where extensions have traditionally been unnecessary. While OS X 10.2 has a flexible attitude toward extensions—using them if they're there, working around them if they're not—rumor has it that future versions of the operating system will require them. As a rule, lowercase extensions are preferable to uppercase ones.

10. *Turn on all Compatibility check boxes.* Just because you're working on a Mac today doesn't mean you won't be using a dedicated UNIX box tomorrow. And if you're among the 95 percent of folks who use Windows, who knows, maybe one of those "I switched to a Mac" testimonials will get through to you. All I know is, it's a cross-platform world and you might as well be ready for anything that comes your way. These check boxes (seen at the bottom of Figure 1-32) make sure that your files can be read on computers using these operating systems.

11. *Let 'er rip.* Click **OK** to send Photoshop on its merry batch-renaming way.

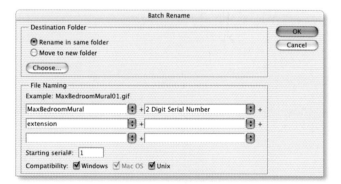

Figure 1-32.

Initially, the thumbnails appear in the same order they did before you chose Batch Rename, with the oldest images at the top and the newer ones at the bottom. If you prefer to resort the files in alphabetical order, just press the F5 key at the top of your keyboard. F5 is the Windows standard for the Refresh command, and Photoshop has adopted it on both the PC and the Mac. Note: If you use an Apple PowerBook, you may have to press both the Function key (fn) and F5.

## Printing Thumbnails

After you back up your images to a CD or some other media, you may find it helpful to print a catalog of thumbnails that you can then toss in a binder or fold into the CD sleeve. And wouldn't you just know it, Photoshop automates this operation with a command called Contact Sheet II, so named because it is the thrilling sequel to a previous Contact Sheet command that frankly needed the attention. But I digress—here's how it works:

1. *Select the Max Mural folder in the File Browser.* Choose **File→Browse** and then open the *Max Mural* folder, which is inside the *Lesson 01* folder inside *Lesson Files-PScs 1on1*. The files should be renamed according to  the steps in the preceding exercise. If you skipped that exercise, that's okay, but your filenames will be different.

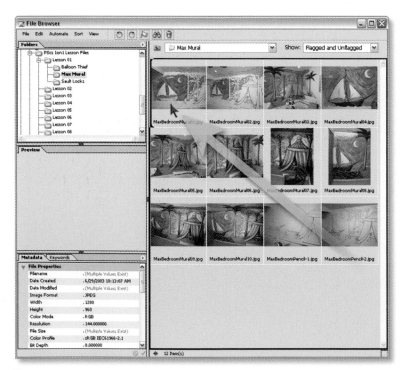

Figure 1-33.

2. *Move the pencil drawings to the top of the sort order.* Assuming that you took my advice and pressed the F5 key at the end of the preceding exercise, the two pencil drawings should appear at the bottom of the thumbnail browser. Select both thumbnails and drag them to the beginning of the group, as shown in Figure 1-33. This way, our photos will print in the desired order.

3. *Deselect all thumbnails.* Photoshop prints just those thumbnails that are selected. So rather confusingly, I think, if you want to print everything, you have to select nothing. Choose **Edit→Deselect All** or press Ctrl+D (⌘-D on the Mac).

4. *Initiate Contact Sheet II.* In the File Browser, choose **Automate→ Contact Sheet II**. Photoshop displays the **Contact Sheet II** dialog box, pictured in Figure 1-34.

5. *Target the File Browser.* Make sure that the **Use** option is set to **Selected Images from File Browser**. Most likely, the option is set this way by default, but better to be safe than sorry.

6. *Specify the page size.* Assuming that you're printing to letter-sized paper, make sure **Units** is set to **Inches** and the **Width** and **Height** values are 8 and 10, respectively. (If you're printing a CD insert, set both values to 4.75 inches.)

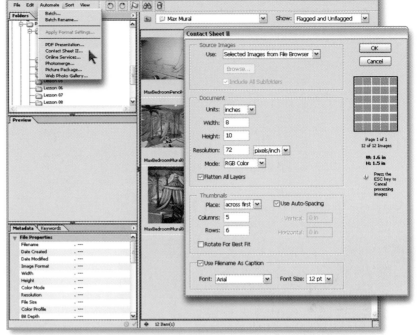

Figure 1-34.

7. *Raise the Resolution.* Raise the **Resolution** value to 300 pixels per inch. This ensures high-resolution, legible output. (I've long argued that this default setting should be changed—for printing purposes, 72 pixels per inch is nuts.)

8. *Set the color mode and flatten all layers.* You'll probably be printing this on an inkjet printer, which is designed to use the RGB color space, so set the **Mode** option to **RGB Color**. For the smallest file size, turn **Flatten All Layers** on. Otherwise, Photoshop generates a layer for every thumbnail and caption, which can make for a rather unruly file.

9. *Set the rows and columns.* We have 12 images in all. So set the **Columns** value to 3 and the **Rows** value to 4. Photoshop updates the preview in the upper-right corner of the dialog box to show you the new approximate configuration.

10. *Let 'er rip.* The remaining options are best left to their default settings. Your dialog box should look like the one shown in Figure 1-35. Confirm that it does, and click the **OK** button to put Photoshop to work.

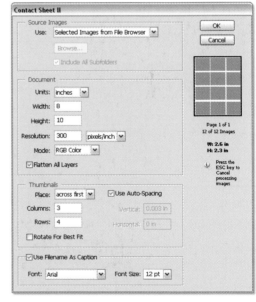

Figure 1-35.

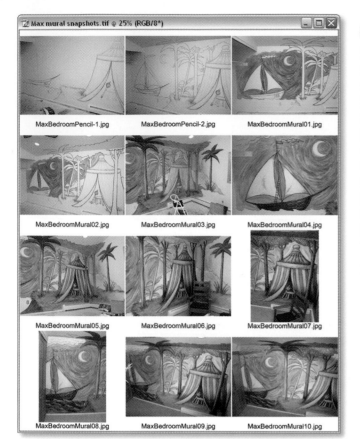

Figure 1-36.

Figure 1-37.

When Photoshop finishes its various activities, you'll see a high-resolution contact sheet like the one in **Figure 1-36**. By virtue of the Color Settings options I suggested in the Preface (Step 11, page xvi), you have a one-layer document in the Adobe RGB color space. Most inkjet printers prefer that you print a flat document (no layers) from the sRGB color space. As it turns out, you can perform both conversions with one command, as I explain in the next step. Mind you, it's not essential that you perform this step, and if for some reason you feel intimidated by it, you can skip it. But performing the step will help to ensure fast, color-accurate printing, so I urge you to continue.

11. *Convert the color space.* Make sure your new contact sheet is the foreground image (in front of the File Browser) and choose **Image→Mode→ Convert to Profile**. In the subsequent dialog box, set the **Profile** pop-up menu in the **Destination Space** area to **sRGB IEC61966-2.1**, as highlighted in Figure 1-37. (IEC61966-2.1 just happens to be the variety of sRGB that Photoshop supports.) Also make sure that:

   • **Engine** is set to **Adobe (ACE)**.

   • **Intent** is set to **Perceptual**, best for continuous-tone images. (If it says Relative Colorimetric, change it.)

   • All check boxes are turned on—in particular, **Flatten Image**, which reduces the layers inside the file.

   Click **OK** to apply the conversion.

12. *Save the contact sheet to disk.* Unlike the other images we've been looking at, the contact sheet exists only in Photoshop's memory. To save it to disk, choose **File→Save** or press Ctrl+S (⌘-S on the Mac) to display the **Save As** dialog box. From here, you can save the file anywhere, in any available format, but I recommend the following (shown in Figure 1-38):

   • Browse to the *Lesson 01* folder you've stored on your hard drive.

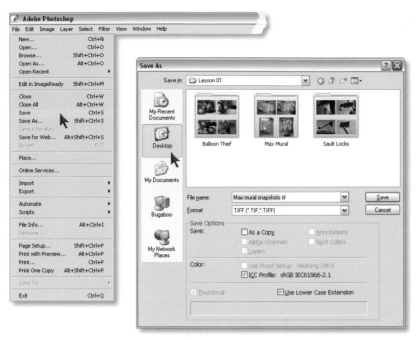

Figure 1-38.

- Select **TIFF** from the **Format** menu. On the PC, the option name is **TIFF** (*.**TIF**;*.**TIFF**). The Tag Image File Format (TIFF) is best suited to high-contrast print documents like this one.

- Name the file "Max Mural Snapshots.tif."

- Make sure the **ICC Profile** check box (called **Embed Color Profile** on the Mac) is turned on.

- If available, the **Use Lowercase Extension** check box should be turned on.

13. *Set the file format options.* Click the **Save** button to save the file to disk. Photoshop next displays the **TIFF Options** dialog box shown in Figure 1-39. Set the **Image Compression** option to **LZW**, which applies harmless but helpful *lossless compression* to the image, thereby reducing the size of your saved file on disk. Set **Byte Order** to **IBM PC** if you plan to use the image on Windows, or to **Macintosh** if you're mostly working on the Mac. (Fortunately, it doesn't really matter which you set; Photoshop and most other programs can read both formats regardless of which platform you use.) Don't worry about the other options; just click **OK**.

Figure 1-39.

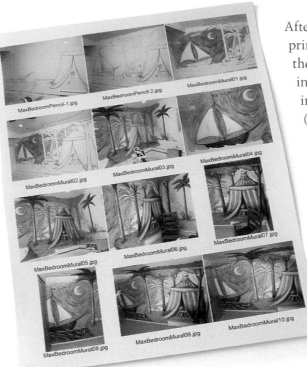

Figure 1-40.

After Photoshop finishes saving the document, you're ready to print the catalog. Make sure your printer is hooked up with the necessary driver software installed, and that it's working properly. It should be loaded with paper and sufficient ink. Then choose **File→Print**. Select the desired settings (as discussed in Lesson 12, "Printing and Output," the optimal settings vary depending on your platform and printer) and then click the **Print** or **OK** button. Assuming everything is working, your printer should deliver a page like the one in Figure 1-40.

FYI, you can also use Contact Sheet II to print ready-to-go pages for a photo album. Even if you prefer to cut the pictures apart and organize them individually, Contact Sheet II is a great way to maximize paper and reduce waste. For bigger snapshots, just print fewer per page by reducing the Columns and Rows values.

## Creating an On–Screen Slideshow

Printing isn't the only way to share your images. Adobe's Portable Document Format (PDF) permits you to share images and other documents with anyone who has a computer and the free Adobe Reader software (available from *http://www.acrobat.com*). Adobe Reader lets you open a PDF file, view it on screen, and even print it. More recent versions of Adobe Reader can even play slideshows that automatically advance from one photo to the next. New to Photoshop CS, the program can now generate such slide shows.

Starting from where we left off in the preceding exercise, here's what you do:

1. *View the Max Mural folder in the File Browser.* Choose **File→Browse** and go to *Max Mural* in the *Lesson 01* folder inside *Lesson Files-PScs 1on1*. The files should  be renamed and recordered according to the steps in the previous exercises. If you skipped these exercises, your filenames will be different.

2. *Deselect all thumbnails.* In the File Browser, choose **Edit→ Deselect All** or press Ctrl+D (⌘-D on the Mac).

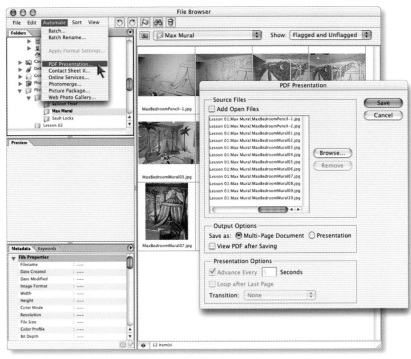

Figure 1-41.

3. *Initiate the PDF Presentation.* Still working in the File Browser menu, choose **Automate→PDF Presentation** to display the **PDF Presentation** dialog box, shown in Figure 1-41.

4. *Specify a slideshow.* Change the **Output Options** setting from **Multi-Page Document** to **Presentation**. Then turn on the **View PDF after Saving** check box.

5. *Set the timing options.* By default, a PDF slideshow is set to advance from one image to the next every five seconds. If you want it to move faster or slower, change the **Advance Every** value. To make the slideshow play repeatedly, turn on **Loop after Last Page**. You can also specify a type of **Transition** that fades one image into the next. But be forewarned, they're all ugly as sin. I say leave the three **Presentation Options** set to their defaults, as in Figure 1-42.

6. *Save the PDF slideshow to disk.* Click the **Save** button to display the Save dialog box. Browse to the *Lesson 01* folder and name the file "Max Mural Slideshow.pdf," as in Figure 1-43. Then click the **Save** button again.

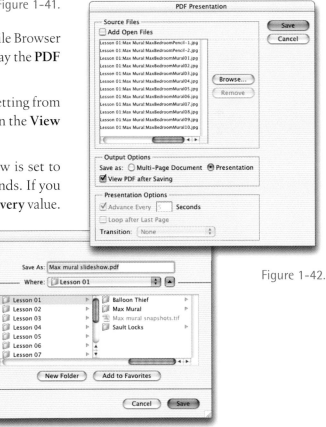

Figure 1-42.

Figure 1-43.

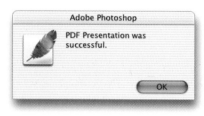

Figure 1-44.

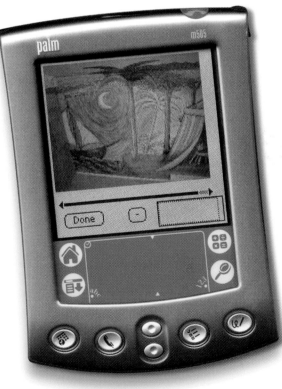

Figure 1-45.

7. *Accept the default PDF Options settings.* Photoshop displays yet another dialog box asking you how you'd like to save your PDF slideshow. The default settings pictured in Figure 1-44 are positively ducky.

8. *Click OK, sit back, and watch the fireworks.* As when creating the contact sheet, Photoshop opens each image in the File Browser and assembles it into a single file. When the process finishes, Photoshop displays a message like the one in Figure 1-45.

Click **OK** and Adobe Reader should launch and play your slideshow. You can either watch as the photos advance automatically, or click in the slideshow to advance manually. To exit the slideshow, press the Esc key.

A PDF slideshow created on the Mac can be played back on the PC (assuming that the PC in question is equipped with Adobe Reader), and vice versa. You can even play the slideshow on a portable electronic device, such as a Pocket PC, Palm Pilot (see Figure 1-46), or Symbian OS cell phone. In the case of handheld playback, you'll need to resize your images in advance to make them considerably smaller; compared with standard desktop computers, portable devices have little memory and itsy-bitsy screens.

Figure 1-46.

# WHAT DID YOU LEARN?

Match the key concept in the numbered list below with the letter of the phrase that best describes it. Answers appear upside-down at the bottom of the page.

## Key Concepts

1. File Browser
2. Thumbnail browser
3. Save Workspace
4. Hide palettes
5. Rotate clockwise/Rotate counterclockwise
6. Export Cache
7. Metadata
8. EXIF
9. Save Metadata Template
10. Batch Rename
11. Contact Sheet II
12. PDF Presentation

## Descriptions

A. A command that saves the descriptions, credits, and keywords assigned to one image so that you can apply them over and over to other images.

B. Any information above and beyond the core image data, including the date the image was last saved, the copyright holder, and how the image was captured.

C. The portion of the File Browser that contains the thumbnail previews.

D. A command used to assign document names, serial numbers, and extensions to multiple image files at a time.

E. A command that saves all transient operations that you perform inside the File Browser to the same folder that contains the image files.

F. A way to free up more room for the File Browser, performed by pressing Shift+Tab.

G. This command saves an on-screen slideshow that plays on a wide variety of computers and electronic devices inside the free Adobe Reader software.

H. A specific kind of metadata saved by most modern digital cameras that records the time and date a photograph was captured as well as various camera settings.

I. This transient File Browser operation stands vertical photographs upright. You can perform it from the keyboard by pressing Ctrl (⌘-on the Mac) and a bracket key, [ or ].

J. The best tool for opening and managing images in Photoshop.

K. The best command for printing images and filenames from the thumbnail browser.

L. A command that saves the position and visibility of palettes, the size of the File Browser, and the position and visibility of panels inside the browser.

## Answers

1J, 2C, 3L, 4F, 5I, 6E, 7B, 8H, 9A, 10D, 11K, 12G

LESSON

2

# HIGHLIGHTS, MIDTONES, AND SHADOWS

**AT HEART**, Photoshop is an image cobbler. Its primary mission is to take a worn photograph, with the pixel-based equivalent of sagging arches and holes in its heels, and make it better. As with shoes, not all images can be repaired; some are hopelessly defective from the moment they leave the factory. But most images have more life left in them than you might suspect. And if anyone can fix them, you and Photoshop can (see Figure 2-1).

Over the course of the next several lessons, we'll examine the many different ways to correct a photograph *in the order that these corrections are best applied*. Pardon my prolonged use of italics, but this last part is important. In addition to telling you how to use Photoshop's tools and commands to their utmost capability, I'll answer a rarely addressed question: When should you do what? Because every change you make to an image builds on the previous adjustment, sequence makes a difference.

Uncorrected shoe

In this lesson, you'll learn how to correct the brightness and contrast of an image. In the next lesson, we'll fix the colors. Later, we'll move on to straightening, cropping, sharpening, and so on. Amend each attribute of your troubled photograph in the order suggested by these lessons, and I swear to you, the results will look as good as they possibly can. This is how the pros do it.

Colors corrected in Photoshop (could still use a real cobbler)

Figure 2-1.

# ABOUT THIS LESSON

## Project Files

Before beginning the exercises, make sure that you've installed the lesson files from the CD, as explained in Step 5 on page xv of the Preface. This should result in a folder called *Lesson Files-PScs 1on1* on your desktop. We'll be working with the files inside the *Lesson 02* subfolder.

In this lesson, we examine Photoshop's most powerful commands, Levels, Curves, and Shadow/Highlight. We'll also look at Photoshop's automatic color fixers, the three Auto commands. You'll learn how to:

## Video Lesson 2: Levels and Curves

The indisputably intuitive Brightness/Contrast command has the unwelcome tendency of leaving an image in worse shape than it found it. As a result, you're better off using more complex commands that give you precise control over highlights, shadows, and midtones.

To see these commands in action, watch the second video lesson included on the CD. To view this video, insert the CD, click the **Start Training** button, and then select **2, Levels & Curves** from the Lessons list on the right side of the screen. During this 9-minute, 21-second movie, you'll learn about Brightness/Contrast, Auto Color, Levels, Curves, and Shadow/Highlight. As you watch, bear in mind that Photoshop makes available the following shortcuts:

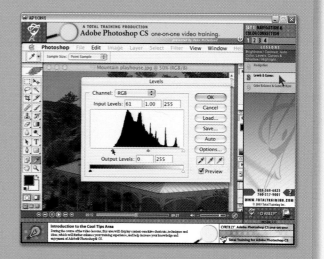

| Command or operation | Windows shortcut | Macintosh shortcut |
| --- | --- | --- |
| Auto Levels | Ctrl+Shift+L | ⌘-Shift-L |
| Auto Color | Ctrl+Shift+B | ⌘-Shift-B |
| Levels | Ctrl+L | ⌘-L |
| Curves | Ctrl+M | ⌘-M |
| Apply an adjustment | Enter | Return |
| Cancel an adjustment | Esc | Esc |
| Undo an adjustment | Ctrl+Z | ⌘-Z |

# Brightness and Contrast

If you've ever done any weight training, you know that you start by exercising your major muscle groups and then work your way down to the small stuff. Not that I'm a fitness expert—in fact, I'm pretty much of the opinion that lugging a pint of ice cream out of the freezer is enough physical labor to justify eating the entire thing—but I gather that you start with squats and leg presses and end by contracting your forehead with very small weights tied to your eyebrows.

Something similar can be said for editing images. You start with the major changes and then work your way down to more detailed adjustments. The biggest changes recruit the most pixels; therefore, they have a tendency to exaggerate any minor changes that precede them. Perhaps more important, big changes quickly reveal flaws in the image, so you can see what other changes need to be made.

The biggest changes tend to revolve around issues of *luminosity*—that is, light colors compared with dark ones. You most often hear this expressed as "brightness and contrast," where *brightness* is how light or dark a group of colors are and *contrast* is the degree of difference between light and dark colors as illustrated in Figure 2-2.

Photoshop pays lip service to this colloquialism with its Brightness/Contrast command. Although exceedingly easy to use, it lacks the predictability and control of Photoshop's more capable functions such as Levels, Curves, and Shadow/Highlight. These tools analyze an image according to three basic attributes—*highlights*, *shadows*, and *midtones*, or what the uninitiated might call light colors, dark colors, and everything in between. Figure 2-3 provides some examples.

Such distinctions not only let you adjust brightness and contrast, but also provide you with *selective control* over an image. You can make the shadows

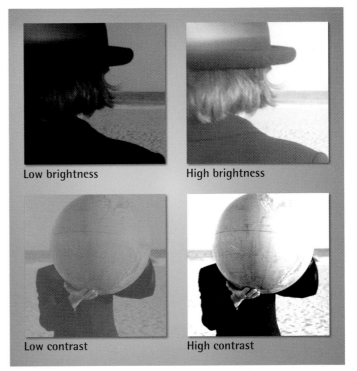

Low brightness    High brightness

Low contrast    High contrast

Figure 2-2.

Figure 2-3.

darker, the midtones lighter, and leave the highlights unchanged. And you can make these changes without upsetting the color balance one iota; or you can adjust luminosity and color values together. Be it red or blue, night or day, sky's the limit.

Figure 2-4.

## Automatic Image Correction

Photoshop offers three commands that correct the brightness and contrast of an image automatically (all labeled Auto in the Image→Adjustments submenu). They don't always do a great job of it—sometimes far from it—but they do the job without any guidance from you. They're like employees who don't ask enough questions. Sometimes they nail the problem, in which case you're glad they didn't bug you. Other times they make a mess of things, in which case you *really* wish they had consulted you. Fortunately, with a bit of intervention on your part, you can make the most of these self-acting drones:

1. *Open a low-contrast image.* Use either **File→Browse** or **File→Open** to find the *Lesson 02* folder inside *Lesson Files-PScs 1on1*. Then open the image called *Low contrast skull.jpg*. Pictured in Figure 2-4, this digital snapshot of a saber-toothed tiger skull suffers from low contrast and a slightly purple color cast, problems the Auto commands are designed to fix.

2. *Duplicate the image three times.* Choose **Image→Duplicate**, and when the **Duplicate Image** dialog box appears, name the new image "Auto Levels," as shown in Figure 2-5. Choose Image→Duplicate again and name the second duplicate "Auto Contrast." Choose Image→Duplicate a third time and name the final image "Auto Color." You should now have four image windows open, all with identical photographs. Each will permit you to see a different automatic image adjustment.

3. *Arrange the windows so you can see each one.* Click the *Low contrast skull.jpg* image window to bring it to the front. Next, choose **View→Zoom Out** or press Ctrl+minus (⌘-minus on the Mac) to reduce the image so it takes up no more than one-quarter of your screen. Choose **Window→Arrange→Match Zoom** to change all windows to this same zoom ratio. Then choose **Window→Arrange→Cascade** to match the window sizes. Now drag the title bars so you can see the images side-by-side. Press the Tab key to hide the toolbox and palettes if necessary.

Figure 2-5.

4. *Apply the Auto Levels command.* Click in the *Auto Levels* image window to make it active. Then choose **Image→Adjustments→ Auto Levels**. In a flash, Photoshop corrects the image. There's no doubt the result (shown in Figure 2-6) is an improvement. But is this the best Photoshop can do? It is, after all, a bit brown. The only way to know whether Photoshop can do better is to try out the other commands.

5. *Apply the Auto Contrast command.* Click in the image window titled *Auto Contrast* to make it active. Then choose **Image→ Adjustments→Auto Contrast**. This time, the brightness and contrast are better, but the skull remains a tad purplish (see Figure 2-7). So far, my money's still on Auto Levels.

6. *Apply the Auto Color command.* Click in the *Auto Color* image window and choose **Image→Adjustments→Auto Color**. Photoshop balances the brightness, contrast, and color-cast in one fell swoop, as shown in Figure 2-8.

The result comes the closest to accurately representing the original scene. But the real question is, do I like it the best? The greenish cast gives it a hospital flavor that I'm not too crazy about. What I'd really like is something midway between this and the Auto Levels adjustment. Fortunately, you can mix the two, as explained in the following step (see page 42).

Figure 2-6.

Figure 2-7.

Figure 2-8.

# The Nature of Channels

To understand how to modify colors in Photoshop, you have to know how color is calculated. And this means coming to terms with the two fundamental building blocks of color, *luminosity values* and *color channels*. Be forewarned, a little math is involved. It's nothing tough—no calculator required—just enough to get us grounded.

For starters, let's consider how things work without color. When you scan a black-and-white photo, the scanner converts it to a *grayscale* image, so called because it contains not just black and white but also hundreds of shades of gray. Because we're in the digital realm, each pixel in the image is recorded as a number, called a luminosity value, or *level*. A value of 0 means the pixel is black; the maximum value (typically 255) translates to white. Other luminosity values from 1 on up describe incrementally lighter shades of gray.

When you add color to the mix, a single luminosity value is no longer sufficient. After all, you have to distinguish not only light pixels from dark, but also vivid colors from drab, yellow from purple, and so on.

The solution is to divide color into its root components. There are several recipes for color, but by far the most popular is *RGB*, short for red, green, and blue. The RGB color model is based on the behavior of light. In the illustration below, we see what happens when you shine three spotlights—one brilliant red, another bright green, and a third deep blue—at a common point. The three lights overlap to produce the lightest color that we can see, neutral white. By adjusting the amount of light cast by each spotlight, you can reproduce nearly all the colors in the visible spectrum.

Now imagine that instead of shining spotlights, you have three slide projectors equipped with slightly different slides. Each slide shows the same image, but one captures just the red light from the image, another just the green, and a third just the blue. Shine the three projectors at the same spot on a white screen and you get the full-color photograph in all its glory.

This is precisely how a digital image works, except that in place of slides, Photoshop gives you *channels*. Each channel contains an independent grayscale image, as shown upper right. To generate the full-color composite, Photoshop colorizes the channels and mixes them together, as illustrated below right. Each channel contains 256 luminosity values—black, white, and the 254 shades of gray in between. But when colored and mixed together, they produce as many as $256^3 = 16.8$ million unique colors. (For a less common scenario that accommodates trillions of colors, see "8 Bits Versus 16 Bits Per Channel" on page 90 of Lesson 3.)

You can access both the full-color composite and the individual channels inside the Levels and Curves dialog boxes. To see what the grayscale channels look like, open an image, choose **Window→ Channels**, and click the **Red**, **Green**, or **Blue** item in the Channels palette. Click **RGB** to return to the full-color composite view.

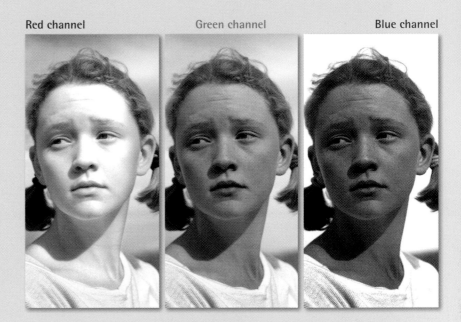

Red channel   Green channel   Blue channel

Red channel   Green channel   Blue channel

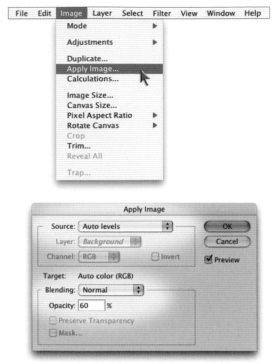

Figure 2-9.

7. ***Blend the Auto Color and Auto Levels images.*** With the *Auto Color* window active, choose **Image→Apply Image**. In the Apply Image dialog box (see Figure 2-9):

- Set the **Source** option to **Auto Levels**, which will mix the *Auto Levels* image with the active *Auto Color* image.

- Skip to the **Blending** option and set it to **Normal**.

- Adjust the **Opacity** value to taste. I ultimately decided to lower the Opacity of the *Auto Levels* image to 60 percent, thus revealing 40 percent of the *Auto Color* image.

Click **OK** to accept your changes and mix the images.

8. ***Save the corrected image.*** After blending the Auto Color and Auto Levels images (the result of which appears beside the original, uncorrected photograph in Figure 2-10), choose **File→Save** or press Ctrl+S (⌘-S on the Mac). The image has never been saved before, so Photoshop will ask you to name the file and specify a location. Because this is a flat image (no layers) based on a JPEG digital photograph, the JPEG file format is a good choice. Click **Save**, specify a **Quality** setting of 10 or higher, then click the **OK** button to complete the Save operation.

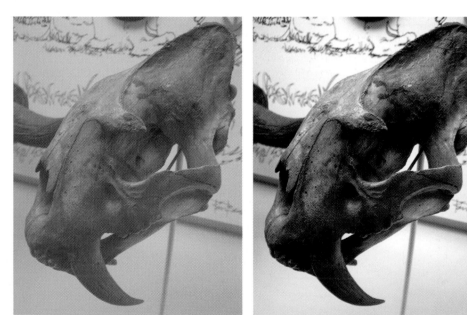

Uncorrected skull      40% Auto Color blended with 60% Auto Levels

Figure 2-10.

By definition, an Auto command adjusts an image without troubling you with the details. But that doesn't mean it applies the same level of correction to one photograph as it does to another. Quite the contrary—each Auto command analyzes an image and corrects it accordingly. A dark image receives different correction than a light one, a yellowish image receives different correction than a bluish one, and so on.

But while every image gets individualized attention, it is modified according to a consistent set of rules. Auto Levels subscribes to one set of rules, Auto Contrast to another, and Auto Color to a third. The following list explains how each command works. But rather than discussing them in the order in which they appear in the Image→Adjustments submenu—as I did in the "Automatic Image Correction" exercise—I'll start with the most basic command, Auto Contrast, and work my way up:

- **Auto Contrast** locates the darkest color in an image and makes it as dark as it can be without changing its color. It then makes the lightest color as light as possible. For example, if the darkest color is blue and the lightest color yellow, as in the building shown below, then the blue becomes a darker blue and the yellow a lighter yellow. The color balance remains unchanged—just what you want when an image is properly colored but not at all what you want when it's not.

- **Auto Levels** makes no attempt to preserve colors. Instead, it analyzes each color channel independently and makes the darkest color in each channel black and the lightest color white. The result is more often than not a shift in color balance. This can be a good thing if the color balance needs fixing. But Auto Levels may go too far, replacing one color cast with another. In the example below, the color cast shifts from pink to blue.

- **Auto Color** can be a bit slower because it tries to do more. Like Auto Levels, it deepens shadows and lightens highlights on a channel-by-channel basis. But where Auto Levels may shift shadows and highlights from one color to another, Auto Color tries to change them to neutral grays. Auto Color also evaluates the midtones in an image. It finds all the midtones that are trending toward gray and then leeches away the color. Given the current state of technology, this is the best method for automatically correcting the color cast of a photo.

Because it attempts to remove color casts from all three brightness regions of an image—shadows, highlights, and midtones—Auto Color frequently outperforms the rest of the Auto pack. But it's by no means foolproof, as the "Automatic Image Correction" exercise illustrates. By testing all three Auto commands, you can decide for yourself which one delivers the most desirable results.

Original image          Auto Contrast          Auto Levels          Auto Color

9. *Close all images.* Now that you've selected and saved your preferred corrected version of the image, you can discard the others. Choose **File**→**Close All** or press **Ctrl+Alt+W** (or ⌘-Option-W). When asked to save changes, click the **No** button on the PC or **Don't Save** on the Mac. If you prefer keystrokes, press N on the PC or D on the Mac.

## Adjusting Brightness Levels

The Auto commands are fine and dandy, but they're no replacement for good old-fashioned manual labor. And when it comes time to roll up your shirtsleeves and smear on the elbow grease, the tool of choice is the Levels command. While not necessarily the most powerful brightness and contrast function in Photoshop's arsenal—as we'll see later, the Curves command outshines it in a few key areas—Levels provides the best marriage of form and function. It lets you tweak highlights, midtones, and shadows predictably and with absolute authority while maintaining smooth transitions between the three.

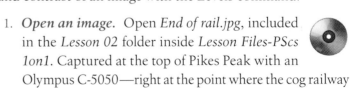

PEARL OF WISDOM

The Levels command is ideally suited to increasing or decreasing brightness values. Where contrast is concerned, Levels is better at increasing contrast than decreasing it. To decrease the contrast of an image—particularly one with overly harsh shadows and highlights—see the sections "Correcting with Curves" (page 51) and "Compensating for Flash and Backlighting" (page 57).

The following exercise explains how to correct the brightness and contrast of an image with the Levels command:

Figure 2-11.

1. *Open an image.* Open *End of rail.jpg*, included in the *Lesson 02* folder inside *Lesson Files-PScs 1on1*. Captured at the top of Pikes Peak with an Olympus C-5050—right at the point where the cog railway drops into the abyss—this image features some atrocious light metering (see Figure 2-11). But don't blame the camera; I dropped it and knocked off a couple of important pieces on the way up the mountain. Fortunately, even though it was damaged, the camera captured enough color information to repair the image in Photoshop.

2. *Duplicate the image.* I often find it helpful to give one of the Auto commands a try before resorting to Levels. (After all, if I can get away with being lazy, more power

to me.) But rather than mess up the original image, better to modify a copy. So choose **Image→Duplicate** and name the new image "Auto Color."

---

If you don't feel like naming the image, you can skip this part. Just press the Alt key (Option on the Mac) when choosing Image→ Duplicate. Photoshop skips the dialog box and names the image *End of rail copy*.

---

3. *Apply the Auto Color command.* Choose **Image→Adjustments→Auto Color**, or better yet, just press Ctrl+Shift+B (⌘-Shift-B on the Mac). The result appears in Figure 2-12. The fact that Photoshop can retrieve this much color and brightness all by itself is flat-out amazing. But I'm afraid it's not good enough. The image remains quite dark with a predominantly blue cast.

4. *Return to the original image.* Click the *End of rail.jpg* title bar to bring that image window to the front.

5. *Choose the Levels command.* Choose **Image→Adjustments→Levels** or press Ctrl+L (⌘-L on the Mac). Photoshop displays the **Levels** dialog box (see Figure 2-13), which contains the following options:

   - The Channel pop-up menu lets you edit the contents of each color channel independently. To edit all channels at once, choose RGB, the default setting.

   - The three Input Levels values list the amount of adjustment applied to the shadows, midtones, and highlights, respectively. The default values—0, 1.00, and 255—indicate no change.

   - The black blob in the middle is the *histogram*, which is a graph of the brightness values in your image. (For more information, read the sidebar, "How to Read and Respond to a Histogram," on page 48.)

   - The two Output Levels values let you lighten the darkest color in the image and darken the lightest color. In other words, they permit you to reduce the contrast. Although useful for dimming and fading, they rarely come into play when correcting an image.

   - The Save button lets you save a collection of settings to disk for later use. Click Load to open a file of such saved Levels settings.

Figure 2-12.

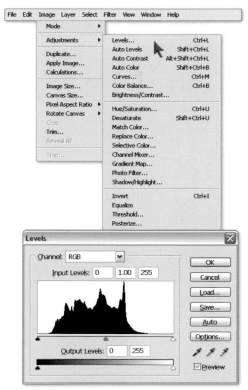

Figure 2-13.

- The Auto button applies the equivalent of the Auto Levels command, which you can then modify as needed. Click Options to apply a different kind of Auto function—such as Auto Color—as well as modify the function's behavior.

- See the three eyedropper tools above the Preview check box? Select an eyedropper and then click in the image window to modify the clicked color. The black eyedropper makes the clicked color black; the white one makes it white; the gray one robs it of color, leaving it a shade of gray.

- Turn on the Preview check box to see your changes applied dynamically to the active image. As you do so, press Ctrl+plus to magnify the image or Ctrl+minus to zoom out. (That's ⌘-plus and ⌘-minus on the Mac.) Press the spacebar to summon the hand tool.

---

Turn off the Preview check box to see what the image looked like before you chose the Levels command. Obvious as this may sound, the Preview option is great for before-and-after comparisons.

---

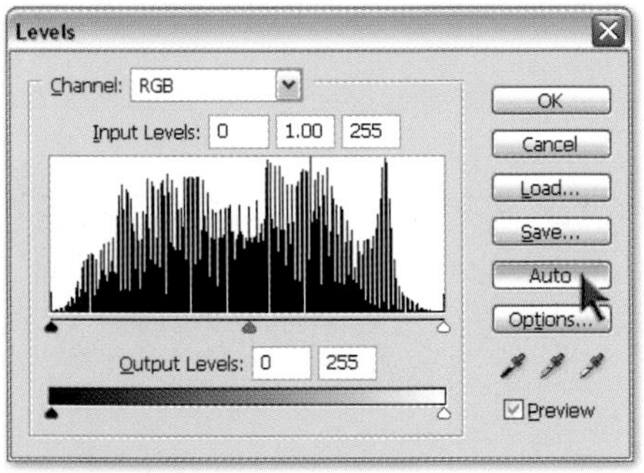

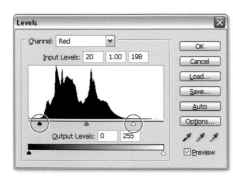

Figure 2-14.

Figure 2-15.

6. **Click the Auto button.** Click the **Auto** button to apply the **Auto Levels** function. The resulting image should look a lot like the Auto Color image you created in Step 3. The histogram stretches to fill the center portion of the dialog box, but the numerical Input Levels values stay the same, as in Figure 2-14. (You'll see why in the next step.) As before, Photoshop's automated adjustment isn't perfect, but it's a good place to start. The difference now is, we can use Levels to tweak the adjustment.

7. **Switch to the Red channel.** Choose **Red** from the **Channel** pop-up menu or press Ctrl+1 (⌘-1 on the Mac). You now see the Red-channel histogram with adjusted Input Levels values, as shown in Figure 2-15.

PEARL OF ● WISDOM

Clicking Auto in Step 6 changed the Input Levels settings on a channel-by-channel basis. So even though you see an altered histogram in the composite view (as in Figure 2-14), you have to visit the individual channels to see the numerical changes.

8. **Nudge the shadows and highlights.** Notice the black and white slider triangles directly below the histogram (highlighted red in Figure 2-15). They correspond to the first and last **Input Levels** values, respectively. In my case, the black slider tells me that any pixel with a brightness of 20 or less will be made black in

the Red channel; the white slider says any pixel 198 or brighter will be made white. (Your values may differ slightly. Remember, 0 is absolute black and 255 is absolute white.) Those values are okay, but I recommend you tighten them up a little—that is, send a few more colors to black or white. Nudge the black value from 20 to 30; nudge the white value from 198 to 168.

---

By *nudge*, I mean literally, using the arrow keys on the keyboard. Highlight the 20 and press Shift+↑ to raise it to 30. Highlight 198 and press Shift+↓ three times to lower the value to 168. Together, these adjustments make the image slightly redder.

---

9. **Raise the midtones value.** Increase the middle **Input Levels** value to 1.23, thus increasing the brightness of the midtones in the Red channel. The result appears in Figure 2-16.

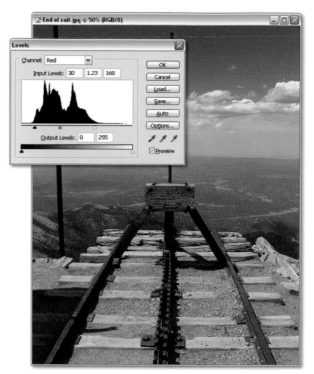

Figure 2-16.

PEARL OF ⬤ WISDOM

The middle Input Levels number and the corresponding gray slider below the histogram are calculated differently than the black and white points. Expressed as an exponent, this so-called *gamma value* multiplies all colors in a way that affects midtones more dramatically than shadows or highlights. The default value of 1.00 raises the colors to the first power, hence no change. Higher gamma values make the midtones brighter; lower values make the midtones darker.

10. **Switch to the Green channel.** Choose **Green** from the **Channel** pop-up menu or press Ctrl+2 (⌘-2 on the Mac).

11. *Adjust the shadows, midtones, and highlights.* Change the three **Input Levels** values to 36, 1.25, and 205. This brightens the green values, as in Figure 2-17.

12. **Switch to the Blue channel.** Choose **Blue** from the **Channel** pop-up menu or press Ctrl+3 (⌘-3).

13. *Adjust the shadows, midtones, and highlights.* This time, change the three **Input Levels** values to 50, 1.26, and 187. The changes to the black and white values darken the Blue channel, while the change to the gamma value lightens the midtones. The result is a slight shift in colors in the evergreens in the background and the dirt beneath the track.

Figure 2-17.

# How to Read and Respond to a Histogram

In the world of statistics, a *histogram* is a kind of bar graph in which the bars vary in both height and width to show the distribution of data. In the Levels dialog box, it's a bit simpler. The central histogram contains exactly 256 vertical bars. Each bar represents one brightness value, from black (on the far left) to white (on the far right). The height of each bar indicates how many pixels correspond to that particular brightness value. The result is an alternative view of your image, one that focuses exclusively on the distribution of colors.

Consider the annotated histogram below. I've taken the liberty of dividing it into four quadrants. If you think of the histogram as a series of steep sand dunes, a scant 5 percent of that sand spills over into the far left quadrant; thus, only 5 percent of the pixels in the image are dark. Meanwhile, fully 25 percent of the sand resides in the big peak in the right-hand quadrant, so 25 percent of the pixels are light. The image represented by this histogram contains more highlights than shadows.

One glance at the image itself (opposite page, top) confirms that the histogram is accurate. The photo so obviously contains more highlights than shadows that the histogram may seem downright redundant. But the truth is, it provides another and very helpful glimpse into the image. Namely, we see where the darkest colors start, where the lightest colors drop off, and how the rest of the image is weighted.

With that in mind, here are a few ways to work with the histogram in the Levels dialog box:

- **Black and white points:** Bearing in mind the sand dune analogy, move the black slider triangle below the histogram to the point at which the dunes begin on the left. Then move the white triangle to the point at which the dunes end on the right. (See the green graph below.) This makes the darkest colors in the image black and the lightest colors white, which maximizes contrast without harming shadow and highlight detail.

- **Clipping:** Take care not to make too many colors black or white. This will result in *clipping*, in which Photoshop renders whole regions of your image flat black or white. That's fine for graphic art but bad for photography, where you need continuous color transitions to convey depth and realism.

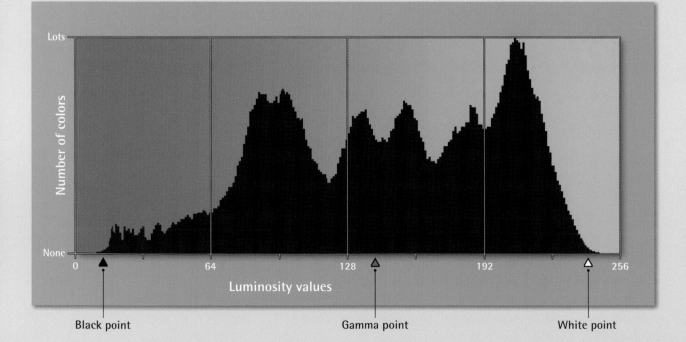

To preview exactly which pixels will go to black or white, press the Alt key (Option on the Mac) as you drag a slider triangle. When dragging the black triangle, any pixels that appear black or any color *except* white (as in the example at the bottom of this page) will be clipped. When dragging the white triangle, Photoshop clips the non-black pixels.

- **Balance the histogram on the gamma:** When positioning the gray gamma triangle, think "center of gravity." Imagine that you have to balance all that sand in the histogram on a teetering board that is poised on this single gray triangle. If you position the gamma properly, you can distribute the luminosity values evenly across the brightness spectrum, which generally produces the most natural results.

Bear in mind that these are suggestions, not rules. Clipped colors can result in interesting effects. An overly dark image may look great set behind white type. But let these suggestions guide your experimentation, and you'll find yourself working more quickly and effectively inside the Levels dialog box.

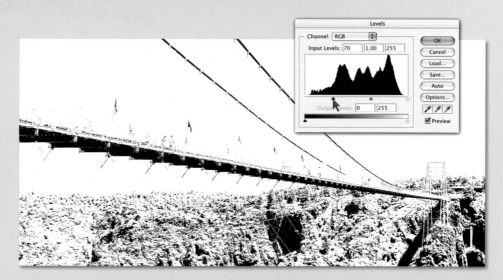

Figure 2-18.

Figure 2-19.

14. *Switch to the RGB composite image.* Choose **RGB** from the **Channel** pop-up menu or press Ctrl+tilde (⌘-tilde on the Mac). The tilde key is the ~ to the left of the 1.

15. *Raise the gamma value.* Advance to the gamma value. (If the gamma value was last active in the Blue channel, it remains active.) Then press Shift+↑ twice to raise the value to 1.2. This lightens the midtones across all color channels, as shown in Figure 2-18.

---

**PEARL OF WISDOM**

Step 15 does a fine job of lightening the image on most PC monitors. But if you're working on a Mac, you may find that it goes a bit too far, leaving the photo looking washed out or overly bright. If so, darken the image by lowering the gamma value to 1.1 or 1.0.

---

16. *Click OK.* Or press Enter or Return to accept your changes and exit the Levels dialog box.

---

The resulting image is significantly brighter than the original photograph, especially where the midtones are concerned. One of the downsides of lightening midtones is that it tends to bleed some of the color out of an image. Fortunately, you can restore color using the Hue/Saturation command, as explained in the next step.

---

17. *Choose the Hue/Saturation command.* Choose **Image→ Adjustments→Hue/Saturation** or press Ctrl+U (⌘-U on the Mac). As we'll see in the "Tint and Color" exercise that begins on page 72 of Lesson 3, Hue/Saturation lets you modify the intensity of colors in an image.

18. *Raise the Saturation value.* Press Tab to advance to the **Saturation** value. Then press Shift+↑ three times to raise the value to +30 percent. Then click **OK** or press Enter or Return. The once drab image is now brimming with color, as shown in Figure 2-19.

The final image is a resounding success. But you may wonder how in the world I arrived at the specific values that you entered into the various Input Levels option boxes. The answer, of course, is trial and error. I spent a bit more time flitting back and forth between the channels and nudging values than the exercise implies, just as you will when correcting your own images. But as long as you keep the Preview check box turned on, you can review each and every modification as you apply it.

That said, my approach wasn't entirely random. Back in Step 11, I didn't know that 36 was the magic shadow value, but I suspected it was somewhere in that neighborhood. The trick is knowing how to read and respond to a histogram, as I explain in the aptly named sidebar "How to Read and Respond to a Histogram" on page 48.

## Correcting with Curves

As a rule, the Auto and Levels commands work best when you want to increase the contrast of an image, not decrease it. Granted, you can darken or brighten midtones. But what if you want to tone down a group of highlights or shine a bit of light into the shadows? To perform these kinds of adjustments, you need more control than the basic three divisions—shadows, midtones, and highlights—can provide. You need to divide shadows and highlights into their component parts. In other words, you need to establish your own brightness divisions.

Which is precisely what the Curves command does. You can set and edit a dozen or more brightness points. Or you can set just three or four, and modify them in ways that Levels simply can't. As we'll see in this exercise, the Curves dialog box lacks a histogram. But thanks to Photoshop CS's new Histogram palette, that's no longer a problem.

1. *Open an image.* Open the image file *Constitution.jpg*, included in the *Lesson 02* folder inside *Lesson Files-PScs 1on1*. Captured in Boston using the same Olympus C-5050 as in the preceding exercise—only before I broke it—the brightly lit image pictured in Figure 2-20 looks ship-shape in most regards. But it has a bit more contrast than I'd like. The direct sunlight results in bright surfaces and a vivid sky set against extremely dark mast lines and shadows. I think we can do better.

Figure 2-20.

2. *Open the Histogram palette.* Choose **Window→Histogram** to display the diminutive **Histogram** palette. Too diminutive, in my estimation. When scaled to fit the width of the other palettes, Histogram permits us to see roughly 75 percent of the 256 brightness bars.

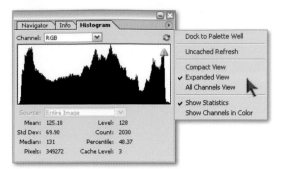

Figure 2-21.

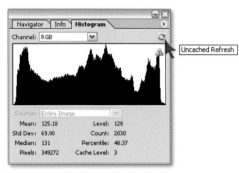

Figure 2-22.

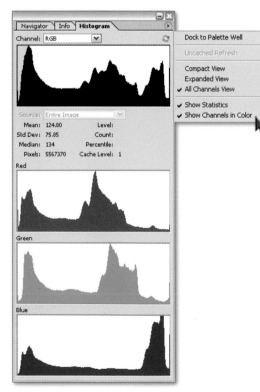

Figure 2-23.

For our purposes, that's not good enough. To expand the palette, click the ⊙ arrow in the upper-right corner and choose **Expanded View,** as in Figure 2-21. Now you can see what you'd normally see in the Levels dialog box.

3. *Refresh the histogram.* Most likely, you'll see a tiny yellow caution icon (⚠) in the upper-right corner of the histogram, which means you're viewing a *cached* (or old and inaccurate) version of the histogram. Caching saves Photoshop some computational effort, but it proves a hindrance when you're trying to gauge the colors in an image. To update the histogram based on the latest and greatest information, click the yellow ⚠ icon or the circular ↻ arrows labeled **Uncached Refresh** in Figure 2-22.

4. *Show all color channels.* If you're a complete histogram freak—and for purposes of this exercise, you are—you'll want to see a separate histogram for each and every color channel. Choose **All Channels View** from the Histogram palette menu. Then choose **Show Channels in Color**, as shown in Figure 2-23. The result is a series of color-coded histograms that you can check at a glance.

---

If screen space is tight, you may have noticed that the Histogram palette consumes the space of the three palettes below it. But click either the Navigator or Info tab—both of which share space with Histogram by default—and Photoshop shrinks the Histogram palette and hides it from view. It's a great space-saving technique when the palette's not in use. However, we need it now, so be sure to click the **Histogram** tab to bring the palette back before proceeding.

---

5. *Choose the Curves command.* Choose **Image→Adjustments→ Curves** or press Ctrl+M (⌘-M on the Mac). Pictured in Figure 2-24, the **Curves** dialog box contains many of the same options found in the Levels dialog box, including the Channels pop-up menu; the Load, Save, Auto, and Options buttons; the eyedropper tools; and the Preview check box. (For explanations of each, see Step 5 of the "Adjusting Brightness Levels" exercise on page 45.) But there are a few differences:

   • The central element of the Curves dialog box is the *brightness graph*, in which you plot points along a line called the *brightness curve*. The curve represents all the brightness values in the image from black in the lower-left corner to white in the upper-right. Click to add a point to the brightness curve, and then drag the point to make that particular value lighter or darker.

- When available, the Input and Output values show the coordinates of the selected point or cursor location in the graph. Input tells the original brightness of the color; Output notes the brightness as it will be when you click OK. As in the Levels dialog box, the brightness of an RGB image is measured from 0 to 255.

- To the right of the Input and Output values are two tools for editing the brightness curve. The first is the point tool. Click in the graph with this tool to add a point to the curve. Then drag the point to bend the curve. The second tool, the pencil, lets you draw freehand curves. For example, if the curve flexes in a way you don't like, switch to the pencil and draw directly inside the graph.

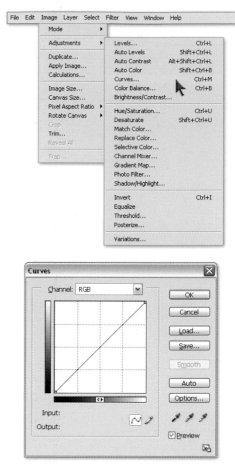

Figure 2-24.

---

Available only when the pencil tool is active, the Smooth button rounds off rough corners in your graph. This is especially useful after Shift-clicking with the pencil tool, which draws straight lines. If one click of the Smooth button doesn't do the trick, click the button again.

---

Now that we have the cursory introductions out of the way, let's see how these options fare in a real-world project.

6. *Expand the brightness graph.* Click the icon in the lower-right corner of the Curves dialog box to expand the brightness graph to 256 pixels wide and just as many tall, as in Figure 2-25. This makes it easier to more precisely drag points on the graph.

---

To increase the number of grid lines, press the Alt key (Option on the Mac) and click in the brightness graph. The result is the 10-by-10 grid shown in Figure 2-25. Alt-click again to restore fewer grid lines.

---

7. *Identify problem areas.* To get a bead on the colors you want to change, move your mouse into the image window to get the eyedropper cursor. Then click and drag in the image window. A "bouncing ball" floats up and down the brightness curve to show you the coordinates of the colors that the eyedropper finds. For example, the bright blues in the sky range between 160 and 190; the dark colors along the side of the ship range between 10 and 60. This helps us get a feel for the specific luminosity values that reside in the highlights, shadows, and midtones of the image.

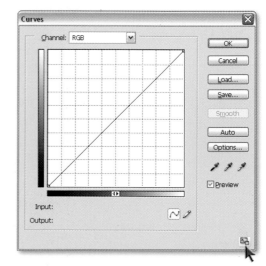

Figure 2-25.

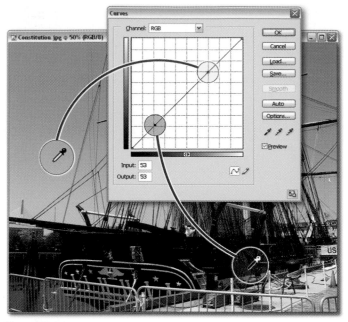

Figure 2-26.

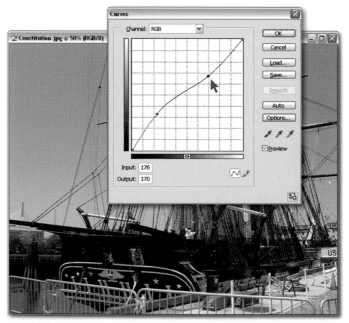

Figure 2-27.

8. ***Add points to the graph.*** Now that you have a rough sense of the color composition of the image, it's time to return to the **Curves** dialog box and adjust the brightness curve. And the first step in modifying the curve is to add a point. You can add a point by clicking anywhere along the diagonal line. But the better method is to lift points directly from the image itself.

---

To do this, press Ctrl (or ⌘ on the Mac) and click in the image window. I recommend Ctrl-clicking once in the sky (highlighted in yellow in **Figure 2-26**) and again along the side of the ship (highlighted in red). You should end up with two points at opposite ends of the diagonal line, which identify key colors in the highlights and shadows of the photograph.

---

9. ***Adjust the Output values.*** To brighten the shadows, drag the first point up a bit. To dim the sky, drag the second point down very slightly. Watch the **Input** and **Output** values as you move the points. To match the results shown in Figure 2-27, do the following:

  - Set the first point to Input: 53 and Output: 83.

  - Set the second point to Input: 176 and Output: 170.

---

A few tricks can make editing points in the brightness graph a lot easier. First, you can activate a point from the keyboard. Press Ctrl+Tab (Control-Tab on the Mac) to advance from one selected point to the next; press Ctrl+Shift+Tab to back up one point. Use the arrow keys to nudge the point in increments of 1; add Shift to raise the increment to 10. The ↑ and ↓ keys change the Output value; ←· and ·→ change the Input value.

---

10. ***Update the histograms.*** Notice that the **Histogram** palette updates as you make your changes, dimming the old histograms and

showing the new ones in black or RGB, as in Figure 2-28. The only downside: the moment you enter the **Curves** dialog box, Photoshop starts working from cached histograms. Refresh them by clicking the ⚠ caution icon or the ↻ update icon on the Histogram palette.

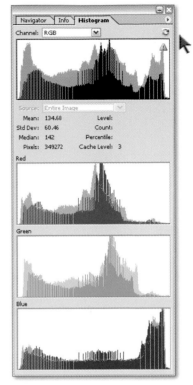

Figure 2-28.

11. *Switch to the Blue channel.* At this point, I'm generally happy with the brightness and contrast of the image. But there still seems to be a preponderance of blue, as verified by the spike on the right side of the Blue histogram in the Histogram palette. (A spike on the right means the channel is light, and therefore dominant; a spike on the left means the channel is dark, or recessive.) To edit the Blue channnel independently, choose **Blue** from the **Channel** pop-up menu in the Curves dialog box or press Ctrl+3 (⌘-3 on the Mac).

12. *Add three points to the graph.* To decrease the brightness of the Blue channel, set points at the following three coordinates (all in effect in Figure 2-29):

   • Input: 128, Output: 128. This first move doesn't change anything; it just anchors the brightness curve in place. The result is a "pivot point" around which you can bend the rest of the line.

   • Input: 230, Output: 215. This adjustment deepens the light blues in the sky.

   • Input: 245, Output: 235. This bends the line more smoothly, which in turn results in smoother color transitions among the lightest colors.

13. *Save your changes.* Click **OK** or press Enter or Return to accept your changes and exit the Curves dialog box.

The contrast of the photograph is now much improved, with more diffused highlights in the sky and dock and better details to the shadows along the near edge of the ship. (To see a before-and-after view, press Ctrl+Z or ⌘-Z a few times in a row.) But while the luminosity values look great, the colors are a little wonky. The easiest way to correct them is with Hue/Saturation.

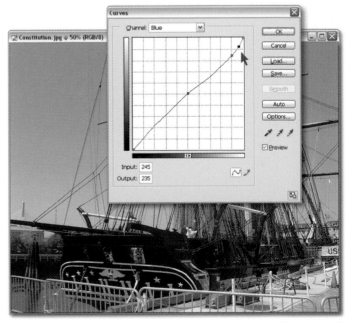

Figure 2-29.

Figure 2-30.

14. ***Display the Hue/Saturation dialog box.*** Choose **Image→Adjustments→Hue/Saturation** or press Ctrl+U (⌘-U on the Mac).

15. ***Adjust the Hue and Saturation values.*** Click in the **Hue** option box and press Shift+↓ to reduce the Hue value to −10 degrees, which pushes the purplish tones of the sky to a more realistic azure (see Figure 2-30). Press Tab to advance to the **Saturation** value and press Shift+↑ twice to raise the value to +20%. Then click **OK**.

Figure 2-31 shows before-and-after views of the adjusted ship. Granted, the transformation isn't as dramatic as the one we saw in the preceding exercise, but with sophistication comes subtlety. And Curves, with its point-by-point approach to brightness and contrast, is Photoshop's master of subtlety. Even so, a close inspection reveals plenty of improvements. The after image exhibits more detail in the shadows, a less overpowering sky, and a more natural overall appearance. That's a subjective judgment, I'll grant you, but I suspect that most people would approve of the adjustment.

Original C–5050 photograph

Adjusted with Curves and Hue/Saturation

Figure 2-31.

# Compensating for Flash and Backlighting

Photography is all about lighting—specifically, how light reflects off a surface and into the camera lens. So things tend to turn ugly when the lighting is all wrong. One classic example of bad lighting is *backlighting*, where the background is bright and the foreground subject is in shadow. Every photographer knows that you adjust for backlighting by adding a fill flash, but even the best of us forget. An opposite problem occurs when shooting photos at night or in dimly lit rooms using a consumer-grade flash. You end up with unnaturally bright foreground subjects set against dark backgrounds.

Whether your image is under exposed or overexposed, the solution is the Shadow/Highlight command. New to Photoshop CS, this marvelous function lets you radically transform shadows and highlights while maintaining reasonably smooth transitions between the two. Here's how it works:

1. *Open an image.* Open *Roman at feed.jpg* from the *Lesson 02* folder inside *Lesson Files-PScs 1on1*. Shot in a dark room with a cheesy consumer flash, this snapshot might as well have been taken in a closet (see Figure 2-32).

Figure 2-32.

2. *Open the Histogram palette.* Choose **Window→ Histogram** to display the Histogram palette. (If the palette was already visible, choosing the command will hide it. Choose the command again to display it.)

3. *Hide the color channels.* Unlike Levels and Curves, the Shadow/Highlight command lacks individual channel controls. Photoshop applies your changes to all channels at once, so there's no point in wasting valuable screen real estate on multiple histograms. Click the ⊙ arrow in the upper right corner of the Histogram palette, and then choose **Expanded View** from the palette menu to see just one large histogram, as in Figure 2-33.

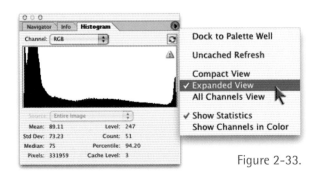

Figure 2-33.

4. *Choose the Shadow/Highlight command.* Choose **Image→Adjustments→Shadow/Highlight**. The resulting **Shadow/Highlight** dialog box contains just two slider bars. The Shadows option lets you lighten the darkest colors; the Highlights option darkens the lightest colors (see Figure 2-34).

5. *Adjust shadows and highlights.* By default, Photoshop is a little bit too enthusiastic about lightening the shadows and not enthusiastic enough about darkening the highlights. To temper the dark colors, reduce the **Shadows** value to 30 percent. Then raise the **Highlights** value to 10 percent (see Figure 2-35).

6. *Show the advanced options.* The Shadow/Highlight dialog box may appear a bit feeble—especially when compared with the likes of Levels and Curves—but it's got a tiger in its tank. To unleash that tiger, select the **Show More Options** check box. Photoshop unfurls the options pictured in Figure 2-36.

Figure 2-35.

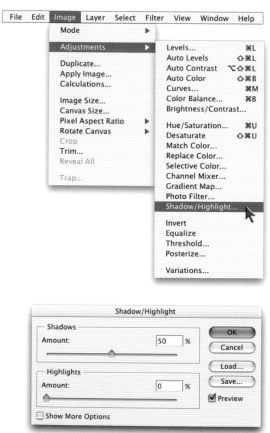

Figure 2-34.

7. *Maximize the Radius values.* The underlying code behind Shadow/Highlight bears a closer resemblance to the filters discussed in Lesson 8, "Adjusting Focus," than it does to Levels and Curves. (In fact, some of Shadow/Highlight's underlying code is based on the High Pass filter, discussed in the "Using Blur to Sharpen" sidebar on page 254.) This means that left to its own devices, the Shadow/Highlight command tends to sharpen an image. To mitigate this, raise both **Radius** values—one under **Shadows** and the other under **Highlights**—to 100 pixels. A large Radius value distributes the effect, resulting in the smoothest possible transitions between our friends the highlights, shadows, and midtones.

8. *Modify the Tonal Width values.* The two **Tonal Width** options control just how many colors Photoshop considers to be shadows and highlights. Because so much of our image is devoted to shadow and so little to highlight, we want to narrow the definition of the former and widen the latter. So reduce the Tonal Width for **Shadows** to 40 percent and increase the Tonal Width for **Highlights** to 70 percent.

9. *Increase the amount of shadow.* Having tempered the shadows by decreasing the Tonal Width and increasing the Radius, they can tolerate a higher **Amount** value. Raise the Amount from 30 percent to 70 percent to increase the brightness of the darkest colors in the photo.

10. *Lower the Color Correction value.* Much like the Saturation value in the Hue/Saturation dialog box (see Step 18, page 50), the **Color Correction** option lets you adjust the intensity of colors. Because the colors in this image are a bit too intense, lower the Color Correction value to +10. Leave the other **Adjustments** values as they are. Figure 2-37 shows the Shadow/Highlight dialog box with the final values entered.

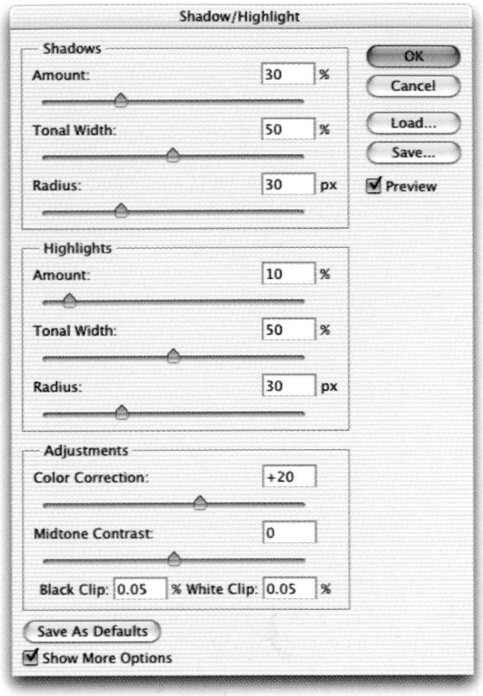

Figure 2-36.

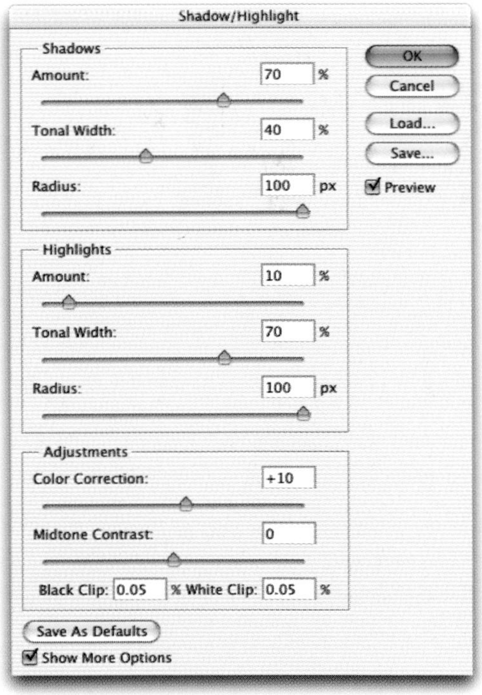

Figure 2-37.

Figure 2-38.

11. **Save your changes.** Click **OK** or press Enter or Return to accept your changes and exit the Shadow/Highlight dialog box.

Shown in Figure 2-38, the result is by no means perfect. In the course of such radical brightness shifts, Shadow/Highlight tends to exaggerate textures and background noise. But the lighting is now significantly more balanced than it was in the original photograph, and you can easily make out details such as the carpeting and the folds in the men's clothing, once clouded in gloom. Shadow/Highlight is the best one-stop method in all of Photoshop for correcting extremely high-contrast images.

# WHAT DID YOU LEARN?

Match the key concept in the numbered list below with the letter of the phrase that best describes it. Answers appear upside-down at the bottom of the page.

## Key Concepts

1. Highlights, shadows, and midtones
2. Red, green, and blue
3. Color channel
4. Auto Levels
5. Auto Contrast
6. Auto Color
7. Apply Image
8. Levels
9. Histogram
10. Gamma value
11. Curves
12. Shadow/Highlight

## Descriptions

A. This command automatically corrects the shadows and highlights of each color channel independently. As a result, it often shifts the color balance.

B. The three brightness ranges that you can edit independently using the Levels command.

C. New to Photoshop CS, this command lets you darken highlights and lighten shadows, just what you need when correcting flash photos.

D. The best tool for manually adjusting the brightness and increasing the contrast of an image on a channel-by-channel basis.

E. Expressed as an exponent, this value multiplies the brightness of an image to lighten or darken midtones.

F. This command both corrects and neutralizes the shadows, highlights, and midtones in an image, making it the most useful of Photoshop's automatic levels-correction functions.

G. A bar graph representation of all brightness values and their distribution in an image.

H. This command automatically corrects the shadows and highlights of an image, but leaves the color balance unchanged.

I. An independent grayscale image that Photoshop colorizes and mixes with other such images to produce a full-color composite.

J. The one command that lets you pinpoint a specific color in an image and make it lighter or darker; best suited to reducing contrast.

K. The three primary colors of light, which mix together to form a full-color image.

L. A command that permits you to merge two open images, particularly useful for blending alternative brightness corrections.

## Answers

LESSON

**3**

# CORRECTING COLOR BALANCE

**DEEP INSIDE** the most primitive recesses of our minds—where thoughts such as "must eat to live" reside— we possess an implicit understanding of luminosity. Sunlight illuminates all things on this planet. Those things reflect highlights and cast shadows. These highlights and shadows permit our eyes to distinguish form, texture, and detail. We need variations in luminosity to see.

By comparison, color is a subjective abstraction. After completing Lesson 2, you could probably provide a concise one-sentence description of the word *midtones*. But could you so elegantly describe *orange* or *purple*, words that you've bandied about since you were a tot? And who's to say what you call orange, I might not call scarlet, amber, or even red?

In day-to-day life, our tenuous understanding of color is generally sufficient. After all, color is mostly window dressing. We don't use it to identify; we use it to clarify. As illustrated in Figure 3-1, you recognize a strawberry by its luminosity; you know whether it's ripe by its color. Millions of people suffer some degree of color blindness and get along with only minor inconveniences—picking unripe strawberries, for example. But if Figure 3-2 is any indication, without variations in luminosity, you'd have a hard time identifying anything.

A strawberry is a strawberry

Red makes it ripe

Figure 3-1.

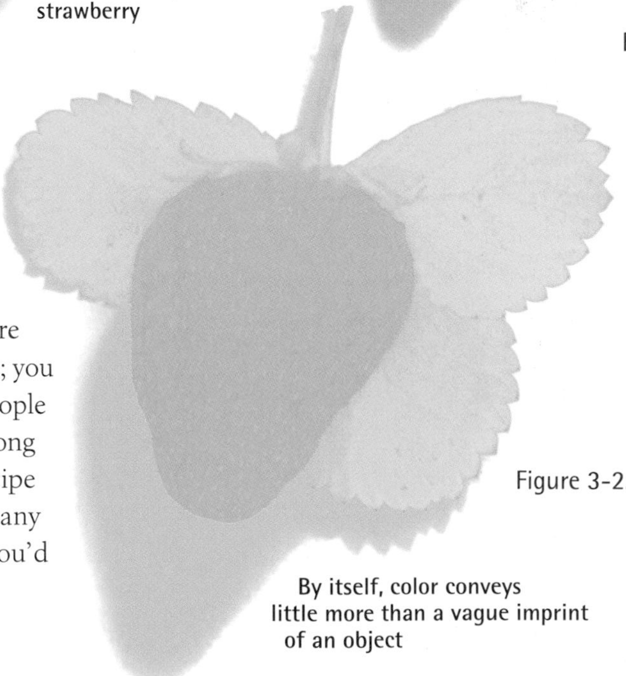

Figure 3-2.

By itself, color conveys little more than a vague imprint of an object

# ABOUT THIS LESSON

## Project Files

Before beginning the exercises, make sure that you've installed the lesson files from the CD, as explained in Step 5 on page xv of the Preface. This should result in a folder called *Lesson Files-PScs 1on1* on your desktop. We'll be working with the files inside the *Lesson 03* subfolder.

This lesson introduces you to Photoshop's most capable color adjustment commands, Variations, Hue/Saturation, and Gradient Map. We'll also explore such concepts as white balance and color temperature when we look at one of Photoshop CS's most powerful capabilities, integrated support for so-called Camera Raw. You'll learn how to:

## Video Lesson 3: Color Balance and Camera Raw

The most obvious command for adjusting color balance is Image→Adjustments→Color Balance. But as noted in the preceding lesson, Photoshop's most obvious solutions are rarely its best. Better are commands that don't have the word *color* or *balance* in their names at all, such as Variations and Hue/Saturation.

To acquaint yourself with these commands, watch the third video lesson on the CD. To view the video, insert the CD, click **Start Training**, and then select **3, Color Balance & Camera Raw** from the Lessons list on the right side of the screen. This 9-minute 36-second movie ends with a look at Photoshop's revamped capability to open and adjust raw files from a digital camera. Shortcuts include the following:

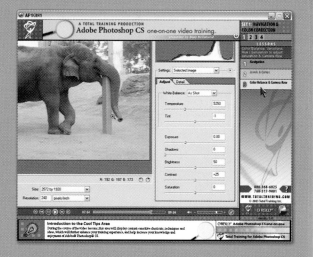

| Command or operation | Windows shortcut | Macintosh shortcut |
| --- | --- | --- |
| Color Balance | Ctrl+B | ⌘-B |
| Variations | Ctrl+Alt+A* | ⌘-Option-A* |
| Hue/Saturation | Ctrl+U | ⌘-U |
| Advance to next option | Tab | Tab |
| Nudge numerical value | ↑ or ↓ | ↑ or ↓ |
| Nudge values in 10× increments | Shift+↑ or ↓ | Shift-↑ or ↓ |

* Works only if you loaded the Deke Keys keyboard shortcuts (as directed in Step 12 on page xvii of the Preface).

Once we enter Photoshop, however, color changes from window dressing to prime commodity. To broker in that commodity, you must know how to take it apart, define the pieces, and reassemble it. Unless you aspire to become a color scientist—such folks do exist—this may seem like an arcane if not downright impossible task. But by the end of this lesson, terms such as hue and saturation will seem so familiar, you may be inclined never to utter the words "orange" or "purple" again.

Figure 3-3.

## What Are Hue and Saturation?

Color is too complex to define with a single set of names or numerical values. After all, if I describe a color as orange, you don't know if it's yellowish or reddish, vivid or drab. So Photoshop subdivides color into two properties, hue and saturation:

- Sometimes called the *tint*, the *hue* is the core color—red, yellow, green, and so on. When you see a rainbow, you're looking at pure, unmitigated hue.

- Known variously as *chroma* and *purity*, *saturation* measures the intensity of a color. By way of example, compare Figure 3-3, which shows a sampling of hues at their highest possible saturation values, to Figure 3-4, which shows the same hues at reduced saturations.

Figure 3-4.

The stark contrast between Figures 3-3 and 3-4 may lead you to conclude that garish saturation values are better. But while this may be true for fruit and candy, most of the real world is painted in more muted hues, including many of the colors we know by name. Pink is a light, low-saturation variation of red; brown encompasses a range of dark, low-saturation reds and oranges. Figure 3-5 shows a collection of browns at normal and elevated saturation levels. Which would you prefer to eat: the yummy low-saturation morsel on the left or the vivid science experiment on the right?

Continuing the trend laid out in the preceding lesson, Photoshop provides several commands that give you selective control over all aspects of color, including hue, saturation, and more specialized attributes. Armed with these commands, you have all the tools you need to get the color balance just right.

**Low-saturation cookie goodness**     **Unfit for human consumption**

Figure 3-5.

## Fixing a Color Cast

One of the most common color problems associated with digital images and photographs in general is *color cast*, a malady in which one color pervades an image to an unrealistic or undesirable degree. For example, an old photograph that has yellowed over the years has a yellow cast. A snapshot captured outdoors using the wrong light setting may suffer a blue cast.

Naturally, Photoshop supplies a solution, and a simple one at that. Designed to remove a prevailing color cast and restore the natural hue and saturation balance to an image, Image→Adjustments→Variations may be Photoshop's most straightforward color adjustment command. Rather than previewing your corrections in the main image window, as other commands do, Variations presents you with a collection of thumbnail previews. Your job is to click the thumbnail that looks better than the one labeled Current Pick. You can click as many thumbnails as you like and in any order.

The following exercise walks you through a typical use for the Variations command:

1. **Open an image.** Open the file named *Color science.jpg*, included in the *Lesson 03* folder inside *Lesson Files-PScs 1on1*. Captured without a flash under colored lights on the set of Total Training for Photoshop Elements—where I played one of those kooky chemists whose specialty is dry ice—this image suffers from what I like to call "A Nutty Preponderance of Red" (see Figure 3-6).

Figure 3-6.

PEARL OF ⬤ WISDOM

The problems with the image in Figure 3-6 bear some resemblance to those that we corrected with the Levels command in Lesson 2 (see "Adjusting Brightness Levels" on page 44). And in truth, you can fix much of what ails this photograph with Levels. But because the main offender here is color cast, Variations is the easier solution. Unlike Levels or any of the other commands from Lesson 2, Variations can recruit information from one channel and bring it into another, an enormous advantage when correcting color balance.

2. *Choose the Variations command.* Choose **Image→**
**Adjustments→Variations**, as shown in Figure 3-7, to
display the gargantuan **Variations** dialog box.

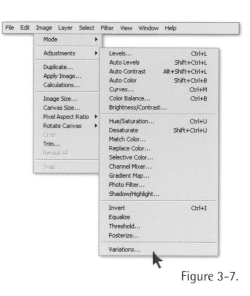

---

By default, Photoshop does not include a shortcut for
Variations. Under Windows, you can access the command
by pressing Alt and typing "Ian." On the Mac, you have to
assign a shortcut using **Edit→Keyboard Shortcuts**. Or you
can use my shortcuts. If you loaded the custom shortcuts
that I recommend in the Preface (Step 12, page xvii), the
shortcut is Ctrl+Alt+A (⌘-Option-A on the Mac).

---

Figure 3-7.

3. *Click the Original thumbnail.* Variations is one of the
few color adjustment commands that automatically
remembers the last adjustment you applied. This is
helpful when revisiting the dialog box if a correction
doesn't quite turn out the way you had hoped. But for
this exercise, you'll want to clear the old correction (if
indeed there was one) and start from scratch. Clicking the top-left thumbnail, the one labeled **Original**,
does exactly that (see Figure 3-8).

4. *Select the Midtones option.* Like Levels, the Variations
command lets you apply your changes to the highlights,
midtones, or shadows in an image. You do so by
selecting one of the first three radio buttons near the
top of the dialog box. When correcting a color cast,
however, you almost always want the default setting,
**Midtones**. (**Shadows** is sometimes useful, **Highlights**
almost never.) Make sure Midtones is selected.

5. *Turn off Show Clipping.* As you adjust hue and saturation, some colors may become unprintable. That
is, they move outside the range reproducible by the
process color inks: cyan, magenta, yellow, and black
(CMYK). These colors are *clipped* to the closest neighboring color. When the **Show Clipping** check box is
on, as by default, Photoshop tries to warn you about
these clipped colors by inverting them. The problem
is, the warning isn't particularly accurate and it blocks
what is already a small view of your image. For my
part, I always turn Show Clipping off.

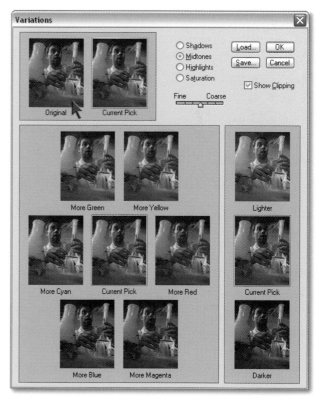

Figure 3-8.

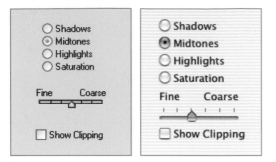

Figure 3-9.

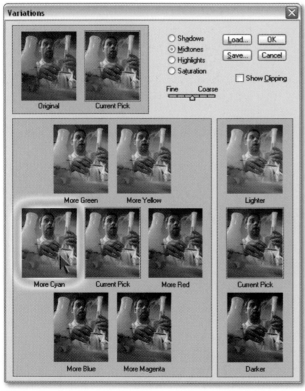

Figure 3-10.

6. *Set the Intensity slider to the middle.* The slider bar labeled **Fine** on one side and **Coarse** on the other lets you modify the intensity of your edits. Under Windows, set the triangle to the exact middle of the slider. Strangely, on the Mac, there is no exact middle. The equivalent setting is two tick marks over from Fine, as in Figure 3-9.

7. *Click the More Cyan thumbnail three times.* When Shadows, Midtones, or Highlights is active, the central portion of the dialog box contains a total of seven thumbnails: six color variations grouped around Current Pick. Click any color variation thumbnail to nudge the image toward a range of hues. So, for example, More Yellow represents not simply yellow, but a whole range of colors—amber, chartreuse, and so on—that have yellow at their center (as you'll learn about in "The Visible Color Spectrum Wheel" on the facing page).

PEARL OF WISDOM

Thumbnails that are arranged across from each other—so that they form a straight line with respect to the central Current Pick thumbnail—represent *complementary colors*. This means they form neutral gray when mixed together. For example, More Yellow appears on the other side of the Current Pick thumbnail from More Blue, so yellow and blue are complementary. In the Variations dialog box, Photoshop treats complementary colors as opposites. In other words, if you click the More Yellow thumbnail, Photoshop adds yellow and subtracts blue.

Our problem color is red, and based on the position of the More Red thumbnail, red's complement must be cyan. We have an awful lot of red to get rid of, so click **More Cyan** three times. (Be sure to get all three clicks in; if you click too fast, Photoshop has a tendency to ignore one.) All the thumbnails, except the one labeled Original, update to reflect the change, as in Figure 3-10.

8. *Click the Lighter thumbnail.* At this point, the image strikes me as a wee bit dark. So click the **Lighter** thumbnail to make the image lighter.

To feel comfortable working in the Variations and Hue/Saturation dialog boxes, you have to understand the composition of a little thing called the *visible color spectrum wheel*. Pictured below, the wheel contains a continuous sequence of hues in the visible spectrum, the saturation of which ranges from vivid along the perimeter to drab gray at the center.

The colors along the outside of the circle match those that appear in a rainbow. But as the labels in the circle imply, the colors don't really fit the childhood mnemonic Roy G. Biv, short for red, orange, yellow, green, blue, indigo, and violet. An absolutely equal division of colors in the rainbow tosses out orange, indigo, and violet and recruits cyan and magenta, producing Ry G. Cbm (with the last name, I suppose, pronounced *see-bim*). Printed in large colorful type, these six even divisions just so happen to correspond to the three primary colors of light—red, green, and blue—alternating with the three primary pigments of print—cyan, magenta, and yellow. (The missing print color, black, is not a primary. Black ink fills in shadows, as we will discuss in Lesson 12.)

In theory, cyan ink absorbs red light and reflects the remaining primaries, which is why cyan appears a bluish green. This is also why More Red and More Cyan are treated as opposites in the Variations dialog box. Similarly, magenta ink absorbs its opposite, green light, while yellow ink absorbs blue.

Of course, Ry G. Cbm is just a small part of the story. The color spectrum is continuous, with countless nameable (and unnameable) colors in between. I've taken the liberty of naming secondary and tertiary colors in the wheel. Since there are no industry standards for these colors, I took my names from other sources, including art supply houses and consumer paint vendors. I offer them merely for reference, so you have a name to go with the color.

The practical benefit is that you can use this wheel to better predict a required adjustment in the Variations dialog box. For example, the color orange is located midway between red and yellow. Therefore, if you recognize that an image has an orange cast, you can remove it by clicking red's opposite, More Cyan, and then clicking yellow's opposite, More Blue.

Photoshop's other color wheel-savvy command, Hue/Saturation, tracks colors numerically. A circle measures 360 degrees, so the Hue value places each of the six primary colors 60 degrees from its neighbors. Secondary colors appear at every other multiple of 30 degrees, with tertiary colors at odd multiples of 15 degrees. To track the difference a Hue adjustment will make, just follow along the wheel. Positive adjustments run counterclockwise; negative adjustments run clockwise. So if you enter a Hue value of 60 degrees, yellow will become green, ultramarine will become purple, indigo will become lavender, and so on. It may take a little time to become comfortable with the wheel, but once it sinks it, you'll want to rip it out of the book and paste it to your wall. Trust me, it's that useful.

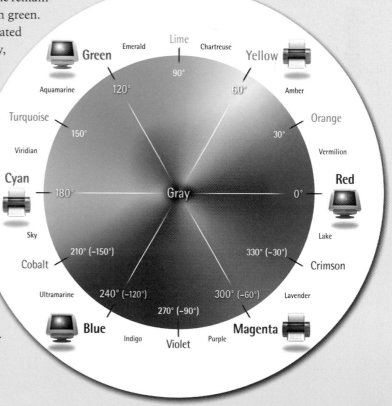

Because the Midtones radio button is active (Step 4), the adjustments you made in the two previous steps affect only the midtone values. Therefore, clicking the Lighter thumbnail is like raising the gamma value in the Levels dialog box (see Step 9 of "Adjusting Brightness Levels," page 47). Shadows and highlights remain untouched.

9. *Adjust the intensity.* Move the **Fine/Coarse** slider triangle one tick mark to the left. (PC or Mac, doesn't matter.) This reduces the intensity of the next step.

10. *Click the More Green thumbnail.* After all these wonderful changes, the image remains a bit too purple. Of the primary colors represented by the thumbnails, the nearest to purple is More Magenta. To remove magenta, click the complementary thumbnail, **More Green**. Because you changed the intensity setting in Step 9, Photoshop's adjustment of greens and magentas is more subtle than in earlier steps.

11. *Select the Saturation option.* So much for the hue and luminosity, now on to saturation. To display the Variations command's saturation controls, select the **Saturation** radio button near the top of the dialog box. Photoshop replaces the thumbnails in the center and right portions of the dialog box with three new ones (see Figure 3-11).

12. *Click the Less Saturation thumbnail.* Currently, the colors in the image are a bit too vivid. Click **Less Saturation** to leech away colors and make them grayer. (The current Fine/Coarse setting, specified in Step 9 above, is fine for this step.)

13. *Click the OK button.* It's hard to judge for sure from a bunch of dinky thumbnails, but the Current Pick image appears more or less on target. Click **OK** or press Enter or Return to exit the dialog box and apply your changes.

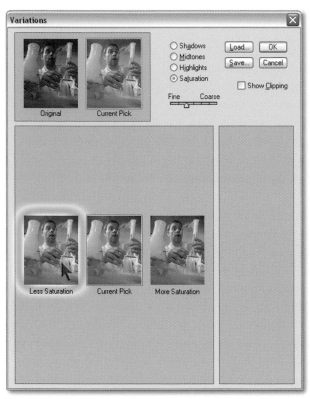

Figure 3-11.

---

Well, as I said, it's hard to judge the accuracy of your color modifications from dinky thumbnails. And sure enough, after clicking OK, it becomes obvious that I didn't quite hit the bull's eye. In fact, I missed by a fair margin. Fortunately, Photoshop lets you back off the last command you applied using the Fade command.

---

14. ***Fade the Variations adjustment.*** Choose **Edit→Fade Variations** or press Ctrl+Shift+F (⌘-Shift-F on the Mac). This brings up the diminutive **Fade** dialog box pictured in Figure 3-12. Reduce the **Opacity** value to 60 percent. Then click **OK** or press Enter or Return.

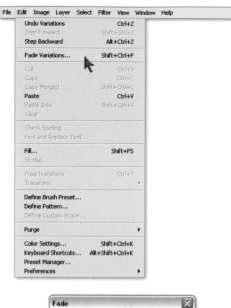

PEARL OF ● WISDOM

The Opacity value acts as an ingredient mixer. If you think of the modified, post-Variations image as one ingredient and the original image as another, Opacity determines how much of each image is used to create the final blend. A value of 100 percent favors the modified image. So 60 percent still gives the modified image the edge, with 40 percent of the original image showing through. Do not construe this to mean that Opacity lessens any specific option applied in the Variations dialog box. Instead, it reduces the effect of the command as a whole. Doubtless, we could have achieved the same outcome by adjusting the Fine/Coarse setting for each and every thumbnail adjustment applied throughout the exercise. But one application of Fade provides better feedback, not to mention heaps more convenience.

Figure 3-13 shows the finished image, unencumbered by color cast, with my natural pale skin tone restored to all its pasty glory. We dry ice chemists don't get out much.

Figure 3-12.

Figure 3-13.

## Tint and Color

Like the Variations command, Image→Adjustments→Hue/Saturation lets you edit a range of colors independently from or in combination with luminosity values. But where Variations permits you to limit your adjustments to brightness ranges (highlights, shadows, and midtones), the Hue/Saturation command lets you modify specific hues. This means you can adjust the hue, saturation, and luminosity of an entire photograph or constrain your changes to, say, just the blue areas. The following exercise provides an example:

1. **Open an image.** Open the *Helicopter & hotel.jpg* file in the *Lesson 03* folder inside *Lesson Files-PScs 1on1.* Having awoken one Los Angeles morning to the unrelenting thrashing of a circling helicopter, I snapped this photo from the window of my hotel room. As shown in Figure 3-14, I was pointed more or less into the sun, so a copious amount of reflected light obscures our view.

2. **Apply the Auto Color command.** This image obviously suffers from low contrast and washed-out shadows. Choose **Image→Adjustments→Auto Color** or press Ctrl+Shift+B (⌘-Shift-B on the Mac).

3. **Fade the Auto Color adjustment.** Auto Color sends the image to the other extreme; it overcorrects the shadows and makes the side of the building too dark. To lighten the shadows, choose **Edit→Fade Auto Color** or press Ctrl+Shift+F (⌘-Shift-F). Then enter an **Opacity** value of 60 percent and click the **OK** button. The result appears in Figure 3-15 on the facing page.

4. **Choose the Hue/Saturation command.** Choose **Image→Adjustments→Hue/Saturation** or press Ctrl+U (⌘-U on the Mac) to display the **Hue/Saturation** dialog box, shown in Figure 3-16.

Figure 3-14.

Figure 3-15.

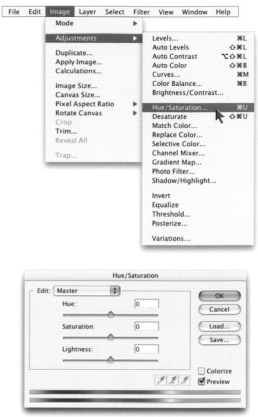

Figure 3-16.

5. **Raise the Saturation value.** Press the Tab key to advance to the **Saturation** value. Then increase the value to +60 percent. This radical adjustment increases the intensity of colors throughout the image.

6. **Lower the Hue value.** The sky and mirrored windows of the building are trending distinctly toward purple. My sense is that they would look better if they trended toward blue. According to the color wheel ("The Visible Color Spectrum Wheel," page 69), shifting the hues from purple to blue is a clockwise rotation, which means a negative value. Press Shift+Tab to select the **Hue** value. Then press Shift+↓ to reduce the value to –10 degrees, which removes the slight purple tint, as in Figure 3-17 on the next page.

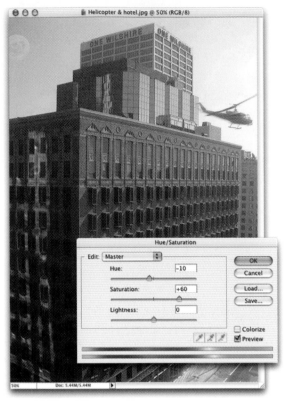

Figure 3-17.

Figure 3-18.

Generally speaking, the dramatic boost to the Saturation value holds up nicely. The red brick of the building looks terrific, as do the yellow reflections and some of the other touches. But the blue sky is just too much. In a lesser piece of software, we'd have to split the difference—that is, come up with a Saturation value high enough to boost the brick but low enough to avoid overemphasizing the sky. Fortunately, Photoshop lets us work on the sky and brick independently.

7. **Isolate the blues.** The Edit pop-up menu at the top of the Hue/Saturation dialog box is set to Master. This tells Photoshop to transform all colors in an image by an equal amount. To limit your changes to just the sky colors, select **Blues** from the **Edit** option instead.

---

Now just because you select Blues doesn't mean you've isolated the *right* blues. The blues of this particular photograph could exactly match Photoshop's definition of blue, but just as likely they lean toward ultramarine, indigo, cobalt, or sky (again, see page 69). Although the Edit pop-up menu doesn't provide access to these colors, it does permit you to precisely nail the hues that reside within the image by moving your cursor into the image window and identifying a specific color by clicking on it. The following step explains how.

---

8. **Confirm the colors in the image window.** The numerical values at the bottom of the dialog box read 195°/225° and 255°\285°. According to the color wheel chart, this tells you Photoshop is prepared to modify the colors between ultramarine (225°) and indigo (255°), centered at blue. The change will taper off as the colors decline to sky (195°) and purple (285°).

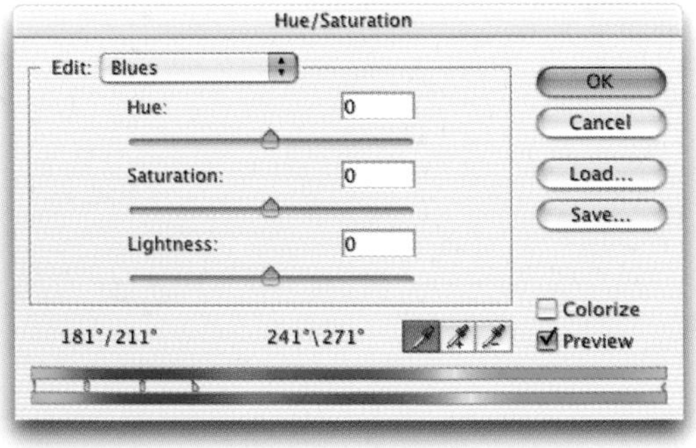

Now move your cursor outside the Hue/Saturation dialog box. It becomes an eyedropper. Click near the moon in the upper-left region of the image. The numbers at the bottom of the dialog box should shift to something in the neighborhood of 180°/210° and 240°\270°, as shown in Figure 3-18. (If your numbers differ by more than 5 degrees, move your cursor slightly and click again.) This translates to a range of cobalt (210°) to blue (240°), with a softening as far away as cyan (180°) and violet (270°). In other words, Photoshop has shifted the focus of the adjustment by –15 degrees; so instead of changing the blues in the image, you're all set to change the slightly greener ultramarines.

Admittedly, this is a lot of theory, but a single click is all it takes to put the theory into practice. And now that we have the colors in the sky properly isolated, it's seems a click well worth making.

9. *Lower the Saturation value.* Reduce the **Saturation** value to –40 percent to take some of the intensity out of the sky. This large Saturation shift may seem to make only a modest difference. But the sky no longer overwhelms other elements of the image, so all is well.

10. *Click OK.* Or press Enter or Return to accept your changes and exit the Hue/Saturation dialog box.

The final image (Figure 3-19) is both more accurate and more dramatic than the original. One might argue that, of the two attributes, drama is given the edge. Well for crying out loud, the photograph has a helicopter in it. If that doesn't call for drama, I don't know what does.

Figure 3-19.

PEARL OF WISDOM

You may have noticed that throughout that entire exercise, we never once touched the Lightness value. And for good reason—it's rarely useful. The Lightness value changes the brightness of highlights, shadows, and midtones by compressing the luminosity range. Raising the value makes black lighter while fixing white in place; lowering it affects white without harming black. It's not the worst luminosity modifier I've ever seen, but Levels, Curves, and Shadow/Highlight provide much better.

# Colorizing a Grayscale Image

One of the major uses for the Hue/Saturation command is colorization. You can override the colors in a color photograph—particularly one in which the colors aren't in great shape. Or, more popularly, you can use the command to add color to a grayscale image. Hue/Saturation makes both tasks a breeze. But its limit of one Hue value and one Saturation value per operation makes it a flimsy tool for the job.

My preferred method for colorizing involves a little-known function called Gradient Map, which allows you to substitute luminosity values with as many hue and saturation values as you like. Problem is, this command is so far outside the mainstream of most Photoshop users' experience, and Hue/Saturation is so commonly employed for colorizing, that I feel compelled to do something I don't normally do in an exercise—compare and contrast. Therefore, in the following steps, we'll make use of both the Hue/Saturation and Gradient Map commands, and you can decide for yourself which is better (even though, truth be told, I'm pretty confident about your verdict).

Figure 3-20.

1. **Open an image.** Open the grayscale image named *Clocks.jpg*, contained in the *Lesson 03* folder inside *Lesson Files-PScs 1on1*. This grayscale image (see Figure 3-20) hails from a black-and-white slide I shot back in high school. (Don't ask how long ago that was; thanks to a non-disclosure agreement with my vanity, I'm not at liberty to say.) I like the worn quality of the slide, so I enhanced it a bit with the Shadow/Highlight command rather than retouching it away. However, it'll look livelier after we add color.

2. **Convert the image to RGB color.** As you may recall from Lesson 2 ("The Nature of Channels," page 40), a grayscale image contains just one channel of information and therefore is incapable of displaying colors. Before you can add color, you have to add the channels. To do so, choose **Image→Mode→RGB Color**, as in Figure 3-21. If you have the **Channels** palette open, you'll see the one Gray channel turn into Red, Green, and Blue, plus the RGB composite. Otherwise, the photo won't look any different because the new channels are identical to the original one, as is necessary to maintain a neutral color balance. But you can take my word for it, the image is now ready for color to blossom.

3. **Choose the Hue/Saturation command.** Press Ctrl+U (⌘-U on the Mac) or choose **Image→Adjustments→Hue/Saturation** to display the Hue/Saturation dialog box.

Figure 3-21.

4. **Turn on the Colorize check box.** Located in the lower-right corner of the dialog box, the **Colorize** check box applies the Hue and Saturation as absolute values. By this, I mean that all pixels are assigned one uniform Hue value and one uniform Saturation value. The moment you turn on Colorize, Photoshop changes the Hue to 0 degrees and the Saturation is 25 percent, which turns the entire image to a low-saturation red, as shown in Figure 3-22.

5. **Adjust the Hue and Saturation values.** At this point, I encourage you to experiment. Enter any **Hue** value documented in the "The Visible Color Spectrum Wheel" sidebar on page 69, and you will see that very color come to life before your very eyes. Meanwhile, a **Saturation** of 0 percent invariably results in gray; 100 percent delivers the most vivid color Photoshop can achieve.

Figure 3-22.

---

And while you experiment, you may want to try out a wonderful little trick called "scrubbing," which is new to Photoshop CS. Move your cursor over the word **Hue** or **Saturation** and drag to scrub the value up or down. Press Shift as you drag to change the value in increments of 10. If you like this technique, take heart—it works in most dialog boxes and palettes. If not, take heart—you don't have to use it.

---

For my part—and you're welcome to follow along with me if you like—I entered a **Hue** of 40 degrees and a **Saturation** of 30 percent. The result is an orange-amber *duotone*, so called because it contains two tones, black and the 40-degree amber (see Figure 3-23).

6. **Cancel the adjustment.** Okay, that was all very interesting, but not good enough. Why? Because the moment you turned on the Colorize check box, you lost all selective control. The Edit pop-up menu dimmed, and thus you lost the ability to adjust the hue and saturation of individual colors. Your best bet is to press the Esc key or click **Cancel** to abandon your changes from Steps 3 through 5, and then turn to the little-known Gradient Map command for a better solution.

Figure 3-23.

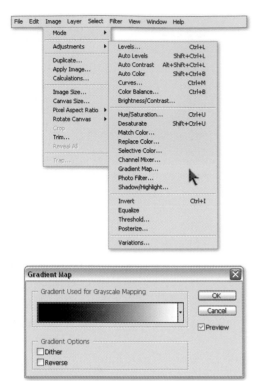

Figure 3-24.

Figure 3-25.

7. ***Choose the Gradient Map command.*** Located with the other color commands in the **Image→Adjustments** submenu (see Figure 3-24), **Gradient Map** substitutes the luminosity values in the image with the colors in a gradient. Strange as this may sound, it's just the ticket for quality colorization. Armed with Gradient Map, you can swap every single gray value, from black to white, for a specific color. And all you need to make this happen is a gradient.

Incidentally, for those who may be wondering, a *gradient* is a continuous fountain of colors. The gradient may transition from black to white, from one color to another, or between a whole slew of colors, as illustrated by the examples in Figure 3-25.

PEARL OF WISDOM

For what it's worth, Photoshop offers yet another colorization function, Image→Mode→Duotone, that lets you print a grayscale image using a combination of two to four colors. Although ostensibly a professional-level tool, I know of few professionals who regularly use it thanks to its arcane implementation. It's a powerful command, and I encourage you to try it— never thwart the enthusiasm of an eager student, I always say—but Gradient Map provides better feedback, more color choices, and the undeniable advantage of a more straightforward approach.

8. ***Load the custom gradients.*** Photoshop's predefined gradients don't work very well for colorization. So I've created a trio of colorization gradients for you to play with. In the Gradient Map dialog box, click the ⬛ arrow to the right of the main gradient bar. This displays a panel of small gradient swatches. Click the ⦿ arrow to the right of the swatches and choose **Load Gradients** from the menu, as in Figure 3-26 on the facing page. After the Load dialog box appears, find the *Lesson 03* folder inside the *Lesson Files-PScs 1on1* folder and open the file called *Gradient maps.grd*. Three new gradient swatches will appear in the Gradient Map dialog box.

9. ***Select the Quadtone Supreme swatch.*** Hover your cursor over the first of the three new swatches. You should see the hint **Quadtone Supreme**. When you do, click to select the swatch. Assuming the **Preview** check box is on (as by default), Photoshop will apply the colors in this gradient to the luminosity values in the image. The gradient progresses from black to very

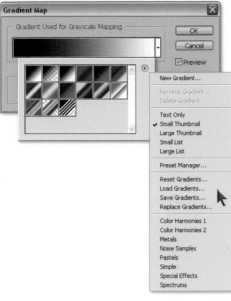

Figure 3-26.

Figure 3-27.

dark magenta followed by a dull red, orange, and finally white, each of which finds a home over the course of the gray values in the photograph, as in Figure 3-27. That's a total of four colors plus white, hence a *quadtone*. (If your image still appears black and white, it's because you didn't convert the image from grayscale to RGB, as explained in Step 2.)

10. ***Open the Gradient Editor.*** A gradient map behaves a lot like the Curves command (see "Correcting with Curves," on page 51 of Lesson 2) because it lets you lighten or darken individual luminosity values. To make brightness adjustments, click inside the gradient bar above the swatches panel to display the **Gradient Editor** dialog box.

Although the dialog box is brimming with options, most of the action centers on the gradient bar. Labeled in Figure 3-28, the gradient bar is festooned with tiny box icons above and below. The boxes above the bar (▮) control the opacity of the gradient, and have no effect on the

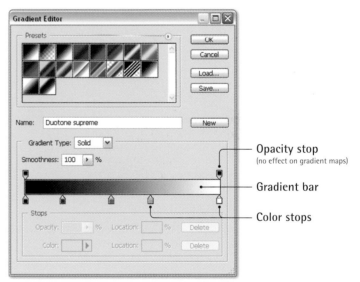

Figure 3-28.

Figure 3-29.

outcome of the Gradient Map command. The boxes below the bar (⬛) let you add key colors to the gradient. Because they determine the position of the colors, they are known as *color stops*.

11. **Edit the gradient.** Click the second color stop from the left—the dark magenta one—to select it. (I know, the swatch looks purple, but if you go by the Hue value, it's magenta. I guess I'm a stickler.) Two options, Color and Location, become available at the bottom of the dialog box. Click the Color swatch if you want to change the color; modify the Location value or drag the color stop to move the color in the gradient. Increasing the Location value darkens the colors in the image; reducing the value lightens them. (This isn't always the case—it depends on the colors in your gradient—but that's how it works in this gradient.)

I recommend that you reduce the **Location** value for the dark magenta color stop to 15 percent. Then click the next color stop over—the dull red one—and change its **Location** to 35 percent. Both changes lighten the image incrementally, just as if you moved points on the brightness graph inside the Curves dialog box.

12. **Save your revised gradient.** Enter "Quadtone Modified" into the **Name** option box and click the **New** button to add a swatch to the end of the **Presets** list (see Figure 3-29).

13. **Click OK.** Click **OK** to accept your changes and return to the **Gradient Map** dialog box.

14. **Try out the other gradients.** To see what other gradients look like when applied to the *Clocks.jpg* image, click the ▾ arrow to the right of the gradient bar and select a different gradient swatch. The images in Figure 3-30 illustrate the two additional gradients I provided—*X-ray invert* and *Wood burn*—as well as one of Photoshop's default gradients, *Copper.* In the last case, I turned on

the **Reverse** check box, which reverses the order of the colors in the gradient and inverts the colors in the image.

15. ***Click OK.*** Once you arrive at a favorite, click the **OK** button or press the Enter or Return key to accept the colorized image. (If the gradient swatch panel is visible, you may have to press Enter or Return twice.)

You can, of course, apply more colorful gradients to an image. But the more you vary the colors, the more psychedelic and convoluted your colorized image becomes. I advise subtle changes. Even small shifts in color can make a big difference.

## Correcting Camera Raw

The final method for correcting colors with Photoshop applies to photographs captured by a midrange or professional-level digital camera and saved in the camera's so-called *raw* format. This raw file represents the unprocessed data captured by the camera's image sensor. Such a file is typically several times larger than the equivalent JPEG file that digital cameras normally use for saving images, but it also contains more information. This means you can shoot fewer pictures at a time, but you capture a wider range of colors and more accurate image detail. Plus, in Photoshop CS, you can open a raw image and correct its colors and luminosity values in a single operation.

Figure 3-30.

PEARL OF WISDOM

At present, Photoshop supports raw files from only a select group of digital cameras sold by Canon, Fuji, Minolta, Nikon, and Olympus. If you recently purchased a camera for under $500, chances are it does not qualify (that is to say, it shoots only JPEG images, which you can open and modify using the techniques outlined in all exercises *except* this one). Note: TIFF files are not considered raw files. If your camera supports both raw and TIFF, raw is the better choice; it offers all the advantages of TIFF and the file sizes are smaller. In most cases, raw camera files end with the suffix CRW, DCR, NEF, ORF, or RAF. Check your camera's documentation for more information.

1. ***Open a raw image.*** Open *Colored objects.orf* in the *Lesson 03* folder inside *Lesson Files-PScs 1on1*. (You have to open the image using Photoshop's Open command or the File Browser; most likely, double-clicking the file from the desktop will not work.) Captured with an Olympus E-20N and saved as an ORF (Olympus Raw Format) file, this five-megapixel picture weighs in at 9.4MB, or about three times the size of an equivalent image saved as a high-quality JPEG file. It also contains slightly more than a billion possible colors, 64 times as many as a typical 16 million-color photograph. To distill these billion colors down to the best 16 million—or round them up to a few hundred trillion (see the upcoming sidebar, "8 Bits Versus 16 Bits Per Channel")—Photoshop displays the Camera Raw window pictured in Figure 3-31.

Figure 3-31.

The window includes a high-resolution preview of the image and a full-color histogram, both of which update as you adjust the color settings. Use the zoom and hand tools in the upper-left corner of the window to magnify and scroll the preview.

The title bar lists the model of camera used to shoot the photo as well as the light sensitivity (ISO), shutter speed, aperture, and focal length in use when the photo was captured. This provides Photoshop with the information it needs to automatically process the image in the event that you decide to skip manual adjustments and go straight for the OK button.

2. *Rotate the image upright.* Click the rotate icon in the lower-right corner of the image preview to rotate the photo 90 degrees clockwise. Or you can press the R key (for rotate right).

3. *Set the White Balance controls.* The color cast of the highlights in a photograph is commonly known as the *white balance*. Because of the trickle-down nature of white balance, you can neutralize a color cast throughout an image using the White Balance controls. Here's how:

   • By default, the **White Balance** option is set to **As Shot**, which refers to the default calibration settings for the specific model of camera. To override this setting, select a lighting condition from the pop-up menu or dial in your own Temperature and Tint values, as follows.

   • The **Temperature** value compensates for the color of the lighting source, as measured in degrees Kelvin. Low-temperature lighting produces a yellowish cast, so Photoshop "cools down" the image by making it more blue. Higher temperature lighting such as shaded daylight produces bluish casts, so Photoshop "warms up" the image by tilting it toward yellow. The closest thing to neutral is direct sunlight, which hovers around 5500 degrees.

   • **Tint** compensates for Temperature by letting you further adjust the colors in your image along a different color axis. Positive values introduce a magenta cast (or remove a green one); negative values do just the opposite.

   This particular image was shot with two light sources, daylight filtered through a rear window and a flash from above. So set the **White Balance** to **Flash**, which results in a **Temperature** of 5500 degrees and a **Tint** of 0, as shown in Figure 3-32 on the next page.

You can also set the white balance using the eyedropper tool in the upper-left corner of the Camera Raw window. Select the eyedropper and click a color in the image that should be white or neutral gray. Photoshop sets the Temperature and Tint values as needed. If you don't like the results, try again. Double-click the eyedropper icon to restore the As Shot values.

4. *Adjust the highlights and shadows.* The Exposure and Shadows values are analogous to the white and black slider triangles in the Levels dialog box (see "Adjusting Brightness Levels," Step 8, page 46). The main difference is that Shadows is measured in luminosity values (where 0 indicates black) and Exposure is computed in terms of f-stops. For example, raising the Exposure to +0.50 simulates opening the lens aperture of the camera a half stop wider.

I recommend raising the **Exposure** value to +0.10, a very slight adjustment in the world of f-stops. Because the image already contains plenty of black pixels, leave **Shadows** set to 0.

Press the Alt key (Option on the Mac) and drag the Exposure or Shadows slider triangle to preview clipped pixels. When you adjust the Exposure, non-black pixels indicate clipped highlights; for Shadows, non-white pixels represent clipped shadows.

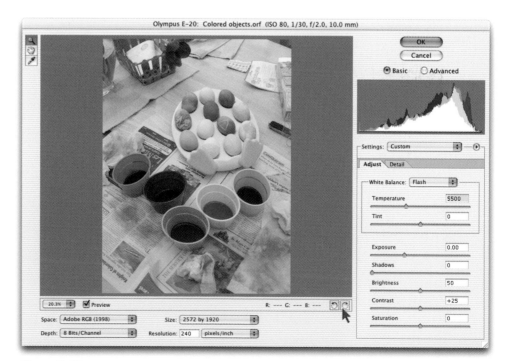

Figure 3-32.

5. *Lower the Brightness setting.* If you're accustomed to the way Levels works, the closest thing to a gamma control in the Camera Raw window is the **Brightness** setting. It's not an exact match, but it does let you adjust midtones using a rough percentage system. Values below 50 compress shadows and expand highlights, thereby lightening an image; values over 50 do just the opposite. In this example, a value of 10 does an excellent job of tempering the overly bright highlights.

6. *Adjust the Contrast and Saturation values.* The remaining slider bars have no equivalents in the Levels dialog box, but I wish they did. The Contrast slider expands or compresses the histogram to increase or decrease the contrast between pixels, respectively. As always, the Saturation value increases or decreases color purity. Enter a **Contrast** value of +30 and a **Saturation** value of +25.

7. *Click the Detail tab.* The three new slider bars in the Detail panel let you sharpen the focus of a photo and smooth away noise artifacts.

---

To best judge the details in your image, double-click the zoom tool icon in the upper-left corner to zoom in to 100 percent. Then press the spacebar and drag the image so you can see a few eggs and some of the newspaper text, as in Figure 3-33.

---

Figure 3-33.

8. *Set the Sharpness and Smoothing values.* Here's how the three **Detail** slider bars work:

- Raise the **Sharpness** value to increase the amount of contrast between neighboring pixels. Unlike the Contrast control, Sharpness doesn't affect the overall histogram; rather, it compares pixels that immediately neighbor each other and increases their difference from one another. (Lesson 8, "Adjusting Focus," contains lots more information.) The result is increased edge definition, which gives the appearance of sharper focus.

- If you increase the Sharpness value too much, you'll increase the contrast between pixels that should be smooth. The result is randomly colored pixels, or *noise*. To soften areas of noise that are the result of variations in lightness and darkness, increase the **Luminance Smoothing** value.

- To soften noise that results from variations in hue or saturation, increase the **Color Noise Reduction** value.

PEARL OF WISDOM

If you plan to make significant changes to an image—particularly changes involving masks, filters, or layers (see Lessons 7, 8, and 9, respectively)— you should leave all three values set to 0 to avoid overly harsh edges and increased noise down the road.

If you don't anticipate any major edits to a photograph, I advise that you crank the Sharpness up to 100 so you can see the image noise at full volume. Then use Luminance Smoothing and Color Noise Reduction to smooth out the rough patches. For this image, my preferred settings are **Sharpness**: 50, **Luminance Smoothing**: 20, and **Color Noise Reduction**: 50.

9. *Select the Advanced option.* Click the **Advanced** radio button located in the upper-right corner of the window to display the **Lens** and **Calibrate** tabs.

10. ***Scroll to the top-left corner of the image.*** Press the spacebar and drag the image down and right until you can see the napkin holder in the upper-left corner of the image. Notice the violet *fringe* along the top of the napkin, highlighted by red arrows in Figure 3-34. You can find a similar fringe along the top of the table if you scroll directly to the right. The center of the image, however, looks fine.

The culprit is a phenomenon known as *chromatic aberration*. Like film cameras, digital cameras may focus one frequency of light differently than another. As a result, luminosity values from one color channel may not align properly with those in another, producing a series of randomly offset colors that manifest themselves as fringes. This misalignment often grows more noticeable around the perimeter of the image, where a camera's lens element creates the most distortion.

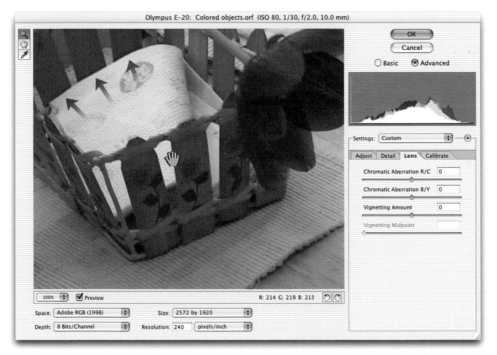

Figure 3-34.

11. *Correct the chromatic aberrations.* To fix this problem, click the **Lens** tab and adjust the following values:

- **Chromatic Aberration R/C** adjusts the size of the Red and Green channels while leaving the Blue channel unmodified. Negative values shrink the image in the Red channel; positive values expand it.

- **Chromatic Aberration B/Y** adjusts the Blue and Green channels. Unlike the previous option, a negative value expands the Blue channel; a positive value shrinks it.

Mixing fringe colors with these options takes some getting used to. But if you stumble on the right formula, you can really nail the problem. In this case, an **R/C** value of −20 and a **B/Y** value of +60 add enough cyan and yellow to completely defeat the violet fringe.

12. *Adjust the corner shading, if desired.* The **Vignetting Amount** option lightens (positive setting) or darkens (negative setting) the perimeter of an image. It's most useful for correcting *vignetting*—an effect that occurs when the corners of an image are shaded by accident or by choice (say, with a lens hood). You can use this option to simulate a gradual vignetting effect as well. The **Vignetting Midpoint** value draws the midpoint of the vignette toward the center of the image (below 50) or out toward the corners (above 50).

This particular photograph does not suffer from vignetting, and I'm not inclined to add any. But I encourage you to experiment as you see fit.

13. *Adjust the Calibrate settings.* On rare occasions, you may want to modify Photoshop's built-in camera profiles by calibrating the Camera Raw settings for your specific device. To do so, click the **Calibrate** tab and adjust the following options:

- **Shadow Tint** lets you change the color cast of shadows in much the same way as the White Balance options change the highlights. Negative values make the shadows more green; positive values trend them toward magenta.

- The three **Hue** values let you add or subtract primary colors inside a limited range. For example, **Red Hue** makes the reds more yellow (positive) or more magenta (negative).

- Use the three **Saturation** sliders to increase or decrease the saturation of a primary color.

This image is sufficiently colorful to accommodate several creative variations on these options. And should you find yourself consumed with interest, I encourage you to set about applying such variations at once. For my part, I am content to adjust the **Shadow Tint** to +15 to subtract just a smidgen of green from the darkest colors.

Press Alt (or Option) and drag the Shadow Tint slider to preview just where the shadows lie and how they will be modified. The color you see is the color that will be added.

14. ***Save your settings.*** My rule of thumb is this: If you spend more than five minutes doing something on a computer, save your work. You never know when Photoshop or your computer will crash and you'll have to perform that work all over again later. In the case of the Camera Raw window, click the ⊙ arrow below the histogram and choose **Save Settings**, as demonstrated in Figure 3-35. Photoshop suggests that you call the setting *Colored objects.xmp*. Click **Save** or press Enter to accept the name and location. From now on, this set of color adjustments will appear in the **Settings** pop-up menu, eagerly awaiting the next time you open a raw image.

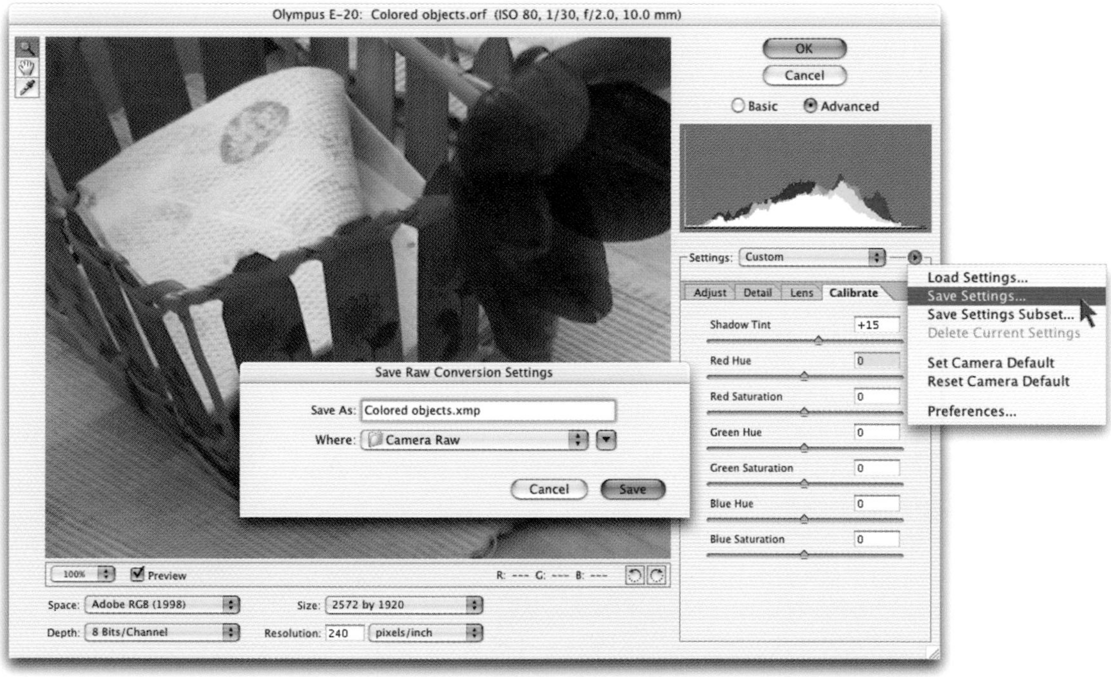

Figure 3-35.

# 8 Bits Versus 16 Bits Per Channel

To understand how color works in an image, you have to start at the very beginning: Your computer is a binary machine. It thinks and communicates entirely in the binary digits 0 and 1, known as *bits*. Pixels began life as single bits, either 0 or 1, black or white. Hence the earliest black-and-white images were called *bitmaps*.

Nowadays, a typical RGB image contains no fewer than 256 luminosity values per color channel, which means a whole

A 24–bit image shown head on, the way we users see it

The same image with
colors mapped into the third dimension

lot of bits. For example, a pixel with 2 bits can be any of 4 colors—00, 01, 10, or 11. Each additional bit doubles the potential of the pixel, so you quickly progress from 8 colors to 16, 32, 64, and so on. A total of 8 bits gets you $2^8 = 256$ colors. Hence, a typical digital photograph is said to be an 8-bit per channel image. Three channels times 8 bits each is 24 bits, which means $2^{24} = 16.8$ million colors.

The name given to the number of bits assigned to a pixel is *bit depth*. So in addition to the height and width of an image, Photoshop sees a third dimension of bit depth associated with each and every pixel, as illustrated on the left.

Various digital cameras and scanners support higher bit depths. The Olympus E-20N supports 10 bits per channel, or 30 bits in all, which translates to $2^{30} = 1.1$ billion colors. Other devices capture 12 bits per channel, 36 bits in all, for $2^{36} = 68.7$ billion colors. Photoshop supports just one higher bit depth, 16 bits per channel, which translates to $2^{48} = 281.5$ trillion colors.

The benefit of so many colors is somewhat theoretical. First, your computer's operating system cannot display more than 16.8 million colors. Second, even an extremely large image—such as that captured with a professional-quality drum scan—might contain at most 100 to 200 million pixels, and most images contain a fraction of that. Given that each pixel can display just one color, that leaves billions or even trillions of colors unused.

The advantage: There are so many potential colors going unused, you can apply multiple radical color transformations without harming your image. It's like a game of musical chairs in which there are a million chairs for every contestant. No one comes within miles of each other, let alone sits in an oc-cupied chair.

Consider the examples in the upper-right figure on the facing page. (Hey, it's an advertisement—the product name is *supposed* to be misspelled.) I start with a photo from a stock image library. Then I choose the Levels command and adjust the

Output Levels values to dramatically reduce the contrast of the image so it can serve as the background for a perfume ad (top middle). Now let's say I lose the original image and the lightened background copy is all I have. If I apply the Auto Color command to restore the highlights and shadows, I can revive a semblance of the original image. But you can see how few colors remain (top right). The corrected image is rife with color banding as well as flat highlights and shadows.

If had I chosen Image→Mode→16 Bits/Channel *before* creating the perfume ad (doesn't do you any good after the colors are lost!), this would not have been a problem. Choosing Auto Color would have restored the image to very nearly its original coloring, as demonstrated by the lower-right example. It would have also produced a much healthier histogram. Whether you're working with 8 or 16 bits per channel, the histogram shows you just 256 levels of brightness. But when you stretch out a squished histogram, the 8-bit histogram reveals gaps and the 16-bit histogram is smooth, as the inset histograms in the examples on the right show.

Photoshop's 16-bit mode has its limitations. The files are twice as large because each pixel contains twice as many bits. You can't save a 16-bit image in the JPEG format; you have to use PSD or TIFF. And you're cut off from most commands in the Filter menu. But if you plan on applying one or more dramatic color adjustments, or if you're merely keen on protecting every single color that you can, working in 16-bit mode can make a big difference in the final appearance of your image.

**Original photograph**  **Lightened using Levels**  **Auto Color produces banding**

**Radically lightened image**  **Auto Color in 8-bit/channnel**  **Auto Color in 16-bit/channnel**

15. ***Modify bit depth and image size.*** The four options below the image preview are complex and obscure. Frankly, there's not much chance you'll want to change any but one of them. That one is the **Size** value, which I recommend you increase one increment to **3072 by 2293** (+).

EXTRA ★ CREDIT

Having said that, I'd like to walk you through all four options and explain how they work, if only so you have a sense for the settings you're leaving intact. If you haven't the stomach for any more information on Camera Raw, I understand. You have my permission to skip to Step 16 on page 94 and be done with it. But if your curiosity remains alive and well, keep reading.

Here's how the four options below the image preview work:

• In almost all cases, you'll want to set the **Space** option to the current RGB working space, which (assuming you followed my directions in Step 11 on page xvi of the Preface) is **Adobe RGB (1998)**. The most compelling reason to change this setting is if you intend to convert the image to 16 bits per channel, in which case ProPhoto RGB provides a wider range of colors.

• Problem is, there's not much upside to converting to 16-bit color. As discussed in the "8 Bits Versus 16 Bits Per Channel" sidebar on page 90, no image can actually handle that many colors. And given that you're doing the lion's share of potentially destructive work *before* opening the image, the real benefit of 16-bit color is rendered irrelevant. So assuming you performed most or all of the color corrections you care to in the previous steps, the **Depth** option is best set to **8 Bits/Channel**.

• **Size** is the one setting I sometimes change. By default, the Size option is set to the maximum number of pixels a specific model of camera can capture. But the number is somewhat misleading. Every one of the cameras that offers a raw format relies on a single image sensor, which means it can capture just one channel of data per pixel. In other words, the camera captures a scant one-third of the colors that it eventually delivers. So stepping up to the next larger size—**3072 by 2293** (+) in the case of our ORF eggs—requires Photoshop to create just 18 percent more pixels than the camera invents automatically. Add the fact that you're scaling the image down from billions of colors to millions, and the interpolation (the amount of new information added) is negligible.

---

The upshot is that you can extract, say, a 7-megapixel image from a 5-megapixel camera with a surprising amount of success. In Figure 3-36, we see a detail from a stepped-up version of the ORF image compared with a similar detail from an image shot at the same time and saved to the JPEG format. The comparison isn't entirely fair since the ORF image has been corrected and the JPEG image has not. But the fact remains, increasing the Size value by one increment may actually result in a slightly sharper photograph.

---

- The **Resolution** value is easily the least important in the Camera Raw window. It affects only the print size; no matter what you set it to, you'll end up with the same number of pixels. Meanwhile, you can always modify the print resolution later using Image→Image Size. Either leave the value as is, or learn more by reading "Changing the Print Size" on page 154 of Lesson 5.

Upsampled to 3072 × 2293 pixels from ORF file    Opened at 2572 × 1920 pixels as JPEG image

Figure 3-36.

16. *Click OK.* After you click the **OK** button, Photoshop imports the image from the camera's raw format and applies the color and focus corrections you specified in the previous steps.

The corrected image appears in Figure 3-37. For the sake of comparison, I include a similar photograph captured a few seconds later under the same lighting conditions and with the same Olympus E-20N, but saved to the JPEG format. (To compare the two images on screen, open *Olympus eggs.jpg* in the *Lesson 03* folder.) The raw image has the advantage of correction, and I could make the JPEG image look significantly better using commands such as Levels and Hue/Saturation. But certain areas, such as the bright spot in the upper-middle section of the table and the chromatic aberrations along the top of the image, would be very difficult to fix and wouldn't look as good as their raw counterparts. Simply put, shooting to a camera's raw format affords you every advantage that Photoshop CS has to offer.

Final color-corrected raw photograph          Uncorrected JPEG image from same camera

Figure 3-37.

# WHAT DID YOU LEARN?

Match the key concept in the numbered list below with the letter of the phrase that best describes it. Answers appear upside-down at the bottom of the page.

## Key Concepts

1. Hue and saturation
2. Variations
3. Red, yellow, green, cyan, blue, and magenta
4. Secondary colors
5. Gradient Map
6. Duotones and quadtones
7. Camera Raw
8. White balance
9. Exposure
10. Luminance Smoothing
11. Chromatic aberrations
12. Bit depth

## Descriptions

A. These incremental steps between Photoshop's primary hues include orange, lime, turquoise, cobalt, violet, and crimson.

B. The predominant color of highlights, usually the result of an uncorrected light source.

C. Varieties of colorized monochrome images, rendered using two and four colors, respectively.

D. The number of digits required to express a single pixel, which in turn determines the potential number of colors in an image.

E. The equally spaced primary colors in Photoshop's rainbow of hues.

F. A designation used to indicate any of several varieties of unprocessed image files captured by midrange and professional-level digital cameras.

G. Measured in f-stops, this option corrects the brightness of highlights in the Camera Raw window.

H. The best tool for colorizing a grayscale image, because it permits you to select three or more colors as well as modify luminosity values.

I. This straightforward command lets you correct an undesirable color cast by clicking thumbnail previews.

J. Color fringes that appear when a digital camera renders one color channel out of alignment with another.

K. In contrast to Color Noise Reduction, this option softens areas of noise that are the result of variations in lightness and darkness.

L. The two ingredients in color: The first is the tint, from red to magenta, and the second is the purity, from gray to vivid.

## Answers

1L, 2I, 3E, 4A, 5H, 6C, 7F, 8B, 9G, 10K, 11J, 12D

# LESSON

# 4

# MAKING SELECTIONS

**MANY COMPUTER** applications let you manipulate elements on a page as objects. That is to say, you click or double-click an object to select it, and then you modify the object in any of several ways permitted by the program. For example, to make a word bold in Microsoft Word, you double-click the word and then click the Bold button. In Adobe Illustrator, you can make a shape bigger or smaller by clicking on it and then dragging with the scale tool. In QuarkXPress, you move a text block to a different page by clicking and dragging it.

The real world harbors a similar affinity for objects. Consider the three sunflowers pictured in Figure 4-1. In life, those flowers are objects. You can reach out and touch them. You can even cut them and put them in a vase.

But while Photoshop lets you modify snapshots of the world around you, it doesn't behave like that world. And it bears only a passing resemblance to other applications. You can't select a sunflower by clicking it—as you could had you drawn it, say, in Illustrator—because Photoshop doesn't perceive the flower as an independent object. Instead, the program sees pixels. And as the magnified view in Figure 4-1 shows, every pixel looks a lot like its neighbor. In other words, where you and I see three sunflowers, Photoshop sees a blur of subtle transitions, without form or substance.

Figure 4-1.

# ABOUT THIS LESSON

## Project Files

Before beginning the exercises, make sure that you've installed the lesson files from the CD, as explained in Step 5 on page xv of the Preface. This should result in a folder called *Lesson Files-PScs 1on1* on your desktop. We'll be working with the files inside the *Lesson 04* subfolder.

This lesson examines ways to select a region of an image and edit it independently of another region using Photoshop's magic wand, marquee, and lasso tools as well as a few commands under the Select menu. You'll learn how to:

## Video Lesson 4: Marquee, Lasso, and Wand

Photoshop's selection tools rank among the program's most fundamental capabilities. Simply put, unless you want to apply an operation to an entire image or layer, you have to first define the area that you want to affect by dragging or clicking with a selection tool.

To see an overview of Photoshop's selection tools, as well as the most common commands from the Select menu,

watch the fourth video lesson on the CD. To view this video, insert the CD, click the **Start Training** button, click the Set **2** button in the top-right corner of your screen, and then select **4, Marquee, Lasso, & Wand** from the Lessons list. The movie lasts 10 minutes and 7 seconds, during which you'll learn about the following tools and shortcuts in the order listed below:

| Tool or operation | Windows shortcut | Macintosh shortcut |
| --- | --- | --- |
| Rectangular or elliptical marquee tool | M (or Shift+M) | M (or Shift-M) |
| Deselect image | Ctrl+D | ⌘-D |
| Feather selection | Ctrl+Alt+D | ⌘-Option-D |
| Inverse (reverse selection) | Ctrl+Shift+I | ⌘-Shift-I |
| Delete selected pixels | Backspace | Delete |
| Lasso or polygonal lasso tool | L (or Shift+L) | L (or Shift-L) |
| Draw straight-sided lasso outline* | Alt-click with lasso tool | Option-click with lasso tool |
| Magic wand tool | W | W |
| Add to a selection | Shift-click with wand tool | Shift-click with wand tool |
| Find intersection of two selections | Shift+Alt-drag with tool | Shift-Option-drag with tool |
| Display Color palette | F6 | F6 |
| Fill selection with foreground color | Alt+Backspace | Option-Delete |

* Works only if no portion of the image is already selected.

So rather than approaching an image in terms of its sunflowers or other objects, you have to approach its pixels. This means specifying which pixels you want to affect and which you do not using *selections*.

## Isolating an Image Element

For example, let's say you want to change the color of the umbrella shown in Figure 4-2. The umbrella is so obviously an independent object that even an infant could pick it out. But Photoshop is no infant. If you want to select the umbrella, you must tell Photoshop exactly which group of pixels you want to modify.

Fortunately, Photoshop provides a wealth of selection functions to help you do just that. Some functions select regions of colors automatically, others require you to painstakingly define the selection by hand. Still others, like the tools I used to describe the bluish regions in Figure 4-3, select geometric regions. All can be used together to forge the perfect outline, one that exactly describes the perimeter of the element or area that you want to select.

As if to make up for its inability to immediately perceive image elements such as umbrellas and sunflowers, Photoshop treats *selection outlines*—those dotted lines that mark the borders of a selection—as independent objects. You can move, scale, or rotate selection outlines independently of an image. You can combine them or subtract from them. You can undo and redo selection modifications. You can even save selection outlines for later use (see Step 26 of "Refining a Selection with a Quick Mask," Lesson 7, page 222).

Selected umbrella

Colorized using Gradient Map

Figure 4-2.

Figure 4-3.

Figure 4-4.

Furthermore, a selection can be every bit as incremental and precise as the image that houses it. Not only can you select each and every pixel inside an image—as a group or independently—you can also specify the degree to which you want to select a pixel—all the way, not at all, or in any of several hundred levels of translucency in between.

This means you can match the subtle transitions between neighboring pixels by creating smooth, soft, or fuzzy selection outlines. In Figure 4-4, I selected the umbrella and the man who holds it and transferred the two to an entirely different backdrop. Not only was I able to maintain the subtle edges between the man and his environment, I was also able to make the darkest portions of his coat translucent so they would blend with the backdrop. Selections take work, but they also deliver the goods.

## Selecting Colored Areas with the Magic Wand

We'll start things off with one of the most automated tools in all of Photoshop, the magic wand. A fixture of Photoshop since its very first release, the magic wand lets you select an area of color with a single click. It works especially well for removing skies and other relatively solid backgrounds, as the following exercise explains.

1. **Open two images.** Open the *PhotoSpin giraffe.jpg* and *Bolivian backdrop.jpg* files, located in the *Lesson 04* folder inside *Lesson Files-PScs 1on1*. Move the images on screen so you can see much of both of them, and then click the title bar for *PhotoSpin giraffe.jpg* to bring it to the front, as illustrated in Figure 4-5 on the facing page. Our goal during this exercise will be to select the giraffe with the magic wand tool and bring it into the *Bolivian backdrop.jpg* image. The fact that the two images come from different continents doesn't bother Photoshop one bit.

Figure 4-5.

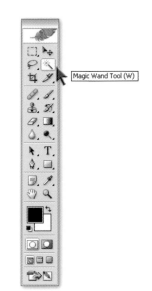

Magic Wand Tool (W)

Figure 4-6.

2. *Select the magic wand tool in the toolbox.* Click the magic wand tool in the toolbox (see Figure 4-6) or press the W key.

3. *Confirm the options bar settings.* Pictured in Figure 4-7, the options bar displays a series of settings for the magic wand. Confirm that they are set as follows:

   • The **Tolerance** value defines how many pixels the wand selects at a time. I discuss this very important option in Step 5. In the meantime, leave it set to its default, 32.

   • Turn on the **Anti-aliased** check box to soften the selection outline just enough to make it look like an organic, photographic boundary. I talk more about this option in Step 13 on page 105.

   • Turn on **Contiguous** to make sure that the magic wand selects uninterrupted regions of color. We'll get a sense of how contiguous selections work in Step 6.

Because this image does not include layers, the Use All Layers check box has no effect.

Tolerance: 32 ☑ Anti-aliased ☑ Contiguous ☐ Use All Layers   Brushes   Tool Presets   Layer Comps

Figure 4-7.

4. ***Click anywhere in the sky.*** For the record, I clicked at the location illustrated by the cursor in Figure 4-8. But unless I missed a spot, you can click just about anywhere and you won't select the entire sky. Which may seem like an odd thing. Here's this tool that selects regions of color, and it can't select what may be the most consistently colored cloudless sky ever photographed. What good is it?

Figure 4-8.

5. ***Raise the Tolerance value.*** The **Tolerance** setting determines how many colors are selected at a time, as measured in luminosity values. By default, Photoshop selects those colors that are 32 luminosity values lighter and darker than the click point. After that, the selection drops off. Given that Photoshop did not select the entire sky, the Tolerance must be too low.

I suggest raising it to 50. The easiest way is to press the Enter key (Return on the Mac) to highlight the value, enter 50, and press Enter again. Note that this has no immediate effect on the selection. Tolerance is a *static* setting, meaning that it affects the next operation you apply, as Step 6 explains.

6. ***Expand the selection using the Similar command.*** The Select menu provides two commands that let you expand the range of a selection based on the Tolerance setting. They both affect any kind of selection, but they were created with the wand tool in mind:

   • Select→Grow reapplies the magic wand, as if we had clicked on all the pixels at once inside the selection with the magic wand tool. In other words, it uses the selection as a base for a larger selection. Grow selects only contiguous pixels—pixels that are adjacent to the selected pixels.

- Select→Similar is almost identical to Grow, except that it selects both adjacent and non-adjacent pixels. So where Grow would select blue sky pixels up to the point it encounters non-blue pixels, such as the giraffe's mane, Similar selects all blue pixels within the Tolerance range regardless of where they lie, including those deep inside the mane.

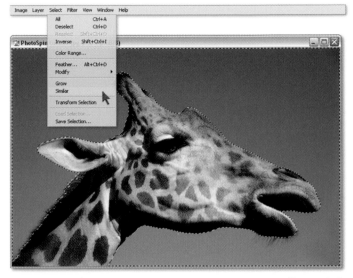

Figure 4-9.

For our purposes, we want to get all the blue pixels, wherever they may reside, so choose **Select→Similar** as shown in Figure 4-9.

7. *Fill out the selection.* This should be sufficient to select the entire sky. But if you miss a spot, press the Shift key and click on that spot in the image window. Shift-clicking with the magic wand adds to a selection.

8. *Reverse the selection.* You may wonder if this approach makes sense. You want to select the giraffe, and yet you've gone and selected the sky. As it turns out, this is by design. It's easier to select a solid-colored sky than a spotty-colored giraffe, and you can always reverse the selection. Choose **Select→Inverse** or press Ctrl+Shift+I (⌘-Shift-I on the Mac) to select those pixels that are not selected and deselect those that are. In this case, the giraffe is selected and the sky is not (see Figure 4-10).

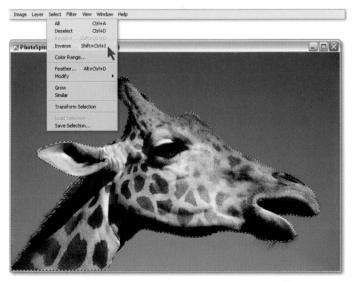

Figure 4-10.

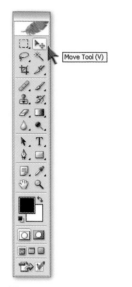

Figure 4-11.

9. **_Select the move tool in the toolbox._** Click the move tool in the toolbox (see Figure 4-11) or press the V key (as in mooV). The move tool lets you move selected pixels within an image or from one image to another.

10. **_Drag the giraffe into the Bolivian backdrop._** This operation is a little tricky, so make sure you read the following paragraph before you begin:

Position your cursor inside the giraffe so it appears as an arrowhead with a little pair of scissors. Then drag the giraffe from the _PhotoSpin giraffe.jpg_ image window into the _Bolivian backdrop. jpg_ image window. Before you release the mouse button, press and hold the Shift key. Finally, release the mouse button and then release the Shift key.

What you just did is called a "drag with a Shift-drop." By pressing Shift, you instructed Photoshop to center the giraffe inside its new background, as shown in Figure 4-12. Had you not pressed Shift, the giraffe would have landed wherever you dropped it. (If you don't quite get it right, press Ctrl+Z or ⌘-Z to undo the operation and try again.)

Figure 4-12.

At this point, you have successfully used the magic wand tool to transfer the giraffe into a new habitat. The only problem is, it doesn't look particularly realistic. In fact, it looks like what it is—a Photoshop montage. If that's good enough for you, then skip ahead to the next exercise, "Using the Marquee Tools," which begins on page 108. But if you want to make this giraffe look like it's really at home, we have a few steps to go.

11. *Select the Background layer in the Layers palette.* The **Layers** palette most likely appears in the bottom-right corner of your screen. If not, choose **Window→Layers** or press the F7 key to open it. You should see two layers, one for the giraffe—an imported selection always appears on a new layer—and another for the background. Click the **Background** layer to make it active, as shown in Figure 4-13.

Figure 4-13.

12. *Apply the Gaussian Blur filter.* To create a more realistic depth of field effect, blur the background. Choose **Filter→Blur→Gaussian Blur**, change the **Radius** value to 12 pixels, and click **OK** (see Figure 4-14). For more on Gaussian Blur, see "Gaussian Blur and Median" on page 257 of Lesson 8.

13. *Zoom in on a few details.* Use the zoom tool to zero in on the giraffe's horns and mane to gauge how well Photoshop selected the image. As you can see in Figure 4-15 on the next page, the selection has some slight problems:

Figure 4-14.

• The horns look a little jagged. But notice that the jagged edges are mitigated by a slight softening effect known as *antialiasing*, a function of the Anti-aliased check box that you turned on back in Step 3. The check box instructed the magic wand to partially select the thin line of pixels around the perimeter of the selection, thus creating a slight fade between the giraffe and its new background. Had you turned Anti-aliased off, the edges of the horns would appear even more jagged.

- Pictured in the right half of Figure 4-15, the mane exhibits a problem called *haloing*, where a foreground image is outlined with a fringe of background color, in this case blue.

The jagged edges aren't perfect, but they look fine when we're zoomed out and they're likely to print fine as well. The haloing is another matter. That should be fixed.

Figure 4-15.

14. *Select the giraffe layer in the Layers palette.* Click the **Layer 1** item to make it active.

15. *Choose the Inner Glow style.* Click the ✿ symbol in the bottom-left corner of the **Layers** palette to display a list of layer effects (see Figure 4-16). Then choose **Inner Glow** to display the large **Layer Style** dialog box.

---

By default, the Inner Glow style creates a glow along the inside edge of a layer, but you can also use it to override a glow by applying a color that's more indigenous to the image, as the next step explains.

---

16. *Adjust the settings to remove the halo.* Here are the settings that I recommend:

- Set the **Blend Mode** to **Color**. This colorizes the fringe pixels rather than making them lighter.

Figure 4-16.

- Reduce the **Opacity** to 50 percent. Because the effect traces the perimeter of the entire giraffe—not just the mane—you want to keep it subtle.

- Click the color swatch, the one above the **Elements** section of the dialog box, to display the **Color Picker** dialog box. Move your cursor into the image window—notice it turns into an eyedropper—and click the orange part of the giraffe's mane to lift a matching color. Then click **OK**.

- In the Elements section, raise the **Size** to 40 pixels to cover the entire mane.

The other options are best left set to their defaults (which is to say, Range set to 50 and all others set to 0). Click **OK** to accept your changes (see Figure 4-17).

The Inner Glow ably corrects the blue haloing, as demonstrated in Figure 4-18. (To learn more about layer styles, read Lesson 11, "Layer Styles and Adjustments.") Save your layered image in the Photoshop (PSD) format and move on to the next exercise.

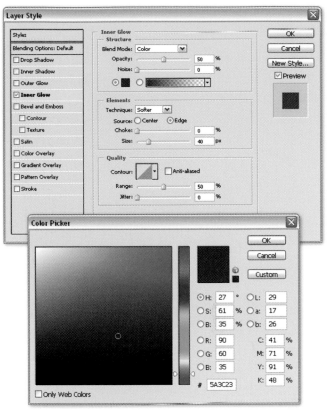

Figure 4-17.

Figure 4-18.

## Using the Marquee Tools

After seeing the magic wand and its ability to select irregular regions of color, you may question the usefulness of a geometric selection tool like the rectangular or elliptical marquee. After all, how many image elements are precisely rectangular or elliptical? The answer is: plenty. Every image begins life as a rectangle, and ellipses are as common as, well, our own Mother Earth.

But it goes beyond that. Both are great for selecting general regions that you want to use for any of a wide variety of purposes, as the following exercise makes clear:

1. **Open three images.** Open the *PhotoSpin red sky.jpg*, *PhotoSpin road.jpg*, and *PhotoSpin moon.jpg* files, all shown in Figure 4-19. These files are located in the *Lesson 04* folder inside *Lesson Files-PScs 1on1*. In the following steps, we'll combine these images into a relatively complex composition using the singularly simple rectangular and elliptical marquee tools. We'll also use the Match Color command to make the colors of the road and moon conform to those of the vivid red sky.

Figure 4-19.

2. ***Select the rectangular marquee tool in the toolbox.*** Bring the *PhotoSpin road.jpg* image to the front and click the rectangular marquee tool in the toolbox (see Figure 4-20) or press the M key. (If you accidentally select the elliptical marquee tool, press the M key again.) The rectangular marquee lets you select rectangular portions of an image.

3. ***Confirm the options bar settings.*** In the options bar, make sure that the **Feather** value is set to 0 and the **Style** is set to **Normal**. These default settings ensure that the marquee tool draws hard-edged rectangles of unconstrained height and width. In other words, they cause the tool to behave normally.

4. ***Select the bottom portion of the image.*** Drag with the rectangular marquee tool to select the bottom portion of the *PhotoSpin road.jpg* image shown in Figure 4-21. Make sure you select all the way to the edges.

Figure 4-20.

---

If you miss a bit of an edge, press the spacebar to temporarily stop drawing the marquee and instead adjust its position. When the spacebar is down, the marquee moves; release the spacebar to continue drawing.

---

Figure 4-21.

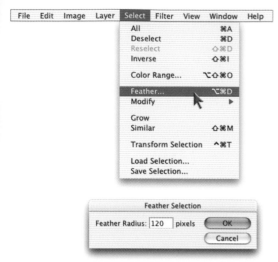

Figure 4-22.

Figure 4-23.

5. **Choose the Feather command.** Choose **Select→Feather** or press Ctrl+Alt+D (⌘-Option-D on the Mac) to display the **Feather** dialog box, which allows you to blur the boundaries of a selection outline. Enter a relatively enormous **Feather Radius** value such as 120 pixels, and click **OK** (see Figure 4-22). This creates a gradual transition between selected and deselected pixels, as we'll see in the next step.

PEARL OF WISDOM

If Feather is so deft at creating gradual transitions, why didn't we use it to fix the edges of the giraffe? The purpose of the Feather command is to blur the edges of a selection so that it has an indistinct boundary. A blurry boundary around a sharply focused giraffe would have looked all wrong. But a road that declines gradually into its background will look great.

6. **Drag the selected road into the red sky image.** You can use the move tool, as in Steps 9 and 10 of the preceding exercise (see page 104). But this time I'd like you to try something different.

Press and hold the Ctrl key (⌘ on the Mac) to get the move tool on the fly. With Ctrl (or ⌘) down, drag the selected portion of the road from *PhotoSpin road.jpg* into the *PhotoSpin red sky.jpg* image window. Before you drop it into place, press the Shift key to center it. Release the mouse button, and then release both keys. You should get the result shown in Figure 4-23.

7. **Bring the moon image to the front.** Click the title bar for *PhotoSpin moon.jpg* to bring it to the front.

8. **Select the elliptical marquee tool.** You can either click the rectangular marquee icon in the toolbox and choose the elliptical marquee tool from the flyout menu or just press the M key. (If you skipped Step 7 on page xv of the Preface, your different preference settings require you to press Shift+M to switch tools.)

9. **Select the moon (and then some).** Drag with the elliptical marquee tool to select an area well outside the moon, as illustrated in Figure 4-24).

Here are three keyboard tricks that can help you define your selection: Press the Alt key (Option on the Mac) while dragging with the elliptical marquee tool to draw from the center of the image out. This lets you align the selection outline evenly around the moon. Press the Shift key to constrain the ellipse to a circle. (The moon is not quite circular, but you still may find Shift helpful.) Press the spacebar to move the ellipse on the fly.

10. *Feather the edges of the selection.* Choose **Select→Feather** or press Ctrl+Alt+D (⌘-Option-D on the Mac). Enter a **Feather Radius** value of 12 pixels and click **OK**. Although you can't tell yet, this blurs the outline around the moon. Granted, it's not as blurry as the super-gradual transition we assigned to the road, but it's blurry nonetheless.

11. *Drag the moon into the red sky image.* Press Ctrl (⌘ on the Mac) and drag the moon into the *PhotoSpin red sky.jpg* image window. This time, instead of pressing the Shift key to center the moon, just drop it in front of the sun directly over the road, as pictured in Figure 4-25).

Figure 4-24.

---

To move an image element after you drop it, press the Ctrl key (⌘ on the Mac) and drag it to the desired location. You can also press the Ctrl key and nudge it using the four arrow keys (↑, ↓, ←, →).

---

12. *Invert the colors in the moon.* Choose **Image→Adjustments→ Invert** or press Ctrl+I (⌘-I on the Mac) to invert the light and dark colors in the moon. The moon turns a deep blue, as shown in Figure 4-26. I like the luminosity values, but I'd prefer to have the colors match the colors of the red sky.

Figure 4-25.

Figure 4-26.

13. *Choose the Match Color command.* Choose **Image→Adjustments→Match Color** to display the **Match Color** dialog box. New to Photoshop CS, this command lets you bring the colors in one image or layer in line with those in another.

14. *Set the Source option to the red sky.* Photoshop needs a *destination* and a *source* for its color modification. The destination is the image you want to change; the source is the image you want to match. At this point, Photoshop already knows the moon is the destination, because it was active when you chose Match Color. But you have to tell it the source.

    Click the **Source** pop-up menu and choose **PhotoSpin red sky.jpg**, the very image you're working on. Next, set the **Layer** to **Background**. Right away, the moon turns to red with a yellow halo, as in Figure 4-27. When everything looks good, click **OK**.

15. *Select the road layer in the Layers palette.* Click the **Layer 1** item to make it active.

16. *Select a thin strip of the road.* Switch to the rectangular marquee tool and draw a selection about half the width of the right side of the road and tall enough to extend into the clouds. The Match Color command will use the area you identify in its next set of calculations.

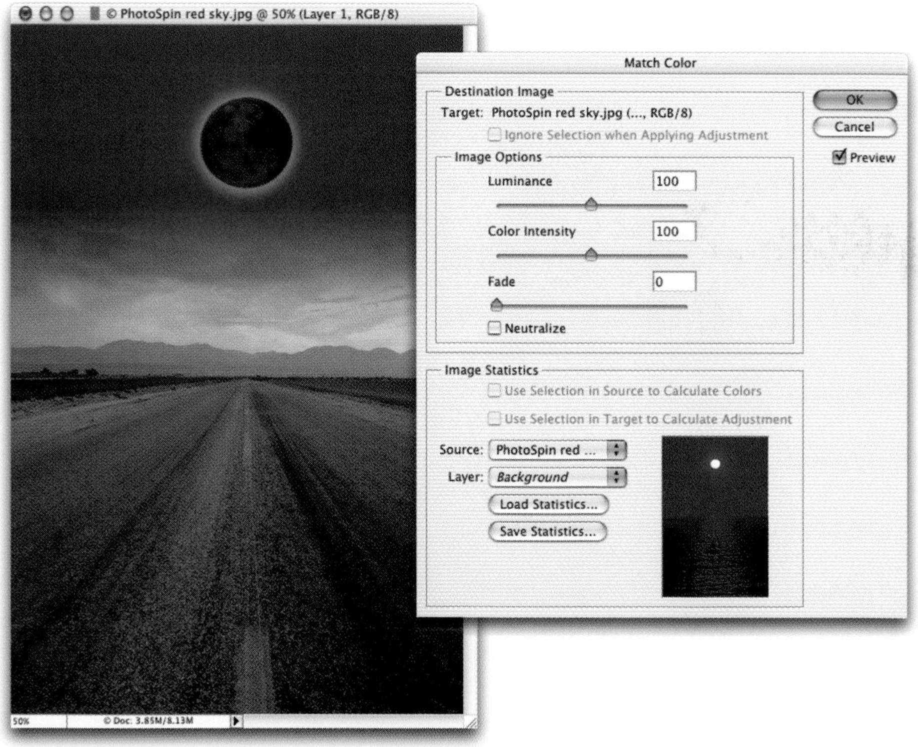

Figure 4-27.

17. ***Choose the Match Color command again.*** This time, press the Alt key (or Option) as you choose **Image→Adjustments→Match Color**. This loads your last settings into the dialog box.

18. ***Adjust the settings as needed.*** The Match Color dialog box addresses a selection in a couple of different ways. It can apply its color modifications to just the selected pixels, as most color adjustment commands do. Or if you prefer, it can use the selection to calculate colors in the source or destination. Here's what you should do:

    - Turn on **Ignore Selection when Applying Adjustment**, which applies the color adjustment across the entire image.

    - For the two check boxes below **Image Statistics**, turn off the first and turn on the second. This uses the selection to calculate the destination colors, but not the source colors.

    - Raise the **Luminance** value to 120 percent.

    - Raise the **Color Intensity** (i.e., saturation) even higher, to 150 percent.

    - Finally, raise the **Fade** value from 0 to 40 percent. This fades the effect of the Match Color command so the reds of the sky blend a bit with the original road colors.

    When your image looks like Figure 4-28, click the **OK** button.

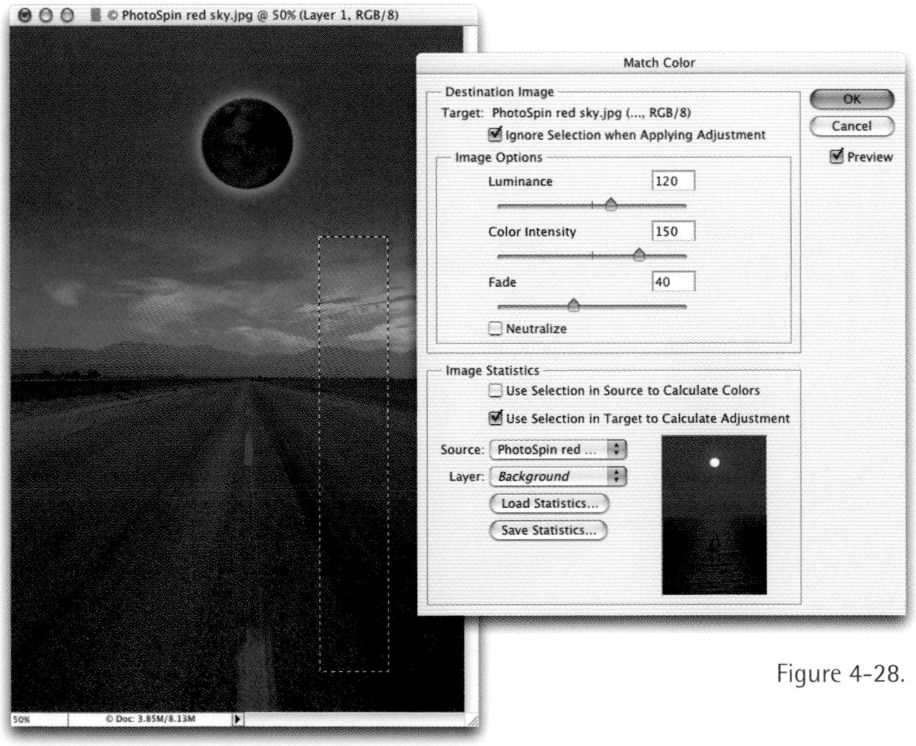

Figure 4-28.

Figure 4-29.

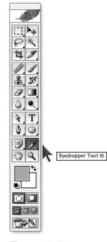

Figure 4-30.

If you like, you can stop now. After all, you've used the rectangular and elliptical marquee tools to great effect, merging three images from completely different photographs into a seamless whole. But the marquee tools can also be used to paint color into an image. In the remaining steps, I explain how to add a jet of color descending from the moon to the road and how to lift color from an image using the eyedropper tool. If you don't feel like following along, skip to the next exercise, "Selecting an Irregular Image," which begins on the next page. Otherwise, we've just seven more steps.

19. ***Draw a new marquee.*** This rectangle should connect the moon to the road, be slightly narrower than the moon, and descend slightly into the road, as shown in Figure 4-29.

20. ***Feather the selection.*** When you choose **Select→Feather**, notice the Feather Radius value is still set to 12 pixels, as you specified back in Step 10. This remains a wonderful setting. To accept it and move on, click **OK**. The corners of the rectangular marquee will appear to round off slightly.

21. ***Select the eyedropper tool.*** Click the eyedropper tool in the toolbox (see Figure 4-30) or press the I key, for I-dropper.

22. ***Eyedrop some amber.*** Armed with the eyedropper, click the brightest, yellowest pixel you can find in the image. The resulting foreground color will most likely fall somewhere in the orange-to-amber range, as in Figure 4-30.

23. ***Hide the selection outline.*** Choose **View→Extras** or press Ctrl+H (⌘-H on the Mac) to hide the animated dotted outline—AKA,"marching ants"—around the marquee.

---

Note that the selection outline is still there; the animated outline is merely hidden so you better see the results of your changes. To redisplay the marching ants, press Ctrl+H or ⌘-H again.

---

24. ***Fill the selection with amber.*** Press Alt+Backspace (Option-Delete on the Mac) to fill the selection with the foreground color. Even though the selection is invisible, Photoshop goes ahead and fills it with amber.

25. ***Fade the amber fill.*** Happily, Photoshop always lets you fade the most recent operation. Choose **Edit→Fade Fill** or press Ctrl+Shift+F (⌘-Shift-F on the Mac) to display the Fade dialog box. Then lower the **Opacity** value to 70 percent and choose **Overlay** from the **Mode** menu. The resulting column of color appears in Figure 4-31.

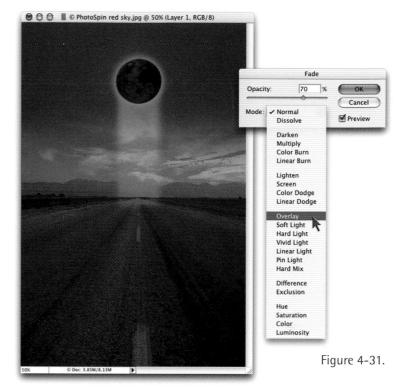

Figure 4-31.

The most amazing aspect of this other-worldly composition is that we managed to pull it off using Photoshop's simplest selection tools, the rectangular and elliptical marquees. Of course, it didn't hurt to soften the transitions with the Feather command. Hopefully, the exercise leaves you with a sense of the many and varied applications for geometric selection outlines in Photoshop.

## Selecting an Irregular Image

The lasso tools let you select irregular portions of an image. The primary lasso tool invites you to drag around an image to trace it freehand. But like freehand tools in all graphics programs, the lasso is haphazard and hard to control. That's why Photoshop also includes a polygonal lasso, which allows you to select straight-edged areas inside an image. Admittedly, the polygonal lasso tool doesn't suit all images, particularly those that contain rounded or curving objects. But as you'll see, the tool is easy to control and precise to boot.

In the following exercise, you'll experiment with both the standard and polygonal lasso tools, and get a feel for why the latter is typically more useful. You'll also get the opportunity to play with a couple of special-effects commands from Photoshop's Filter menu.

1. ***Open an image.*** Open the *Denver Public Library.jpg* file located in the *Lesson 04* folder inside *Lesson Files-PScs 1on1*. This image captures an amazing work of architecture with a terribly dull backdrop, as shown in Figure 4-32 on the very next page. A structure like this should always be paired with a dramatic sky. Fortunately, Photoshop excels at dark and stormy nights.

Figure 4-32.

Figure 4-33.

2. **Click the lasso tool in the toolbox.** Or press the L key. As I say, the lasso tool (Figure 4-33) can be difficult to control. But I'd like you to experience the tool for yourself so you can decide what you think of it firsthand.

3. **Try dragging around the library building.** The portion of the building I'd like you to select appears highlighted in Figure 4-34. Trace along the red line to select the area inside the building. (The green area represents the region outside the selection.)

   The lasso is exceedingly flexible, scrolling the image window to keep up with your movements and permitting you to drag outside the image to select the extreme edges. But if you're anything like me, you'll have a heck of a time getting halfway decent results out of it.

4. **Deselect the image.** Assuming your selection looks like garbage, choose **Select→Deselect** or press Ctrl+D (⌘-D on the Mac) to throw it away and start over. If, on the other hand, your selection outline looks great, give yourself a gold star and skip to Step 7.

Figure 4-34.

5. *Select the polygonal lasso tool in the toolbox.* Click the lasso icon to display a flyout menu of addition tools and then choose the polygonal lasso. Or just press the L key (or Shift+L if you skipped the Preface). Either way, the polygonal lasso lets you select straight-sided areas inside an image.

6. *Click around the roof of the library.* The yellow arrowheads in Figure 4-35 point to the eight corners at which you need to click. Start by clicking at the corner labeled **❶**. (There's no special reason to start at this particular corner; it just seems as good a point of reference as any of the others.) Then move the cursor down to corner **❷**. As you do so, a straight line connects the cursor to **❶**. Make sure this line follows the line of the roof, then click to set the corner in place. Keep clicking the corners in the order indicated in the figure.

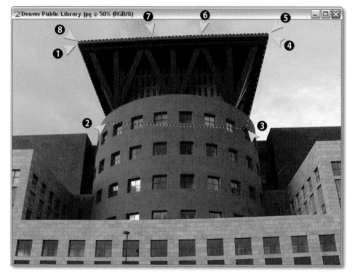

Figure 4-35.

After you click at corner **❽**, you have two options for completing the selection:

- Click on corner **❶** to come full circle and close the selection outline.

- Double-click at point **❽** to end the selection and connect points **❶** and **❽** with a straight segment.

7. *Select the elliptical marquee tool.* The central tower of the building is a cylinder, and the top of a cylinder is elliptical. You could try to select the rounded edges using the lasso. Or you could use a tool better suited to ellipses. Press the M key a couple of times or select the elliptical marquee from the toolbox flyout menu.

8. *Select the cylindrical top of the building.* This is another tricky step, so read the following paragraph before you begin:

Press the Shift key and drag with the elliptical marquee tool to add the new ellipse to the existing straight-sided selection. (Shift always adds, Alt or Option subtracts.) After you begin your drag, you can release the Shift key.

Figure 4-36.

Figure 4-37.

As you drag, remember that you can press the spacebar to move the ellipse on the fly. When you get it into position, release the spacebar and continue dragging. When the ellipse is properly sized (as in Figure 4-36), release the mouse button.

9. *Select the polygonal lasso.* Click the lasso icon in the toolbox and select the polygonal lasso tool from the flyout menu. Or press the L key to return to the tool.

10. *Select the lower portion of the cylinder.* Press the Shift key and click around the perimeter of the central building. It should take you just four clicks (see Figure 4-37).

So far, everything we've drawn has been a crisp-edged selection. The only softening is due to Photoshop's default antialiasing, which minimizes jagged transitions. But let's say you want all future edges to be fuzzy. In the case of this image, for example, we have yet to select the horizontal portion of the building at the bottom of the photo. And for purely aesthetic reasons, I think it'd be terrific if this area sported a blurry selection outline. This requires adjusting the lasso tool's Feather value, as in the next step.

11. *Raise the Feather value in the options bar.* Press the Enter or Return key to highlight the **Feather** value. Then enter 6 and press Enter or Return again. Like most of the values in the options bar, this one has no influence over the existing selection; instead, it affects the next selection outline you create.

12. *Increase the size of the image window.* Size the window so that you can see a generous amount of empty gray pasteboard around all sides of the image. Zoom out with the zoom tool if necessary.

13. *Select the main building elements.* Press the Shift key and click around the lowest elements of the building. To make sure you select everything, click outside the image in the gray pasteboard, as illustrated in Figure 4-38.

14. *Send the selection to its own layer.* With the entire building now selected, choose **Layer→New→Layer via Copy**, or press Ctrl+J (⌘-J on the Mac) to send it to its own layer.

15. *Select the Background layer in the Layers palette.* Make sure the **Layers** palette is visible. (If necessary, choose **Window→ Layers** to display it.) Then click the **Background** layer in the palette to make the lowest layer active. Now let's set about transforming the background into the dark and stormy night that I promised at the outset of the exercise.

16. *Lift some dark blue from the windows.* To make the dark and stormy night, we'll be using a filter that relies on the active foreground color. This means changing the foreground color to something dark and stormy, such as deep blue. Begin by selecting the eyedropper tool in the toolbox or pressing the I key. Then click on a dark blue pixel in one of the front and center windows in the cylindrical portion of the library. In the wink of an eye, the foreground color becomes dark blue.

Figure 4-38.

17. ***Apply the Fibers filter.*** Choose **Filter→Render→Fibers** to open the **Fibers** filter dialog box. New to Photoshop CS, this filter draws rough vertical lines of color in the foreground and background colors. In our case, the dark blue and white create an effect similar to rain. The default values shown in Figure 4-39 are fine, so click **OK** to accept.

18. ***Apply the Difference Clouds filter.*** Choose **Filter→Render→Difference Clouds** to merge a cloud pattern into the Fibers rain and create a dark, nasty storm.

19. ***Repeat Difference Clouds a few times.*** Pressing Ctrl+F (⌘-F on the Mac) repeats the most recently applied filter. Each additional application of Difference Clouds inverts the background and applies more clouds. To achieve the effect shown in Figure 4-40, I pressed Ctrl+F a total of five times in a row.

Given that rain rarely falls strictly in back of a building, you could add a layer of Fibers rain in front of the structure as well. But frankly, I prefer the look of the stormy sky when isolated to the background. It makes the library seem safer—more like a cozy, kooky, mad-scientist's hangout—the kind of place where you can curl up and read a really scary book.

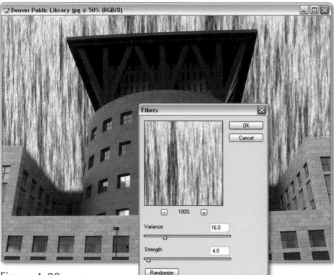

Figure 4-39.

Figure 4-40.

The final lasso tool, the magnetic lasso, is one of the most amazing selection tools in Photoshop's arsenal. No kidding, this tool can actually sense the edge of an object and automatically trace it, even when contrast is low and background colors vary. But as miraculous as this sounds, the magnetic lasso has never won the hearts and minds of Photoshop users the way, say, the magic wand has. Why? Part of the reason is that it requires you to work too hard for your automation. Perhaps worse, the tool makes a lot of irritating mistakes. Even so, the magnetic lasso can work wonders, especially when tracing highly complex edges set against relatively evenly colored backgrounds.

Select the magnetic lasso from the lasso tool flyout menu. As when using the polygonal lasso, click along the edge of the image element that you want to select to set a point. Next, move the cursor—no need to drag, the mouse button does not have to be pressed—around the image element. As you move, Photoshop automatically traces what it determines is the best edge and lays down square *anchor points*, which lock the line in place. In the figure below, I clicked the bottom-left corner of the library's trapezoidal roof and then moved the cursor up and around to the right.

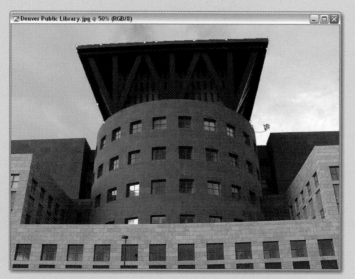

Some other techniques:

- If the magnetic lasso traces an area incorrectly, trace back over the offending portion of the line to erase it. Again, just move your mouse; no need to press any buttons.

- Anchor points remain locked down even if you trace back over them. To remove the last anchor point, press Delete or Backspace.

- Photoshop continuously updates the magnetic lasso line until it lays down a point. To lock down the line manually, just click to create your own anchor point.

- Of the various options bar settings, the most useful is Width, which adjusts how close your cursor has to be to an edge to "see" it. Large values let you be sloppy, small values are great for working inside tight, highly detailed areas.

---

The best thing about this setting is you can change it on the fly. While working with the magnetic lasso, press [ to make the Width value smaller; press ] to make it larger.

---

- Double-click or press Enter to complete the selection. You can also click the first point in the shape. Press the Esc key to cancel the selection.

Photoshop's smartest lasso tool is clearly the most challenging to use. But it's usually worth the effort. And remember, you can always combine it with other tools.

# Drawing Precise Curves

The final category of selection tools is the most exacting, the most demanding, and the most obscure. Known collectively as the *path tools*, these let you draw and adjust free-form outlines one segment at a time. The process is less like drawing and more like building a shape with an erector set. In the right hands, the path tools can result in sculpted, organic outlines that precisely follow the edges of even the most complex image elements. But as the experts will tell you, it can be tedious, irksome work. I must admit, despite years of experience and heaps of admiration, I turn to these tools as instruments of last resort.

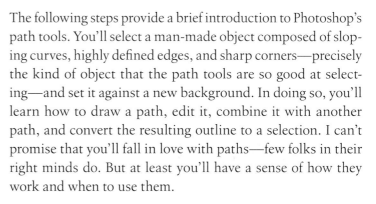

PEARL OF WISDOM

If you have experience with a 2-D illustration program—such as Adobe Illustrator, Macromedia FreeHand, or CorelDraw—then the path tools will seem like old acquaintances, if not bosom buds. They are, in fact, modeled after the tool that introduced 2-D computer drawing as we know it today, Illustrator's groundbreaking pen tool.

The following steps provide a brief introduction to Photoshop's path tools. You'll select a man-made object composed of sloping curves, highly defined edges, and sharp corners—precisely the kind of object that the path tools are so good at selecting—and set it against a new background. In doing so, you'll learn how to draw a path, edit it, combine it with another path, and convert the resulting outline to a selection. I can't promise that you'll fall in love with paths—few folks in their right minds do. But at least you'll have a sense of how they work and when to use them.

Figure 4-41.

1.  *Open an image.* Open the file *Trash bird.psd* located in the *Lesson 04* folder inside *Lesson Files-PScs 1on1*. Shot at that least computerized of all possible events, the County Fair, this happy, little trash can just screams, "Kids, I'm unsanitary! Come rub your hands all over me!" Honestly, it was lousy with flies. Just imagine how many diseases you'll avoid by selecting it from a distance (see Figure 4-41).

2. **Select the ellipse tool in the toolbox.** The filthy pelican's nearly circular head is the simplest shape, so we'll start with it. Click and hold the rectangle tool icon to display the flyout menu pictured in Figure 4-42. Then choose the ellipse tool, which lets you draw oval path outlines, perfect for the filthy pelican's nearly circular head.

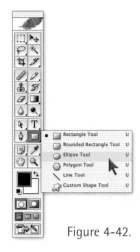

Figure 4-42.

3. **Click the Paths button in the options bar.** Pictured in Figure 4-43, the Paths button ensures that the ellipse tool draws a path outline as opposed to a colored shape layer. (Although shape layers are related to paths, they serve a completely different purpose, as I explain in Lesson 10, "Text and Shapes.")

Figure 4-43.

4. **Trace around the bird's head.** Draw a circular shape around the pelican's head. As when using the marquee tools, you can press the spacebar to temporarily freeze the shape's size and reposition it on the fly. You won't be able to perfectly align the ellipse to the head—the head is a bit skewed, after all—so just get it roughly in place, as in Figure 4-44.

5. **Enter the free transform mode.** Right-click inside the path (on the Mac, Control-click) to display a shortcut menu. Then choose **Free Transform Path**. Or just press Ctrl+T (⌘-T) to invoke the **Free Transform** command under the **Edit** menu. Either way, Photoshop enters the free transform mode, which lets you scale, rotate, and slant a path.

Figure 4-44.

Figure 4-45.

Figure 4-46.

6. **Skew the path to fit the head.** Press and hold the Ctrl key (or ⌘ on the Mac) and drag each of the four side handles—highlighted in red in Figure 4-45—to slant the oval to better fit the pelican's head. When you get a good match, press Enter (Return on the Mac) to apply your changes.

---

When working in the free transform mode, Ctrl-dragging (or ⌘-dragging) a side handle moves it independently of the opposite side, thus skewing the shape. Ctrl-drag a corner handle to distort the shape. Both techniques are useful when fitting ellipses and other geometric paths to image elements.

---

7. **Display the Paths palette.** Click the **Paths** tab in the **Layers** palette, or choose **Window→Paths**. This displays the **Paths** palette, which is where all path outlines in Photoshop reside.

Note that the Paths palette contains several path outlines. The first three are paths that I've drawn for you. The last, **Work Path**, is the path you just drew. Photoshop automatically names it and temporarily includes it as part of the file. If, however, you deactivate the path and draw a new one, you will lose the slanted oval. To protect the path outline, you must rename it.

8. **Name the new path.** Double-click the **Work Path** item to display the **Save Path** dialog box, shown in Figure 4-46. Name the path "Pelican Outline" and click **OK**. The path is now a permanent part of the file and will be saved to disk the next time you choose File→Save.

Now we have the head. But that's just a small part of the waterfowl receptacle. The next several steps explain how to modify this path and combine it with the rest of the body.

9. **Select the pen tool.** Click the pen tool in the toolbox (see Figure 4-47) or press the P key. The pen tool lets you modify existing paths, as well as add straight and curved segments.

Figure 4-47.

10. **Insert points into the ellipse outline.** First make sure the ellipse is selected. Four square points should appear around the shape. If not, press the Ctrl key (or ⌘ on the Mac) and click anywhere along the outline of the ellipse to make it active.

Then release the key and move the pen cursor over the path outline. Notice that the cursor gets a small + sign, indicating that it's ready to add points to the shape. Click at the two spots along the outline that I've indicated in red in Figure 4-48. These *anchor points* mark locations at which the path arcs or changes direction. In this case, the anchor points mark where the circular outline of the head meets the neck and beak.

11. **Delete the bottom point.** Press Ctrl (or ⌘) to temporarily access the white arrow tool and click the point at the bottom of the path, highlighted in red in Figure 4-49. Then release Ctrl and press the Backspace or Delete key to delete it. A circular path should now travel a bit more than half way around the bird's head.

Figure 4-48.

PEARL OF    WISDOM

Pressing Ctrl isn't the only way to select the white arrow tool. You can also access the tool from the black arrow tool flyout menu, or by pressing the A key twice in a row. But when drawing paths, it's more efficient to press and hold Ctrl (or ⌘) because it involves less work than manually switching tools and it allows you to keep working in a specific area of your image without losing your place.

The next phase of the exercise is to combine the pelican head with its body. Before we can do that, we must bring the two together in the Paths palette. This is a little tricky, so I've broken it into four steps (Steps 12 though 15). After that, we'll join head and body together.

12. **Copy the Partial path.** Go to the **Paths** palette and Alt-click (or Option-click) the **Partial** item. This displays and selects the path in one operation. This path outline traces most of the pelican. I drew it point-for-point with the pen tool, as you'll learn to do in just a moment.

Figure 4-49.

Figure 4-50.

13. ***Copy the path.*** Choose **Edit→Copy** or press Ctrl+C (⌘-C on the Mac).

14. ***Switch back to the path in progress.*** In the Paths palette, click the **Pelican Outline** item— that is, the path outline you named in Step 8 on page 124.

15. ***Paste the path.*** Choose **Edit→Paste** or press Ctrl+V (⌘-V). Photoshop shows the two paths together, as illustrated in Figure 4-50. But they remain disconnected. We will connect them in the next few steps.

16. ***Click the anchor point on the inside edge of the beak.*** Use the pen tool, which should still be active, to click the point that I've highlighted in red in Figure 4-51. When you click an endpoint with the pen tool, it activates the path outline and prepares it to receive more points and segments.

17. ***Click to set the next point.*** If you zoom in on the image, you'll notice a tiny straight edge along the inside of the top beak. Click the right side of the edge, at the point that I've highlighted in blue in Figure 4-51. This new

Figure 4-51.

point is called a *corner point*, because it acts as a corner in the path. Photoshop draws a straight segment between the new corner point (blue) and the one you clicked in the previous step (red).

18. **Drag from that same point.** Again click the point that you just finished clicking, but this time drag from it in the direction indicated by the green arrow in Figure 4-52. The result is a circular *control handle*, which causes a line segment to curve in the direction of the handle. Think of it as a lever that bends the segment toward it. We'll see just how useful that can be in the next step.

19. **Drag to add a smooth point.** Move the cursor midway up the bottom edge of the top beak, to the point highlighted in red in Figure 4-53. Next, click and drag up and to the right, as indicated by the green arrow. Two control handles emanate from the point, one under your cursor and one opposite the cursor. The result is a continuous arc, or *smooth point*. Photoshop draws a curved segment between the new smooth point and the corner point you made in the previous step.

Figure 4-52.

Figure 4-53.

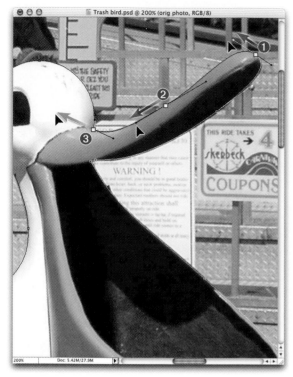

Figure 4-54.

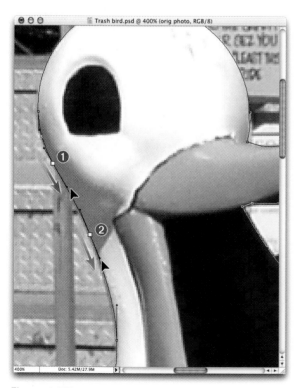

Figure 4-55.

20. ***Add more smooth points.*** Click and drag at the spot marked ❶ in Figure 4-54, in the direction indicated by the green arrow, to add a smooth point at the tip of the beak. Do the same to add another smooth point at the spot marked ❷.

---

If a segment doesn't curve just the way you want it to, don't worry. You can always edit it after that fact. While drawing the path, press and hold the Ctrl key (⌘ on the Mac) to access the white arrow tool, which lets you adjust individual anchor points and control handles. Then drag the point or handle you want to modify. When you're ready to again edit the path, release the Ctrl key (or ⌘ key) and continue drawing the path.

---

21. ***Join the two path outlines.*** Now to join the beak to the head. First, move your cursor over the right-hand point in the partial ellipse, marked ❸ in Figure 4-54. The pen cursor gets a little anchor point next to it, indicating that you're about to join paths. Press the Alt key (or Option on the Mac) and drag from the point as indicated by the green arrow.

By pressing Alt (or Option) as you drag, you ensure that Photoshop joins the two paths with a curved segment that ends with a corner point. The control handle emanates from its point in the opposite direction of your drag. Strange as it may seem, this is the way the pen tool works across all Adobe applications.

22. ***Close the path.*** A gap remains along the left edge of the path outline. To close it, drag from the point marked ❶ in Figure 4-55. It may be hard to see the control handle—it's almost parallel to the path outline—so drag in the direction indicated by the green arrow. Then drag at the spot marked ❷, again as indicated by the green arrow, to create a continuous and precise closed path.

23. ***Save your image.*** Why risk losing all that work? Choose **File→Save** or press Ctrl+S (⌘-S on the Mac) to update the file on disk. You haven't changed a single pixel in the document, so there's no risk of overwriting any important data.

If this is your first experience with the pen tool, you may feel like you've been put through the proverbial wringer. No doubt about it, this is one of Photoshop's more daunting and challenging functions. That's why I'm going to give you permission to jump ship if you so desire. Even though we haven't really done anything with our path, you've seen how the pen tool works, which is the ultimate point of the exercise. Then again, if you decide to stick it out, you have my assurance that it gets much easier (not to mention more fun) from here. Plus you'll actually get to *do* something with the path, which makes for a more satisfying experience.

24. ***Load the path as a selection.*** With the Pelican Outline path selected, click the dotted circle icon (⬡) at the bottom of the **Paths** palette, highlighted in Figure 4-56. This hides the path and loads it as a selection.

> Better yet, you can load a path as a selection by pressing the Ctrl key (⌘ on the Mac) and clicking its name in the Paths palette. I like this approach for two reasons: First, you can load any path, not just the active one. Second, this same technique works for layers and channels, as we'll see in future lessons.

Figure 4-56.

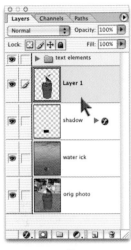

25. ***Switch to the Layers palette.*** Click the **Layers** tab or press F7. Note that this image contains a handful of layers that I've created for you in advance. We'll be putting these layers to work in the remaining steps.

Figure 4-57.

26. ***Send the selection to an independent layer.*** Choose **Layer→New→Layer via Copy**, or press the keyboard shortcut Ctrl+J (⌘-J on the Mac).

27. ***Adjust the order and visibility of the layers.*** In the Layers palette, drag **Layer 1** above the layer called Shadow. Then click in the eyeball column to the left of **Shadow**, **Water Ick**, and **Text Elements** to turn each of these items on. (Little 👁 icons will spring up where you click.) Your Layers palette should look like the one in Figure 4-57.

28. ***Merge Layer 1 and the Shadow layer.*** With Layer 1 active, choose the **Merge Down** command from the **Layer** menu. This combines Layer 1 with the Shadow layer below it, thus imbuing the former with a fetching drop shadow, as shown in Figure 4-58. (We'll learn more about creating and editing drop shadows in Lesson 11.)

Figure 4-58.

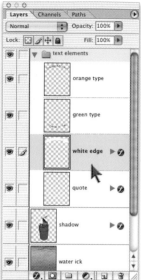

Figure 4-59.

Figure 4-60.

The layered composition looks great, in a putrid-pelican-trash-can sort of way. But one problem: The green "Thanx for the trash" text doesn't stand out very well from its background. It needs the same white edges as the orange headline above it. Fortunately, Photoshop's selection commands make this a snap.

29. *Select the White Edge layer.* Click the ▶ in front of **Text Elements** to twirl the folder open. Inside, you'll find four layers. Click **White Edge** to make it active, as in Figure 4-59.

30. *Load the Green Type layer as a selection.* Press the Ctrl key (or ⌘) and click the **Green Type** layer in the Layers palette. This converts the letter outlines to a selection.

31. *Expand the selection.* Choose **Select→Modify→Expand** to increase the size of the selection outline by a specified amount. In the **Expand Selection** dialog box, enter a value of 12 pixels and click the **OK** button.

32. *Smooth off the sharp corners.* Choose **Select→Modify→Smooth** to round out the corners of the selection outline. Enter 6 pixels into the **Smooth Selection** dialog box and click **OK**.

33. *Fill the selection with white.* First, press the D key to restore Photoshop's default foreground and background colors, which are black and white, respectively. Then press Ctrl+Backspace (⌘-Delete on the Mac) to fill the selected area with the background color, white.

The utterly and completely fabulous result appears in Figure 4-60. Thanks to the power of the pen tool—as well as a few of Photoshop's other selection goodies—our once grubby bird bin is now a vibrant, cheerful, sassy character, well deserving of even the most fastidious child's unmitigated devotion.

# WHAT DID YOU LEARN?

Match the key concept in the numbered list below with the letter
of the phrase that best describes it. Answers appear upside-down
at the bottom of the page.

## Key Concepts

1. Magic wand
2. Tolerance
3. Grow and Similar
4. Move tool
5. Antialiasing
6. Feather
7. Match Color
8. Polygonal lasso
9. Anchor point
10. Pen tool
11. Control handle
12. Smooth

## Descriptions

A. A slight softening effect applied most commonly to selection outlines to simulate smooth transitions.

B. Use this tool to select free-form, straight-sided areas in an image.

C. A setting in the options bar that determines how many colors the magic wand selects at a time, as measured in luminosity values.

D. New to Photoshop CS, this command permits you to bring the colors in one image or layer into agreement with those in another.

E. This special kind of lever attracts the line segment in a path outline, bending it to form a fluid curve.

F. Accessible by pressing Ctrl on the PC or ⌘ on the Mac, this tool permits you to move selected pixels, even between images.

G. Click with this tool to select regions of color inside an image.

H. The most precise of Photoshop's selectors, this tool lets you draw free-form outlines one segment at a time.

I. This command blurs the edges of a selection outline to create fuzzy transitions.

J. A spot in a magnetic lasso or path outline that marks a location at which the outline arcs or changes direction.

K. These commands expand the range of a selection to include additional adjacent or nonadjacent pixels, respectively.

L. Located in the Select menu, this command rounds off the corners in a jagged or straight-sided selection.

## Answers

1G, 2C, 3K, 4F, 5A, 6I, 7D, 8B, 9J, 10H, 11E, 12L.

# CROP, STRAIGHTEN, AND SIZE

I SUPPOSE IT'S possible that on some planet, there are those who believe that the perfect photograph is one that needs no editing. On this far-flung world, programs like Photoshop are tools of last resort. The very act of opening a photograph in an image editor is a tacit declaration that the photo is a failure. Every command, tool, or option applied is regarded as a mark of flimflam or forgery.

But that's hardly the case here on Earth. Despite oft-voiced (and occasionally reasonable) concerns that modern image editing is distorting our perception of places and events, image manipulation has always been part and parcel of the photographic process. And there's no better example of this than cropping.

Since long before computers were widely available and eons before Photoshop hit the market, it has been common practice among professional photographers to frame a shot and then back up a step or two before snapping the picture. This way, you have more options when it comes time to crop. Of course, nothing says you have to crop the image the way you first framed it; as illustrated in Figure 5-1, you can crop it any way you want to. And that's just the point. Even back in the old days, photographers shot their pictures with editing in mind because doing so ensured a wider range of post-photography options.

## Whole-Image Transformations

If image editing is the norm, then the norm for image editing is whole-image transformations. This includes operations such as scale and rotate applied to an entire image at a time. While this may sound like a dry topic, whole-image transformations can produce dramatic and surprising effects.

The image you framed

The image you shot

The image you cropped

Figure 5-1.

# ABOUT THIS LESSON

## Project Files

Before beginning the exercises, make sure that you've installed the lesson files from the CD, as explained in Step 5 on page xv of the Preface. This should result in a folder called *Lesson Files-PScs 1on1* on your desktop. We'll be working with the files inside the *Lesson 05* subfolder.

In this lesson, we explore ways to crop, straighten, and resize digital photographs using a small but essential collection of tools and commands. You'll learn how to:

- Automatically crop and straighten a group of images scanned together . . . . . . . . . . . . . . page 136

- Measure the angle of a crooked photo and rotate it in the opposite direction . . . . . . . page 139

- Use the crop tool to straighten an image and crop extraneous background information . . . . . . page 144

- Adjust the resolution of an image and select the best interpolation setting . . . . . . . . . . . . page 150

## Video Lesson 5: Image and Canvas Size

The exercises in this lesson deal with one of the most fundamental topics in Photoshop: changing and managing the number of pixels in an image. To fully understand this topic, you must come to terms with the concepts of *image size* and *canvas size*. Both describe the number of pixels in an image, but in different ways.

For an introduction to these key concepts—as well as the commands named for them—watch the fifth video lesson on the CD. To view this video, insert the CD, click the **Start Training** button, click the Set **2** button in the top-right corner of your screen, and then select **5, Image & Canvas Size** from the Lessons list. The movie lasts 8 minutes and 39 seconds, during which time you'll learn about the following tools, commands, and shortcuts:

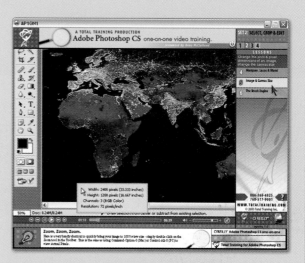

| Tool, command, or operation | Windows shortcut | Macintosh shortcut |
| --- | --- | --- |
| View pixel dimensions of image | Alt-click Doc: item | Option-click Doc: item |
| Show or hide the Info palette | F8 | F8 |
| Image Size | Ctrl+Alt+I* | ⌘-Option-I* |
| Crop tool | C | C |
| Canvas Size | Ctrl+Alt+C* | ⌘-Option-C* |
| Proceed button | P | P |

* Works only if you loaded the Deke Keys keyboard shortcuts (as directed in Step 12 on page xvii of the Preface).

More important, the whole-image transformation forces you to think about basic image composition and ponder some important questions:

- The image in Figure 5-2 is clearly at an angle, but just what angle is it? A label in the image says it's off by 47.7 degrees. Why am I so confident this number is exactly right?

- After I rotate the image, I have to crop it. But as illustrated in Figure 5-3, which of several methods should I use? And which, if any, is best suited to this image?

- Finally, once the crop is complete, there's the problem of scale. Should I reduce or increase the number of pixels? Or should I merely reduce the resolution to print the image larger, as in Figure 5-4?

So many questions. Fortunately, this lesson contains the answers.

Figure 5-2.

Figure 5-3.

Figure 5-4.

## The Order in Which We Work

At this point, you may wonder why I've waited until Lesson 5 to talk about such a fundamental topic as cropping. Given that we're addressing topics in the order you actually apply them, wouldn't it make more sense to first crop an image and then correct its brightness, contrast, and color balance, as discussed in Lessons 2 and 3? The answer is in some cases yes, but in more cases no.

---

**PEARL OF WISDOM**

Scaling an image changes the number of pixels. Straightening an image changes the orientation of pixels. Both operations throw away pixels and make up new ones—a process called *interpolation*—which is best performed after you get the colors in line. In fact, interpolation can actually help a color adjustment by smoothing out the rough transitions sometimes produced by commands such as Shadow/Highlight and Hue/Saturation.

---

On its own, cropping does not require interpolation, and may therefore be applied in advance of color adjustments. However, Photoshop offers a few functions that crop and interpolate an image all at once, in which case, you're better off applying the color adjustments first.

So by way of general advice, get your color adjustments out of the way first, and then set about cropping and straightening the image.

## Auto Crop and Straighten

Photoshop CS offers a new method for straightening and cropping that is applicable specifically to scanned images, particularly those captured by a flatbed scanner. Photoshop can now open a crooked image, rotate it upright, and crop away the area outside the image— all automatically, without so much as batting an eye. Better yet, Photoshop can work this magic on multiple images at a time.

You begin by taking a handful of printed images and throwing them down on a flatbed scanner. Then, rather than using the scanner's software to assign each image to a separate file, go ahead and scan all images as a group to a single file. Figure 5-5 shows me scanning a total of seven images using a Umax PowerLook 3000, from both the hardware and software perspectives. Called *gang scanning*, this previously ill-advised technique works wonders in Photoshop CS. The goal of this exercise is to take this very gang scan and extract the individual images inside Photoshop.

1. ***Open the scanned image.*** Open *The gang.jpg* included in the *Lesson 05* folder inside *Lesson Files-PScs 1on1*. You'll see a collection of seven images of various shapes and sizes—some photographs, some printed artwork—as in Figure 5-6. Miraculously, Photoshop can work on them all at once.

PEARL OF WISDOM

Note that Figure 5-6 shows the actual file produced by the scanner. The PowerLook 3000 is distinct in that the glass that holds the images moves as the sensor zips back and forth beneath it. The blue background is a mat that anchors the images in place. Despite my scanner's unusual design, this real-life exercise should match your experiences when straightening and cropping your own scanned photos.

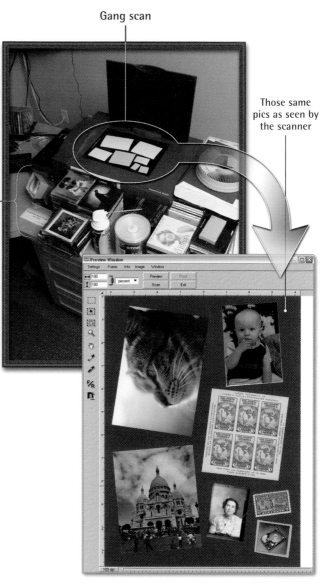

Gang scan

My incredibly orderly, roomy desktop

Those same pics as seen by the scanner

Figure 5-5.

Figure 5-6.

Adobe Photoshop

| File | Edit | Image | Layer | Select | Filter | View | Window | Help |

New...                    Ctrl+N
Open...                   Ctrl+O
Browse...            Shift+Ctrl+O
Open As...
Open Recent                        ▸

Edit in ImageReady   Shift+Ctrl+M

Close                    Ctrl+W
Close All             Alt+Ctrl+W
Save                     Ctrl+S
Save As...           Shift+Ctrl+S
Save a Version...
Save for Web...  Alt+Shift+Ctrl+S
Revert                       F12

Place...

Online Services...

Import                             ▸
Export                             ▸

Automate                           ▸     Batch...
Scripts                            ▸     PDF Presentation...
                                         Create Droplet...
File Info...      Alt+Shift+Ctrl+I
Versions...                              Conditional Mode Change...
                                         Contact Sheet II...
Page Setup...       Shift+Ctrl+P         Crop and Straighten Photos
Print with Preview...  Alt+Ctrl+P        Fit Image...
Print...               Ctrl+P            Multi-Page PDF to PSD...
Print One Copy  Alt+Shift+Ctrl+P         Picture Package...
                                         Web Photo Gallery...
Jump To                            ▸
                                         Photomerge...
Exit                     Ctrl+Q

Figure 5-7.

2. *Choose the Crop and Straighten Photos command.* Amazingly, that's all there is to it. The moment you choose **File→Automate→ Crop and Straighten Photos** (see Figure 5-7), Photoshop takes over. You may see a progress bar as Photoshop loads the plug-in from disk. Then the windows start flying as the program duplicates, rotates, and crops each image. All you have to do is sit back and watch. If all of Photoshop was this easy, I'd be out of a job.

3. *Review the cropped images.* In less than a minute on most systems, the Crop and Straighten Photos command makes order from chaos. In all, the command generates seven separate image windows, each named *The gang copy* followed by a number, in the order shown in Figure 5-8. Note that Photoshop analyzes the images from top to bottom. This is why the photo of my son Sammy, which is slightly higher than the cat, comes up first.

Photoshop really does a swell job of straightening the images, even managing to accurately evaluate pictures with irregular edges, such as the perforated stamp and the clipped magazine photo of the hard drive. But it doesn't know when an image is on its side. That means the cat photo still needs work.

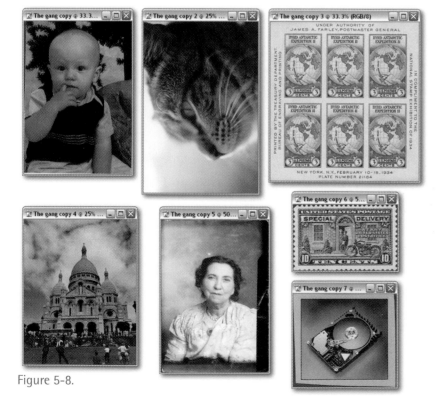

Figure 5-8.

4. *Rotate the cat photo.* Click the title bar for the cat photo, *The gang copy 2.* Then choose **Image→Rotate Canvas→90° CW.** Alternatively, if you loaded the custom Deke Keys short-cuts that I recommend in Step 12 on page xvii of the Preface, you can press Ctrl+Shift+Alt+] (⌘-Shift-Option-] on the Mac). This rotates the entire image, changing it from vertical to horizontal (see Figure 5-9).

5. *Save the images.* Photoshop does not automatically save the images it generates; you have to do that manually. So go ahead and save the files you might want to use later. The JPEG format with a high Quality setting is fine for the photographs.

But because JPEG modifies image details in its attempt to minimize the file size, it is not well suited to high-contrast artwork, such as the stamps. You may prefer to save these images as TIFF files.

If an image (such as the hard drive) requires further cropping or you simply aren't happy with Photoshop's choices, turn to one of the techniques documented in the upcoming exercises.

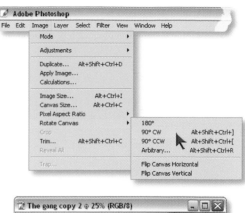

## Straightening a Crooked Image

The Crop and Straighten Photos command works wonders on an image that was scanned crooked, but it doesn't work worth a hill of beans on an image that was shot crooked. For example, consider the bridge detail in Figure 5-10. Clearly, I shot it a few degrees off plumb (left). But applying Crop and Straighten Photos makes it even worse (right). Without an obvious rectangle to work with, the command goes haywire.

Figure 5-9.

When straightening a crooked photo—digital or otherwise—the better solution is Image→Rotate Canvas→Arbitrary. This command permits you to rotate an entire image by a specific numerical increment, accurate to 0.01 degree. Of course, the trick is to figure out

Figure 5-10.

Figure 5-11.

how much rotation to apply. You do this using the measure tool, as we'll see in the following exercise:

1. ***Open a crooked photograph.*** Open the file named *Suspension tower.jpg* located in the *Lesson 05 folder* inside *Lesson Files-PScs 1on1*. At first glance, the photo doesn't look so bad. After all, you have to allow some slanting for perspective. But believe me, if this bridge tower were a mast, we'd all be tumbling toward the starboard side. Our job is to straighten it.

2. ***Duplicate the image.*** Choose **Image→Duplicate** to copy the image. Name the duplicate "Tower Upright" (see Figure 5-11) and click **OK**. We'll straighten the duplicate version of the image; then in Step 7, we'll call on the original to assist in cropping away the excess pixels produced by the rotation.

3. ***Select the measure tool in the toolbox.*** Click and hold the eyedropper icon near the bottom of the toolbox and choose the measure tool from the flyout menu (see Figure 5-12). This tool lets you measure the distance and angle between two points. Handy for us, it also shares that angle information with the Arbitrary command.

4. ***Drag inside the image with the measure tool.*** For the best results, drag along the edge of an image element that should be exactly horizontal or vertical.

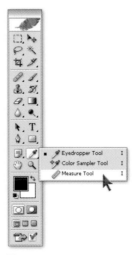

Figure 5-12.

You might be tempted to drag down the middle of the tower, which ought to be vertical, but finding your way through the latticework is nearly impossible. Better to drag along the bottom of the bridge, which ought to be horizontal, as illustrated in Figure 5-13. After you draw the line, feel free to drag the endpoints to get the line exactly right.

As you work with the measure tool, the options bar notes the angle (**A**) and distance (**D1**) of the line. Angle is the inclination of the line, which translates to the number of degrees the line is "out of plumb" (off from absolute vertical or horizontal). Distance is the length of the line, measured in our case in pixels. When straightening an image, **D1** is of no concern; only **A** matters.

If you drag from left to right, as I did, the **A** value will be something like −3.8 degrees. But if you drag from right to left, the **A** value will be more in the neighborhood of 176.2 degrees. Which is correct? As it turns out, both. Which should you use to rotate the image? Neither, because Photoshop will do it for you in the very next step.

5. *Choose the Arbitrary rotation command.* Choose **Image→Rotate Canvas→Arbitrary**. Or, if you loaded the Deke Keys shortcuts I recommend in the Preface (Step 12, page xvii), you can press Ctrl+Shift+Alt+R (⌘-Shift-Option-R on the Mac). The **Rotate Canvas** dialog box appears, bearing an Angle value that is the opposite of the **A** value tracked by the options bar. In my case, the value is 3.79 degrees counter-clockwise (see Figure 5-14), which is the same as −176.21 clockwise. The angle of your measure line —and thus your Angle value—may be slightly different. But as long as the difference is just a few fractions of a degree, all should be fine. Click **OK** to accept the rotation.

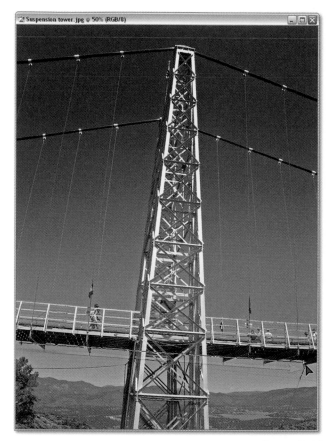

Figure 5-13.

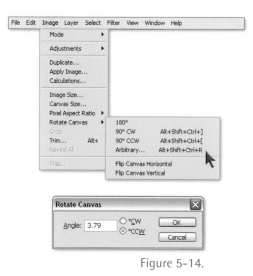

Figure 5-14.

Figure 5-15.

Your image should now be upright. But in expanding the boundaries of the image to include the rotated photograph, the Arbitrary command exposed empty wedges around the corners (see Figure 5-15). (The wedges appear in the background color, which is white by default.) Naturally, you need to crop away the wedges, but how? Ideally, Photoshop would provide an automatic way to delete all the wedges without taking away any more of the image than is absolutely necessary, but it doesn't. Fortunately, you can work around this oversight using Canvas Size and a little math, as the remaining steps explain.

6. *Choose the Canvas Size command.* Once again, assuming you loaded my shortcuts (Step 12, page xvii), press Ctrl+Alt+C (⌘-Option-C on the Mac). Otherwise, choose **Image→Canvas Size**. This displays the **Canvas Size** dialog box shown in Figure 5-16, which lets you scale the boundaries of an image—the so-called *canvas*—without resizing the image itself. If you make the canvas

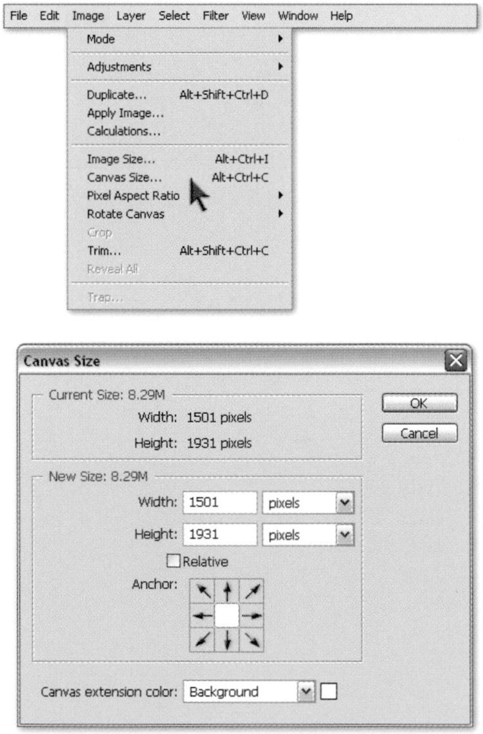

Figure 5-16.

smaller, you crop the image; if you make it larger, you add to the wedges. Naturally, we want to make the canvas smaller.

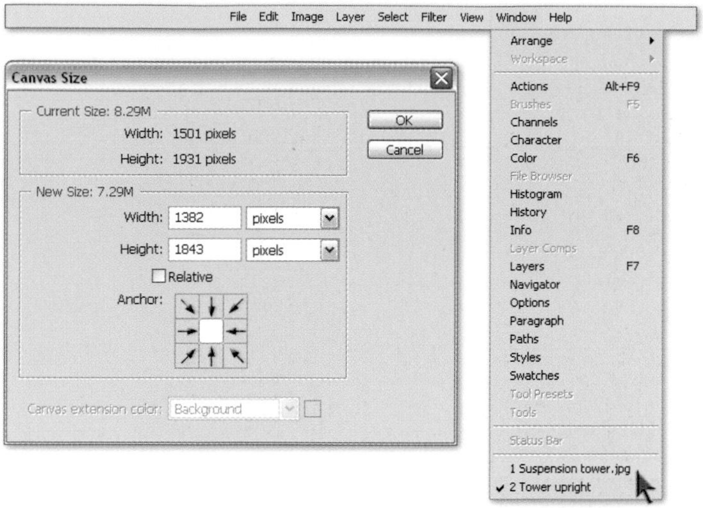

7. *Choose Window→Suspension tower.jpg.* On occasion, Photoshop lets you choose menu commands from within dialog boxes. Even with the Canvas Size dialog box open, for example, you still have access to the Window menu. By choosing an open image, such as **Window→Suspension tower.jpg**, you load its exact canvas dimensions—in this case, 1382 pixels wide by 1843 pixels tall, as shown in Figure 5-17. (As mentioned in the video lesson, you should be working in pixels.)

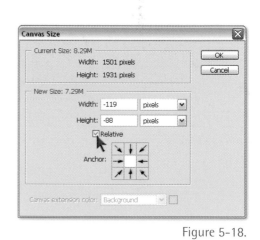

Figure 5-17.

8. *Turn on the Relative check box.* Selecting **Relative** changes the Width and Height values so that, instead of showing the absolute dimensions of the canvas, they show the number of pixels that will be added or cropped away. In this case, the Width and Height values change to –119 and –88 respectively (see Figure 5-18). Your numbers may differ slightly, depending on the amount of rotation you accepted in Step 5.

PEARL OF WISDOM

Why should you care about the dimensions of the original canvas compared to the post-rotation canvas? Because they provide insight into the size of the wedges. As an image rotates, it extends half into the old canvas and half into the new. This means each wedge is exactly twice the width or height of the relative difference between the old and new canvas dimensions. Upshot: All we have to do is multiply by 2.

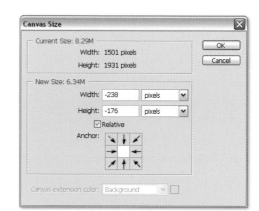

Figure 5-18.

9. *Double the Width and Height values.* If you can do the math in your head, go for it. If not, get a calculator. (Both Windows and the Mac have one.) For my part, $119 \times 2 = 238$ and $88 \times 2 = 176$. So I change the **Width** value to –238 pixels and the **Height** to –176 (see Figure 5-19). Whatever your values, a minus sign should precede each number. This ensures that Photoshop crops the image instead of adding to it.

Figure 5-19.

Figure 5-20.

10. *Click the OK button.* After you do, Photoshop displays an alert message asking whether you're sure you want to reduce the canvas size and crop the image. Click **Proceed** to tell Photoshop to bug off. Pictured in Figure 5-20, the end result is a straight, precisely cropped bridge, with not so much as a sliver of a wedge in sight.

## Using the Crop Tool

If an image requires cropping, then the aptly named crop tool is your best bet. It lets you draw and scale the canvas boundary directly in the image window (as opposed to working numerically, as with the Canvas Size command). You can also rotate the boundary to accommodate a crooked image. It really is one-stop cropping.

1. *Open an image.* Open *Observation hut.jpg* located in the *Lesson 05* folder inside *Lesson Files-PScs 1on1*. Pictured in Figure 5-21, this digital

Figure 5-21.

snapshot is obviously crooked. But it's also too *wide*—that is, we're backed too far away from the scene. Plus, I find the right-hand edge distracting. On first glance, it looks like a post cuts through the tower in the background, when in fact we're seeing a window reflection. Fortunately, we'll manage to solve every one of these problems by straightening and cropping the image with the crop tool.

2. *Select the crop tool in the toolbox.* Click the crop tool in the toolbox (see Figure 5-22) or press C for Crop, not to mention Clip, Cut, and Curtail.

3. *Draw the crop boundary.* Drag inside the image window to draw a rectangle around the portion of the image you want to keep, as demonstrated in Figure 5-23. As you do so, you enter the *crop mode*. From this point until you press Enter or Esc, most of Photoshop's commands and palettes are unavailable. You have now made a commitment to cropping.

Figure 5-22.

Figure 5-23.

As with the marquee tools, you can adjust the position of the crop boundary on the fly by pressing and holding the spacebar. But don't get too hung up on getting things exactly right. You can easily move and resize the crop boundary after you draw it, as demonstrated in Step 5.

Figure 5-24.

4. *Change the shield attributes in the options bar.* Photoshop indicates the area that will be cropped away by covering it with a translucent *shield*. Black by default, the shield is too dark to suit this particular image. Go to the options bar and click the **Color** swatch to display the **Color Picker** dialog box. Then set the color to white and click **OK**. I also recommend lowering the **Opacity** value to 35 percent, as illustrated in Figure 5-24.

5. *Move and scale the crop boundary.* Drag inside the crop boundary to move it. Drag the dotted outline or one of the eight square handles surrounding the crop boundary to scale it (that is, change its size). Also worth noting:

   • Press the Shift key while dragging a corner handle to scale the crop boundary proportionally.

   • Press the Alt key (Option on the Mac) while dragging to scale with respect to the center of the boundary. In other words, the corners move but the center stays in place.

6. *Rotate the crop boundary.* To rotate the crop boundary, move your cursor outside the boundary and drag. Because you want to straighten the image, you need to rotate the boundary in the opposite direction of your intended rotation. Rotating the crop boundary counterclockwise, for example, ultimately rotates the image clockwise.

To straighten the image, you'll need a frame of reference. I suggest that you drag the right edge of the crop boundary until it intersects the sliding glass door near the top of the tower. Then rotate the boundary to match the angle of the doorway, as demonstrated in **Figure 5-25**. (Don't worry that the right edge is now in the wrong place; we'll fix that in a moment.)

Note that Photoshop rotates the boundary around a central origin point, labeled in Figure 5-25. To rotate around a different spot, drag the origin from the center of the boundary to the desired location.

To monitor the angle of the rotation, choose **Window→Info** to display the **Info** palette. Then note the angle value (**A**) in the upper-right corner of the palette. I finally settled on an angle of 3.2 degrees.

7. *Make any last-minute tweaks.* You'll at least need to move the right edge of the boundary back to the right of the tower. But feel free to move, scale, and rotate the crop boundary as much as you like until you get it exactly the way you want it. My final boundary appears in Figure 5-26 on the next page.

8. *Save your changes.* Click the check mark in the options bar or press the Enter or Return key to accept your changes. Photoshop crops away the pixels outside the boundary and rotates the image upright.

Origin point

Rotate cursor

Figure 5-25.

Figure 5-26.

Shown in Figure 5-27 below, the result is a more legible, engaging photograph, nicely framed by the elements around the left, right, and top edges. However, it might look even better if set against a matte. Fortunately, we can create a lovely matting effect by "uncropping" the image—or adding to the canvas—using the Canvas Size command.

9. *Copy the image to a new layer.* Choose **Layer→ New→Layer via Copy** or just press Ctrl+J (⌘-J on the Mac).

10. *Choose the Canvas Size command.* Choose **Image→ Canvas Size** or press Ctrl+Alt+C (⌘-Option-C) to display the Canvas Size dialog box.

Figure 5-27.

11. *Change the Width and Height values to 50 pixels each.* Make sure that the **Relative** check box is turned on, so that the Width and Height values add to the existing canvas. Values of 50 pixels each will extend the canvas 25 pixels (half of 50) in all directions.

12. *Assign a canvas color.* Go down to the **Canvas Extension Color** option and choose **Other**. Inside the Color Picker dialog box, change the **H**, **S**, and **B** values to 210, 10, and 40, respectively, to get the blue gray shown in Figure 5-28. Click **OK** to exit the Color Picker, and then click **OK** again to extend the canvas size.

13. *Give the matte a beveled edge.* Go to the **Layers** palette. (If necessary, choose **Window→Layers** or press F7 to bring the palette to front.) Make sure Layer 1 is active. Then click the ⊘ icon at the bottom of the Layers palette and choose **Bevel and Emboss**, as shown in Figure 5-29, to display the immense **Layer Style** dialog box.

14. *Apply the Outer Bevel effect.* Choose **Outer Bevel** from the **Style** pop-up menu at the top of the dialog box. This ensures that the bevel extends out from the image into the matte. From there, you can either accept the default settings, or enter the custom settings shown in Figure 5-30. When you're finished, click **OK**.

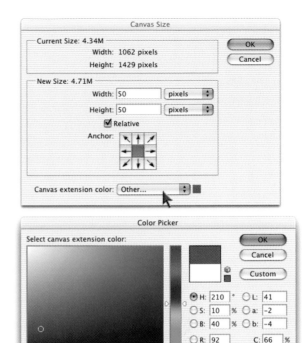

Figure 5-28.

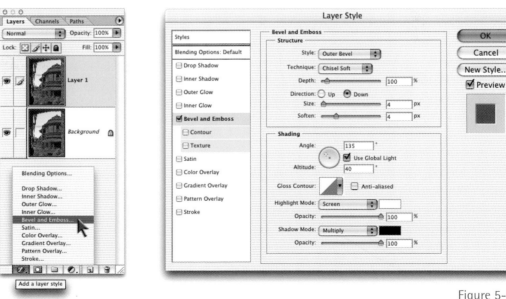

Figure 5-29.

Figure 5-30.

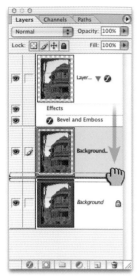

Figure 5-31.

Figure 5-32.

15. *Copy the Background layer to a new layer.* Click the **Background** item in the Layers palette to select the layer that contains the matte color. Then once again press Ctrl+J (⌘-J on the Mac) to clone the image to a new layer.

16. *Choose Image→Canvas Size.* Or press Ctrl+Alt+C (⌘-Option-C) to again display the **Canvas Size** dialog box. Then do the following:

    • Make sure **Relative** is turned on.

    • Change the **Width** and **Height** values to 150 pixels apiece.

    • Click the **Other** color swatch and lower the **B** value to 30. (The H and S values should still be 210 and 10, respectively.)

    • Click **OK** to exit the Color Picker, and then click **OK** again to extend the canvas size.

17. *Duplicate the Bevel and Emboss effect.* In the **Layers** palette, drag the **Effects** item and drop it immediately below the **Background copy** layer, as demonstrated in Figure 5-31. This copies the effect from the top layer to the middle layer, creating another layer of matting.

The result is the double-matte effect that appears in Figure 5-32. Granted, we ventured a bit outside our mandate toward the end of this exercise, but all's fair in creating a beautiful image. In case you're curious, we examine layers in full detail in Lesson 9, "Building Layered Compositions." For more information on Bevel and Emboss and other effects, read Lesson 11, "Layer Styles and Adjustments."

## Resizing an Image

Now we leave the world of rotations and canvas manipulations in favor of what may be the single most essential command in all of Photoshop: Image→Image Size. Designed to resize an entire image all at once—canvas, pixels, the whole shebang—Image Size lets you scale your artwork in two very different ways. First, you can change the physical dimensions of an image by adding or deleting pixels, a process called *resampling*. Second, you can leave the quantity of pixels unchanged and instead focus on the *print resolution*, which is the number of pixels that print within an inch or millimeter of page space.

Whether you resample an image or change its resolution depends on the setting of a check box called Resample Image. As we'll see, this one option has such a profound effect on Image Size that it effectively divides the command into two separate functions. In this next exercise, we explore how and why you might resample an image. To learn about print resolution, read the "Changing the Print Size" sidebar on page 154.

1. *Display the status bar.* If you're working on a PC, make sure the status bar is visible at the bottom of the screen. If it isn't, choose **Window→Status Bar**. (Macintosh users can skip this step.)

2. *Open the image you want to resize.* Open the file named *Enormous chair.jpg*, included in the *Lesson 05* folder inside *Lesson Files-PScs 1on1*. Shown in Figure 5-33, this 21-foot tall rocking chair is not only enormous in real life, but also contains the most pixels of any file we've seen so far (not including layers).

3. *Check the existing image size.* To see just how many pixels make up the image, press the Alt key (Option on the Mac) and click the box that lists the size of the image file in megabytes, Doc: 17.5M/17.5M. This box is located on the left side of the status bar, or in the lower-left corner of the image window on the Mac.

Figure 5-33.

Alt-clicking the box displays a flyout menu that lists the size of the image in pixels, along with its resolution. Pictured in Figure 5-33 on the preceding page, the image measures 2,250 pixels wide by 2,720 pixels tall, for a total of 2,250 × 2,720 = 6.12 million pixels. When printed at 300 ppi, the image will measure 7.5 inches wide by a little more than 9 inches tall.

4. *Magnify the image to the 100 percent zoom ratio.* Double-click the zoom tool icon in the toolbox. Then scroll around until you can see the sign tacked to the front of the chair. Pictured in Figure 5-34, the text on the sign is exceedingly legible—explaining the whats and the whens of the rocking chair, while inexplicably omitting the whys—a testament to the high resolution of the photograph. But there's also a lot of noise (see Step 8 of the "Correcting Camera Raw" exercise, Lesson 3, page 86). So even though we have scads of pixels, they aren't necessarily in great shape.

5. *Decide whether all these pixels are really necessary.* This may seem like a rather cerebral step, but it's an important one. Resampling amounts to rewriting every pixel in your image, so weigh your options before you plow ahead.

In this case, the image contains 6.12 million pixels, just sufficient to convey crisp edges and fragile details such as the text on the sign. But these pixels come at a price. Lots of pixels consume lots of space in memory and on your hard drive, plus they take longer to transmit, whether to a printer or via email or the Web.

So let's say you want to email this image to a couple of friends. Your friends may want to print the photo, but surely they can print it smaller than 7.5 by 9 inches or at a lower resolution. But chances are they won't print the image at all; they'll just view it on screen. A high-resolution monitor can display 1,600 by 1,200 pixels, a mere 30 percent of the pixels in this photo.

Conclusion: Resampling is warranted. This is a job for Image Size.

Figure 5-34.

6. *Choose the Image Size command.* Choose **Image→Image Size**. Alternatively, if you loaded my shortcuts as suggested on page xvii of the Preface, you can access the command from the keyboard by pressing Ctrl+Alt+I (⌘-Option-I on the Mac). Pictured in Figure 5-35, the ensuing **Image Size** dialog box is divided into two parts:

   - The Pixel Dimensions options let you change the width and height of the image in pixels. Lowering the number of pixels is called *downsampling*; raising the pixels is called *upsampling*. We'll be downsampling, by far the more common practice.

   - The Document Size options control the size of the printed image. They have no effect on the size of the image on screen or on the Web.

7. *Turn on the Resample Image check box.* Located at the bottom of the dialog box, this option permits you to change the number of pixels in an image.

8. *Select an interpolation setting.* To the right of the Resample Image check box is a pop-up menu of interpolation options, which determine how Photoshop blends the existing pixels in your image to create new ones. When downsampling an image, only three options matter:

   - When in doubt, select Bicubic, which calculates the color of every resampled pixel by averaging the original image in 16-pixel blocks. It is slower than either Nearest Neighbor or Bilinear (neither of which should be used when resampling photographs), but it does a far better job as well.

   - Bicubic Smoother compounds the effects of the interpolation to soften color transitions between neighboring pixels. This helps suppress film grain and noise.

   - Bicubic Sharper results in crisp edge transitions. Use it when the details in your image are impeccable and you want to preserve every nuance.

   Because this particular image contains so much noise, **Bicubic Smoother** is the best choice.

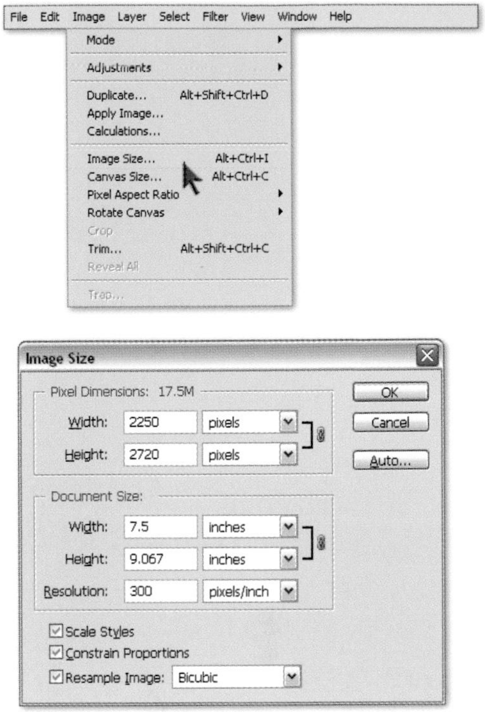

Figure 5-35.

# Changing the Print Size

As often as not, you have no desire to change the number of pixels in an image; you just want to change how it looks on the printed page. By focusing exclusively on the resolution, you can print an image larger or smaller without adding or subtracting so much as a single pixel.

For example, let's say you want to scale the original *Enormous chair.jpg* image so that it prints 10 inches wide by 12 inches tall. Would you upsample the image and thereby add pixels to it? Absolutely not. The Image Size command can't add detail to an image; it just averages existing pixels. So upsampling adds complexity without improving the quality. There are times when upsampling is helpful—when matching the resolution of one image to another, for example—but they are few and far between.

The better solution is to modify the print resolution. Try this: Open the original *Enormous chair. jpg.* (This assumes that you have completed the "Resizing an Image" exercise and saved the results of that exercise under a different filename, as directed by Step 15 on page 156.) Then choose Image→Image Size and turn off the Resample Image check box.

Notice that the Pixel Dimensions options are now dimmed and a link icon (⑧) joins the three Document Size values, as in the screen shot below. This tells you that it doesn't matter which value you edit or in what order. Any change you make to one value affects the other two, so you can't help but edit all three values at once. For example, change the Width value to 10 inches. As you do, Photoshop automatically updates the Height and Resolution values to 12.089 inches and 225 ppi, respectively. So there's no need to calculate the resolution value that will get you a desired set of dimensions; just enter one of the dimensions and Photoshop does the math for you.

Click OK to accept your changes. You will notice that the image looks exactly the same as it did before you entered the Image Size dialog box. This is because you changed the way the image prints, which has nothing to do with the way it looks on screen. If you like, feel free to save over the original file. You haven't changed the structure of the image; you just added a bit of sizing data.

To learn more about printing—including how you can further modify the print resolution using the Print with Preview command—consult Lesson 12, "Printing and Output."

9. *Turn on the Constrain Proportions check box.* Unless you want to stretch or squish your image, leave this option turned on. That way, the relationship between the width and height of the image—known as the *aspect ratio*—will remain constant.

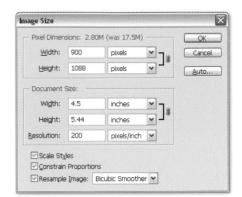

Figure 5-36.

10. *Specify a Resolution value.* When Resample Image is checked (Step 7), any change made to the Resolution value affects the Pixel Dimensions values as well. So if you intend to print the image, it's a good idea to get the Resolution setting out of the way first. Given that we're emailing the image and we're not sure if it'll ever see a printer, a **Resolution** of 200 ppi should work well enough.

11. *Adjust the Width or Height value.* The Pixel Dimensions have dropped to 1,500 by 1,813 pixels. But given that most screens top out at 1,600 by 1,200 pixels, that's still too big. Reduce the **Width** value to 900 pixels, which changes the **Height** value to 1,088 pixels. This also reduces the Document Size to 4.5 by 5.44 inches (see Figure 5-36), plenty big for an email picture.

12. *Note the new file size.* The Pixel Dimensions header should now read 2.80M (was 17.5M), where the M stands for *megabytes*. This represents the size of the image in your computer's memory. The resampled image will measure 900 × 1,088 = 979,200 pixels, a mere 16 percent of its previous size. Not coincidentally, 2.8M is precisely 16 percent of 17.5M. The complexity of a file is directly related to its image size, so this downsampled version will load, save, print, and email much more quickly.

13. *Click OK.* Photoshop reduces the size of the image on screen and in memory. As verified by Figure 5-37, the result continues to look great when printed, but that's in part because it's printed so small. The real test is how it looks on your screen.

Figure 5-37.

14. *Magnify the image to the 300 percent zoom ratio.* Use the zoom tool to zoom in on the sign, as in Figure 5-38. The letters are rougher—no surprise given the lower number of pixels—but they remain legible. And the photo overall is less grainy. Downsampling with the Bicubic Smoother setting (Step 8, page 153) goes a long away toward smoothing away the noise.

Figure 5-38.

15. *Choose File→Save As.* Or press Ctrl+Shift+S (⌘-Shift-S on the Mac). Then give the file a new name or save it to a different location. The reason I have you do this is to emphasize the following very important point:

PEARL OF WISDOM

At all costs, you want to avoid saving your downsampled version of the image over the original. *Always* keep that original in a safe place. I don't care how much better you think the downsampled image looks; the fact remains, it contains fewer pixels and therefore less information. The high-resolution original may contain some bit of detail you'll want to retrieve later, and that makes it worth preserving.

# WHAT DID YOU LEARN?

Match the key concept in the numbered list below with the letter
of the phrase that best describes it. Answers appear upside-down
at the bottom of the page.

## Key Concepts

1. Cropping
2. Whole-image transformations
3. Interpolation
4. Gang scanning
5. Measure tool
6. Canvas
7. Shield
8. Origin point
9. Print resolution
10. Downsampling
11. Bicubic Smoother
12. Aspect ratio

## Descriptions

A. A quick and dirty method of capturing several images with a flatbed scanner to a single file and then sorting them out using Photoshop CS's new Crop and Straighten command.

B. A means of cutting away the extraneous portions of an image to focus the viewer's attention on the subject of the photo.

C. An interpolation setting that makes a special effort to suppress film grain, noise, and other artifacts.

D. The number of pixels that will print within a linear inch or millimeter of page space.

E. The process of throwing away pixels and making up new ones by averaging the existing pixels in an image.

F. To change the physical dimensions of an image by reducing the number of pixels.

G. To straighten a photo with this tool, drag along an edge that should be exactly horizontal or vertical.

H. The translucent film of color that covers the portions of an image that will be deleted after you apply the crop tool.

I. The relationship between the width and the height of an image.

J. Operations such as Image Size and the Rotate Canvas commands that affect an entire image, including any and all layers.

K. The center of a rotation or other transformation.

L. The boundaries of an image, as measured independently of the contents of the image itself.

## Answers

1B, 2J, 3E, 4A, 5G, 6L, 7H, 8K, 9D, 10F, 11C, 12I

# PAINT, EDIT, AND HEAL

SO FAR, WE'VE seen a wealth of commands that correct the appearance of an image based on a few specifications and a bit of numerical input. On balance, there's nothing wrong with these commands, and many are extraordinarily useful. But all the automation in the world can't eliminate the need for old-fashioned, roll-up-your-sleeves, slather-on-the-elbow-grease, sometimes-toil-some-but-always-rewarding artistic labor.

Such is the case with painting and retouching in Photoshop. Whether you want to augment a piece of artwork or fix the details in a photograph, it's time to give the commands a slip and turn your attention to the toolbox. Photoshop devotes fully one third of its tools—all those in the second section of the toolbox (see Figure 6-1)—to the tasks of applying and modifying colors in an image. The idea of learning so many tools and putting them to use may seem intimidating. And because they require you to paint directly in the image window, they respond directly to your talents and dexterity, not to mention your lack thereof. Fortunately, despite their numbers, the tools are a lot of fun. And even if your fine motor skills aren't everything you wish they were, there's no need to fret. I'll show you all kinds of ways to constrain and articulate your brushstrokes in the following exercises.

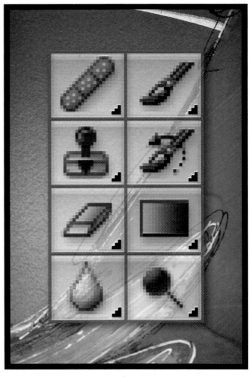

Figure 6-1.

## The Essential Eight, Plus Two

Clicking and holding on any one of the icons pictured in Figure 6-1 produces a flyout menu of additional tools, 20 in all. Of those, 16 are *brush-based*. Select such a tool and drag in the image window to create a brushstroke of colored or modified pixels. The remaining 4 tools are modeled after the selection tools discussed in Lesson 4. You either click to replace colored regions, as with the magic wand, or drag to change free-form areas, as with the lasso.

# ABOUT THIS LESSON

## Project Files

Before beginning the exercises, make sure that you've installed the lesson files from the CD, as explained in Step 5 on page xv of the Preface. This should result in a folder called *Lesson Files-PScs 1on1* on your desktop. We'll be working with the files inside the *Lesson 06* subfolder.

The exercises in this lesson explain how to use Photoshop's paint, edit, and healing tools to brush color and effects into an image. You'll learn how to:

## Video Lesson 6: The Brush Engine

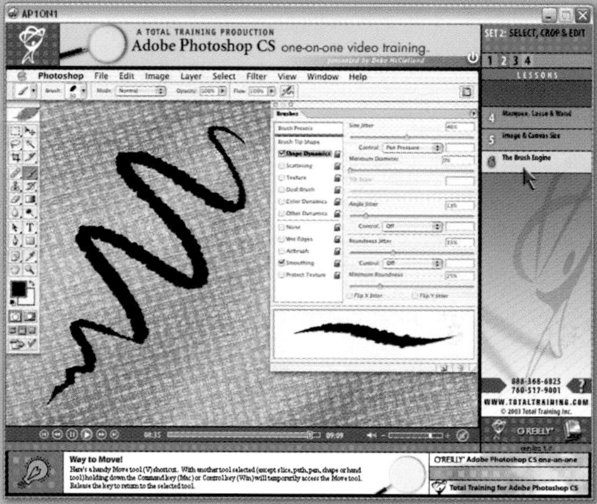

Many of Photoshop's paint, edit, and heal tools rely on a common group of options and settings that Adobe calls the *brush engine*. These options dictate the thickness, fuzziness, and lumpiness of a brushstroke. You can even assign tapered ends to a brushstroke, as shown on the right.

You adjust brush engine settings from the options bar and the dedicated Brushes palette. To get a feel for how these settings work, watch the sixth video lesson on the CD. Insert the CD, click the **Start Training** button, click the Set **2** button in the top-right corner of your screen, and then select **6, The Brush Engine** from the Lessons list. Clocking in at 9 minutes and 9 seconds, this video introduces you to the following tools, palettes, and shortcuts:

| Tool or operation | Windows shortcut | Macintosh shortcut |
| --- | --- | --- |
| Brush tool | B | B |
| Hide the Brush pop-up palette | Enter | Return |
| Incrementally enlarge the brush | right bracket, ] | right bracket, ] |
| Incrementally shrink the brush | left bracket, [ | left bracket, [ |
| Make the brush harder | Shift+] | Shift-] |
| Make the brush softer | Shift+[ | Shift-[ |
| Show or hide the Brushes palette | F5 | F5 |

Brush-based or otherwise, you don't need to learn every one of these tools. As with everything in Photoshop, some tools are good, some tools are bad. In this lesson we focus on what I consider to be the Essential Eight brush-based tools: the paintbrush (AKA, the brush tool); the history brush; the dodge, burn, sponge, smudge, and color replacement tools; and the healing brush. We also look at two selection-type tools, the paint bucket and the patch tool.

This emphasis on brushes may lead you to think that tools such as the paintbrush and sponge are best suited to creating original artwork. Although it's true that many people create artwork from scratch in Photoshop, it's not really what the program's designers had in mind. The real purpose of these tools is to help you edit photographic images or scanned artwork, and that's how we'll use them in this lesson.

Figure 6-2.

## The Three Editing Styles

Photoshop lets you use the tools in the second section of the toolbox to apply and modify colors in three ways:

- The first group of tools, the *painting tools,* comprises the paintbrush, the paint bucket, and others. They permit you to paint lines and fill shapes with the foreground color. I drew the lines in Figure 6-2 with the paintbrush while switching the foreground color between black and white.

- *Editing tools* is a catch-all category for any tool that modifies rather than replaces the existing color or luminosity of a pixel. The burn tool darkens pixels, the smudge tool smears them, and the color replacement tool swaps out hue and saturation values, as demonstrated in Figure 6-3.

Figure 6-3.

Figure 6-4.

Figure 6-5.

- The *healing tools*—the healing brush, patch tool, and history brush among them—permit you to clone elements from one portion or state of an image to another. The history brush clones pixels from an older version of the image. The healing brush and patch tool go a step better, merging the cloned details with their new backgrounds to create a gradual or seamless match, as illustrated in Figure 6-4.

## Coloring Scanned Line Art

Photoshop is possibly the best program on this or any other planet for manipulating digital photographs. But it's also a very capable program for creating original art and coloring scanned artwork. This latter proficiency is especially valuable because it exploits the best aspects of traditional and digital media:

- It's easier to draw on paper with a pencil and pen than it is to sketch on screen, if only because you can see the entire sheet of paper all at once without zooming or panning.

- Meanwhile, it's easier to add colors in Photoshop than hassle with conventional paints or assemble fussy mechanicals.

How you add colors depends on the effect you want to achieve. In this exercise, we approach this topic in two stages. First you'll clean up a piece of scanned line art and apply color to the lines. Then you'll fill in the shapes, introduce a photographic background, and apply a texture or two. Throughout the entire process, you won't harm a single stroke in the original drawing. It really is the best of all worlds.

1. *Open the scanned artwork.* Go to the *Lesson 06* folder inside *Lesson Files-PScs 1on1* and open *Butterfly.tif*, which contains  a sketch that I drew with a common, run-of-the-mill Sharpie on a piece of cheap copier paper, as pictured in Figure 6-5. While these are admittedly low-tech art tools, I prefer them to anything Photoshop has to offer. The image is somewhat misnamed—after all, it's only half a butterfly. But we'll take care of that in the next few steps.

2. *Double the width of the canvas.* Before you can create the right half of the butterfly, you need to expand the canvas to give yourself room to work. Choose **Image→Canvas Size** to display the Canvas Size dialog box. (If you loaded the shortcuts I recommended in Step 12 on page xvii of the Preface, press Ctrl+Alt+C or ⌘-Option-C instead.) Then make the following changes, as shown in Figure 6-6:

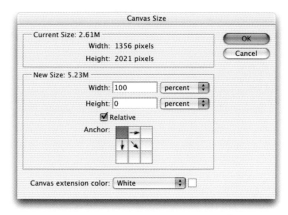

Figure 6-6.

- To add to the existing canvas size, turn on the **Relative** check box.

- Change the unit of measure to **Percent**.

- Set the **Width** value to 100. This will add 100 percent of the existing image width to the canvas, making it twice as wide.

- Click one of the three left-hand boxes inside the **Anchor** area to anchor the butterfly to the left side of the image and add new canvas to the right.

- Change the **Canvas extension color** to **White**, on the off chance it isn't white already.

- Click **OK** to make your changes.

3. *Select the butterfly with the rectangular marquee tool.* Click the rectangular marquee tool in the toolbox or press the M key, and then select the butterfly. Don't worry about being precise. Just draw a generous selection around the black outline and include a small white margin.

4. *Clone the selection and move it to the right.* Press the Ctrl, Shift, and Alt keys (⌘, Shift, and Option on the Mac) and drag the butterfly selection to the right. Hold those keys down until you release the mouse button. (Incidentally, Ctrl gets you the move tool, Alt clones the selection, and Shift constrains the angle of your drag.) You should now see two copies of the butterfly aligned with each other horizontally.

5. *Choose the Free Transform command.* Choose **Edit→ Free Transform** or press Ctrl+T (⌘-T on the Mac) to enter the *free transform mode*. This mode lets you scale, rotate, skew, or flip the selection.

6. **Right-click and choose Flip Horizontal.** If your Macintosh mouse doesn't have a right mouse button, press Control and click to bring up the shortcut menu, then choose **Flip Horizontal**. After Photoshop flips the selection, as shown in Figure 6-7, press Enter or Return to accept the transformation.

---

Technically, you can flip the selection in one step by choosing **Edit→ Transform→Flip Horizontal**. Although this is arguably a quicker technique, I prefer to enter the free transform mode for two reasons: First, I'll do anything to avoid a submenu. Second, as we'll see at length in Lesson 9, "Building Layered Compositions," the free transform mode lets you apply multiple transformations in one operation, so entering the mode is a good habit to get into.

---

7. **Nudge the selection into position.** As long as you don't go and click somewhere or choose another command, your selection should be *floating* above the surface of the image. This means you can move it without harming the underlying original. Press the ← key to nudge the selection 1 pixel or Shift+← to nudge it 10 pixels. Use these two key combinations to nudge the right half of the butterfly over the left half.

Figure 6-7.

---

If pressing the arrow key moves the selection outline without affecting the butterfly, then your selection is no longer floating. Press the Ctrl key (⌘ on the Mac) and ← to move the selection and get it floating again.

---

The obvious problem with trying to align the two halves of the butterfly is that you can't see through the white margins of the right half to line it up with the left half (see Figure 6-7). Although you could erase the white margin by Alt-clicking in the margin with the magic wand tool, that would likely mess up the edges of your line art. Better to make the white go away temporarily using the Fade command.

8. *Apply the Darken blend mode.* Choose **Edit→Fade** or press Ctrl+Shift+F (⌘-Shift-F on the Mac). Introduced in Lesson 3 (see Step 14, page 71), the Fade command lets you combine a corrected image with its original. But it also lets you blend a floating selection with its background. This time, instead of changing the Opacity value, I want you to change the **Mode** option to **Darken**. Then click **OK**.

---

The Darken mode drops out the whites and ensures a seamless merging of the black lines in the artwork. You may need to nudge the selection with the ← and → keys to get the butterfly's halves to match up properly, as shown in **Figure 6-8**. Zoom in to 100 percent for the most accurate view.

---

So much for the base art, now to color it. As I mentioned at the outset, we'll be coloring the artwork in five stages. The first stage, coloring in the lines, requires you to select the lines and send them to a separate layer. Based on what you learned in Lesson 4, your natural tendency might be to reach for the magic wand tool. But there's a simpler way that produces better results.

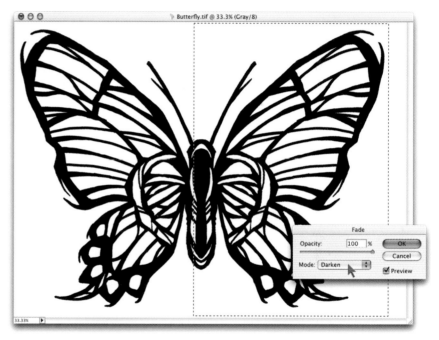

Figure 6-8.

9. *Go to the Channels palette.* If necessary, choose **Window→ Channels**. Because I scanned the artwork as a grayscale image, the palette lists one channel, **Gray**.

---

To see a larger view of this channel, right-click in the empty space below it (inside the palette) and choose **Large**, as shown in **Figure 6-9**.

---

Figure 6-9.

10. ***Load the channel as a selection.*** One of the fantastic things about channels is that you can convert them to selection outlines. Anything that's white becomes selected; anything that's black becomes deselected. To load the selection, press the Ctrl key (⌘ on the Mac) and click anywhere on the **Gray** item in the Channels palette.

---

This is one of those weird times in Photoshop where a shortcut—in this case, Ctrl- or ⌘-clicking—is your primary means for performing an operation. This is not to say it's the *only* way; if you prefer, you can click the far left icon at the bottom of the Channels palette, the one that looks like ⬭. But there is no equivalent menu command. None. I swear, sometimes it's like the whole program is one big secret passageway.

---

After you Ctrl- or ⌘-click, you should see marching ants all over the place. Every white pixel inside the image is now selected. There's just one small problem. You want to select the black lines, not the white background. So...

11. ***Reverse the selection.*** Choose **Select→Inverse** or press Ctrl+Shift+I (⌘-Shift-I on the Mac). Photoshop deselects the white pixels and selects the black ones.

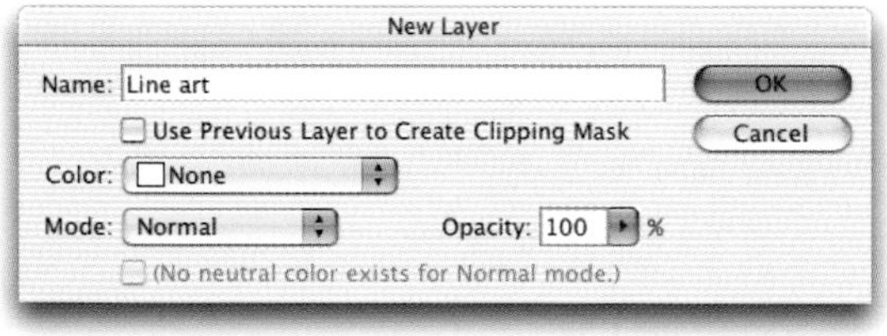

12. ***Make a new layer.*** Choose **Layer→New→Layer** or press Ctrl+Shift+N (⌘-Shift-N) to add a new layer to your image. Inside the **New Layer** dialog box, name the layer "Line Art" (as in Figure 6-10), and click **OK**.

Figure 6-10.

13. ***Fill the selection with black.*** The selection transfers to the new layer automatically. Press the D key to reset the default colors, black and white. Then press Alt+Backspace (Option-Delete on the Mac) to fill the selection with black. The black lines are now relegated to their own layer.

---

If you prefer commands, you can avoid the shortcut by choosing **Edit→Fill**, changing the **Use** option to **Foreground Color** or **Black**, and clicking the **OK** button. Of course, you'd have to be out of your mind to do that, but it is an option.

---

14. ***Select the Background layer.*** Click the **Layers** tab or press F7 to bring up the **Layers** palette. Then click the **Background** item to make it active.

15. **Deselect and fill with white.** Now that we have the butterfly transferred in all its glory to the Line Art layer, you can get rid of the background butterfly. Press Ctrl+D (⌘-D on the Mac) to deselect the artwork. Then press Ctrl+Backspace (⌘-Delete) to fill the Background layer with white. (Or, if you prefer the long way, choose **Edit→Fill**, change **Use** to **Background Color** or **White**, and click **OK**.)

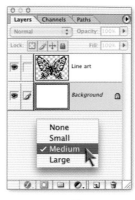

Figure 6-11.

As long as we're in the Layers palette, we might as well make these thumbnails bigger, too. Right-click in the empty space below the layer name and choose **Medium**, as in **Figure 6-11**.

16. **Lock the transparency of the Line Art layer.** Click the **Line Art** layer to select it. Then click the first **Lock** icon—the one that looks like a checkerboard (⬚)—near the top of the Layers palette. This prevents you from changing the opacity of individual pixels in the layer. The opaque pixels stay opaque, the transparent pixels stay transparent; all you can change is the colors. The upshot is that any brushstroke you apply will appear strictly inside the lines.

17. **Convert the image to RGB.** Currently, the image is a single-channel grayscale image. That's perfect for scanning black-and-white line art because it keeps the file size to a minimum. However, it also means we can't paint in color—unless you count shades of gray as color. To open up the spectrum, choose **Image→Mode→RGB Color**.

PEARL OF WISDOM

At this point, Photoshop brings up a message that's very easy to ignore. But don't. Photoshop is telling you that it wants to flatten your artwork and toss out all the work you did in Steps 9 through 16. Ostensibly, this clumsy solution is intended to avoid the color shifts that sometimes result when recalculating blend modes. The problem is, those shifts are most likely to occur when converting between RGB and CMYK, and they simply can't happen when converting from grayscale to RGB. So be very sure to click **Don't Flatten**, or press the D key.

18. **Select the paintbrush tool.** Click the paintbrush tool in the toolbox (see Figure 6-12) or press the B key. Photoshop offers two painting tools, the paintbrush—AKA, the brush tool—and the pencil. The pencil paints jagged lines, making it most useful for changing individual pixels. The paintbrush is more versatile, permitting you to modify the sharpness of a line and tap into a wealth of controls that the pencil can't touch. In other words, when you want to paint, get the paintbrush.

Figure 6-12.

19. ***Select a color and a brush.*** Choose **Window→Color** or press the F6 key to display the **Color** palette and dial in your favorite butterfly-painting color. I decided on red, which is **R**: 255, **G**: 0, and **B**: 0. Next, go to the options bar and click the ⊡ arrow to the right of the word **Brush** to bring up a pop-up palette of brush options.

- Adjust the **Master Diameter** value to change the size of the brush. For our purposes, a large brush works well, something in the neighborhood of 150 to 200 pixels.

- Use the **Hardness** value to adjust the softness of the brush. A Hardness of 100 percent results in an antialiased brush (mostly sharp with a tiny bit of softness). I'd like you to set the Hardness to 0 percent to create a fuzzy brush.

- Alternatively, you can ignore both the Master Diameter and Hardness values, and select a predefined brush from the scrolling list.

To hide the pop-up palette and accept your changes, press Enter or Return. Or just start painting in the image window. (Press the Esc key to hide the palette and abandon your changes.)

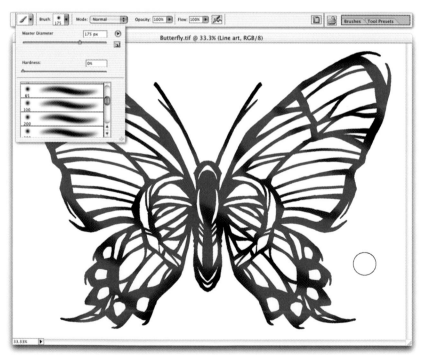

You can change the brush attributes incrementally from the keyboard using, of all things, the bracket keys. Press [ to reduce the brush diameter; press ] to raise it. Press Shift+[ to make the brush softer; press Shift+] to make it harder. These shortcuts may seem weird, but when used properly, they're enormous time savers.

20. ***Paint inside the butterfly.*** Paint as much of the butterfly as you like, wherever you like. As you do, Photoshop confines your brushstrokes to the interior of the line art, as shown in Figure 6-13.

Figure 6-13.

By now, you should have a pretty clear idea of how to assign color to scannned line art. To add more colors, select a different foreground color from the Color palette and keep painting. For a more efficient approach, try the following steps, which document how to add a random collection of colors in a single brushstroke. Or you can skip ahead to the next exercise, "Adding Fills and Textures," which begins on page 171.

21. *Bring up the Brushes palette.* If you're hungry for more brush options, it's time to visit the **Brushes** palette. Either click the **Brushes** tab in the dock at the upper-right corner of the screen or press the F5 key. Click an item in the left-hand column to switch to a different panel of options, and then manipulate the settings on the right. The bottom quarter of the palette contains a preview showing how the changes you made would affect a sample brushstroke.

22. *Select Scattering from the left-hand list.* Then increase the **Scatter** value to 100 percent. This separates the spots of color laid down by the paintbrush to create the effect previewed in the left half of Figure 6-14.

23. *Select Color Dynamics from the list.* The Color Dynamics settings cause the color laid down by the paintbrush to randomly fluctuate according to Jitter values. More Jitter means more random behavior. Set the **Hue Jitter** to 100 percent, the **Saturation Jitter** to 25 percent, and the **Brightness Jitter** to 50 percent, as in the right half of Figure 6-14. You may notice that the preview remains unchanged. This is nothing to worry about. The preview doesn't track the color of a brush, just its size and shape.

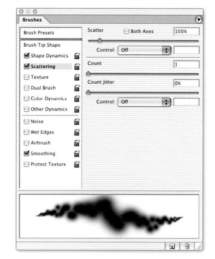

Figure 6-14.

24. *Paint around the butterfly.* Increase the brush diameter to 400 pixels. (As you press the ] key, you can track the specific diameter value in the options bar.) Then paint all around the perimeter of the butterfly. The effect will look something like the image in Figure 6-15, with random dollops of color darting in and out of view. This one edit goes a long way toward off-setting the rigid symmetry of the insect. Naturally, I'm all for that. The only reason the butterfly is symmetrical in the first place is because I was too lazy to draw the other half.

25. *Turn off Scattering and Color Dynamics.* Click the check boxes inside the Brushes palette. The settings remain in place in case you want to revisit them later, but the functions are turned off.

26. *Switch to black and choose the Overlay mode.* Press D to re-store black as the foreground color. Then choose **Overlay** from the **Mode** pop-up menu in the options bar. The Overlay mode will paint with black while maintaining some of the most vivid colors that you added in previous steps.

Figure 6-15.

27. *Paint inside the bug's body.* Paint the body and the two antennae—and try to do it in one stroke. Otherwise, you risk making the colors too dark.

28. *Press 5 to reduce the Opacity value to 50 percent.* You can also select the Opacity value and enter 50. But just pressing the 5 key is so much more convenient.

---

When using one of the paint or edit tools, you have only to press a number key to change the Opacity value in 10 percent increments. Press 1 for 10 percent, 2 for 20 percent, and so on. Press 0 for 100 percent. Press two numbers in a row to enter a specific value, such as 6-7 for 67 percent.

---

29. ***Paint the tips of the wings.*** Paint along the top and bottom edges to give the wings a bit of a toasting, as shown in Figure 6-16. This time, it's okay to paint in multiple strokes. For added contrast, press the X key to swap the foreground and background colors. Then paint inside the wings to brighten them.

30. ***Save your artwork.*** This has been a long exercise, so it's probably a good idea to save your work. To avoid replacing the original file, choose **File→Save As**. The native PSD format is generally best when saving layers, so choose **Photoshop** from the **Format** menu. Then click the **Save** button.

Figure 6-16.

## Adding Fills and Textures

We now begin the second part of our look at coloring scanned line art. But this time, instead of coloring the lines themselves, we'll color the spaces between the lines, as well as add depth and shading.

1. ***Open the revised butterfly composition.*** Open the *Colored lines.psd* file located in the *Lesson 06* folder inside *Lesson Files-PScs 1on1*. This image contains the painted butterfly line art that I saved in Step 30 (above) plus a few additional layers that we'll integrate over the course of the following steps.

2. ***Make a new layer.*** Click the **Line Art** layer in the **Layers** palette to make it active. Next, press Ctrl+Shift+N (⌘-Shift-N) to add a new layer to your image. Name the layer "Colored Fills" and click **OK**.

3. ***Move the new layer backward.*** In the Layers palette, drag the **Colored Fills** layer immediately under the **Line Art** layer, as in Figure 6-17. Or you can press Ctrl+[ (or ⌘-[ on the Mac). When combined with Ctrl or ⌘, the bracket keys move the active layer behind or in front of other layers in the image.

Figure 6-17.

Figure 6-18.

4. *Select the paint bucket tool in the toolbox.* Click and hold the gradient tool icon (sixth tool on the right) to display the flyout menu pictured on the left in Figure 6-18. Then choose the paint bucket. We'll use the paint bucket tool to fill the areas inside the lines with color.

5. *Open the Swatches palette.* Choose **Window→Swatches** to view the **Swatches** palette (see Figure 6-19), which you can use to save frequently used colors.

6. *Choose Load Swatches from the palette menu.* Shown in Figure 6-19, the **Load Swatches** command lets you load a collection of color presets from disk. Find the file called *The vivid 24.aco* in the *Lesson 06* folder inside *Lesson Files-PScs 1on1*. Then select it and click the **Load** button. As shown in Figure 6-20, Photoshop adds 24 colors to the bottom of the Swatches palette, each of which represents a 15-degree interval along the perimeter of the color wheel (see "The Visible Color Spectrum Wheel" on page 69 of Lesson 3). These vivid hues are the colors we'll use to fill the butterfly.

7. *Set the paint bucket options.* Go to the options bar and assign the following settings:

   • The **Fill** option should be **Foreground**, so the paint bucket fills an area with the foreground color.

   • When working with independent layers, the **Mode** and **Opacity** options are best set to **Normal** and 100 percent,

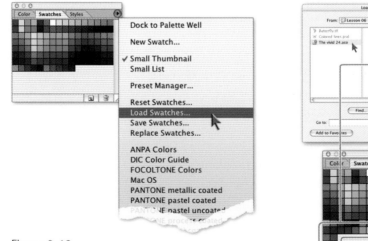

Figure 6-19.

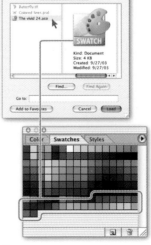

Figure 6-20.

respectively. This ensures that the colors in the Colored Fills layer cover up the colors behind them. If you later decide to apply a blend mode or opacity setting, you can apply it to the layer (as described in Step 18 on page 177).

- The paint bucket is essentially a magic wand tool that colors pixels instead of selecting them. So not surprisingly, it offers many wand-like options. First and foremost among these is Tolerance, which controls how many colors the paint bucket fills at a time. (To learn more, see "Selecting Colored Areas with the Magic Wand," Step 5, page 102.) Raise the **Tolerance** value to 100. This will help fill in tight corners and crevices.

- Leave **Anti-aliased** and **Contiguous** turned on. The latter is especially important because Photoshop would otherwise fill in all white spaces at once (which as we'll see, is not what we want to do).

- If you were to click inside the image at this point, the paint bucket would fill the entire window, from stem to stern. This is because the active Colored Fills layer is empty; it contains no outlines to hold the paint. To make the paint bucket "see" the outlines on the Line Art layer, turn on the **All Layers** check box. Now the paint bucket will fill just one shape at a time.

The screen detail in Figure 6-21 highlights the two options (**Tolerance** and **All Layers**) that I ask you to change from their default settings.

8. *Select a color from the Swatches palette.* I recommend that you start with a light color such as yellow and work your way up. Because light colors produce the subtlest effects, you can use them the most and make some fast progress up front.

---

To confirm the name of a color in the Swatches palette, hover your cursor over it. This will help you distinguish yellow from, say, amber or chartreuse. (Note that Show Tool Tips must be on in the Preferences dialog box for this trick to work.)

---

Figure 6-21.

9. **Click inside the lines.** Armed with the paint bucket, click a few of the gaps inside the butterfly line art to fill the areas with the foreground color, in this case yellow. As shown in Figure 6-22, I clicked in 20 areas in all, spread more or less evenly throughout the image. In each case, Photoshop applies the yellow pixels to the active layer, Colored Fills, while staying inside the lines defined by the Line Art layer.

10. **Fill in the other colors.** Exactly which colors you use and where you apply them is up to you. Of the two versions of the artwork in Figure 6-23 on the opposite page, the first shows how I applied the 6 primary colors (yellow, green, cyan, blue, magenta, and red); the second shows the additional 18 secondary and tertiary colors, plus black and white.

Figure 6-22.

My approach was mostly random. But there are a few things here and there that I'd like you to notice:

- I tried to spread the colors out as much as possible, so that very few neighboring areas received the same color. There are exceptions, of course, and you can do as you like. It's ultimately an aesthetic choice.

- To better distinguish the wings, I filled all the areas inside the butterfly's body with black. (Remember, to make the foreground color black, just press the D key.) The result doesn't look very good right now, but it will later.

- The five oval areas along the bottom of each wing appear to have no color in them. But they are in fact filled with white. This will help distinguish these areas from the background art in future steps. To make the foreground color white, press the D key followed by the X key.

Naturally, you won't love every color you apply. It's perfectly okay to change your mind, but not with the paint bucket tool. Although fine for filling transparent areas, the bucket doesn't fare nearly so well when switching from one color to another.

With the preceding Pearl in mind, here are a couple of ways to swap out a fill color:

- If you catch a mistake right away, press Ctrl+Z (⌘-Z) to undo the fill. Then select a different color and again click with the paint bucket.

- To change a color applied with an earlier click, first select the color with the magic wand. Then choose **Select→Modify→ Expand**, enter 4 pixels, and click **OK**. This selects an area slightly larger than the fill color. Now select a new color for the fill and press Shift+Alt+Backspace (Shift-Option-Delete on the Mac). This special keyboard shortcut recolors just the filled pixels in the selection and leaves the transparent pixels alone.

11. *Magnify the image.* Press Ctrl+plus (⌘-plus) a few times to get a closer look at the image. After some inspection, you may be able to make out fine white cracks between the fills and the line art, especially in very sharp corners, as witnessed in Figure 6-24 on the next page. The high Tolerance value that you specified in Step 7 helps mitigate this, but no Tolerance setting can make it go away entirely.

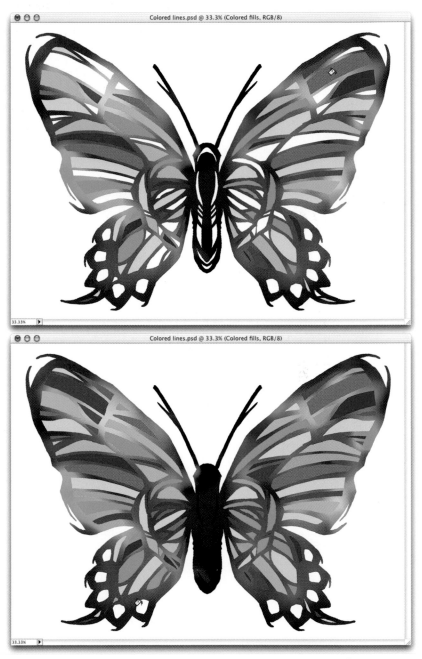

Figure 6-23.

Figure 6-24.

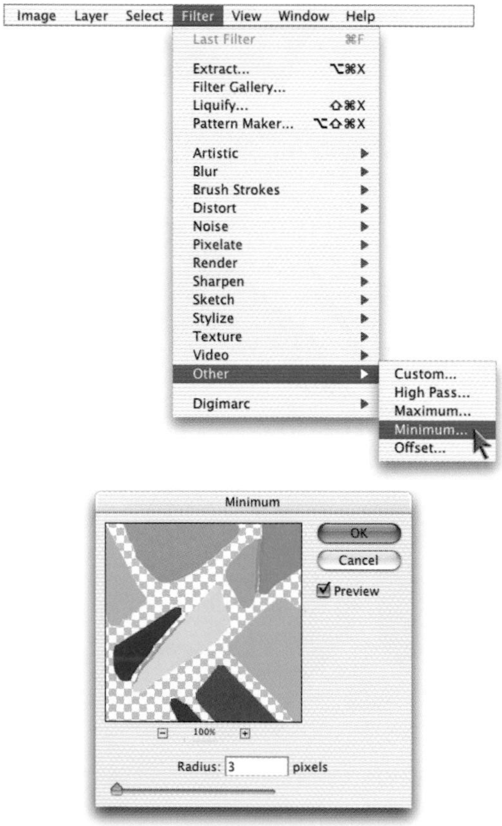

Fortunately, you can expand the fill using one of Photoshop's more obscure functions, the Minimum filter. Originally designed to expand dark areas inside an image, it has the added (and arguably more useful) effect of expanding the size of objects on a layer.

12. *Choose the Minimum command.* Choose **Filter→Other→Minimum** to display the **Minimum** dialog box. Then raise the **Radius** value to expand the fill objects in 1-pixel increments, as in Figure 6-25. Be forewarned that this command can also mess up colors in an image, so turn on the **Preview** check box and keep a close eye on the changes you make inside both the dialog box and the image window. In the case of this particular image, a Radius value of 3 pixels works best; anything higher, and the colors start to ooze into each other. When you're satisfied, click the **OK** button to apply the command.

13. *Move the Photocomp layer to the back of the stack.* Click the **Photocomp** layer in the **Layers** palette to activate the layer and reveal an eyeball icon (👁) to the left of it. This displays the layer, which contains a composite of photographs and effects that I created in advance.

   Choose **Layer→Arrange→Send to Back** to move the Photocomp layer to just above the Background layer. Or press the shortcut Ctrl+Shift+[ (⌘-Shift-[ on the Mac).

14. *Select the Colored Fills layer.* Click the Colored Fills layer or press Alt+] (Option-] on the Mac) to make the brightly colored interiors active.

   Now to add some texture to the Colored Fills layer. The combination of colors inside the line art looks a little like stained glass, so I decided to emphasize the effect by setting a pattern layer into Colored Fills by way of something called a *clipping mask* (about which we'll learn more in Lesson 9, "Building Layered Compositions").

Figure 6-25.

15. **Add a Pattern layer.** Along the bottom of the Layers palette, between the little folder and the little page, is a ⬤ icon. Press the Alt key (Option on the Mac) and click this icon. Then choose **Pattern**, as shown in Figure 6-26.

16. **Name the layer and make it part of a clipping mask.** The Alt (or Option) key forces the display of the **New Layer** dialog box. Name the new layer "Glass." Then turn on the check box **Use Previous Layer to Create Clipping Mask** (as in Figure 6-27) and click **OK**.

17. **Select the Metal Landscape pattern.** Inside the **Pattern Fill** dialog box, click the ▾ arrow to the right of the pattern preview and choose the fourth swatch on the bottom row, which Photoshop calls Metal Landscape, as labeled in Figure 6-28. Then raise the **Scale** value to 200 percent and click **OK** to create the layer.

18. **Change the blend mode and opacity.** Choose **Hard Light** from the blend mode pop-up menu at the top of the Layers palette (see Figure 6-29). Also change the **Opacity** value to 40 percent. The result is a series of fracture lines inside the cut glass of the Colored Fills layer.

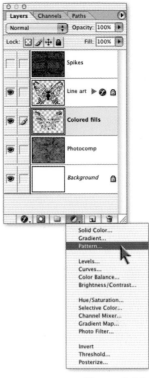

Figure 6-26.

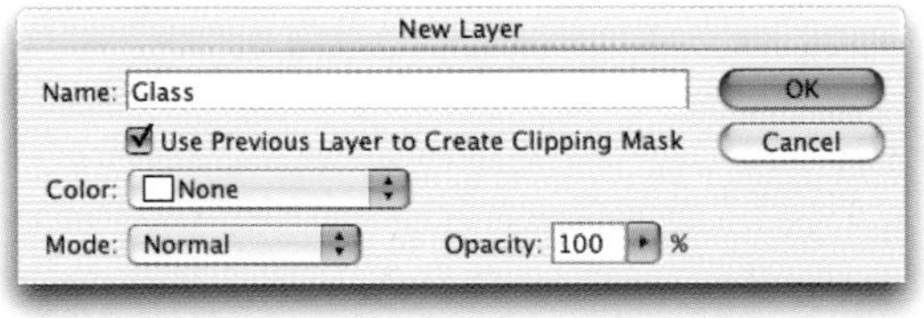

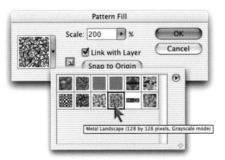

Figure 6-27.

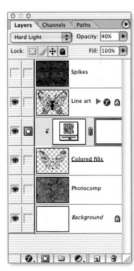

Figure 6-28.

Figure 6-29.

Figure 6-30.

Figure 6-31.

19. *Set the blend mode for the Colored Fills layer to Screen.* Click **Colored Fills** in the Layers palette to make it active again. Then choose **Screen** from the blend mode pop-up menu. Photoshop reduces the saturation of the colors in the active layer by bleaching them into those of the Photocomp layer behind them, thus achieving the bright glass effect pictured in Figure 6-30.

Note that the fracture lines extend into the ovals at the bottom of the wings as well as the cuts inside the body, all thanks to the white and black fills combined with the pattern and blend modes. Modify a single fill, pattern, or blend mode and the effect would be compromised.

20. *Click the Spikes layer at the top of the stack.* In the Layers palette, click the word **Spikes**, as in Figure 6-31. This both turns on the layer and makes it active. The layer covers the artwork with a modified photo of a fortified wooden door from the PhotoSpin stock image library. This just so happens to be the same image upon which I based the Photocomp layer, so my hope is that the two layers will echo each other.

21. *Create a clipping mask.* Choose **Layer→Create Clipping Mask** or press the keyboard shortcut Ctrl+G (⌘-G on the Mac) to group the Spikes layer with the Line Art layer immediately below it. The result: the contents of the Line Art layer mask those of the Spikes layer, once again revealing the layers below.

22. *Set the blend mode to Multiply.* With the Spikes layer still active, choose **Multiply** from the blend mode pop-up menu at the top of the Layers palette. Photoshop burns the photo of the fortified door into the hand-painted butterfly outlines, creating a dark combination of the two, as seen in Figure 6-32.

Figure 6-32.

My only remaining issue with the artwork is that the interior portion of the bug's body appears too light, so that it competes for attention with the wings. The solution is to darken the open body fragments using existing information from the Colored Fills layer. Not interested? Skip ahead to "Dodge, Burn, Sponge, and Smudge" on page 181. Interested? Just eight more steps:

23. *Load the Colored Fills layer outlines as a selection.* Like channels, layer outlines can be converted to selection outlines. Press the Ctrl key (⌘ on the Mac) and click anywhere on the **Colored Fills** item in the Layers palette.

24. *Find the intersection of the existing selection and the body.* Select the rectangular marquee tool. Then press the Shift and Alt keys (Shift and Option on the Mac) and drag around the insect's body, as demonstrated in Figure 6-33 on the very next page. Be careful to get all of the bug's body without cutting into the wings' fills. If necessary, press the spacebar as you drag to properly align the marquee.

25. *Make a new layer.* Press Ctrl+Shift+N (⌘-Shift-N) to add yet another layer to your image. Name the layer "Body Dark" and click the **OK** button.

26. *Fill the selection with black.* Press the D key to restore the default foreground color, black. Then press Alt+Backspace (Option-Delete on the Mac) to fill the selection with black.

27. *Deselect the image.* Now that the selection is filled, the selection outline is redundant. Press Ctrl+D (⌘-D) to get rid of it.

28. *Reduce the Opacity value.* Press the 4 key, or change the **Opacity** value in the Layers palette to 40 percent. The result is a darker butterfly body.

29. *Twirl open the Line Art layer.* Notice that the Line Art layer has a small ▶ next to it (between the layer name and the *ƒ*). Click the ▶ to twirl the layer open and reveal its layer styles, as in Figure 6-34.

30. *Turn on the layer styles.* Click the box to the left of the word Effects to display the eyeball icon (👁) and turn on the drop shadow and other layer styles for the Line Art layer. For more information about layer styles, read Lesson 11, "Layer Styles and Adjustments."

And lo these many steps later, we arrive at the image in Figure 6-35 on the facing page. What was once a mere caterpillar of a sketch has emerged full grown into the world as a finished piece of artwork, complete with color and texture, thanks to the finishing capabilities of Photoshop.

Figure 6-33.

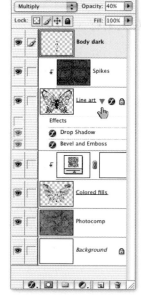

Figure 6-34.

Figure 6-35.

## Dodge, Burn, Sponge, and Smudge

We now move from painting to editing. And by *editing*, I mean using Photoshop's tools to modify the colors, luminosity values, and color transitions in a photographic image. We start with Photoshop's core editing tools, which are as follows:

- The dodge tool lightens pixels as you paint over them.

- The burn tool darkens pixels as you paint over them. If you're having problems keeping the dodge and burn tools straight, just think of toast—the more you burn it, the darker it gets.

- The sponge tool adjusts the saturation of colors, making them either duller or more vivid.

- The smudge tool smears colors. Used in moderation, it can be useful for smoothing out harsh transitions.

- New to Photoshop CS, the color replacement tool replaces one set of colors with another. It was designed to fix red-eye, but as we'll see, it does much more.

There are other edit tools, but these are the ones you're most likely to use. (Two others, blur and sharpen, are so poorly implemented as to be virtually useless—and I say "virtually" only as a courtesy

Figure 6-36.

to those who have the courage to try and prove me wrong.) The following exercise explains how to use the five edit tools and the paintbrush to solve some common retouching problems.

1.  *Open the photo of some poor sap who requires an emergency makeover.* Open the image titled *Yours truly.jpg* in the *Lesson 06* folder inside *Lesson Files-PScs 1on1*. The file features an all too accurate head shot of me, your gruesome-looking author, pictured in horrifying detail in Figure 6-36. In his *Maxims for the Use of the Over-educated*, Oscar Wilde wrote, "A subject that is beautiful in itself gives no suggestion to the artist. It lacks imperfection." In that regard at least, my face is extremely suggestive. In that same volume, Wilde wrote, "Those whom the gods love grow young." Well, the gods may not love me in real life, but they're going to fawn all over me in Photoshop. *The Picture of Dorian Gray* has nothing on this program.

---

If you don't want to use my face—and who can blame you—use a picture of yourself, a loved one, or a dire enemy. The specific concerns may be different, but the general approach will be the same. One potential difference: Because my flesh tones trend toward glow-in-the-dark white boy, my face needs a little dodging and a whole lot of burning. If the face you're working on is rich in melanin, it may require just the opposite.

---

2.  *Click the dodge tool in the toolbox.* Located directly above the **T** (see Figure 6-37), the dodge tool is the first of Photoshop's *toning tools*. To get the dodge tool from the keyboard, press the O key.

3.  *Reduce the Exposure value to 30 percent.* Located in the options bar, the **Exposure** value controls the intensity of edits applied by the dodge tool. In my experience, the default value of 50 percent is too extreme for most editing work. Press the 3 key to take it to 30 percent.

4.  *Drag over the image details you want to lighten.* In my case, I started with my nose—my big old splotchy, freckly nose. I reduced the brush diameter a few notches (to, say, 40 pixels) and dragged inside the eyes, teeth, and eyelids. I also dragged over the smile lines trailing away from my nose. Figure 6-38 on the opposite page shows the areas that received my attentions in color. (Unaffected areas are overlaid in blue-gray.) Feel free to follow my lead or go your own way.

Figure 6-37.

The biggest mistake people make when working with the edit tools is to push things too far. For example, it's tempting to take my coffee-stained teeth (positive note: no food stuck inside them) and scrub them until they're pearly white. But if you do that, my newly brilliant smile will look unnatural. Better to make small adjustments—one or two passes at most—so that you leave the shadows intact. We'll get rid of the yellow in Step 14.

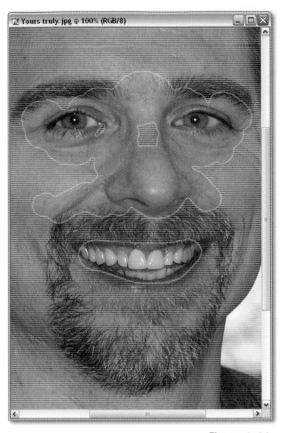

5. **Bring up the History palette.** If it's not already visible on screen, choose **Window→History**. The **History** palette tracks the most recent commands and tools you applied to an image, thus permitting you to step back to one of several previous *states* (how the image looked at different stages in the recent past). In other words, the History palette lets you undo multiple operations. And as if that's not enough, you can brush back portions of a previous state using the history brush.

It's this last option that makes the History palette so useful when retouching an image. After painting in an edit effect, you can turn around and erase portions of it with the history brush—provided, that is, that you manage your history states properly. By default, Photoshop tracks the last 20 operations. But as Figure 6-39 shows, it's easy to click and drag more than 20 times with the dodge tool without even noticing. And once a state gets bumped off the History list, there's no restoring it. Of course, you could raise the number of history states, but doing so can dramatically slow down Photoshop when applying large-scale adjustments. A much better practice is to get in the habit of saving significant points in the adjustment of an image—such as when you finish using a certain tool—as *snapshots*.

Figure 6-38.

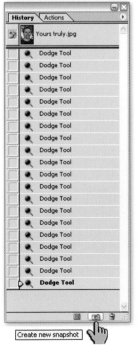

6. **Create a snapshot of the current state.** Press the Alt key (or Option) and click the camera icon (📷) at the bottom of the History palette, as shown in Figure 6-39. Name the new snapshot "Dodged Image" and click **OK**. The snapshot appears at the top of the History palette and will steadfastly refuse to roll off, even after 20 more operations.

7. **Select the burn tool in the toolbox.** Click and hold the dodge tool icon to display a flyout menu and then choose the little hand icon that represents the burn tool, as in Figure 6-40 on the following page. Or if you prefer, press Alt (or Option) and click the dodge icon to advance to the next tool. Or just press the O key (or Shift+O if you skipped the Preface).

Figure 6-39.

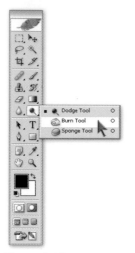

Figure 6-40.

8. **_Reduce the Exposure value to 20 percent._** Again, the default Exposure value is 50 percent, far too radical for burning. Press the 2 key to permit yourself more subtlety and flexibility.

9. **_Drag over the image details you want to darken._** The burn tool adds shadows, and shadows give an image volume, depth, and form. I started by increasing the brush diameter several notches (200 to 300 pixels) and dragging up and down both sides of my face, including over the ears. Then I reduced the brush to around 80 pixels and painted under my eyebrows, nose, cheekbones, and chin; along the sides of my nose; and over my thinning hair, as indicated by the full-color areas in Figure 6-41. Basically, use the burn tool anywhere you would apply makeup.

Don't worry about dragging over the same spots with the burn tool as you did with the dodge tool. If they require burning, edit away. About the worst that can happen is you can undersaturate color values, but that's something you can remedy later with the sponge tool.

Figure 6-41.

Attention Caucasians: The burn tool can serve as a nifty tanning aid, but as always, don't overdo it. A few brushstrokes are all that stands between plausibly augmented skin tones and surreal George Hamilton territory, as in Figure 6-42.

10. ***Brush away any mistakes.*** After you've toasted any and all desired details with the burn tool, you may want roll back the effects of the tool using the history brush. Here's how: Click in front of the **Dodged Image** state in the History palette to set it as the source of the history brush edits. Then click the history brush in the toolbox (see Figure 6-43) and paint to restore details to their pre-burned appearance.

For example, while I was careful to avoid painting with the burn tool inside my eyes or teeth (see Figure 6-41), the blurry edges of the brush couldn't help but affect them. By painting with the history brush and a small brush diameter, I managed to restore the post-Step 4 brightness of eyes, teeth, and anything else that appeared too dark.

Healthy glow
Beyond the realm of possibility

Figure 6-42.

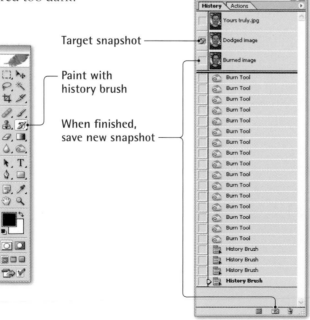

Target snapshot

Paint with history brush

When finished, save new snapshot

Figure 6-43.

Figure 6-44.

Figure 6-45.

11. ***Create another snapshot.*** Having arrived successfully at another juncture in the editing process, press Alt (or Option) and click the 📷 icon at the bottom of the History palette. Name this snapshot "Burned Image" and click **OK**.

12. ***Select the sponge tool in the toolbox.*** Now to modify the saturation levels. Press Alt (or Option) and click the burn tool icon to advance to the next toning tool, the sponge. Or press the O key (Preface skippers, press Shift+O).

13. ***Reduce the Flow value to 30 percent.*** Though it's calculated differently, the **Flow** value in the options bar serves the same purpose as the dodge and burn tools' Exposure value—it modifies the intensity of your brushstrokes. In my experience, the default value of 50 percent is too much. Press the 3 key to knock it down to 30 percent.

14. ***Drag in the image to leech away aberrant colors.*** Make sure the **Mode** option in the options bar is set to **Desaturate**. Then drag inside the teeth. A couple of passes gets rid of most of the yellow and leaves the teeth a more neutral white. (Be sure to leave behind some yellow. Gray teeth won't look right.) I also dragged over some of the more lurid pinks in the eyelids, ears, and lips, as well as some unusually orange patches in the forehead (see the colored areas in Figure 6-44).

15. ***Switch the Mode option to Saturate.*** You can also increase the saturation of colors using the sponge tool. After choosing **Saturate** from the **Mode** pop-up menu in the options bar, click a few times inside each of the irises. This brings out both the green and the red-eye. We'll remedy the latter in a moment.

16. ***Create another snapshot.*** Not essential, but always a good idea. Alt-click (or Option-click) the 📷 icon at the bottom of the History palette, name this snapshot "Sponged Colors," and click **OK**.

17. ***Select the smudge tool in the toolbox.*** Click and hold the blur tool icon—the one that looks like a drop of water—to display a flyout menu of *focus tools*. Then choose the smudge tool (see Figure 6-45). Or press the R key three times—once to select blur and twice more to advance to smudge. (If you skipped the Preface, press R and then Shift+R twice to get the smudge tool.)

18. *Reduce the Strength value and change the Mode setting.*
The smudge tool's default settings are designed to create
painterly effects. If you want to use it to edit an image, you
need to rein the tool in a bit. Press the 2 key to reduce the
**Strength** value in the options bar to
20 percent. Then choose **Lighten** from
the **Mode** pop-up menu (see Figure
6-46). Now the tool will smear light
colors into dark ones and not the other
way around.

Figure 6-46.

19. *Drag in the image to smear colors.* Press the ] key a couple
of times to increase the brush diameter to 30 pixels. Then
drag across my bottom lip to smooth over the grooves and
make the skin look more hydrated. Be sure to trace along
the lip, as demonstrated by the area highlighted in color in
Figure 6-47. (Dragging across will recruit colors from the
teeth and whiskers.) In all, you may have to drag across the
lip three or four times to give it that "Just ChapStick'ed"
look. I also painted across some of the more pitted portions
of my skin (illustrated in Figure 6-47).

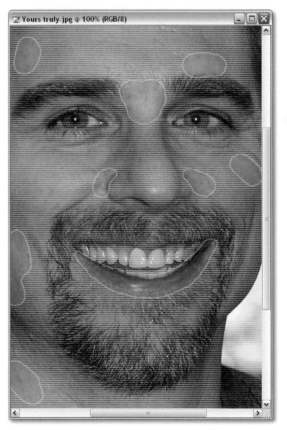

Figure 6-47.

---

To limit the area affected by the smudge tool, draw a selection
outline. For example, if you lasso the lower lip, you can drag
anywhere you please inside the image but affect only the lower lip.
This technique works for all the paint and edit tools, including the
paintbrush. But it's especially useful when using the smudge tool,
which is unique in that it can smear colors from deselected pixels
even as it modifies selected ones.

---

20. *Create yet another snapshot.* I called mine "Smudged
Colors." Heads up: This is the last time I'll remind you to
create a snapshot in this exercise. But it is a really great habit.
It's like saving a document—you do it in part to protect
yourself in case something goes wrong.

PEARL OF WISDOM

Speaking of saving, it's worth bearing in mind that Photoshop does *not*
save anything tracked by the History palette. This goes for snapshots as
well as individual states. If you want to save a particular snapshot, drag
it onto the left-hand icon at the bottom of the History palette, which
duplicates it to an independent image. Then use File→Save to save the
image to disk.

We've now seen all the tools mentioned in the name of this exercise, "Dodge, Burn, Sponge, and Smudge," and all but one of the tools I promised in the introduction. The one remaining feature is Photoshop CS's new color replacement tool. If you've had enough of editing, skip to the final exercise, "Healing and Patching," which begins on page 191. To learn how to fix a few more details in my uniquely imperfect face—including red-eye—complete the remaining steps.

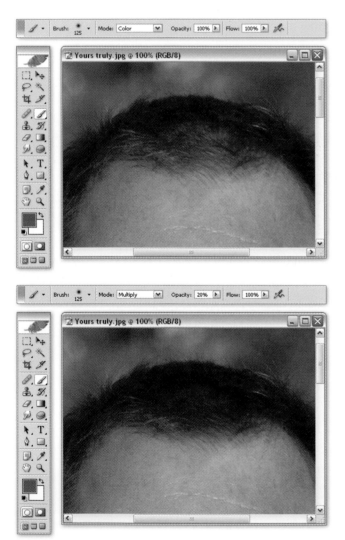

Figure 6-48.

21. **Click the paintbrush in the toolbox.** Or press B. We'll use this tool to fill in my fine hair.

22. **Eyedrop a representative hair color.** With the paintbrush active, press the Alt key (Option on the Mac) to temporarily access the eyedropper, and then click on a color in one of the rare full portions of my hair. To see what color you lifted, bring up the **Color** palette. Mine was in the neighborhood of **R**: 100, **G**: 90, **B**: 80. But there is so much variation to the hair, and depending on how much you burned the hair back in Step 9, you may end up with something entirely different. Feel free to use the color you eyedropped or dial in the number suggested above—either should work fine.

23. **Paint the scalp using the Color mode.** Change the **Mode** setting in the options bar to **Color**. Or press the keyboard shortcut, Shift+Alt+C (Shift-Option-C on the Mac). Change the brush diameter to 125 pixels. Then paint the top of my scalp to get the effect shown at top in Figure 6-48.

24. **Paint some more using the Multiply mode.** Choose **Multiply** from the **Mode** menu, or press Shift+Alt+M (Shift-Option-M). Press 2 to lower the **Opacity** value to 20 percent. Then paint short strokes in the light areas of the scalp to darken them up, as shown in the bottom image in Figure 6-48.

25. **Select the color replacement tool in the toolbox.** Your final task is to remove the red-eye caused by the camera's flash. Click and hold the band-aid below the crop tool icon in the toolbox and choose the color

replacement tool from the flyout menu (see Figure 6-49). Or press the J key three times. (If you skipped the Preface, press J and then Shift+J twice instead.)

26. ***Eyedrop a representative iris color.*** Press Alt (or Option) and click on a color inside one of the irises of my eyes. The resulting RGB values should be something like **R**: 120, **G**: 100, **B**: 75.

27. ***Paint inside each of the pupils.*** Zoom in to one of the pupils and paint over it. Just like that, the red-eye goes away. Paint the other pupil as well. Some of the red pixels are tenacious, so you may have to paint an area more than once. For the sake of comparison, before and after views appear in Figure 6-50.

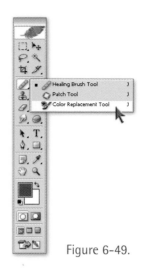

Figure 6-49.

Red-eye may be easily removed using the color replacement tool's default settings, but it's hardly the only purpose for the tool. It's also great for evening out the color of splotchy skin. But before you take this step, you have to adjust a few settings.

28. ***Change the Mode, Sampling, and Tolerance settings.*** Increase the brush diameter to 60 pixels and reduce the **Hardness** setting to 0 percent. (Remember, that's ] and Shift+[ from the keyboard.) Then do the following:

- Set the **Mode** option to **Hue**, which replaces the core hues while leaving the saturation values intact.

- Change the **Sampling** option from Continuous to **Once**, as in Figure 6-51. The Once setting tells Photoshop to replace only those colors that match the pixel at which you began to drag. It's a way of constraining the tool so it replaces fewer colors at a time.

- Press 2 to reduce the **Tolerance** to 20 percent. (On the PC, you have to press Esc to deactivate the Sampling option and then press 2.) Again, this limits the number of colors affected at a time.

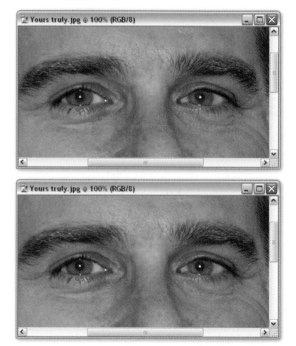

Figure 6-50.

Figure 6-51.

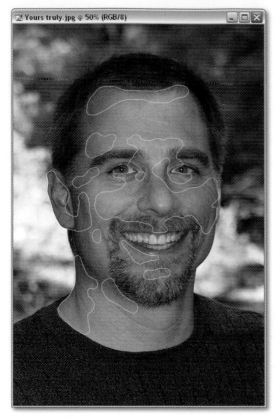

Figure 6-52.

29. *Eyedrop a flesh tone.* Press the Alt (or Option) key and click in one of the areas of my skin that trends toward orange as opposed to pink. A good color to match is **R**: 205, **G**: 165, **B**: 150.

30. *Paint away the pinks in the skin.* Paint over the pink areas in the eyelids, cheeks, and nose, as well as the more understated pinks of the neck, ears, and forehead, all outlined in Figure 6-52. As you do, these areas will turn a uniform fleshy peach color, as if my face were coated in a forgiving layer of foundation.

---

When working on large areas with the color replacement tool, it's easy to inadvertently recolor details that you don't want to—in this case, the eyes, lips, gums, teeth, hair, sweater, and background. The best solution is to tag the Smudged Colors snapshot (Step 20, page 187) as the source state and then paint away your mistakes with the history brush. Another option is to change the **Limits** setting in the options bar to **Find Edges**. This tells the color replacement tool to observe strict edges as you paint. It makes the tool more precise, but it also requires you to apply more brushstrokes to get the same results, which means more work.

---

31. *Continue to adjust details as needed.* Don't expect to be able to retouch an image in one pass. After all, a change made with the color replacement tool might beg you to make another with the burn tool, which in turn requires you to take up the sponge tool, and so on. In short, expect to revisit all these tools as you create that near-perfect image.

As you work back and forth inside your image, here are a few techniques and words of advice:

- The dodge and burn tools affect specific color ranges. By default, the **Range** menu in the options bar is set to **Midtones**, which changes the midtones and protects the highlights and shadows. If you prefer to adjust the lightest or darkest colors, choose **Highlights** or **Shadows** instead. In Figure 6-53, I set the burn tool to Highlights to darken the perimeter of the background.

- The dodge and burn tools are interchangeable. Just press the Alt key (Option on the Mac) to darken with the dodge tool or lighten with the burn tool. This is a great way to take the settings assigned to one tool—such as a brush diameter and Range setting—and apply them to the opposite function.

- The dodge, burn, sponge, and smudge tools work best when used with a soft brush (typically, a **Hardness** value of 50 percent or lower). The color replacement tool can go either way, hard or soft.

- Feel free to cheat. Just because you have all these edit tools doesn't mean you have to use them. For example, my lower lip was resolutely determined to remain a bright crimson despite my best efforts. So I selected it with the lasso tool and used the Hue/Saturation command to nudge it more toward red and bring down the saturation. It doesn't matter how you get there as long as it works.

Frankly scary original

After a big dose of edit tools

Figure 6-53 compares the original photograph to the edited version. Now you know why I never let an image out of my studio without a proper retouching.

Figure 6-53.

## Healing and Patching

The edit tools are well suited to a wide variety of retouching scenarios. But they can't create detail where none exists. To fix dust and scratches or cover up blemishes and wrinkles, you need tools that can paint imagery on top of imagery. Tools like the healing brush and patch tool:

- The healing brush paints one section of an image onto another. As the tool clones the source detail, it mixes it with the color and lighting that surrounds the brushstroke, thereby mending the offending detail seamlessly.

- The patch tool clones like the healing brush. But instead of painting with the tool, you select areas as you would with the lasso.

The following exercise shows you how to use these powerful tools to fix a variety of photographic woes, ranging from rips and tears to blemishes and age spots.

Figure 6-54.

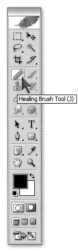

Figure 6-55.

1. **Open a broken image.** Open the file *PhotoSpin bluebeard.psd* located in the *Lesson 06* folder inside *Lesson Files-PScs 1on1*. Available in perfect condition from PhotoSpin's Ed Simpson International People collection, this particular version of the photo appears so tragically scratched because I scratched it. I printed the image to a continuous-tone Olympus P-400 image printer. Then I folded the output once vertically and again horizontally, scored the crease with a pair of scissors, pressed it flat, and scanned it into Photoshop. The result appears in Figure 6-54. The image is representative of the worst sorts of photographic wounds, directed both at the subject of the photo and the medium.

2. **Click the healing brush in the toolbox.** True to its mission, the healing brush looks like a band-aid (see Figure 6-55). If you're performing this step on the heels of the last exercise, Alt-click (or Option-click) the color replacement tool icon to switch to the healing brush. Or press the J key.

3. **Confirm the default settings.** In the options bar, make sure **Source** is set to **Sampled** and the **Aligned** check box is off. Sampled tells Photoshop to clone pixels from a spot inside an image (as you'll specify in the next step); turning Aligned off lets you clone several times in a row from that one pristine spot.

---

If these options are not set properly, you can restore the default settings by choosing the **Reset Tool** command from the pop-up menu on the far left side of the options bar. The highlighted ▾ and ◉ arrows in Figure 6-56 show the path to this very useful command.

---

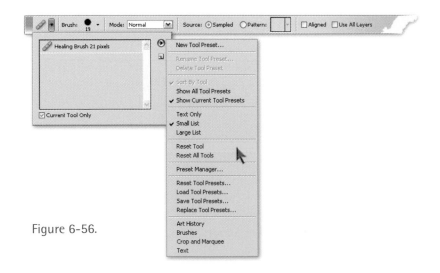

Figure 6-56.

4. *Set the source point for the healing.* The healing brush uses a *source point* to clone from one portion of an image to another. To set the source point, press the Alt key (Option on the Mac) and click at the spot below the left cheek (his right) as indicated by the crosshairs in Figure 6-57.

5. *Heal the giant mole.* Increase the brush diameter a couple of notches (say, to 30 pixels) and drag over the giant mole up and to the left of the source point. As you drag, Photoshop shows you what the patch looks like if you were merely to clone the source detail, as illustrated by the first image in Figure 6-58. But the moment you release the mouse button, Photoshop blends the source detail and destination perimeter to create a seamless mend, as witnessed by the second image in Figure 6-58.

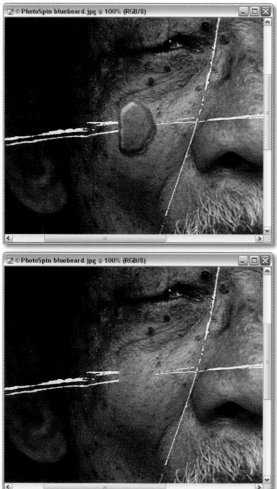

Figure 6-58.

Figure 6-57.

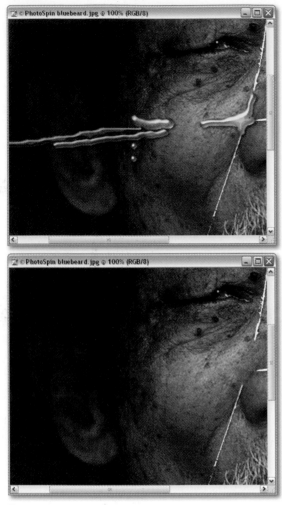

Figure 6-59.

6. **Heal the left part of the scratch.** Press [ to reduce the brush diameter to 20 pixels. Then do the following:

- Drag over the top-right fragment of the left-hand scratch, indicated by the yellow brushstroke in the top image in Figure 6-59. (Note that the brushstroke colors in this figure are for illustration purposes only; your brushstrokes will appear normal.)

- Next, press [ again to reduce the brush diameter to 10 pixels and drag along the bottom fragment, as indicated in cyan in the figure.

- In a separate brushstroke, drag along the remaining portion of the left-hand scratch, indicated in purple.

- Finally, drag around the area indicated in green.

In each case, I started my brushstroke on the right and dragged to the left. If you're right handed, this may seem backward. But it's important to follow my lead in this case; if you drag from left to right, you will clone the vertical scratch and mar your image.

PEARL OF WISDOM

If you look at the options bar, you'll see that you're using a hard brush, which is as it should be. A hard brush prevents the healing tool from incorporating distant and unrelated details into its mended pixels. In this case, the hard brush permits you to skirt between scratch lines without incorporating the white from one line into the healing for another. Just make sure each of your brushstrokes completely covers a scratch without crossing or touching another one.

But even the best of automated results fall short of perfect. For my part, I can clearly see rows of inconsistent pixels running through the old man's cheek and ear (see the spotlighted example in Figure 6-60). Known as *scarring*, these bad seams tell the world that your image has been modified. Fortunately, you can re-heal an area by painting over it once, twice, or as many times as you like.

7. ***Move the source and paint short strokes.*** Using the healing brush effectively is all about selecting a good source point. The previous source worked well across the forward portion of the cheek, but then we ran into a bad spot. Thankfully, when one source fails, you can switch to another one. Sources generally work best when set in an area that closely resembles the *destination* (the area that you want to heal).

    - To heal inside the ear, for example, Alt-click (Mac users, Option-click) inside the top portion of the ear and then drag over the scarred section.

    - To heal in the face, set the source point in the lower area of the cheek where the flesh is relatively smooth.

    - To heal the black background, Alt-click somewhere in the black background. If you get some haloing along the edge of the ear—a function of Photoshop recruiting ear colors into its healing algorithm—Alt-click along the edge of the ear and paint again.

    Keep your brushstrokes short. When using larger brushes, individual clicks can be very effective. I finally arrive at the revised cheek and ear shown in the bottom image in Figure 6-60. I can still make out some scarring, and the inner edge of the ear doesn't quite line up, but the bad stuff is sufficiently shadowed that few folks (if any) are likely to notice.

8. ***Set a new source.*** Now to fix the nearly vertical scratch in the bottom half of the image. Scroll down. Then press Alt (or Option) and click just to the left of the scratch along the red hat strap, as shown on the left in Figure 6-61 on the following page.

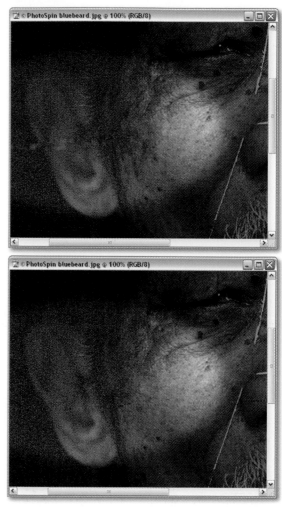

Figure 6-60.

9. ***Click and Shift-click to draw straight lines.*** Set the brush diameter to 20 pixels. Click at the point where the scratch intersects the red strap, indicated by the yellow target in the right image in Figure 6-61. Then press the Shift key and click midway up the scratch, at the point indicated by the cyan target in the figure. Photoshop connects the two points with a straight line of healing, which I've colorized in orange below. Finish off the scratch by Shift-clicking just left of the nose, indicated by the purple target.

10. ***Heal the bottom of the scratch.*** That still leaves an inch or so of scratch at the bottom of the image. Once again, click where the strap intersects the scratch (yellow target in Figure 6-61) to reset the relationship between the source and destination points. Then press Shift and click down and to the left to heal away the scratch.

11. ***Fix scars and repeated details.*** If you look hard enough, you can make out repeated details around the nose and mouth. But the bigger problems occur near the collar and among the whiskers, as highlighted on the left side of Figure 6-62. To fix

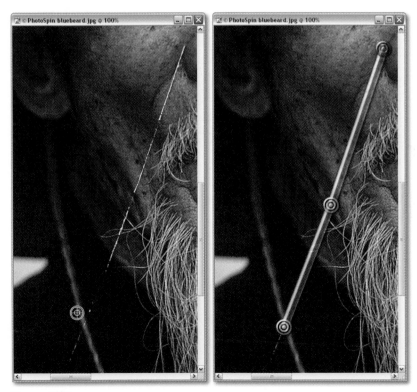

Figure 6-61.

these, you'll need to source very similar areas—meaning collar-to-neck transitions and whiskers at similar angles—and paint them in using very small brushes, as small as 6 or 7 pixels in diameter. To build up the two horizontal whiskers, I sourced what little remained intact of one, clicked to double its width, sourced that, clicked again, and so on. It takes a little patience, but in the end, you can build something out of nothing (shown on the right in the figure).

---

When using the healing brush, the options bar offers a handful of Mode options, but it lacks an Opacity setting. Fortunately, you can vary the opacity of a brushstroke after the fact. Immediately after painting a line with the healing brush, choose **Edit→Fade Healing Brush**. Then adjust the **Opacity** value to your liking and click **OK**.

---

12. *Select the patch tool in the toolbox.* We now turn our attention from the healing brush to its companion, the patch tool. Click and hold the healing brush to bring up a flyout menu of additional options. Then choose the patch tool, as in Figure 6-63. Or press the J key (Shift+J if you skipped the Preface).

Figure 6-63.

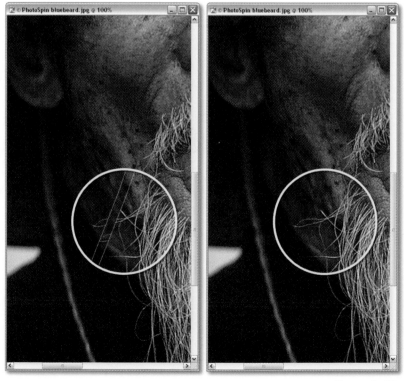

Figure 6-62.

13. *Confirm the default settings.* In the options bar, make sure **Patch** is set to **Source** and **Transparent** is turned off.

14. *Drag around the portion of the image you want to heal.* Initially, the patch tool works exactly like the lasso. To select an area inside the image, just drag around it. Be sure to select slightly outside the area you want to heal. You need a bit of margin for the tool to operate properly.

---

Need a polygonal patch tool? No problem. Press Ctrl+D (⌘-D on the Mac) to make sure nothing is selected. Then press and hold the Alt key (Option on the Mac) and click to set points in a straight-sided selection outline. I used this technique to select the scratch line at the top of the image, as shown on the left side of Figure 6-64. Notice that I kept my outline loose, selecting a few pixels of margin around the scratch.

---

15. *Choose View→Snap To→Document Bounds.* When turned on (as by default), **Snap To→Document Bounds** forces selection outlines and other objects to snap into alignment with the boundaries of the image. Normally, that's fine. But because

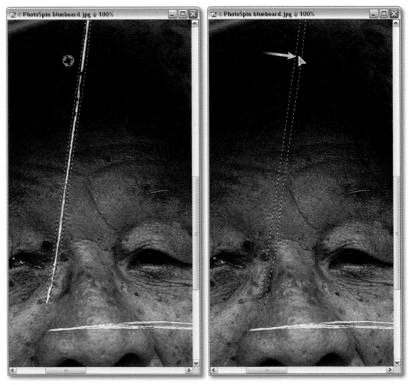

Figure 6-64.

you're already working close to the boundaries and you want to move the selection without constraint, it's best to turn it off.

16. ***Drag the selection to source another portion of the image.*** Drag the selection outline just slightly to the right and down, to a portion of the image that is not scratched. In Figure 6-64, I dragged about 30 pixels to the right and 10 pixels down. Photoshop shows you a live preview of the cloning operation on the fly. Release the mouse button to apply the healing effect.

---

One of the downsides of using the patch tool is that the selection outlines cover up the mended edges and thus interfere with your ability to judge the quality of your edit. Fortunately, you can hide the selection outline by choosing **View**→**Extras** or pressing Ctrl+H (⌘-H on the Mac).

---

17. ***Select the magic wand in the toolbox.*** The patch tool functions like a selection tool, but that's just a convenience function. Its healing powers translate to any kind of selection. To heal the final scratch, press W to select the magic wand.

18. ***Turn Contiguous off.*** In the options bar, make sure the **Tolerance** value is set to 32 and **Anti-aliased** is turned on, as by default. To select the entire scratch all at once, turn off the **Contiguous** check box.

19. ***Click anywhere along the remaining scratch.*** You can click just about anywhere. But you might as well make it easy on yourself and click at the thickest point in the scratch, on the tip of the man's nose. Photoshop selects the entire scratch along with lots of light pixels throughout the image.

20. ***Deselect everything except the scratch.*** Click the rectangular marquee tool in the toolbox to select it. Then press the Shift and Alt keys (Shift and Option on the Mac) and drag around the scratch as shown in Figure 6-65. (If needed, press the spacebar to move the marquee so you encompass the entire scratch, all the way to the right-hand edge of the image.)

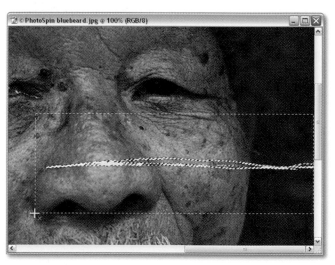

Figure 6-65.

As you may recall from Video Lesson 4, "Marquee, Lasso, and Wand" (see page 98), pressing Shift and Alt finds the intersection of one selection outline and another. In this case, it finds the intersection of the marquee and the wand selections, thus deselecting everything outside the marquee.

21. ***Choose the Expand command.*** Choose **Select→Modify→ Expand** to bring up the **Expand** dialog box, then enter 3 and click **OK**. This expands the selection to include just enough margin to make the healing function work properly.

22. ***Select the patch tool.*** Now that the selection is ready to go, press the J key to return to the patch tool.

23. ***Drag the selection to source another portion of the image.*** Drag the selection outline to an area free of scratches. I dragged my outline about 40 pixels down and 5 pixels to the left, as shown in Figure 6-66. Make sure the edge of the face previewed inside the selection matches the edge outside the selection. Then release the mouse button to complete the operation.

24. ***Clean up with the healing brush.*** The patch tool did a pretty good job of healing both the top and right-hand scratches. But there are a few rough edges. To clean them up, press J a couple of times to switch back to the healing brush. Then press Ctrl+D (⌘-D on the Mac) to deselect the image. Alt-click (or Option-click) to set a source and get to work.

If you're looking for additional practice, the healing brush is an excellent tool for cleaning up blemishes, and this image gives you lots to work with. For my part, I went ahead and painted over most of the moles and age spots. But I left the wrinkles. Wrinkles add character, and this particular gentleman wears them well.

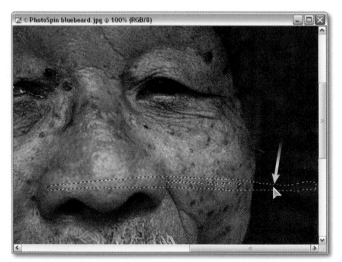

Figure 6-66.

The one remaining problem is that left eye (his right). The top eyelid droops so that it covers virtually the entire iris, not to mention the pupil. I have this overwhelming urge to mend the eye, but it's easier said than done. After all, there's really nothing to clone from. The following steps explore this special retouching scenario, in which we'll heal the eye from an independent layer. If you've had enough healing for one day, skip to the end-of-lesson quiz on page 203 and test your knowledge.

Figure 6-67.

25. *Select the Replacement Eye layer.* Go to the **Layers** palette (press F7 if necessary) and click the **Replacement Eye** layer. A disembodied eye appears above the bad one, as pictured in Figure 6-67. This is nothing more than a copy of the right eye placed on an independent layer, flipped, and slightly rotated and scaled. Let's see what happens if we heal from it.

26. *Set the source point on the Replacement Eye layer.* With the Replacement Eye layer active, press the Alt key (Option on the Mac) and click in the highlight of the eye (the tiny bright spot) to set the source for your healing.

27. *Select the Background layer.* Go to the Layers palette and click **Background**. Yes, the healing brush permits you to clone between layers. (This is not true for the patch tool, just so you know.)

28. *Click on the bad eye.* Center your cursor on the highlight in the bad eye—a much bigger target—and click. Don't drag, just click. I know, it doesn't look right, but trust me. For the moment, all you're doing is establishing a relationship between the source and destination points. You'll see, it'll work out splendidly in the end.

29. *Turn on the Aligned check box.* Located in the options bar, this check box locks in the relationship between source and destination points that you established in the previous step. From now on, you can paint as many separate strokes as you like and all parts of the eye will remain properly aligned.

30. *Paint over the eye.* Start wherever you like and paint as much as you like. Just be sure to keep the source point well inside the confines of the Replacement Eye layer; otherwise, you'll get a flat edge where the layer ends. In the left half of Figure 6-68 (next page), I've highlighted my various brush-strokes as one big cyan mass; the sourced area appears green. On the right, we see the healed result. Photoshop not only

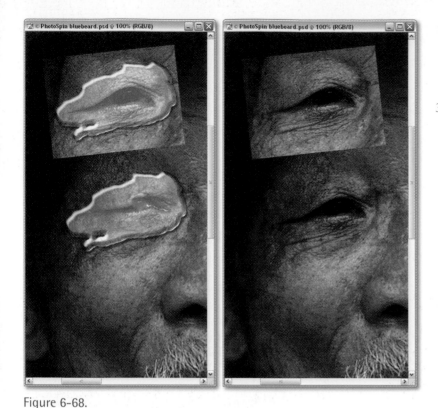

Figure 6-68.

replaced the bad eye with the good, it blended the edges and matched the deeper shadows and ambient colors of the destination.

31. ***Turn off the Replacement Eye layer.*** Or, if you prefer, delete the layer by dragging it to the trash icon at the bottom of the Layers palette. Use **File→Save As** to save your changes. Figure 6-69 compares the original version of the image—that is, the one I purposely damaged—to the document as it appears after I healed it inside Photoshop. If you search hard enough, you can find a few scars and flaws. And the eyes are a bit more symmetrical than they would be in real life. But I suspect most people would have no idea this image has been tampered with at all.

Figure 6-69.

# WHAT DID YOU LEARN?

Match the key concept in the numbered list below with the letter
of the phrase that best describes it. Answers appear upside-down
at the bottom of the page.

## Key Concepts

1. Edit tools
2. Floating selection
3. Lock transparency
4. Jitter
5. All Layers
6. Minimum
7. Snapshot
8. Dodge and burn
9. Sponge tool
10. Color replacement tool
11. Source point
12. Patch tool

## Descriptions

A. A pair of edit tools that lighten and darken portions of an image as you paint.

B. An option in the Layers palette that limits your edits to the existing opaque pixels in a layer.

C. Drag a selection outline to heal the selected area, whether it was created with this tool or some other selection function.

D. When using the paint bucket, turn on this check box in the options bar to fill areas of line art on an independent layer.

E. Decreases or increases the saturation of an image, depending on the Mode setting in the options bar.

F. A special kind of state in the History palette that remains available well after 20 operations.

G. A loose collection of tools that modify the existing color or luminosity of a pixel without altogether replacing its content.

H. The spot from which the healing brush samples information when repairing a flaw in an image.

I. An image element that hovers above the surface of the image, permitting you to move or transform it without harming the underlying original.

J. A command in the Filter menu that can be used to expand the size of objects on a layer, especially useful with solid colors.

K. A new feature in Photoshop CS that gets rid of red-eye and evens out flesh tones.

L. A series of percentage values in the Brushes palette that permit one or more attributes to vary randomly over the course of a brushstroke.

## Answers

1G, 2I, 3B, 4L, 5D, 6J, 7F, 8A, 9E, 10K, 11H, 12C

# CREATING AND APPLYING MASKS

**IF YOU'RE LIKE** most Photoshop users, you've at least heard of *masks*. Or perhaps you've heard them called *friskets* or *mattes* or *alpha channels* or any of a half dozen other occupation-specific variants. But whatever you call them, the purpose of masks is to block out one portion of an image and reveal another, as illustrated in Figure 7-1.

Essentially, what I've done in Figure 7-1 is select the woman's face and move it into the mirror. But I never could have achieved such an accurate selection if I had relied exclusively on the lasso, wand, and pen tools. This is because masking lets you use the colors and luminosity values inherent in the image to define a selection outline. In effect, you use the image to select itself. Masking takes some getting used to, but once you do, no selection tool is as accurate or efficient.

## Seeing through Photoshop's Eyes

In real life, we have a natural sense of an object's boundaries. You may not be able to make out an individual flower in a crowded garden from a distance, but get in close enough, and you can trace the exact border in your mind (see Figure 7-2, page 207). So why does Photoshop have such a hard time with it? Why can't you just say, "Pick the flower," instead of painstakingly dragging around every single leaf, stem, and petal?

The source image

The destination

The mask

The composite

Figure 7-1.

# ABOUT THIS LESSON

## Project Files

Before beginning the exercises, make sure that you've installed the lesson files from the CD, as explained in Step 5 on page xv of the Preface. This should result in a folder called *Lesson Files-PScs 1on1* on your desktop. We'll be working with the files inside the *Lesson 07* subfolder.

In this lesson, you'll immerse yourself gradually in the world of masking, starting with automated techniques, moving on to extraction, and then finally taking on calculations and channel masking. You'll learn how to:

- Isolate a complex image element using the Color Range command . . . . . . . . . . . . . . page 209

- Modify a selection outline as a mask using the provisional quick mask mode . . . . . . . page 214

- Erase an entire background in a single pass using the Extract command . . . . . . . . . . page 223

- Assemble a professional-quality mask with the Calculations command and toning tools . . . . page 230

- Match the lighting and edges of a masked image with its new background . . . . . . . . . . page 238

## Video Lesson 7: Just What Is Masking?

This lesson explores two related functions in Photoshop, extractions and more traditional channel-based masks. To *extract* an image is to delete the background pixels and convert the foreground image to a new layer. A *mask* is an independent channel that can be converted to a selection outline and saved for later use. Of the two, masks are the more flexible, but both have their merits.

To learn just what these merits are, as well as see how the two functions compare, watch the seventh video lesson included on the CD. Insert the CD, click the **Start Training** button, click the Set **3** button in the top right corner of the screen, and then select **7, Just What Is Masking?** from the Lessons list. The 9-minute, 40-second movie explores the following commands and shortcuts:

| Command or operation | Windows shortcut | Macintosh shortcut |
|---|---|---|
| Extract | Ctrl+Alt+X | ⌘-Option-X |
| Draw straight lines in Extract window | Shift-click | Shift-click |
| Move a selection | Ctrl-drag | ⌘-drag |
| Revert image to saved appearance | F12 | F12 |
| Color Range | Ctrl+Shift+Alt+O* | ⌘-Shift-Option-O* |
| Add to Color Range selection | Shift-drag in image window | Shift-drag in image window |
| Make mask foreground color black | X | X |
| Return to RGB composite image | Ctrl+tilde (~) | ⌘-tilde (~) |
| Load mask as selection outline | Ctrl-click mask in Channels palette | ⌘-click mask in Channels palette |

\* Works only if you loaded the Deke Keys keyboard shortcuts (as directed in Step 12 on page xvii of the Preface).

Well the truth is, you can, provided you know how to speak Photoshop's language. It may require a long conversation, and there may be some misunderstandings along the way. But with a little time, a bit more patience, and a lot of experience, you'll learn to translate your vision of the world into something Photoshop can recognize as well.

When you see the flower, you know exactly where it begins and where it ends.

Figure 7-2.

As you may recall from Lesson 2 (see "The Nature of Channels," page 40), Photoshop never actually looks at the full-color image. Assuming that you're working in the RGB mode, the program sees three independent grayscale versions of the image, one for each color channel. A mask is just another kind of channel, one in which white pixels are selected and black pixels are not. So if any one of those channels contains a very light foreground subject against a very dark background, you've got yourself a ready-made mask.

More likely, however, each channel contains some amount of highlights, some amount of shadows, and lots of midtones in between. But that's okay, because the strengths of one channel can compensate for the weaknesses of another. Take the sunflower, for example. If you inspect the individual color channels, you find that each highlights a different portion of the image. The petals are brightest in the Red channel, the stem is well-defined in the Green channel, and the sky is lightest in the Blue channel (see Figure 7-3).

High contrast, light petals and head    Uniform brightness, great detail    Generally dark with bright sky

Figure 7-3.

Duplicating the Blue channel and inverting it makes the sky dark and other portions of the image light, a step in the right direction. Combining channels with Image→ Calculations permits you to emphasize portions of the image, such as the flower (Figure 7-4, left) or stem (middle). From there, it's just a matter of selecting the pieces you like, splicing them together, and adjusting contrast values. After a few minutes of tinkering—a process that I explain in detail later in this lesson—I arrived at the rough mask shown on the right side of Figure 7-4. Another five to ten minutes later, the mask was complete.

Invert Blue, combine with Red    Invert Blue, combine with Green    5 minutes of hacking pieces together

Figure 7-4.

Photoshop gives you the raw information you need to accurately define the edges in the image. Then it's up to you to figure out how to assemble the pieces. Fortunately, you can do so using not just a few selection tools, but virtually every function in Photoshop's arsenal. And because a mask is a channel that can be saved as part of a TIFF or native PSD file, you can recall or modify the selection outline any time you like.

## Using the Color Range Command

Photoshop's Color Range command uses a masking metaphor to generate selection outlines. In this regard, it serves as a bridge between the worlds of selections and masks, not to mention as a wonderful introduction to our lesson.

Essentially an enhanced version of the magic wand, Color Range lets you adjust the range of colors you want to select until you arrive at an acceptable, if not perfect, selection outline. And it does so dynamically, so there's no need to start a selection over again the way you sometimes must with the wand. Finally, Color Range interprets luminosity values in a more sophisticated manner than the wand, which results in smoother, more credible selection outlines.

1. **Open two images.** Open the *Duckbill in tent.tif* and *The planets.psd* image files located in the *Lesson 07* folder inside *Lesson Files-PScs 1on1*. 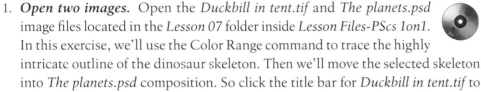 In this exercise, we'll use the Color Range command to trace the highly intricate outline of the dinosaur skeleton. Then we'll move the selected skeleton into *The planets.psd* composition. So click the title bar for *Duckbill in tent.tif* to make sure that image is in front, as in Figure 7-5.

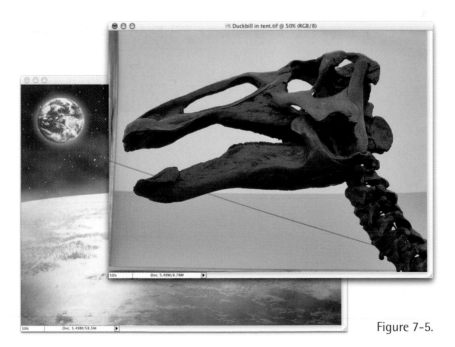

Figure 7-5.

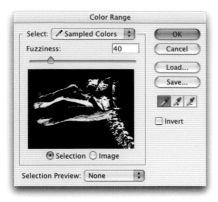

Figure 7-6.

2. ***Press the D key.*** By now, you know this resets the foreground color to black. But what you might not know is that the Color Range command uses the foreground color as the basis of a selection. You don't always have to start with black; it merely assures that you and I begin on the same foot.

3. ***Choose the Color Range command.*** Choose **Select→Color Range**. Alternatively, if you loaded the custom keyboard shortcuts I recommend in the Preface (Step 12, page xvii), you can press Ctrl+Shift+Alt+O (⌘-Shift-Option-O on the Mac). Either way, you get the **Color Range** dialog box, shown in Figure 7-6.

The central portion of the dialog box features a black-and-white preview, which shows you how the selection looks when expressed as a mask. The white areas represent selected pixels; the black areas are deselected; and the gray areas are somewhere in between. This might seem like a weird way to express a selection outline, but it's actually more precise than the marching ants we saw back in Lesson 4. Where marching ants show the halfway mark between selected and deselected pixels, a mask shows the full range of a selection, from fully selected to not selected to somewhere in between.

Figure 7-7.

4. ***Click somewhere in the background above the dinosaur.*** When you move the cursor into the dinosaur image window, it changes to an eyedropper. Click to establish a base color for the selection. In our case, the tent ceiling behind the dinosaur divides into two main bodies of color: light gray at the top and a slightly darker gray toward the bottom. I'd like you to click in the light gray above and to the left of the animal's long nose. This resets the base color from black to a very light color, thus inverting the mask preview, as in Figure 7-7.

5. ***Raise the Fuzziness value to 90.*** Like the magic wand's Tolerance value (see "Selecting Colored Areas with the Magic Wand," Step 5, page 102), the **Fuzziness** value spreads the selection across a range of luminosity values that neighbor the base color. Lowering the value contracts the selection; raising the value expands the selection.

Fuzziness improves on Tolerance in two important ways. First, whereas the static Tolerance value modifies the next selection, the dynamic Fuzziness value changes the selection in progress. Second, the magic wand selects all colors that fall inside the Tolerance range to the same degree, but Color Range gradually fades the selection over the course of the Fuzziness range. As a result, Fuzziness produces gradual, organic transitions.

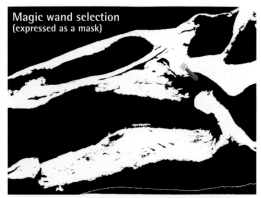

y

PEARL OF WISDOM

In the comparative illustrations in Figure 7-8, I rendered the selections as colorized masks, better to see the transitions from black (not selected) to white (selected). In both cases, the Tolerance and Fuzziness values were set to 90. The cursors show the common location at which I clicked to set the base color. (Note, this is not a step, so please don't click there yourself. If you do, reset the base color as instructed in Step 4. Then move on to Step 6.)

6. **Add a base color to the selection.** To add base colors to the selection, press the Shift key and click or drag inside the image window. For our purposes, Shift-click in the area of medium gray near the lower-left corner of the image window, as indicated by the eyedropper in Figure 7-9. This expands the selection to include more midtones, including a few inside the skull.

Figure 7-8.

PEARL OF WISDOM

It's worth pointing out that Shift-clicking produces a different effect than raising the Fuzziness value. When you Shift-click, you increase the number of colors that are fully selected (white in the mask). In contrast, the Fuzziness value affects partially selected pixels (gray in the mask).

7. **Check your mask in the image window.** The mask preview inside the Color Range dialog box is helpful, but its dinky size makes it hard to accurately gauge a selection. To better judge the quality of your work, choose **Grayscale** from the **Selection Preview** pop-up menu, as in Figure 7-10 on the next page. Photoshop fills the image window with the mask preview, permitting you to zoom in (Ctrl+plus on the PC or ⌘-plus on the Mac) and see every little detail of your prospective selection.

Figure 7-9.

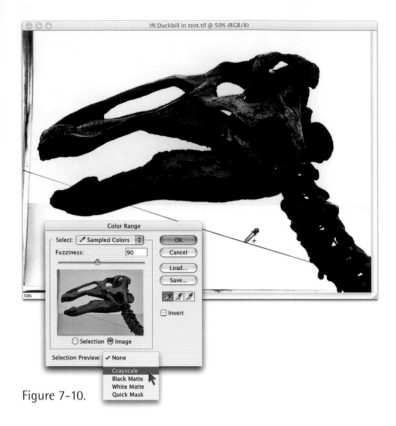

Figure 7-10.

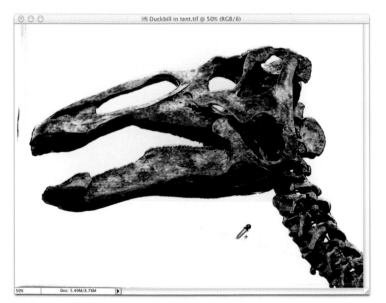

Figure 7-11.

To see the mask preview and image at the same time, click the **Image** radio button directly under the preview. The preview box switches from a thumbnail of the mask to a thumbnail of the full-color image (again, see Figure 7-10).

8. ***Add any detail that still needs to be selected.*** For example, we need to get rid of that diagonal support cable. Press Shift and click on the cable, as indicated by the eyedropper in Figure 7-10. Color Range samples the base color and adds the cable to the selection.

   Depending on where you Shift-click, Photoshop selects some or all of the cable. But in my case, it goes too far, selecting well into the skeleton, as shown in Figure 7-11. If this happens to you—as it likely will—you have two options. (For the moment, don't do them; just read about them.)

   • Press the Alt key (Option on the Mac) and click a color in either the image window or preview to deselect an area related to that base color. The problem is, this technique often overcompensates by deselecting too many pixels.

   • Choose Edit→Undo Color Sample or press Ctrl+Z (⌘-Z on the Mac). Great feature, but bear in mind that you have just one level of undo inside the Color Range dialog box. Use it wisely.

9. ***Choose the Undo Color Sample command.*** Given that you have just one level of undo, and Alt-clicking to subtract from a selection probably won't work, your best bet is to invoke **Undo** now before it's too late. Press Ctrl+Z (⌘-Z on the Mac) to return to where you were after Step 7.

10. **Click the Invert check box.** As we did when selecting the giraffe in Lesson 4 (see Step 8, page 103), we've gone and selected the background instead of the element we want to select. And wouldn't you just know it, we did it for exactly the same reason: because the background is easier to select. To get the foreground element instead, just turn on **Invert**. Now the skeleton turns white and the background black, as in Figure 7-12.

11. **Click the OK button.** Color Range uses the base colors and Fuzziness value to deliver a selection outline in the image window. Note, you will not see a mask; instead, you get a standard marching ants-style selection, ready for immediate use.

12. **Drag the selected skeleton into the planets backdrop.** Press and hold the Ctrl key (⌘ on the Mac) to get the move tool and drag the selected skeleton from *Duckbill in tent.tif* into *The planets.psd* image window. Before you drop it into place, press and hold Shift to center it. Release the mouse button and then release both keys. You should get the result shown in Figure 7-13.

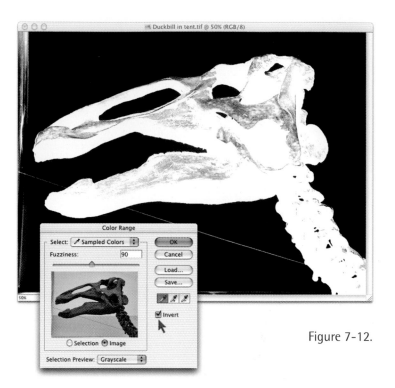

Figure 7-12.

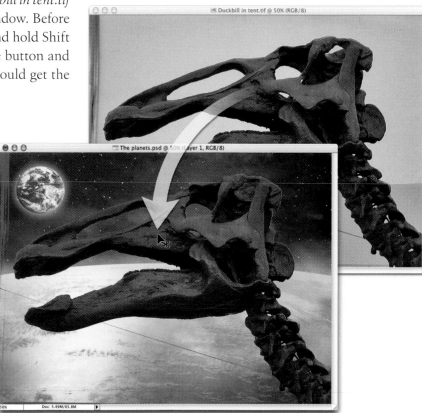

Figure 7-13.

The resulting composition is commendable. The Color Range command managed to trace a pretty complicated outline and omit all the right holes. But while I'd give Photoshop an A for effort, the implementation is imperfect. Portions of the dinosaur that should be opaque are translucent. As illustrated by Figure 7-14, the edges are fringed by hot yellow artifacting captured by the camera. And then there's that darn support cable.

13. ***Choose the Undo command.*** Choose **Edit→Undo→Drag Selection** or press Ctrl+Z (⌘-Z) to abandon the imported skeleton. Before we can introduce the dinosaur into his new home, his selection has to be refined. And we'll be doing just that in the next exercise.

Figure 7-14.

## Refining a Selection with a Quick Mask

Photoshop's *quick mask mode* is nothing more than an alternate way to view and edit a selection outline. You enter the mode to view the selection as a mask, edit the mask as desired, and then exit the mode to see the updated selection outline. The mask remains available only as long as you stay in the quick mask mode, but during that time, you have access to Photoshop's full range of masking options. Frankly, there's nothing particularly "quick" about the quick mask mode—you can spend as long making a quick mask as any other kind of mask. The fact that it's temporary is what sets it apart.

The quick mask mode works especially well in combination with the Color Range command. Color Range establishes the rough selection outline and then quick mask refines it. The goal of this exercise is to finesse the selection you began in the last exercise. For example, portions of the dinosaur that should be opaque are translucent, the edges are fringed with yellow, and there's that darn cable in the picture. We'll address all these issues, and more, using quick mask.

1. ***Open those same two images.*** If you're performing these steps immediately after the others, and you still have both images open and the skeleton remains selected, bring the *Duckbill in tent.tif* file to front and skip to Step 5. Otherwise, open *Duckbill in tent.tif* and *The planets.psd*, both in the *Lesson 07* folder inside *Lesson Files-PScs 1on1*.

2. *Choose the Color Range command.* Make sure the *Duckbill in tent.tif* file is in front. Then choose **Select→Color Range** or press Ctrl+Shift+Alt+O (⌘-Shift-Option-O on the Mac).

3. *Load the Color Range settings.* Click the **Load** button inside the Color Range dialog box. Then locate the file *Duckbill settings.axt* in the *Lesson 07* folder and click **Load** (or double-click the filename). This opens the settings that I applied back in the preceding exercise (Step 11, page 213).

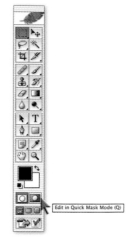

4. *Invert and accept the selection.* When you save a collection of Color Range settings, Photoshop stores the base colors and Fuzziness value. It does not remember the setting of the Invert check box. So Invert may be on or off, depending on the last selection you created with the Color Range command. Regardless, make sure **Invert** is turned on. Then click **OK**.

Figure 7-15.

5. *Click the quick mask icon in the toolbox.* Click the ⬜ icon near the lower-right corner of the toolbox, as demonstrated in Figure 7-15. Or just press the Q key. Either way, Photoshop coats the deselected portion of the image with a red overlay, based on a traditional *rubylith*, a kind of film commonly used in the old days to stencil photographs and line art.

6. *Change the color overlay.* Just because the overlay is red doesn't mean it has to stay that way. In this case, the red doesn't contrast well with the warm colors in the dinosaur bones. So double-click the ⬜ icon in the toolbox to display the **Quick Mask Options** dialog box. Click the color swatch to open the Color Picker, change the **H** value to 180 degrees (giving you cyan, the complement to red), and click **OK**. You can also change the Opacity value if you want, but I left mine at 50 percent (see Figure 7-16). Then click **OK** to accept your changes.

7. *Click the brush tool in the toolbox.* The most basic tool for editing a quick mask is the brush tool. Click its icon in the toolbox or press the B key to get it.

Figure 7-16.

If you're performing this exercise on the heels of Lesson 6, in which we last used a randomized scatter brush, you'll need to restore the default settings for the brush tool. First, click the ▾ arrow next to the brush icon on the far left side of the options bar. Then click the ⊙ arrow on the right side of the pop-up palette and choose the **Reset Tool** command. (For an illustration, see Figure 6-56 back on page 192.)

8. *Set the foreground color to black.* It probably is black already, but press the D key just to make sure. Regardless of the color of the quick mask overlay—red, cyan, whatever—painting with black adds to the mask and therefore deselects areas; painting with white adds to the selection. (As when editing any mask, you can't paint in color because you're working with the equivalent of a grayscale image.)

9. *Set the brush diameter and hardness.* I found it best to use a 20-pixel brush. And you definitely want the **Hardness** set to 100 percent to avoid introducing incongruously soft edges. (If you reset the brush in Step 7, press the ] key to increase the brush diameter one increment; then press Shift+] four times to maximize the hardness.)

Figure 7-17.

10. *Paint away the diagonal support cable.* The support cable is a straight line, so you can paint over it by clicking at one end of the cable and then Shift-clicking at the other end. Photoshop will draw a straight brushstroke between the two points, highlighted in purple in Figure 7-17. Keep your click and Shift-click points very close to the edge of the skeleton, as demonstrated by the yellow targets. Repeat the process to paint away the upper-left portion of the cable.

Notice that even though black was your foreground color, you actually painted a faint cyan brushstroke. That's because both black and the translucent cyan overlay represent masked pixels. Had you been painting in white, you would have erased the cyan. This will make more sense as you experiment further with the quick mask mode.

11. **Bring up the Channels palette.** Even though you changed the overlay from red to cyan, you're probably still having problems telling which portions of the dinosaur are masked and which are not. Fortunately, you can view the mask independently of the full-color image from the Channels palette. Click the **Channels** tab or choose **Window→Channels**.

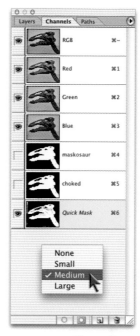

Figure 7-18.

Note that the Channels palette contains the usual RGB and Red, Green, and Blue items. But it also contains a couple of surplus, so-called *alpha channels*, Maskosaur and Choked. Each represents a saved selection outline you can load at will (as we'll witness first-hand by the end of this exercise). The last item, *Quick Mask*, is just that—the quick mask itself. The fact that the item is in italics tells you that it's temporary and lasts only as long as you stay in the quick mask mode.

To enlarge the channel thumbnails a bit, right-click in the empty portion of the palette and choose **Medium**, as shown in Figure 7-18. (If your Macintosh mouse doesn't have a right button, press Control and click.)

12. **Hide the RGB image.** The eyeballs (👁) in the Channels palette tell us that we're seeing the RGB channels and the quick mask together, hence the cyan overlay. Click the 👁 icon in front of **RGB** to turn it off. Now you see the quick mask by itself, in its true form, as a grayscale image (see Figure 7-19). It's now easy to see the large areas of black and white, as well as the inconsistent grays that need to go one way or the other.

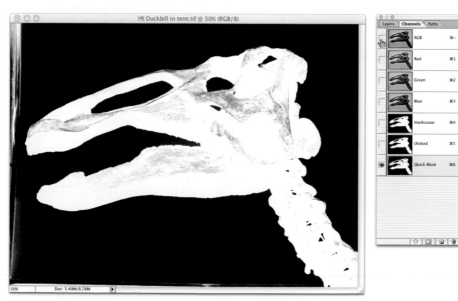

Figure 7-19.

The problem with the mask is that it has too many grays. Some need to be sent to black, others white. And what better way to increase the contrast of an image than with the Levels command?

13. ***Increase the contrast of the mask.*** Choose **Image→Adjustments→Levels** or press Ctrl+L (⌘-L on the Mac) to display the Levels dialog box shown in Figure 7-20. Increase the first **Input Levels** value to 90, which sends everything with a luminosity value of 90 or lower to black. Reduce the third Input Levels value to 135, which turns just about all the light colors to white. Then click **OK**. The result is a sharper, more precise selection, with a ring of antialiased pixels remaining in the range of luminosity values between 90 and 135.

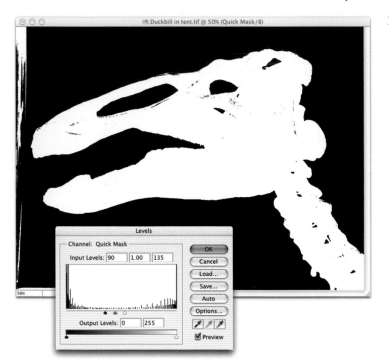

Figure 7-20.

14. ***Restore the RGB image.*** In the **Channels** palette, click the blank square in front of **RGB** to again view image and quick mask together and inspect the mask for problems. You'll see that we've dealt with two of the three issues that diminished the original Color Range selection: The cable is now gone, and most of the interior of the skeleton is opaque. (We'll clean up the remaining spots in Step 17.) But we continue to have fringing around the outer edge of the skeleton. The problem is that the selection is slightly too big for the dinosaur. The solution is to contract, or *choke*, the mask.

I find it very helpful to turn the full-color image on and off periodically as I work in the quick mask mode. Thankfully, you can do it from the keyboard. Just press the tilde key (~, just above Tab) to hide the RGB image. Press tilde again to bring the image back.

15. ***Choose the Gaussian Blur command.*** Choose **Filter→Blur→Gaussian Blur**, change the **Radius** value to 2 pixels, and click **OK**. Photoshop blurs the mask, and in doing so, smoothes out rough transitions and spreads the edges. This latter effect permits us to ex-

pand or contract the edges with precise control, as in the next step. (For more information on Gaussian Blur, see "Gaussian Blur and Median" on page 257 of Lesson 8.)

16. ***Again, increase the contrast.*** Press Ctrl+L (or ⌘-L) to display the Levels dialog box. Set the first **Input Levels** value to 170 and the third to 195. Then click **OK**.

    This time, we made most of the colors black, which has the effect of choking the mask and moving the edges inward. Very few values are permitted to remain gray, but that's okay because blurring the image gave us such a wealth of grays to work with. The net result is that we continue to have softer edges than we did by the end of Step 14, as Figure 7-21 illustrates.

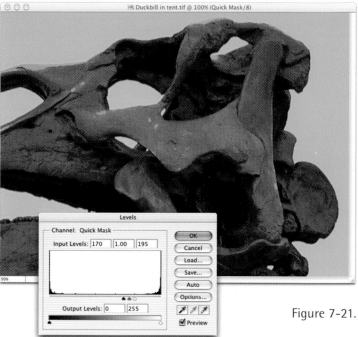

17. ***Clean up the skeleton with the brush tool.*** Press the X key to make the foreground color white. Then paint away any spots of cyan inside the dinosaur's skull and spine that shouldn't be there. (Be careful: A few of the spots represent holes between the bones and should stay.) If you're feeling ambitious, you can clean up a few of the edges along the top of the skull as well. Just make sure you stay well inside the edge so you don't bring back any of that fringing.

Figure 7-21.

18. ***Fix the image boundaries with the rectangular marquee.*** If you zoom out from the image, you'll notice some garbage along the left and bottom boundaries of the image. Press M to select the marquee tool. (Yes, you have full access to the selection tools when editing a mask.) Select the left and bottom areas as shown in Figure 7-22. Then press Ctrl+Backspace (⌘-Delete on the Mac) to fill them with the background color, black.

19. ***Exit the quick mask mode.*** Either click the white ▢ icon near the lower-left corner of the toolbox or press the Q key. Photoshop immediately converts the mask to a marching ants-style selection outline.

Figure 7-22.

20. ***Again drag the skeleton into the planets backdrop.*** Press the Ctrl key (⌘ on the Mac) and drag the selection from *Duckbill in tent.tif* into *The planets.psd* image window. Before you drop, press and hold Shift. The result appears in Figure 7-23.

The figure below may make all the work you've done appear a bit subtle. But zoom in on your image and you'll see just how perfect things really are. Frankly, it's stunning just how good this selection has turned out.

Figure 7-23.

EXTRA ★ CREDIT

The skeleton looks swell in its new home, but you have to wonder why it's there. That is to say, what's a dinosaur skeleton doing miles above the surface of a planet that hovers so close to Earth? The remaining steps reveal the answer. Don't care about the answer? Skip to the "Extracting a Photographic Element" exercise on page 223. Care deeply? Then onward we go.

21. ***Add a Gradient Overlay style.*** Let's begin our process of discovery by adding a bit of drama. Go to the **Layers** palette and choose **Gradient Overlay** from the layer style pop-up menu, as shown in Figure 7-24.

22. ***Adjust the gradient settings.*** To give the dinosaur skeleton a darker aspect, as if obscured by shadows, apply the following settings (all of which appear in Figure 7-24):

- Set the **Blend Mode** to **Multiply** and the **Opacity** to 70 percent. This ensures that the gradient darkens its background, as with a shadow.

- Make sure the **Gradient** bar shows black to white. If not, click the ⬝ arrow and select the black-to-white gradient.

- Rotate the **Angle** value to –146 degrees.

- Move the gradient a bit to the right by dragging it directly in the image window.

When you're done, click **OK** to accept the newly shaded dinosaur. The result is a shadow that fades from upper right to lower left, as if the skeleton is very close to us, deep in the foreground.

23. ***Turn on the Features and Caption layer sets.*** In the **Layers** palette, you'll see that a couple of folders are turned off. Click to the left of them to bring back their eyeballs (👁) and make them visible. The Features folder contains several layers that make up the dinosaur's eye and spindly hands. The Caption folder displays a passage of text that explains the hideous monster's dreadful plans (see Figure 7-25).

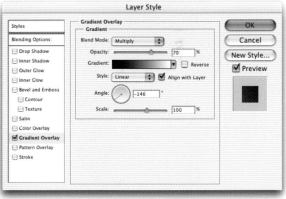

Figure 7-24.

Figure 7-25.

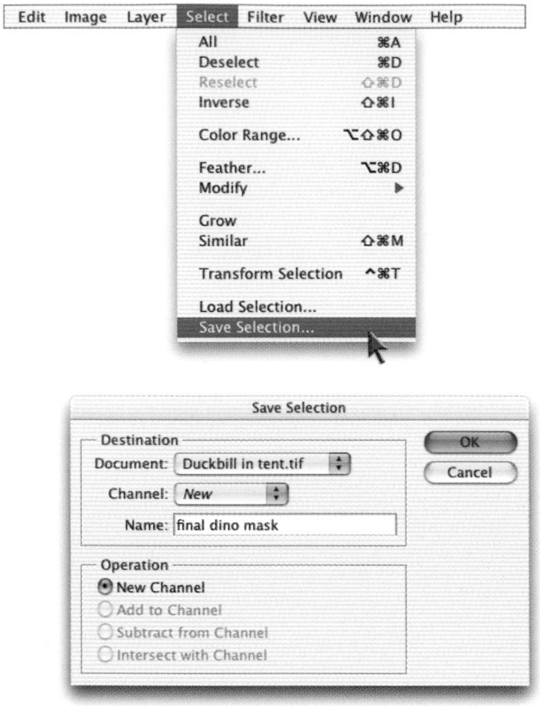

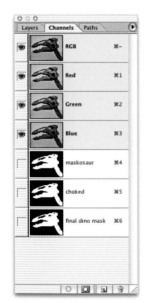

Figure 7-26.

Figure 7-27.

24. **Save your artwork.** Choose **File→Save As** and name your masterpiece "Dinosaur Planet.psd."

See, this race of raving mad dinosaurs actually moved their planet closer to Earth. We didn't notice—they did it during some sort of astronomer's holiday—so now we're in big trouble. I'd tell you what happpens next, but I'd only ruin the stirring climax that's in store for us in Lesson 9. Well anyway, I promised at the outset of the Extra Credit section that I'd explain what this composition is all about, so I knew you'd want to know.

25. **Return to Duckbill in tent.tif.** If that image is worth saving, then certainly all the hard work you put into making the selection outline is worth saving, too.

26. **Save the selection.** Choose **Select→Save Selection**. In the **Save Selection** dialog box, enter a **Name** for the new alpha channel, which I called "Final Dino Mask," as in Figure 7-26. The other settings are fine as is, so click **OK**.

Go back to the **Channels** palette and notice that the final item now reads **Final Dino Mask** (see Figure 7-27). If you like, you can now press Ctrl+D (⌘-D on the Mac) to deselect the image. After all, it's all backed up, pixel for pixel, in this new channel.

27. **Compare your masks.** To reload a mask, press the Ctrl key (⌘ on the Mac) and click anywhere on its channel. This allows you to load and compare multiple variations of a selection so you can decide which one's best. In this case, I created my earlier selections, Maskosaur and Choked, using lesser techniques than those we ultimately employed in this exercise. So Final Dino Mask rules the day.

28. **Save your changes.** Choose **File→Save** or press Ctrl+S (⌘-S) to update the *Duckbill in tent.tif* file on disk. You have now saved your selection outline for all time.

PEARL OF    WISDOM

Incidentally, although masks can be stored to alpha channels and then saved with an image, not all file formats support them. Only TIFF, PDF, and the native Photoshop PSD format can save multiple alpha channels per image. (The popular JPEG format can't save so much as a single alpha channel.) My recommendation is this: If you want to save a flat image (no layers) with channels, use TIFF. If the image also contains layers, use the PSD format instead.

# Extracting a Photographic Element

One of the biggest problems that arises when transferring an image from one background to another is fringing. The edges of every element in a photograph incorporate ambient colors from the photograph's background. So when you move an element to another background—or replace the background with another color, as in Figure 7-28—the edges have an alarming habit of retaining their original coloring. The result is a sharp and defiant border that screams, "This image does not belong here! It is a stranger to this shabby composition!"

Photoshop's solution is the Extract command. When you *extract* an image, you erase its background and leech out the fringe coloring from the old background. The process is hardly perfect—it permanently erases pixels, and the tools aren't as expertly implemented as I'd like—but on occasion, it comes through with flying colors. Or more accurately, without them.

In the following exercise, we'll extract the foreground subject from one photograph and place it against a handful of foreign backgrounds. Foreground and backgrounds contain a range of different colors, providing us with a chance to judge just how well Extract can work.

1. ***Open an image and a prospective background.*** This time around, the files are *PhotoSpin buffalo.jpg* and *Vacation destinations.psd* located in the *Lesson 07* folder inside *Lesson Files-PScs 1on1*. First, observe that the animal in Figure 7-29 on the following page is truly a buffalo, not a bison, for those of you who are sticklers on such topics. (I myself am not. I went to an institution of higher learning where bison are called "buffs," and thus I stand before you, incapable of tellling one animal from the next.) Second, and more to the point, the buffalo's background is as smooth as it is pervasive. The Extract command functions best with smooth backgrounds; busy textures tend to mix it up.

Buffalo in its native habitat

When the background is replaced, the ambient color survives

Figure 7-28.

Figure 7-29.

2. **Choose the Extract command.** Make sure that the *PhotoSpin buffalo.jpg* window is in front, and then choose **Filter→Extract** or press Ctrl+Alt+X (⌘-Option-X on the Mac). Photoshop displays the **Extract** window, which behaves like a separate extraction utility, complete with its own tools and options, as pictured in Figure 7-30.

The center of the window features a large preview of the image. You can zoom it or scroll it using the standard navigation tricks introduced in Video Lesson 1, "Navigation" (see page 4). Strangely, however, the window lacks scroll bars or any mention of a zoom ratio percentage. So it's difficult to know if you're seeing all of the image or how many pixels are being interpolated away. So be sure to zoom and scroll around frequently to stay apprised of where you are.

3. **Click the edge highlighter tool.** Or press the B key (so used because the edge highlighter behaves like the pencil in the main toolbox). The tool is active by default, but I reckon it's a good idea to know what tool you're using, so give it a click to say hello.

Figure 7-30.

4. *Set the brush diameter.* By default, the diameter is 20 pixels. You can change this by entering a new **Brush Size** value (under Tool Options, upper right). Or press the ] key to increase the diameter in 2-pixel increments. For my part, I started with a **Brush Size** of 30 pixels.

5. *Trace around the perimeter of the buffalo.* Make sure you can see the far left side of the image, every pixel of it. Then begin dragging from the top left point in the buffalo's back. Trace along the back, taking care to center the brush on the border between the buffalo and grass. Then trace over the double hump of horns at the top of the head. Stop at the point marked with the cyan target in Figure 7-31.

6. *Change the highlight color.* By default, the line that you draw is colored green, which is hard to see against a green background. Change the **Highlight** option (under Brush Size) to **Red** to make the line red instead.

7. *Shift-click around the right horn (the beast's left).* Reduce the brush diameter to 20 pixels. Then click at the last point you drew. From here on, press Shift and click in short segments around the inner and outer portions of the horn, until you get to the end of the red line shown in Figure 7-31. Photoshop draws straight lines between each Shift-click.

PEARL OF  WISDOM

When tracing the buffalo, feel free to take breaks—you don't have to outline the entire animal in one drag. Press Ctrl+Z (⌘-Z) if you make a mistake. You also have an eraser tool available to you (press E to get it) in case you make a big flub. It doesn't matter if the line grows or gets lumpy in places, so retrace areas if necessary.

Figure 7-31.

8. *Paint around the ear and right side.* The ear is the hairiest part, so raise the **Brush Size** value to 50 pixels to get it all in. Then drag around the ear and all the way down the right side of the body (the animal's left) until you reach the very bottom.

9. *Paint with the Smart Highlighting function.* We still have one area to paint, that tiny sliver of green between the ear and the horn on the right-hand side. You could paint it freehand with a very small brush, but Extract gives you a better way to paint fine details. Turn on the **Smart Highlighting** check box, and then paint along the sliver and watch the tool work its magic. Even though your brush diameter is still 50 pixels, Smart Highlighting manages to draw a thin, precise line.

10. *Click the fill tool.* Or press the G key to get the second tool down, the one that looks like a paint bucket. This tool tells Extract what portion of the image to keep and what to erase.

11. *Click inside the buffalo.* The fill tool coats the interior of the buffalo in translucent blue, as shown in Figure 7-32.

---

If the blue spills outside the red outline, there's a break somewhere in the outline (possibly along an edge that is scrolled out of view). Find the break, paint it in with the edge highlighter tool (as in Step 5, page 225), and then try filling the buffalo again.

---

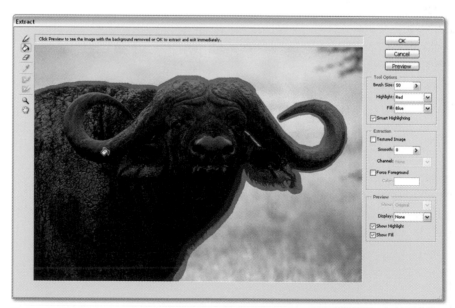

Figure 7-32.

12. ***Click the Preview button.*** After you achieve an unbroken outline and a contained fill, click **Preview** to see what the extraction will look like right inside the Extract window. The checkerboard pattern (see Figure 7-33) represents transparent pixels—that is to say, those that will be erased.

Figure 7-33.

13. ***Select a Display setting.*** Once Photoshop finishes calculating the preview, examine the extracted edges for defects. If the checkerboard pattern is too noisy to make sense of the image, try one of the other settings from the **Display** pop-up menu. Choose a **Matte** setting to see the image against a solid colored background. Choose **Mask** to see the extraction expressed as a grayscale mask; white is opaque, black is transparent.

---

Press the F key to cycle between the different Display settings.

---

14. ***Apply the edge touchup tool.*** You have two ways to fix any problems you may find. Press the T key to select the edge touchup tool, which automatically adjusts pixels that fall inside your original red highlight line (Steps 5 through 9). I found this tool especially helpful at increasing the contrast around the horns. But because it sharpens the transitions, you probably won't want to use it around the ears and other hairy areas.

To move the edge in or out from the buffalo, press and hold the Ctrl key (⌘ on the Mac) as you drag. It's a weird technique, but it sometimes comes in handy. You can also increase or decrease the intensity of the tool by pressing a number key, 0 being the most intense and 1 being the least. (The dialog box doesn't provide any direct feedback—for example, there is no corresponding numerical option—so you have to accept your changes on faith.)

15. *Apply the cleanup tool.* Press C to select the cleanup tool. Then drag to erase pixels. Press the Alt key (or Option key) and drag to make pixels opaque. I found this tool most useful for fixing some of the messy edges around the animal's body and ears. I also used it to shift some of the edges around the horns that had stubbornly resisted the edge touchup tool.

I find the cleanup tool most useful in the Mask mode. Drag to paint with black, Alt-drag (or Option-drag) to paint with white. The final mask view should look nice and clean—free of stray gray pixels in the predominantly black and white areas—as shown in Figure 7-34.

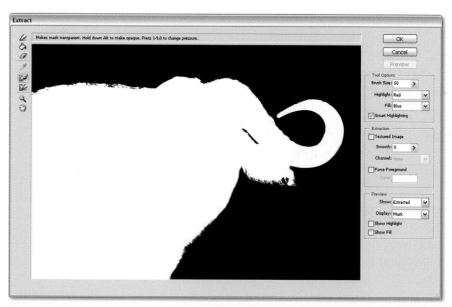

Figure 7-34.

16. ***Click the OK button.*** Like Color Range, the Extract command does not deliver a mask, but nor does it give you a selection outline. Instead, it transfers the extracted element to its own layer and completely eliminates the background.

---

Despite your best efforts, the Extract command may erase pixels you wanted to keep. In my case, I lost pixels across the top of the back and horns, as well as the very tip of the right horn. Fortunately, the history brush can bring them back.

---

17. ***Bring back lost pixels with the history brush.*** Press the Y key to select the history brush. Then select a small, sharp brush—say, 20 pixels with **Hardness** cranked all the way up to 100 percent. Now zoom in tight and paint to bring back the pixels you lost. If you end up bringing back patches of green, undo and try again.

18. ***Drag the buffalo into the Mt. Rushmore backdrop.*** When you're done with the history brush, press the Ctrl key (⌘ on the Mac) and drag the new buffalo layer from *PhotoSpin buffalo.jpg* into the *Vacation destinations.psd* image window. No need to press Shift this time around; just drop when ready. Once inside the Mt. Rushmore image, Ctrl-drag (or ⌘-drag) the buffalo to move it into the approximate position shown in Figure 7-35.

19. ***Turn on the other layers.*** Thanks to its relative lack of color fringing, the buffalo is comfortable anywhere, including some of America's hottest vacation destinations, pictured in Figure 7-36 on the next page. To see the versatile bovine in action for yourself, go to the **Layers** palette and turn on the **Glacier Bay** layer

Figure 7-35.

Figure 7-36.

and then the **Carnegie Deli** layer. The lighting may not entirely match, but the edges look terrific. In fact, I come across just one subtle patch of fringing around the right ear (the animal's left). If this bothers you—and bear in mind, it barely shows up in print—perform the following two steps.

20. ***Lock the transparency of the buffalo layer.*** Click the layer name (presumably **Layer 0**) in the Layers palette to make sure it's active. Then press the / key to lock the transparency.

21. ***Hand-paint the ear.*** Press the B key to get the brush tool. Then press the Alt key (Option on the Mac) and click inside a dark portion of the ear to lift a representative color. Set the **Mode** to **Color** and the **Opacity** to 50 percent. Select a soft brush and paint over any overly green hairs to reinstate the buffalo's natural red coloring. If one pass of the brush doesn't do the trick, give it a second pass. The 50 percent Opacity lets you build up color incrementally.

## Defining a Mask from Scratch

Working with automated commands such as Color Range and Extract is all very well and good. But the true power of masking resides in its ability to use an image to select itself. Although this approach requires a lot more thought and experimentation, the irony is, it frequently takes less time than monkeying around in the quick mask mode and less patience than trying to get Extract to function properly. In other words, once you get the hang of it, manual masking is actually easier than the automatic options. Plus, wouldn't you know it, the manual approach delivers better results.

This next exercise shows how to take a couple of color channels from an RGB photograph and combine them to produce a complex, naturalistic mask. And just for fun, we'll be using this technique to select those wispiest of all image details, individual strands of hair. That's right, using this technique, you can select a detail that's a single hair wide. Enjoy.

1. **Open a couple of photographs.** The specific images in question are *Senior photo.tif* and *Backyard blur.jpg*, both in the *Lesson 07* folder inside *Lesson Files-PSCS 1on1*. The first is a high school senior (in case you were expecting someone more advanced in years) from the PhotoSpin image library. The second is a purposely out-of-focus snapshot of my backyard that I captured about a minute ago off the deck of my studio. Totally different lighting conditions, not to mention different cameras and different depths of field, but you'll soon see how the two can work together splendidly. Click the title bar of the *Senior photo.tif* image to bring it to the front, as in Figure 7-37.

Figure 7-37.

2. **Survey the color channels.** Go to the **Channels** palette and click on the individual channel names **Red**, **Green**, and **Blue**. (For the moment, ignore the two alpha channels, Gradient and Final Mask.) Or press the keyboard shortcuts Ctrl+1, Ctrl+2 and Ctrl+3 (⌘-1, 2, and 3 on the Mac). This permits you to peruse the channels and decide which ones are the best candidates for building a mask. The three channels appear slightly colorized in Figure 7-38.

---

PEARL OF WISDOM

You're looking for the two channels that represent the biggest extremes—that is, extreme contrast between shadows and highlights as well as extreme contrast between each other. In our case, the best candidates appear to be Red and Blue, as is fairly typical in portrait photography. The Red channel contains the most contrast; the Blue channel has the distinction of being most unlike Red.

---

3. **Return to the RGB composite view.** Now that we've decided on our channels, click **RGB** in the Channels palette or press Ctrl+tilde (⌘-tilde on the Mac) to make the full-color image active.

Figure 7-38.

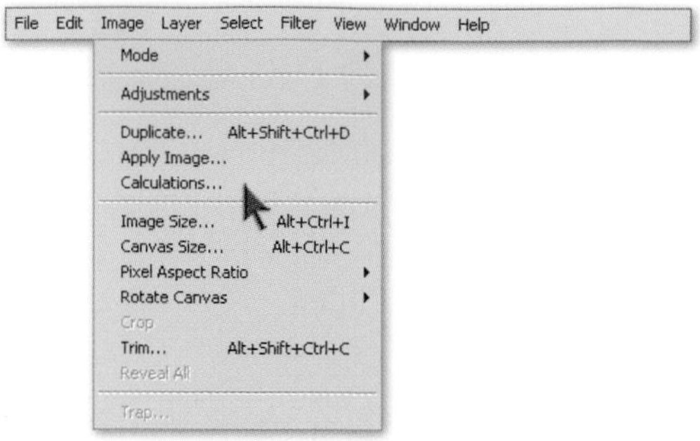

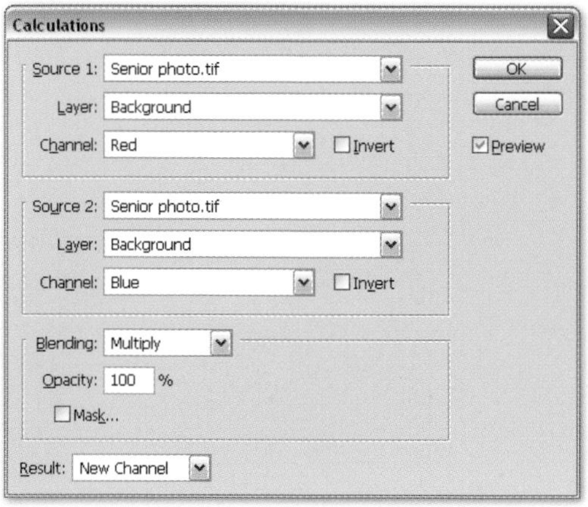

Figure 7-39.

4. **Choose the Calculations command.** Choose **Image→ Calculations** to display the **Calculations** dialog box (see Figure 7-39). This command lets you mix two channels to form a new alpha channel using a blend mode and an Opacity value. Back in the days before layers, this command's equivalents were how you mixed just about everything. Now, Calculations is relegated almost exclusively to the creation of masks.

---

This is a rather elaborate dialog box, so it's a good idea to turn on the **Preview** check box, if it's not turned on already. With Preview on, you can observe the results of your changes in the full-image window.

---

5. **Select the desired Source channels.** You can think of the Calculations dialog box as layering one channel on top of another. Source 2 is the background channel; Source 1 is the channel in front. This means Source 1 is in a position of emphasis and should therefore contain the channel with the highest contrast. Accordingly:

   - Make sure the **Source 1** and **Source 2** pop-up menus are set to **Senior photo.tif**.

   - This is a single-layer document, so both **Layer** options are automatically **Background**. No need to change them.

   - Set the first **Channel** option to **Red**. Set the second one to **Blue**, as shown in Figure 7-39.

6. **Experiment with Invert and Blending.** This is the least predictable step in the process because the ideal settings vary radically depending on the composition of your image. Bear in mind, the goal is to select the foreground subject by making it white against a deselected black background. So more than likely, you'll need to invert the luminosity values in at least one of the channels and maybe both. Blend modes that inherently invert the image, such as Difference and Subtract, are also useful.

I include a few of my experiments (with slight colorization, to better convey gray values) in Figure 7-40:

- In the first image, I turned on the Invert check box for both channels and set the Blending option to Multiply. This generates a light foreground and a dark background, but I'd like to increase the contrast.

- Next, I turned off Invert for the Blue channel and set the Blending option to Difference. This delivers nice black edges, but the highlights remain too dark.

- Finally, I turned off Invert for the Red channel and turned it on for Blue. Then I set Blending to Subtract. This particular blend mode subtracts the luminosity values in the Red channel from those in the inverted Blue channel. It also comes with an Offset value that, when positive, adds brightness across the image. I raised the value to 50, which elevates the luminosity and helps prevent some of the rampant clipping inherent with Subtract.

Incidentally, none of these variations is particularly flattering, and it's only going to get more gruesome as the exercise progresses. Masks are not pretty things; don't share them with your clients.

Red Blue Multiply

Red Blue Difference

Red Blue Subtract, Offset: 50

Figure 7-40.

7. *Assign the ideal settings.* In this case, my last experiment comes the closest to a finished mask. So, as shown in Figure 7-41:

- Turn off the first **Invert** check box, turn the second one on.

- Change **Blending** to **Subtract**.

- Set the three numerical values to 100 percent, 50, and 1 respectively, as shown on the right.

- The **Result** setting should be **New Channel**. This tells Photoshop to add an alpha channel to hold your mask.

When you've done all that, click **OK**.

Figure 7-41.

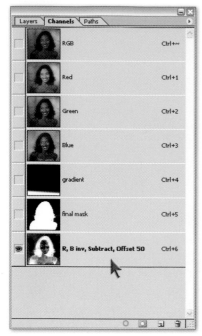

Figure 7-42.

8. **Name the new alpha channel.** Double-click the **Alpha 1** item in the **Channels** palette. I like to name my channels after how I created them, so I called mine "R, B Inv, Subtract, Offset 50" (see Figure 7-42), but you can call yours whatever you want. Then press Enter or Return to accept the new name.

Notice that this is actually the third alpha channel in this document. The first, Gradient, contains a gradient we'll be using to combine masks in Steps 13 and 14 on the facing page. The second, Final Mask, contains our final destination. To see what the end result looks like, click the channel or press Ctrl+5 (⌘-5 on the Mac).

9. **Duplicate the new channel.** Click the last channel in the list and drag it onto the tiny page icon at the bottom of the Channels palette (⬚, to the left of the trash icon). This duplicates the channel. Double-click the new channel and rename it "First Levels Adjustment."

Why duplicate the channel? To protect yourself. When working in a single channel, you don't have access to layers. This means you can't experiment with different options and merge them together. So the best way to give yourself space to backtrack and make different choices is to duplicate the alpha channel between steps. Then you always have your incremental channels to come back to. An image can contain 56 channels, so you've got lots of room to work.

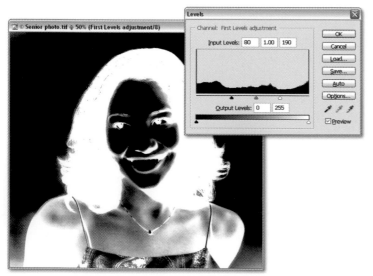

Figure 7-43.

10. **Increase the contrast of the hair.** Choose **Image→Adjustments→Levels** or press Ctrl+L (⌘-L on the Mac). Increase the first value to 80 and reduce the third value to 190. Then click **OK**. As shown in Figure 7-43, this does a great job of increasing the contrast between the hair and the background. But the transitions between the shoulders and background are weak, ultimately fading into a wishy-washy gray at the bottom of the image. The obvious question is, why not find a better combination of Levels values? Because there isn't one. We can accommodate either the hair or the shoulders, but not both. Unless, that is, we call in another channel.

11. ***Again duplicate the sixth channel.*** Go back to the channel you created in Steps 4 through 8 (the one I called **R, B Inv, Subtract, Offset 50**) and drag it onto the ⬚ icon at the bottom of the Channels palette. Again, Photoshop duplicates the channel. Rename it "Second Levels Adjustment."

12. ***Increase the contrast of the shoulders.*** Press Ctrl+L (⌘-L) to display the **Levels** dialog box. Change the first value to 170 and the third to 190 and then click **OK**. This leaves just 20 luminosity values to express the grays, not nearly enough variations to maintain the subtle transitions between strands of hair. But it works well for the area below the shoulders (see Figure 7-44).

13. ***Click the Gradient channel.*** Created in advance by me, this alpha channel marks the point where the two Levels adjustment channels diverge. The black area indicates where the First channel is good; the white area is best expressed in the Second channel. We can blend the two channels using Calculations.

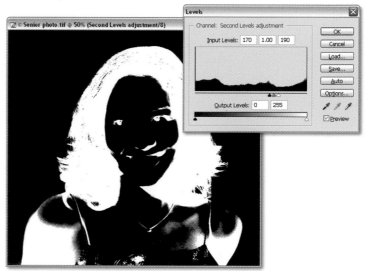

Figure 7-44.

14. ***Choose the Calculations command.*** Choose **Image→Calculations** to display the **Calculations** dialog box. Then set the options as follows:

- Set the **Channel** option for **Source 1** to **Second Levels Adjustment**.

- Set the **Channel** option for **Source 2** to **First Levels Adjustment**.

- Turn off both **Invert** check boxes.

- Set **Blending** to **Normal**.

- Turn on the **Mask** check box and then change the final **Channel** setting to **Gradient**.

Click the **OK** button to create the new alpha channel (see Figure 7-45).

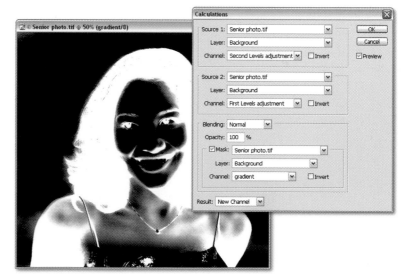

Figure 7-45.

15. *Name the new alpha channel.* Double-click the newest **Alpha 1** item in the **Channels** palette to highlight the channel's name. Then call it "Gradient Mask Combo" to indicate that alpha channels were combined using a gradient mask.

    Now all that's left is to clean up the alpha channel by painting inside the image window. But instead of using the brush tool, we'll be lightening and darkening pixels with the dodge tool.

16. *Select the dodge tool in the toolbox.* Or press the O key. For convenience's sake, we'll use this one tool to do both the dodging and burning.

17. *Change the Range setting in the options bar to Highlights.* You can do this from the keyboard by pressing Shift+Alt+H (Shift-Option-H on the Mac). This restricts the dodging to only the lightest colors in the mask. Also, increase the **Exposure** to 50 percent and enlarge the brush diameter to somewhere between 150 and 200 pixels. For the smoothest results, keep the brush soft (**Hardness**: 0 percent).

18. *Drag over the areas that should be white.* Paint the light grays in the shoulders and the outer edge of the hair. (Don't worry about the central stuff such as the face; we'll delete that wholesale in a moment.) Drag as many times as you need to, but be careful not to lighten too much. Used in excess, the dodge tool can expand the selection too far from the natural edges of the hair.

19. *Change the Range to Shadows.* You can do this by pressing Shift+Alt+S (or Shift-Option-S). This will restrict the changes to the darkest colors.

20. *Alt-drag over the areas that should be black.* If you're working on a Mac, press the Option key and drag. As you may recall from Lesson 6, pressing Alt or Option when dragging with the dodge tool burns the image (last paragraph, page 190). This permits us to continue to use the same brush size and Exposure settings that we established in previous steps.

---

As ever, beware of overdoing it. Overdarkening can choke the selection and result in transitions that are too sharp. You can rarely go wrong by leaving too many gray pixels, especially around the edges of hairs.

---

21. ***Lasso the central portion of the image.*** Now to round up all that extraneous junk in the center of the image. Press the L key to get the lasso tool. Then drag around the interior details. In Figure 7-46, I pressed Alt (or Option) and clicked with the lasso tool to draw a polygonal selection. (Feel free to use the polygonal lasso if you prefer.)

22. ***Fill the selection with white.*** Press D for the default colors, which are foreground white and background black when working in a mask. Then press Alt+Backspace (Option-Delete on the Mac) to make the face, neck, dress, and straps go away. The result appears in Figure 7-47.

    In all likelihood, you'll find a faint light spot in the upper-left corner of your mask. Select that area with the rectangular marquee tool and press Ctrl+Backspace (⌘-Delete on the Mac) to fill it with black.

23. ***Save your alpha channels.*** Press Ctrl+S (⌘-S on the Mac) or choose **File→Save** to save the changes made to your image, including all four new alpha channels.

Don't go closing the document. More discoveries await you in the next exercise.

Figure 7-46.

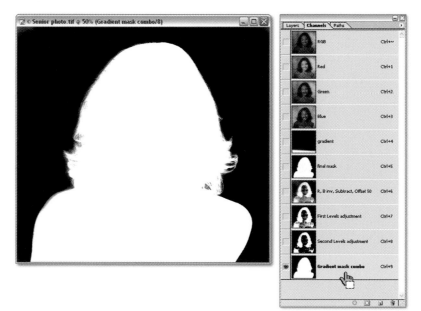

Figure 7-47.

# Putting the Mask in Play

At this point, I'd say you owe yourself a pat on the back. Whether you know it or not, you just finished making one of the Most Closely Held Secrets of the Photoshop Masters, a professional-level mask. I mean, how easy was that? Okay, so it took a few more steps than the Extract command. But truth be told, I strung things out a bit in the dodge and burn section. Besides, wait until you get a load of how well this baby works.

In the following steps, you'll use the mask you created in the previous exercise to select the kid and set her against the blurry backyard. Then you'll adjust her fleshtones to match her new background and modify the ambient color in her hair. The result is about as perfect a composite as computer imaging affords.

1. *Open the photographs.* If the photos are already open (per my instructions at the end of the last exercise), skip to the next step. However, if for some reason you had to close the images, go ahead and open *Senior photo.tif* and *Backyard blur.jpg* from the *Lesson 07* folder inside *Lesson Files-PScs 1on1*. Even if you didn't save your changes (Step 23 on the preceding page), I have a finished mask ready and waiting for you.

2. *Load the final mask as a selection.* Inside the **Channels** palette, press the Ctrl key (⌘ on the Mac) and click the **Gradient Mask Combo** channel that you named back in Step 15 on page 236. If you would prefer to work from my mask, Ctrl-click the **Final Mask** item instead.

---

If you prefer commands, choose **Select**→**Load Selection** and then choose **Gradient Mask Combo** from the **Channel** menu. If you hate commands and desire even speedier keyboard techniques, press Ctrl+Alt+9 (⌘-Option-9 on the Mac) to load the Gradient Mask Combo channel, or Ctrl+Alt+5 (⌘-Option-5) to load my Final Mask.

---

3. *Switch to the RGB image.* You may already be there. If not, click on the **RGB** item at the top of the Channels palette or press Ctrl+tilde (or ⌘-tilde). The image name in the title bar should end with the parenthetical *RGB/8.*

4. ***Drag the young woman into the blurry background.*** Press the Ctrl key (⌘ on the Mac) and drag the selection from *Senior photo.tif* into the *Backyard blur.jpg* image window. Once inside the backyard document, Ctrl-drag (or ⌘-drag) the kid to move her into the approximate position shown in Figure 7-48.

5. ***Match the teen to her background.*** It's one thing to have independent foreground lighting; strobes create it all the time. But it's another to have a purple color cast against an amber backdrop. To match the images, choose our friend from Lesson 4, **Image→Adjustments→ Match Color**. Then make the following changes:

   - Set the **Source** option to **Backyard blur.jpg** and the **Layer** option to **Background**. This tells Photoshop to gather the source colors from the amber backdrop.

   - Increase the **Fade** value to 60 percent to create what I consider to be the ideal mix of foreground and background colors.

   Click the **OK** button to invoke the change shown in Figure 7-49.

Figure 7-48.

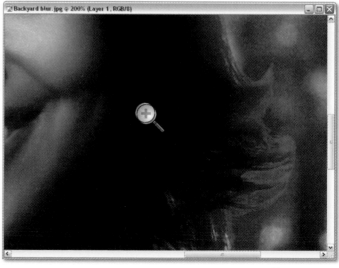

Figure 7-49.

6. ***Inspect the edges of the masked image.*** Zoom in on your image and scroll around the teen's head to see the transitions. With the exception of the occasional blue reflection, the shoulders look pretty good. But the hair suffers some unacceptably harsh transitions, as Figure 7-50 attests. Known as *edge artifacts*, such transitions are virtually impossible to avoid in the masking mode. Even if you were bound and determined to do so, it would likely require painting individual hairs—such a waste when easier solutions are available to you in the compositing phase.

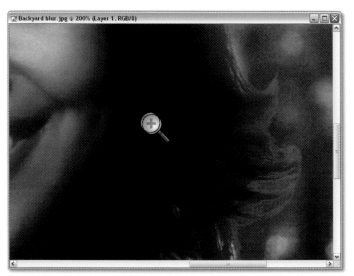

Figure 7-50.

7. ***Apply the Multiply blend mode to the layer.*** Press F7 to switch to the **Layers** palette. Press the 3 key to reduce the **Opacity** value to 30 percent. Then select **Multiply** from the upper-left pop-up menu, or press Shift+Alt+M (Shift-Option-M on the Mac). This burns the hair and other details from the top layer into the background, as shown in Figure 7-51.

Although this step may fix the edges, it also does wonders to mess up the image. To reinstate the portrait, you'll need another layer.

8. ***Create a copy of the layer.*** Choose **Layer→ New→Layer via Copy** or press Ctrl+J (⌘-J).

Figure 7-51.

9. **Reinstate the Normal blend mode.** Press 0 to return to 100 percent **Opacity**. Then choose **Normal** from the ⊙ pop-up menu at the top of the Layers palette. Or you can press Shift+Alt+N (Shift-Option-N on the Mac).

PEARL OF ⬤ WISDOM

The image looks like it did at the end of Step 6. The difference is that you now have two layers—one to blend the edges and another to represent the detail. The trick is making them interact. The remaining steps explain how to use the Contract and Feather commands to mask away the perimeter pixels from the top layer to reveal the multiplied pixels in the layer below.

10. **Load the selection outline for the layer.** Press the Ctrl key (⌘ on the Mac) and click on the top layer in the Layers palette, presumably **Layer 1 Copy**. This traces the edges of the layers with a highly accurate selection outline.

11. **Choose the Contract command.** Choose **Select→Modify→Contract**, enter a value of 4 pixels, and click **OK**. This shrinks the size of the selection outline by an even increment all the way around the perimeter of the layer.

12. **Choose the Feather command.** Choose **Select→Feather**, enter a **Feather Radius** value of 2 pixels, and click **OK**. This blurs the selection outline by half the previous Contract amount, which will soften the transitions between the pixels in Layer 1 Copy and Layer 1 below.

13. **Click the layer mask icon.** Click the second-to-left icon along the bottom of the **Layers** palette, ▢, to convert the selection into a layer mask. The upshot is that everything outside the selection is masked away (see Figure 7-52).

Figure 7-52.

14. ***Inspect the revised edges.*** Again, zoom in on the image and scrutinize the transitions between the foreground pixels and those in the background. As shown in Figure 7-53, we can make out individual strands of hair. Plus, the hair merges evenly and organically with its new environment. This is an image that whispers, "I was born here. This is where I live."

Figure 7-53.

Don't think for a moment that this is the only way to mask an image. To explore other techniques, consult the *Photoshop CS Bible, Professional Edition* (Wiley Publishing) or my DVD series "Total Training for Adobe Photoshop CS" (Total Training).

# WHAT DID YOU LEARN?

Match the key concept in the numbered list below with the letter of the phrase that best describes it. Answers appear upside-down at the bottom of the page.

## Key Concepts

1. Masking
2. Color Range
3. Fuzziness
4. Mask preview
5. Quick mask mode
6. Alpha channel
7. Save Selection
8. Extract
9. Edge touchup tool
10. Calculations
11. Subtract
12. Edge artifacts

## Descriptions

A. This enhancement to the magic wand tool lets you adjust the range of colors you want to select and see the results dynamically.

B. Any channel beyond the core color channels, used almost exclusively in Photoshop to hold masks.

C. A tool in the Extract dialog box that automatically adjusts pixels along the edges of the extracted image element.

D. A special masking blend mode that subtracts the luminosity values in the Source 1 channel from those in the Source 2 channel.

E. A method for creating a selection outline as an independent channel, which you can then edit and save like any other image.

F. A command that erases the pixels outside an image element and leeches the fringe coloring conveyed by the original background.

G. This dynamic setting in the Color Range dialog box gradually fades the selection over a range of luminosity values.

H. Harsh transitions along the edge of a layer that belie your masking efforts and are best fixed when compositing the image against a new background.

I. A dialog box thumbnail or image that shows an ongoing selection outline as a grayscale image, where white selects and black deselects.

J. Saves the selection outline as an alpha channel, which can be saved with any image file stored in the TIFF or PSD format.

K. Press the Q key to view and modify the selection outline as a rubylith overlay.

L. A command in the Image menu that lets you blend two channels to form a new alpha channel that will eventually serve as a mask.

## Answers

1E, 2A, 3G, 4I, 5K, 6B, 7J, 8F, 9C, 10L, 11D, 12H

# ADJUSTING FOCUS

**WHEN AN IMAGE** is formed by the camera lens, its
focus is defined. The moment you press the shutter release, you
accept that focus and store it as a permanent attribute of the photograph. If the photograph is slightly out of focus, it stays out of
focus. No post-processing solution can build more clearly defined
edges than what the camera actually captured, or fill in missing or
murky detail.

So how is it that we can do a lesson on adjusting focus? We fake
it. While Photoshop can't reach back into your camera and modify
the lens element for a better shot, it can *simulate* the appearance of
worse or better focus. It can compare neighboring pixels to enhance
or impair what edges exist inside an image. Your eyes think they
see a differently focused image, but really they see an exaggerated
version of the focus that was already there.

## The Subterfuge of Sharpness

Focus puts every detail in its proper place, like the unmitigated
perfection of objects you see in real life with natural or corrected
20/20 vision. But photography rarely matches this perfection. Film
remains a very capable medium to this day, and yet even large-format
film suffers some amount of *grain*, the visual lumpiness typically
created by the tiny particles of silver in the film's emulsion. The
equivalent of grain in digital cameras is *noise*, the term given to
the random flecks of color created by a camera's internal circuitry.
Unrelated but equally vexing, most digital cameras capture only a
single channel of information per pixel—red, green, *or* blue, but
never all three at once. The camera has to average this spotty data
to generate the full-color photograph, which adds more random
color variations into the image. The upshot is the focus you perceive in a photograph is in part an illusion. What we mistake for

# ABOUT THIS LESSON

## Project Files

Before beginning the exercises, make sure that you've installed the lesson files from the CD, as explained in Step 5 on page xv of the Preface. This should result in a folder called *Lesson Files-PScs 1on1* on your desktop. We'll be working with the files inside the *Lesson 08* subfolder.

In this lesson, I explain ways to modify the perceived focus of a photograph to account for slight blurriness, grain, noise, and other imperfections. You'll learn how to:

- Amplify the edge detail in an image using the Unsharp Mask filter . . . . . . . . . . . . . .page 249

- Use the Radius value and High Pass filter to achieve the best possible sharpening effect. . . . . .page 254

- Soften details and smooth away harsh transitions using Gaussian Blur and Median . . . .page 257

- Sharpen only the detail in a grainy or noisy photograph with the help of an edge mask. . . . . .page 266

## Video Lesson 8: Filtering Basics

In a program that seems to pride itself on its crowded menus, Photoshop's Filter menu is the most jam-packed of them all. Its commands (known generically as *filters*) range from extremely practical to wonderfully frivolous to just plain lame. This lesson is about the best of the filters, those that let you correct images by modifying their edges.

To get a sense for how the corrective filters work—as well as how to repeat a filter and adjust its results after applying it—watch the eighth video lesson on the CD. Insert the CD, click the **Start Training** button, click Set **3** in the top-right corner of your screen, and then select **8, Filtering Basics** from the Lessons list. The 9-minute, 39-second movie contains information about the following commands and shortcuts:

| Command or operation | Windows shortcut | Macintosh shortcut |
|---|---|---|
| Zoom the picture in the image window | Ctrl+plus or minus | ⌘-plus or minus |
| Adjust selected value incrementally | ↑ or ↓ | ↑ or ↓ |
| Adjust selected value by 10x increment | Shift+↑ or ↓ | Shift-↑ or ↓ |
| Advance to next (or previous) value | Tab (or Shift+Tab) | Tab (or Shift-Tab) |
| Fade last-applied filter | Ctrl+Shift+F | ⌘-Shift-F |
| Restore undone states in History palette | Ctrl+Z | ⌘-Z |
| Reapply last-applied filter | Ctrl+F | ⌘-F |
| Reapply filter with different settings | Ctrl+Alt+F | ⌘-Option-F |

continuous detail is really a blend of independent and often very differently colored pixels.

Fortunately, Photoshop permits you to exploit this illusion. Consider the photos in Figure 8-1. The first is a detail from a high-resolution image that was shot to film and then scanned. The focus is impeccable, but even so, you can make out film grain in the magnified inset. The second and third images show Photoshop-imposed variations. Softening blurs the pixels together; sharpening exaggerates the edges. Softening bears a pretty strong resemblance to what really happens when an image is out of focus. Sharpening is a contrast trick that exploits the way our brains perceive definition, particularly with respect to distant or otherwise vague objects. A highly defined edge with sharp transitions between light and dark tells us where an object begins and ends.

This is not to impugn Photoshop's sharpening capabilities. Photography itself is a trick that simulates reality, very specifically geared to human eyes and brains. If Photoshop's sharpening augments that trick, more power to it. I just want you to know what you're doing. After all, the magician who knows his bag of tricks is better equipped to perform magic.

Real focus                    Photoshop-imposed softening          Photoshop-imposed sharpening

Figure 8-1.

## Sharpening, Blurring, and Averaging

In this lesson, we'll be looking at Photoshop's three basic varieties of focus manipulations—sharpening, blurring, and averaging. Each is the function of a handful of *corrective filters*, commands under the Filter menu that compare neighboring pixels in an attempt to fix what ails an image. Sharpening, blurring, and averaging are served by groups of commands under the Sharpen, Blur, and Noise submenus. But in each case, one command rules the roost. If Photoshop had just three filters, these would be them:

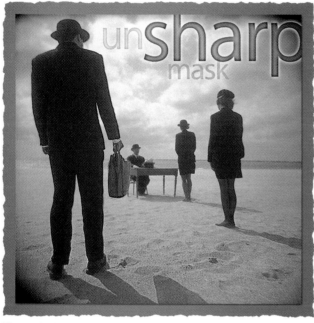

Figure 8-2.

- The Unsharp Mask filter finds areas of high contrast in an image—the so-called *edges*—and increases their contrast still further. The result is more pronounced drop-offs between one detail and another (see Figure 8-2).

- Illustrated in Figure 8-3, Gaussian Blur softens the transitions between pixels. If you were to put a big black square next to a big white square and apply a generous amount of Gaussian Blur, you'd get a gradient. Named after 19th-century mathematician Karl Frederic Gauss, the filter is pronounced *gows*-sian, not *gosh*-ian. If you hear someone pronounce it wrong, remind them, "Gosh, no—it's Gauss."

Figure 8-3.

- The Median filter calculates a few million circles inside an image—large overlapping circles, one centered about each and every pixel—and averages the colors of the pixels inside those circles. (You specify how big the circle gets.) The result: Everything gets round and plastic, as in the gooey Figure 8-4. Goodbye noise, but also goodbye edges. We'll see how to make Median work for us in the exercises.

We'll also touch on a few ancillary edge filters that play key supporting roles in adjusting focus, all of which are demonstrated in Figure 8-5:

- Find Edges traces an image with dark lines. Higher contrast edges translate to thicker lines; non-edges turn white.

- High Pass sends all non-edges to gray. The filter gets its name from its underlying mechanics: It filters out low-contrast areas while letting high-contrast edges pass through.

- Maximum expands the areas of maximum luminosity—that is to say, the lightest colors in the image. In Figure 8-5, I used the Maximum filter to inflate the white forms of the people beyond their previously traced edges.

The Filter menu contains more than 100 commands in all. And while many of them let you apply splendid effects, these few are the ones you need on a regular basis to adjust the focus of your images.

## Sharpening an Image

The job of the filters in the Filter→Sharpen submenu is to sharpen the perceived focus of a photograph. I say "perceived" because, naturally, they can't *really* modify the focus—only a camera lens can do that. But filters can (and do) detect the edges in an image and trace dark and light pixels around those edges to accentuate the contrast. Our eyes read the enhanced edges as sharply defined details.

Of the four Sharpen filters, only one, Unsharp Mask, lets you control the amount of sharpening you apply to an image. As a result, it does everything the other three

Figure 8-4.

Figure 8-5.

filters do—which isn't much, frankly—plus a whole lot more. Unsharp Mask derives its name from an old and largely abandoned traditional darkroom technique in which a photographic negative was sandwiched together with a blurred, low-contrast positive of itself and printed to photographic paper. Ironically, this blurred positive (the "unsharp" mask) accentuated the edges in the original, resulting in the perception of sharpness.

---

To learn how Unsharp Mask's arcane origins translate to the way the function works in Photoshop, read the upcoming sidebar "Using Blur to Sharpen."

---

In the meantime, the goal of this exercise is to learn how to put the Unsharp Mask command to everyday use.

Figure 8-6.

1. *Open a couple of soft images.* Go to the *Lesson 08* folder inside *Lesson Files-PScs 1on1* and you'll find two photos of an unconscious young tabby, *Sleepy kitten.jpg* and *Sloppy kitten.jpg* (see Figure 8-6). I shot both pictures at a nearby farm. The kitten slept in a pen, so I had to position the camera lens between links in the surrounding fence. Unfortunately, my companions included an army of enthusiastic preschoolers who would, without warning, grab the fence and shake it until their mothers made them stop. When I captured the first photo, *Sleepy kitten.jpg*, the fence was in between shakes. Not so lucky on the second photo—I got smacked.

   The result: The first image is soft, meaning that it's a little off from its ideal focus, most likely a function of me moving the camera after focusing it. The second image, however, looks blurred because the camera was moving when I took the shot. This makes a big difference in how we approach the images and just how much good we can do.

2. *Bring one of the soft images to front.* We'll start with *Sleepy kitten.jpg*, so click its title bar to make sure that the first image is active.

3. *Choose the Unsharp Mask command.* I often say that if I had to keep just one command in the Filter menu, it would be **Filter→ Sharpen→Unsharp Mask**. That's why I gave it a keyboard shortcut. If you loaded the Deke Keys shortcuts as advised in Step 12 on page xvii of the Preface, press Ctrl+Shift+Alt+U (⌘-Shift-Option-U on the Mac).

4. ***Turn on the Preview check box.*** Pictured in Figure 8-7, the **Unsharp Mask** dialog box supports all the previewing options that I demonstrated in the video. It includes a cropped preview of the effect inside the dialog box. When the **Preview** check box is on, Photoshop applies the effect in real time to the larger image window as well.

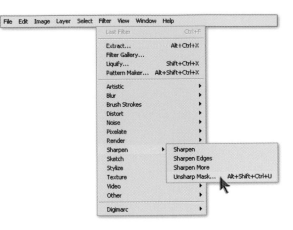

As elsewhere in Photoshop, the Preview check box is an essential tool for gauging the results of your numerical settings. I can think of only two reasons to turn off Preview: first, if you want to compare before-and-after versions of an image, and second, if you're working on a very large image and Photoshop just can't keep up with your changes.

5. ***Click in the image window.*** This centers the preview inside the dialog box. I recommend clicking on the cat's forward-facing paw. In any case, you want to center on some detail that you'd like to bring into sharper focus. Drag inside the preview box to further adjust the view.

6. ***Set the previews to different zoom ratios.*** Set the image window to the 100 percent view size and the preview to 50 percent, or vice versa. This way you have two views into the results of your changes.

Why 100 and 50 percent? Because the first shows you how the image looks if displayed on screen, and the other more closely represents its appearance when printed (at which point more pixels are packed into a smaller space). Also worth noting, 50 percent is an interpolated zoom, meaning that Photoshop properly smoothes over pixel transitions. By comparison, odd zoom ratios such as 67 and 33 percent are jagged and misleading.

Figure 8-7.

7. ***Raise the Amount to 200 percent.*** This is merely a temporary value that exaggerates the effect and permits us to see what we're doing.

8. ***Specify a Radius value of 2.5 pixels.*** Even though **Radius** is the second value, I recommend starting with it because it's really the hinge pin of the sharpening operation. Unsharp Mask simulates sharper edges by drawing halos around the edges (see "Using Blur to Sharpen"). The Radius value defines the thickness of those halos. Thin halos result in a precise edge; thick halos result in a more generalized high-contrast effect. A few examples appear in Figure 8-8 on the next page.

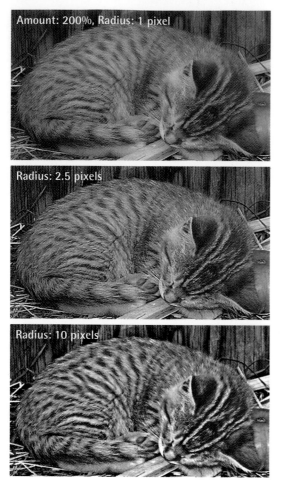

Figure 8-8.

For everyday sharpening, the best Radius value is the one you can just barely see. Naturally, this varies depending on how your final image will be viewed:

- If you intend to display the image on screen (say, for a Web page), enter a very small value, such as 0.5 pixel.

- For medium-resolution printing, a Radius of 1.0 to 2.0 pixels tends to work best.

- For high-resolution printing, a Radius of 2.0 or higher results in sharp edges. (For more information on print resolution, read Lesson 12, "Printing and Output.")

The examples in Figure 8-8 were printed at 334 pixels per inch, so the 2.5-pixel Radius delivers the best edges. A smaller Radius value most likely looks better on your screen, but for now, I'd like you to pretend you're going to print, so enter 2.5.

---

Use the up and down arrow keys to nudge the value by its smallest increment, 0.1 in the case of Radius, 1 in the case of Amount and Threshold. Add Shift to nudge 10 times that increment.

---

9. ***Lower the Amount value to 100 percent.*** The **Amount** value is the easiest to understand—it controls the degree to which the image gets sharpened. Higher Amount values result in more crisply defined edges. The effects of the Amount value become more pronounced at higher Radius values as well. So where 200 percent may look dandy with a Radius of 1 pixel, the image may appear jagged and noisy at a Radius of 2.5. An image subject to too high an Amount value is said to be *over-sharpened*, as is presently the case for our tabby.

   Press Shift+Tab to highlight the Amount value. Then press Shift+↓ a few times in a row to nudge the value down in increments of 10 percent. Figure 8-9 on the facing page shows a few examples. For my money, the final setting is the best fit.

10. ***Leave Threshold set to 0.*** The final value, **Threshold**, decides whether or not neighboring pixels are factored into the sharpening equation. Threshold is measured in luminosity levels; the default, 0, means that neighboring pixels have to be at least 0 levels different from each other to be considered a potential

edge. In other words, all pixels are sharpened uniformly. Higher Threshold values rule out more and more pixels. For those of you who enjoy symmetry in your software, the Threshold value measures colors just like the magic wand's Tolerance setting (see Step 5, page 102). Only instead of including pixels, as Tolerance does, Threshold rules them out.

In theory, the Threshold value helps avoid sharpening grain and other artifacts. In practice, it just doesn't work. Because Threshold is an on or off proposition—pixels get sharpened or they don't—any value large enough to produce a visible effect does as much to create grain as defeat it. For example, a Threshold of 40 calls out random flecks in the kitten's fur, shown in Figure 8-10 at 100 and 200 percent.

For more on Threshold, including a better way to defeat film grain, see the "Using an Edge Mask" exercise, which begins on page 266.

11. ***Click the OK button.*** Confirm that your values match those shown in Figure 8-11, and away you go.

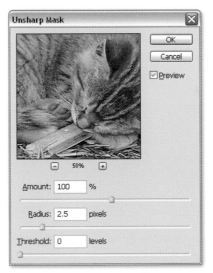

Figure 8-9.

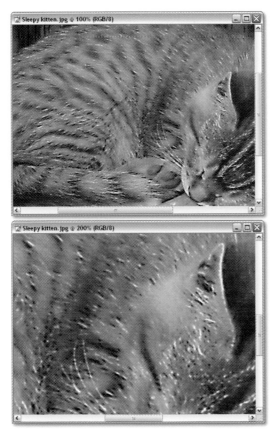

Figure 8-10.

Figure 8-11.

# Using Blur to Sharpen

The "unsharp" in Unsharp Mask is a function of the softly tapering halo applied by the Radius value. Once you understand this, you can master the art of focus in Photoshop.

Consider the line art in the figure below. The top-left example features dark lines against a light background. The other three images are sharpened with increasingly higher Radius values. (Throughout, the Amount value is set to 200 percent.) In each case, the Unsharp Mask filter traces the dark areas inside the lines (the brown areas) with a blurry dark halo and the light areas outside the lines (the green areas) with a blurry light halo. The thickness of these halos conforms to the Radius value. So all Unsharp Mask does is increase the contrast by tracing halos around edges.

Given that the Radius value is all about blurring, it's no surprise that this option also appears in the Gaussian Blur dialog box (see "Gaussian Blur and Median," which begins on page 257), where it once again generates halos around edges. In fact, if we were to trace the lineage of these filters, Gaussian Blur is Unsharp Mask's grandparent. The missing family member in between is an obscure command called High Pass.

Why should you care? Because Unsharp Mask's parent, High Pass, is a more flexible sharpening agent than its progeny.

Try this: Go ahead and open *Sleepy kitten.jpg.* (If it's still open from the "Sharpening an Image" exercise, press F12 to revert the image to its original appearance.) Now press

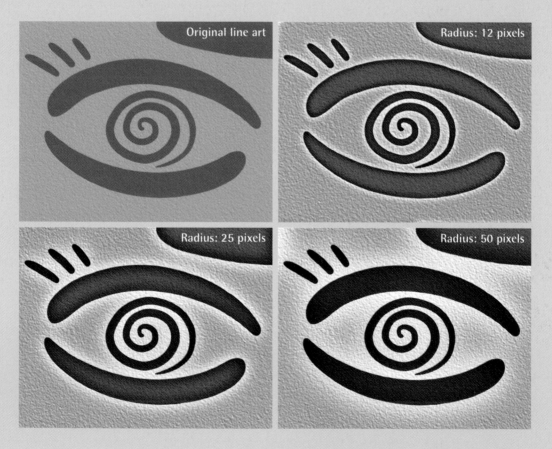

Ctrl+J (or ⌘-J) to copy the image to an independent layer. Next, choose Filter→Other→High Pass. Pictured below, the High Pass dialog box contains a single option, Radius. Change this value to 2.5 pixels, the same Radius you applied in the exercise using Unsharp Mask. Then click OK.

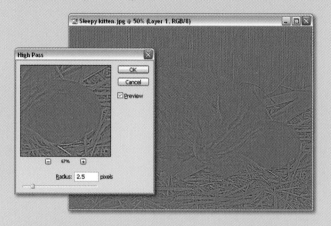

Looks like a big mess of gray, right? But there are tenuous edges in there. To bring them out, press Ctrl+L (or ⌘-L) to display the Levels dialog box. Change the first and third Input Levels values to 75 and 180, respectively, as in the figure below. Then click OK.

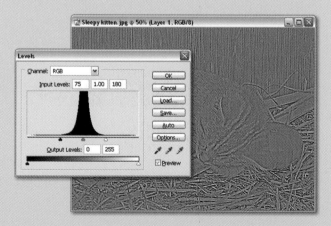

Still looks terrible. But what you're looking at are the very same light and dark halos that Unsharp Mask creates. To apply those halos to the original photograph, go to the Layers palette and choose Overlay from the top left pop-up menu. Just like that, Photoshop drops out the grays, blends in the edges, and makes it all better, as shown below. The result is almost exactly what you'd get if you applied Unsharp Mask with a Radius of 2.5 and an Amount of 200 percent. (In other words, the current High Pass layer is twice as strong as the equivalent Unsharp Mask.) In other words, the photograph is oversharpened just as it was at the outset of Step 9 on page 252. To match the more pleasing Amount value of 100 percent that we eventualy settled on in the exercise, reduce the layer's Opacity setting to 50 percent.

Why go through all this just to get the same effect we achieved in the exercise? Because now you have a floating layer of sharpness whose Amount you can change at any time just by modifying the layer's Opacity setting. This means you can change your mind well into the future, as opposed to being locked into the static result of Unsharp Mask. Sure, it's an unusual approach, and it takes a bit of experience to get it down pat. But the additional flexibility you gain is well worth the effort.

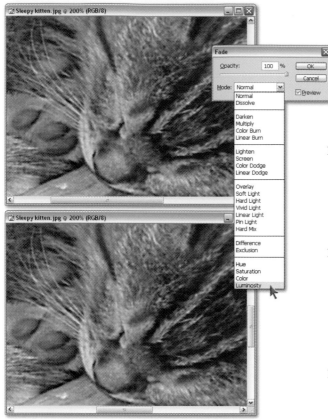

Figure 8-12.

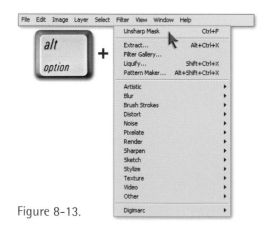

Figure 8-13.

If you zoom in on the image and look closely, you'll notice that in addition to the sharpened detail, Unsharp Mask has pulled out a few aberrant colors (Figure 8-12 top). The filter can't distinguish color detail from luminosity detail, so it exaggerates the contrast between both. To return the colors to their previous appearance while keeping the sharpness, do the following.

12. *Fade the effect using Luminosity.* Press Ctrl+Shift+F (⌘-Shift-F) to display the **Fade** dialog box. Then choose **Luminosity** from the **Mode** pop-up menu and click **OK**. Photoshop merges the new sharpness with the original colors (Figure 8-12 bottom).

13. *Bring the blurry image to up front.* That pretty well fixes the first photograph. Now what can we do about the second? Well, sad to say, not a whole lot. To see for yourself, bring the *Sloppy kitten.jpg* image up front by clicking its title bar or choosing its name from the bottom of the **Window** menu.

14. *Again display the Unsharp Mask dialog box.* But don't choose Filter→Sharpen→Unsharp Mask. Instead, bring up the Filter menu and notice that the first command now reads Unsharp Mask, as in Figure 8-13. As I explained back in Video Lesson 8, "Filtering Basics" (see page 246), choosing this command would reapply the filter with the same settings as before. However, don't do that. Instead, press and hold the Alt key (Option on the Mac) and then choose **Filter→ Unsharp Mask**. Or better yet, press the keyboard shortcut Ctrl+Alt+F (⌘-Option-F). Photoshop revisits the dialog box, permitting you to apply the filter with different settings.

15. *Raise the Amount value.* This image requires more sharpening than the first one. So click inside the **Amount** box and press Shift+↑ several times to increase the value in 10 percent increments. As you do, Photoshop increases the sharpness of the image, but it also brings out more and more of the diagonal lines of noise associated with the motion blur, as shown in Figure 8-14 on the facing page.

For my money, an Amount of 200 percent gets things as close to focused as they're going to get. What about raising the Radius value? Doesn't really help. Might not Threshold reduce the noise? As I said, that option doesn't work under the best of conditions, and it doesn't stand a chance against the directional noise produced by a motion blur. My experience: This is as good as it gets.

Figure 8-14.

16. ***Wipe away the tears and get on with your life.*** Click **OK** to accept your revised **Amount** value of 200 percent. It's not so bad, right? In fact it looks kind of cool.

Not satisfied? Then grab your camera, go back to that farm, and try your best to talk that kitten into sleeping on that pumpkin just one more time. And be quick about it because, I swear, when those preschoolers land they move in fast and furious.

## Gaussian Blur and Median

The Unsharp Mask filter has a strange name, but its purpose is clear. It makes a photograph appear more sharply focused. But what good are the Gaussian Blur and Median filters? One blurs the focus of an image, something you actively avoid when shooting a photo. The other averages the colors of neighboring pixels, as if the image were rendered in candle wax and melted. Why would you want to take an image with sharply focused details and gum it up?

Because details are not always good, especially when they're unwanted or unflattering. An unwanted detail might be a hair on a jacket or a fingerprint on a glass. These are details you clean away before you snap a picture (assuming you notice them, that is). Then there are the unflattering details, the ones we can't clean away, the flaws that are ingrained into every square inch of exposed flesh. Entire multibillion dollar industries—cosmetics, dermatology, plastic surgery—are founded on the principle that we'd just as soon withhold such details from public scrutiny. So where focus is concerned, give me the eyes of an eagle, but make those around me blind.

Photography only makes matters worse. Film adds grain, prints add texture, and scanners add dust. Even a properly trained camera can make humankind's most beautiful representatives appear riddled with imperfections. As we'll see, even make-up may not protect and sometimes it makes matters worse.

Some photographic problems demand the kind of meticulous attention documented in the second half of Lesson 6, "Paint, Edit, and Heal." But others just need a little bit of generalized focus removal. That's when you bring in Gaussian Blur to soften the details and Median to smooth over the harsh transitions—which, coincidentally, are the goals of the following exercise.

1. **Open an image that needs some TLC.**  For this exercise, I'd like you to open *Some softening required.jpg* in the *Lesson 08* folder inside *Lesson Files-PScs 1on1*. Therein, we chance upon the two astonishing denizens of the unconventional captured in Figure 8-15. So dramatic, so cheerful, so festive. But at the risk of sounding catty, I can't help but think that a change of razor blades might have made all the difference. Or perhaps it's the glitter combined with a landscape of generous pores. Whatever the case, Photoshop's blurring and averaging functions can make these lads every bit as pretty as they intended to be.

2. **Select a large elliptical area.** Press M twice (or M, Shift+M if you skipped the Preface) to select the elliptical marquee tool. Then drag from one corner of the image to the other to select a large portion of the image, roughly the size of the marching ants outline shown in Figure 8-16 on the facing page.

Figure 8-15.

3. *Choose Select→Feather.* Or you can press Ctrl+Alt+D (⌘-Option-D on the Mac). Enter a **Feather Radius** value of 120 pixels and click **OK**.

4. *Choose Select→Inverse.* Or press the keyboard shortcut Ctrl+Shift+I (⌘-Shift-I). Photoshop deselects the area inside the ellipse and selects the area outside.

5. *Choose the Gaussian Blur filter.* Choose **Filter→Blur→Gaussian Blur**. Or, if you loaded the shortcuts I suggested in Step 12 on page xvii of the Preface, you can take advantage of the keyboard shortcut Ctrl+Shift+Alt+G (⌘-Shift-Option-G on the Mac). However you get there, once you do, enter a **Radius** value of 250 pixels and click **OK**. Photoshop blurs the outer pixels to the maximum extent allowed, as shown in Figure 8-17.

Figure 8-16.

The word *Gaussian* refers to the non-linear nature of the blur. The colors blur dramatically inside the circles formed by the Radius value and more gradually toward the outsides. The result is a tapering effect that ensures smooth transitions between blurred areas of color. The Feather command (applied in Step 3) is likewise a Gaussian function, one that ensures smooth transitions between selected and deselected pixels.

Figure 8-17.

6. *Choose Edit→Fade.* Or press Ctrl+Shift+F (⌘-Shift-F on the Mac). Then choose **Linear Dodge** from the **Mode** pop-up menu, change the **Opacity** value to 50 percent, and click **OK**. The result is the subtle but vibrant vignette pictured in Figure 8-18 on the next page.

Figure 8-18.

Figure 8-19.

7. *Deselect the image.* The easiest way: Ctrl+D (or ⌘-D).

8. *Revisit the Gaussian Blur dialog box.* Press the Alt key (Option on the Mac) and choose **Filter→Gaussian Blur** or press Ctrl+Alt+F (⌘-Option-F) to reapply the filter with a different Radius value (see Figure 8-19).

9. *Change the Radius value.* Enter a **Radius** of 6 pixels and click **OK**.

10. *Choose Edit→Fade.* Or press Ctrl+Shift+F (⌘-Shift-F). Choose **Soft Light** from the **Mode** pop-up menu and click **OK**. This both enhances the contrast and reduces the effect of the blur (see Figure 8-20 on the opposite page).

The colors may look a bit garish, but you've already made a big dent in the roughness of the image, while maintaining an image that appears uniformly focused. So you can appreciate the degree of change, the following steps let you compare the original image with the present one.

11. *Go to the History palette.* Click the **History** tab or, if the palette is hidden, choose **Window→History**.

12. *Click the snapshot at the top of the palette.* Or click the **Open** state. Either way, Photoshop shows you the "before" version of the image.

Figure 8-20.

13. **Choose Edit→Undo State Change.** Or press Ctrl+Z (⌘-Z on the Mac). This restores all your recent changes to the image, creating an "after" view (see Figure 8-21).

---

At this point (and until you perform the next step), you can flip back and forth between the before and after views just by pressing Ctrl+Z (or ⌘-Z). It's a fantastic way to track the progress of an image.

---

One note of caution: If you elect to take advantage of the preceding tip, be sure you restore the after view of the image before moving on to the next step!

**EXTRA ★ CREDIT**

We've made terrific progress, but we're not out of the woods yet. I'm still concerned about some rough patches in the lightest portions of the image. If you don't share my concern, move on to the next exercise, which begins on page 266. But if you (like me) are just itching to smooth out those light areas with Median and Gaussian Blur, then away we go.

14. **Choose Select→Color Range.** Click inside the whitest areas of the fellow's face on the right. Then press Shift and drag over other light portions of his face,

Figure 8-21.

including the pink swath across his cheek. Be careful to avoid any shadows. Raise the **Fuzziness** value to 100. (If Lesson 7 was the last time you used the Color Range command, you'll also need to select the **Selection** option and choose **None** from the **Selection Preview** pop-up menu.) Your mask preview should look like the one in Figure 8-22. Once it does, click **OK**.

Figure 8-22.

Figure 8-23.

Given that the details of this image are in rough shape, it stands to reason that a selection outline based on the image is rough as well. And so it is with the one you just created. You could smooth it out using Select→Modify→Smooth or Feather, but neither of these commands lets you preview your changes. Worse yet, because all you have to work with are marching ants, you can't effectively gauge your changes after the commands are applied. Better to consult the quick mask mode.

15. **Enter the quick mask mode.** Click the ▢ icon in the toolbox or press the Q key.

16. **View the mask by itself.** Press the tilde key (~) or go to the **Channels** palette and turn off the 👁 in front of **RGB**. You should now see the grayscale mask shown in Figure 8-23.

17. **Choose the Median command.** To smooth over the stray pixels and compression artifacts rampant in this mask, choose **Filter→Noise→Median** and enter a **Radius** value of 6 pixels and click **OK** (see Figure 8-24).

---

**PEARL OF ● WISDOM**

I've mentioned how the Median filter averages pixels, but what does that mean in this case? It merges neighboring clusters of pixels and rounds off sharp corners. When applied to a mask, Median produces *exactly the same effect* as applying Select→Modify→Smooth to a selection outline (see Step 32 of "Drawing Precise Curves," Lesson 4, page 130). The difference is, armed with a mask and a filter, you can see what the heck you're doing.

---

18. *Choose Filter→Blur→Gaussian Blur.* Although Median smoothes pixels, it has no effect on the sharpness of an image. Harsh or jagged transitions remain every bit as abrupt. To soften things a bit, choose the **Gaussian Blur** filter and enter a **Radius** value of 3 pixels. Then click **OK**.

PEARL OF WISDOM

Just as Median is the masking equivalent of Smooth, Gaussian Blur is the equivalent of Feather. The only difference: Feather works on selection outlines; Gaussian Blur works on images. That, and Gaussian Blur shows you what's going on.

19. *Exit the quick mask mode.* Smooth and soft, the mask is good to go. Click the ⬚ icon in the toolbox or press the Q key to return to marching ants and the full-color image.

20. *Send the selection to its own layer.* Choose **Layer→New→Layer via Copy** or press Ctrl+J (⌘-J on the Mac).

Now you need to smooth and soften the layer. For the sake of demonstration, I want you to apply higher values than you might normally so you can see what's really going on (even if it does result in a little over-softening).

21. *Choose Filter→Noise→Median.* Enter a **Radius** of 12 pixels—double the value from Step 17—and click **OK**. Why double? Because I saw what a 6-pixel radius did in the quick mask mode and I want to make twice that much of a difference this time around.

22. *Choose Filter→Blur→Gaussian Blur.* Again, you need to soften the results of your smoothing. So choose **Gaussian Blur** and enter a **Radius** of 6 pixels, twice the value in Step 18. Then click **OK**. The result appears in Figure 8-25.

Figure 8-24.

Figure 8-25.

23. *Reduce the opacity of the layer.* Press the 3 key to change the **Opacity** value to 30 percent. You can also experiment with the blend mode if you like, but then you run the risk of exaggerating the saturation or contrast. For this particular example, the Normal mode works just fine.

24. *Compare before and after views.* Go to the **History** palette and click the opening snapshot at the top of the list. Then press Ctrl+Z (⌘-Z) to switch between the before and after views, shown magnified in Figure 8-26.

If you think you went too far with the smoothing and softening, further reduce the opacity of the layer. If you don't think you went far enough, nudge the value up a few percent.

PEARL OF WISDOM

One of the most striking differences between the before and after views is the latter's increased saturation. Hot, vivid colors happen to work well for this particular image. But if you prefer to maintain consistent saturation values, then you must seek out the Hue/Saturation command.

Before          After

Figure 8-26.

25. ***Add a Hue/Saturation layer.*** Because you need to adjust multiple layers at a time, you must use a special kind of color correction known as an adjustment layer (discussed in the "Creating and Modifying Adjustment Layers" exercise, Lesson 11, page 405). Click the ⊘ icon at the bottom of the **Layers** palette and choose **Hue/Saturation**, as shown in Figure 8-27.

26. ***Reduce the Saturation value.*** Inside the familiar Hue/Saturation dialog box, enter a **Saturation** value of –20 percent and click **OK**.

Photoshop creates a new Hue/Saturation layer that reduces the saturation values of both layers below it. Pictured in Figure 8-28, the resulting composition provides a good match to the colors in the original image, while retaining the smoothness and softness of its more highly saturated predecessor.

27. ***Save your composition.*** Choose **File→Save As** and save the image in the native Photoshop PSD format. This saves all three layers, including the adjustment layer you added in the last step. For more information on adjustment layers, read Lesson 11, "Layer Styles and Adjustments."

Figure 8-27.

Figure 8-28.

# Using an Edge Mask

Now that you've had ample opportunity to see the Unsharp Mask, Gaussian Blur, and Median filters in action, let's combine their efforts to create that most essential of all sharpening assistants, the *edge mask*—that is, a mask that highlights the true visual edges in an image.

The idea is this: On its own, Unsharp Mask recognizes edges entirely according to the degree of contrast between neighboring pixels. So a high-contrast color transition gets more attention than a low-contrast transition. This scheme works fine for well-focused images shot and digitized using modern, professional-level equipment. But the success rate drops when confronted by less "clean" photos shot with consumer cameras or scanned from damaged or worn source material. Such images contain random *artifacts*—film grain, noise, dust, scratches, compression patterns, or any other variety of pixels that don't convey information about the subject of the photo. To the Unsharp Mask filter, an artifact looks like any other edge. So the worst of the grain and dust in your image appears more amplified after sharpening.

This exercise begins with a quick look at just how dismally the Unsharp Mask filter fares when confronted by heavy-duty artifacting. After that, we'll build an edge mask and get the job done right.

1. *Open a vintage photograph.* Open the file *Plains dwellers.jpg* located in the *Lesson 08* folder inside *Lesson Files-PScs 1on1*. Scanned from a print positive, this 80-year-old image is a terrific example of the staying power of traditional media. Pictured in Figure 8-29, the photo is stained, pitted, faded, and creased, but it's still here and very much readable. Let's hope anything remotely like that can be said 80 years from now about the CD that contains this file. In case you're curious, this is a family photo. That's my grandmother smiling (somewhat unusual for this crowd) on the right.

2. *Choose Filter→Sharpen→Unsharp Mask.* If you loaded my custom shortcuts (Step 12, page xvii), press Ctrl+Shift+Alt+U (⌘-Shift-Option-U).

3. *Specify the desired Amount and Radius values.* I suggest an **Amount** of 250 percent and a **Radius** of 1.2 pixels. The result is an image marked by sharply defined edges and even more sharply defined film grain, as illustrated in Figure 8-30. Like turning up the treble on an AM radio, Unsharp Mask brings out the static.

Figure 8-29.

Figure 8-30.

4. ***Raise the Threshold and Amount values.*** For demonstration purposes, I suggest a **Threshold** of 25 and an **Amount** of 500. The purpose of Threshold is to circumvent the static. In this case, the Unsharp Mask filter ignores the subtler edges and affects only the edges where neighboring colors differ by at least 25 luminosity levels. As shown in Figure 8-31, this eliminates some grain, but by no means all of it. Meanwhile, you lose a lot of the real edges. The net result is a pockmarked effect that looks anything but sharp.

5. ***Click the Cancel button.*** Or press the Esc key. That dog ain't hunting, so best to abandon it. But if Threshold doesn't work, what does? The solution is to use some of Photoshop's sensitive edge-detection filters to create a custom edge mask.

6. ***Bring up the Channels palette.*** A mask needs an alpha channel. So click the **Channels** tab to make the palette visible.

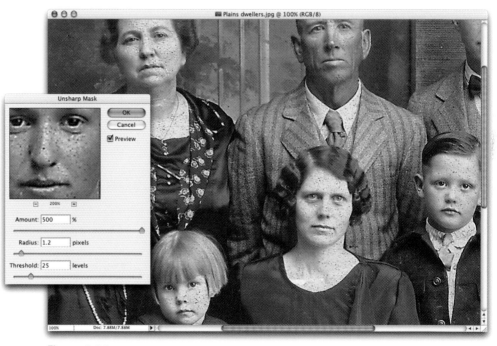

Figure 8-31.

7. *Duplicate a channel.* Because this is a monochrome photo, one color channel looks much like another. But as a rule of thumb, the Green channel is the most representative of the details in an image, so drag the **Green** item onto the ▣ icon at the bottom of the **Channels** palette. If you find yourself working in a grayscale image, duplicate the Gray channel instead.

8. *Name the new alpha channel.* Double-click the **Green copy** item and name it "Edge Mask."

9. *Choose Image→Adjustments→Levels.* Or press Ctrl+L (⌘-L on the Mac). Then change the first and third **Input Levels** values to 60 and 170, respectively, as in Figure 8-32. Click the **OK** button to accept your settings. The idea is that most of the really horrible pitting is located in the lightest areas of the image. So by getting rid of those light areas right off the bat, we do ourselves an invaluable favor in later steps.

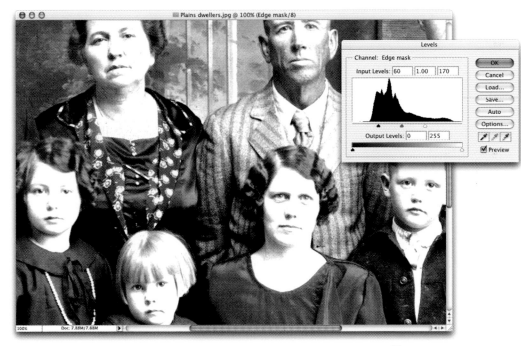

Figure 8-32.

10. **Choose Filter→Stylize→Find Edges.** This unique and simple filter traces the edges in the alpha channel, making areas of high contrast black and areas of low contrast white, as in Figure 8-33. Alas, if only the Unsharp Mask's Threshold option was capable of doing anything remotely as sophisticated. But perhaps it's better that it doesn't. As we'll see, pursuing this task manually leads to much better results than we could hope to achieve with any automated function.

Figure 8-33.

11. **Choose the Invert command.** Eventually, you want to select the edges, which means you need the edges to be white and the non-edges to be black. So choose **Image→Adjustments→Invert** or press Ctrl+I (⌘-I on the Mac) to make it so.

12. **Choose the Maximum filter.** The white edges are a bit too skinny in their current state, so we need to thicken them up. And the best way to expand the highlights in a mask is to apply **Filter→Other→Maximum**. Enter a **Radius** of 2 pixels (no decimals allowed) and click the **OK** button.

The light areas are clearly bigger than they were before, but the filter seems to have generated a bunch of squares (Figure 8-34 left). In expanding the highlights, Maximize is forced to magnify individual pixels, so the tiny square pixels turn into bigger squares. The solution is to round off the squares, a job uniquely suited to Median.

13. *Choose Filter→Noise→Median.* Enter the same **Radius** as in the last step, 2 pixels, and click **OK**. Median smoothes the square into circles, resulting in more or less continuous lines (Figure 8-34 right). But the transitions are very sharp. We need some softening.

Figure 8-34.

14. *Choose Filter→Blur→Gaussian Blur.* As always, we follow up Median with Gaussian Blur. This time around, enter a **Radius** value of 4 pixels, double the last value, and click the **OK** button. The mask is officially a blurry mess, but it affords you the gradual transitions you need to sharpen the edges accurately.

15. **Again apply the Levels command.** There are still too many stray pixels drifting around the mask. To tighten things up, press Ctrl+L or ⌘-L to invoke the **Levels** command. Change the first and third **Input Levels** values to 140 and 215, respectively, as in Figure 8-35. Then click **OK**.

The mask-in-progress pictured in Figure 8-35 is looking really good. The edges are white, the non-edges are black. There are a few stray spots, which you can clean up with the brush tool if you have a mind to. Our more pressing concern, however, is the fact that the Levels command has gone and sharpened our previously blurry mask. In other words, we have to reapply Gaussian Blur.

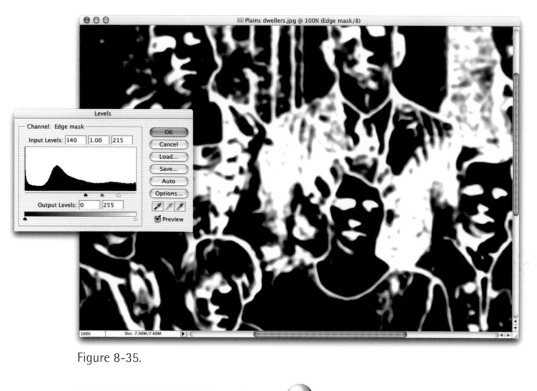

Figure 8-35.

PEARL OF WISDOM

For those of you who are thinking, "Deke, we seem to be driving in circles. Is this really the most efficient route?" the answer is yes. Step 14 used Gaussian Blur to soften the effects of Maximum and Median, Step 15 brought in Levels to erase away some remaining non-edges, and now we need Gaussian Blur again.

16. ***Reapply Gaussian Blur.*** The last Radius value of 4 pixels was fine, so choose the first command in the **Filter** menu or press Ctrl+F (⌘-F on the Mac) to reapply the filter. The final mask appears in Figure 8-36.

17. ***Load the mask as a selection.*** Press the Ctrl (or ⌘) key and click the **Edge Mask** channel in the **Channels** palette. Alternatively, you can press Ctrl+Alt+4 (⌘-Option-4) since this is the fourth channel in the image.

Figure 8-36.

18. ***Switch to the RGB image.*** Click the **RGB** item at the top of the Channels palette or press Ctrl+tilde (or ⌘-tilde). The selection stays with you.

19. ***Hide the selection outline.*** Press Ctrl+H (or ⌘-H) to hide the marching ants so you can better see what you're doing.

20. ***Choose Filter→Sharpen→Unsharp Mask.*** Reestablish the settings I recommended back in Step 3 on page 266—that is, an **Amount** of 250 percent and a **Radius** of 1.2 pixels. Then click **OK**. The utterly marvelous result appears in Figure 8-37 on the next page. Granted, the grain and pits remain, and a few even get amplified, but you can always tidy those up later using the healing brush and other retouching tools, as I discussed back in Lesson 6.

Figure 8-37.

At this point, you image looks as good as it's going to get. You may therefore consider the project complete. However, given my enthusiasm for the High Pass filter in the sidebar "Using Blur to Sharpen" (see page 254), I reckon I owe you a real demonstration of just how swell the filter can be. In the remaining, purely optional steps, we'll mimic the Unsharp Mask operation using the slower but more flexible High Pass approach.

21. *Choose Edit→Undo Unsharp Mask.*  This undoes the Unsharp Mask filter applied in Step 20 so that we can resharpen the image with High Pass.

22. *Send the selection to its own layer.*  Choose **Layer→New→Layer via Copy**, or press Ctrl+J (⌘-J on the Mac).

23. *Choose Filter→Other→High Pass.*  Then enter a **Radius** of 1.2 pixels, matching the Unsharp Mask value from Step 20. Click **OK** to turn the edgework an ugly gray, as in Figure 8-38 on the facing page. I know, it's hard to love High Pass at first. But as you'll see, it's a real performer.

24. *Choose the Levels command.*  To bring out the edges in the layer, press Ctrl+L (⌘-L on the Mac) to bring up the **Levels** dialog box. Then change the first and third **Input Levels** values to 105 and 150, respectively, and click **OK**. The layer remains predominantly gray, but now it has edges, as witnessed in Figure 8-39.

Figure 8-38.

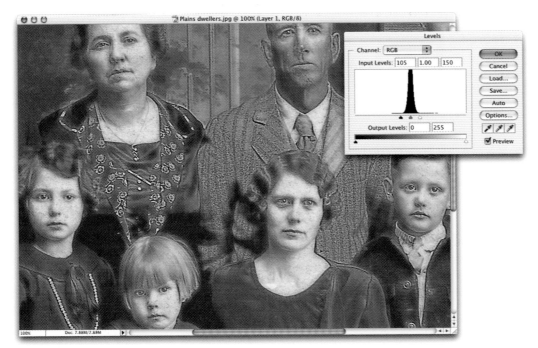

Figure 8-39.

You may notice that these Input Levels values are different from the ones I recommended in the "Using Blur to Sharpen" sidebar. Different Radius values require different Levels adjustments. In the sidebar, the Radius was larger, 2.5 pixels, so the Input Levels were looser, 75 and 180. For what it's worth, I'm just responding to what I see in the histogram.

25. ***Choose the Overlay blend mode.*** Press F7 to display the **Layers** palette and then choose **Overlay**. Or, assuming one of the selection tools is active, press Shift+Alt+O (Shift-Option-O on the Mac).

26. ***Reduce the Opacity setting to 50 percent.*** If a selection tool is active, press the 5 key. We now have nearly exactly the same sharpening effect we had in Step 20. (The Opacity may be off a percent or two, but otherwise, it's the same.) Plus, the sharpening exists on a separate layer, so you can modify its blend mode and opacity well into the future.

Just for reference, Figure 8-40 shows how the edge mask effect (right) compares with the inferior sharpening performed back in Steps 3 and 4 (left and middle). I have yet to encounter a grainy or noisy image in which an edge mask has not easily justified the effort I put into making it.

27. ***Choose File→Save As.*** To preserve your layer and alpha channel, save the image in Photoshop's native PSD format.

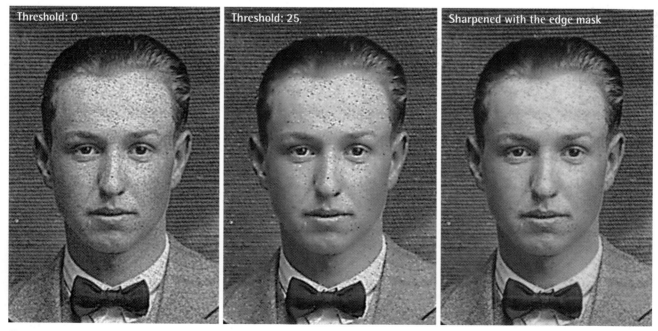

Figure 8-40.

# WHAT DID YOU LEARN?

Match the key concept in the numbered list below with the letter
of the phrase that best describes it. Answers appear upside-down
at the bottom of the page.

## Key Concepts

1. Focus
2. Corrective filters
3. Edge
4. Unsharp Mask
5. Radius
6. Threshold
7. High Pass
8. Gaussian
9. Median
10. Edge mask
11. Artifacts
12. Find Edges

## Descriptions

A. This simple filter traces around the high-contrast areas in an image with lines of varying thickness and opacity.

B. The thickness of the effect applied by a filter, often expressed as a softly tapering halo.

C. The clarity of the image formed by the lens element and captured by the camera.

D. A selection outline used to distinguish artifacts from the true details in a photograph.

E. This option decides whether or not neighboring pixels are factored into the sharpening equation, a question better settled by an edge mask.

F. Commands in Photoshop's Filter menu that are designed to detect edges and correct focus.

G. Named for a 19th-century mathematician, this interpretation of the Radius value provides for smooth transitions between pixels.

H. A filter named for a traditional technique in which a photographic negative is combined with a blurred version of itself.

I. Any of several varieties of random pixels that don't convey information about the subject of the photo, including film grain, noise, and dust.

J. A ridge formed by areas of extreme contrast between neighboring pixels.

K. A filter that mimics the functionality of Unsharp Mask by retaining areas of high contrast and sending low-contrast areas to gray.

L. Photoshop's primary noise-removal filter averages the colors of neighboring pixels in sweeps defined by the Radius value.

## Answers

1C, 2F, 3J, 4H, 5B, 6E, 7K, 8G, 9L, 10D, 11I, 12A

# BUILDING LAYERED COMPOSITIONS

EVERY IMAGE begins life as a few channels of data—most commonly, one each for red, green, and blue—fused into a single pane of pixels (see Figure 9-1). Whether it comes from the least expensive digital camera or a professional-level drum scanner, the image exists entirely on one layer. One and only one full-color value exists for each and every pixel, and there is no such thing as transparency. Such an image is said to be *flat*.

But as soon as you begin combining images, you add layers. Each layer serves as an independent image, which you can stack, transform, or blend with other layers.

A document that contains two or more layers is called a *layered composition*. There's no need to wait until a certain point in the editing cycle to build such a composition—you can add layers to a document any old time you like, as we have several times in previous lessons. But layers have a way of becoming even more useful after some of the basic editing work is out of the way. That's why I've waited until now to show you the many ways to create and manage layers in Photoshop.

Three channels combine to make one layer

Figure 9-1.

## The Benefits and Penalties of Layers

Photoshop's reliance on layers makes for an exceedingly flexible (if sometimes confusing) working environment. As long as an image remains on a layer, you can move or edit it independently of other layers in the composition. Moreover, you can create relationships between neighboring layers using a wide variety of blending options

# ABOUT THIS LESSON

## Project Files

Before beginning the exercises, make sure that you've installed the lesson files from the CD, as explained in Step 5 on page xv of the Preface. This should result in a folder called *Lesson Files-PScs 1on1* on your desktop. We'll be working with the files inside the *Lesson 09* subfolder.

In this lesson, we'll explore all facets of building a layered composition, from transformations to stacking order, from blend modes to knockouts, from clipping masks to layer comps. You'll learn how to:

- Edit the contents of individual layers and move them forward or backward in the stack . . . . . . . page 283

- Scale, rotate, distort, link, and align layers . . . . . page 291

- Use layer masks, blending options, and knockouts to change the appearance of a layer without altering a single pixel . . . . . . . . . . . page 306

- Save the visibility, position, and appearance of layers using layer comps . . . . . . . . . . . . . page 319

## Video Lesson 9: Layers at Work

Layers are nothing more than independent images that you can set to interact with each other from the Layers palette. But what a difference they make. By relegating image elements and effects to independent layers, you give yourself the flexibility to adjust your artwork well into the future.

To get a sense of how layers work in Photoshop and see a brief sampling of the benefits they can provide, watch the ninth video lesson on the CD. Insert the CD, click the **Start Training** button, click the Set **3** button in the top-right corner of your screen, and then select **9, Layers at Work** from the Lessons list. The movie lasts 8 minutes and 46 seconds, during which time you'll learn about the following operations and shortcuts:

| Operation | Windows shortcut | Macintosh shortcut |
|---|---|---|
| Show or hide the Layers palette | F7 | F7 |
| Float selection | Ctrl-drag selection | ⌘-drag selection |
| Mix floater with underlying image | Ctrl+Shift+F | ⌘-Shift-F |
| Convert floater to independent layer | Ctrl+Shift+J | ⌘-Shift-J |
| Reduce layer opacity to 50 percent | 5* | 5* |
| Restore layer opacity to 100 percent | 0 (zero key)* | 0 (zero key)* |
| Mask active layer with layer below | Ctrl+G | ⌘-G |

* Works only if selection tool is active.

and masks, all of which work without changing the contents of the layers in the slightest.

But layers come at a price. Because they are actually independent images, each layer consumes space both in memory and on your hard drive. Consider the following example:

- I start with an image from the Corbis image library that measures 2,100 by 2,100 pixels, or 7 by 7 inches at 300 pixels per inch (see Figure 9-2). Each pixel takes up 3 bytes of data. The result is a total of 4.41 million pixels, which add up to 12.6MB in memory. Because the image is flat, I can save it to the JPEG format, which compresses the file down to 3.7MB at the highest quality setting.

- I introduce another image from the Corbis collection that measures the very same 2,100 by 2,100 pixels. Photoshop puts the image on its own layer. I apply the Multiply blend mode to get the effect shown in Figure 9-3. The image size doubles to 25.2MB in memory. I can no longer save the layered composition in the JPEG format because JPEG doesn't permit layers. Thus, I save it in the native Photoshop (PSD) format instead. The Photoshop format lacks JPEG's exceptional compression capabilities, and so the file on disk balloons to 25.7MB.

- I then add a series of image and text layers to fill out the composition, as pictured in Figure 9-4 on the next page. Because the layers are smaller, and the text layers are defined as more efficient vectors (see Lesson 10), the size of the image grows only moderately in memory (34.4MB) and barely at all on disk (26.2MB).

So as you add layers, your composition gets bigger. And as your composition gets bigger, Photoshop requires more space in memory and on disk to manage the file. Generally speaking, you can let Photoshop worry about these sorts of nitty gritty details on its own. But bear in mind, no matter how sophisticated your computer, its memory and hard disk are ultimately finite. And if either the memory or (worse) the hard disk fill up, your ability to edit your marvelous multilayer creations may come to a skidding halt.

Flat image, 2100 × 2100 pixels
12.6MB in memory, 3.7MB on disk (saved in JPEG format, Quality 12)

Figure 9-2.

Second layer, full 2100 × 2100 pixels
25.2MB in memory, 25.7MB on disk (saved in native PSD format)

Figure 9-3.

# How to Manage Layers

Fortunately, a few precautions are all it takes to keep layered compositions on a diet and Photoshop running in top form:

- First, don't let your hard disk get anywhere close to full. I recommend keeping at least 1GB available at all times, and more than that is always welcome. (Consult your computer's documentation to find out how to check this.)

- Back up your Photoshop projects regularly to CD-R or some other storage medium. This not only preserves your images, but also permits you to delete files from your hard disk if you start running out of room.

- As you work in Photoshop, you can keep an eye on the size of your image in memory by observing the Doc: values on the left side of the status bar. (If the status bar is hidden, choose Window→Status Bar. On the Mac, look to the lower-left corner of the image window.) The value before the slash tells you the size of the image if flattened; the value after the slash tells you the size of the layered composition.

- You can reduce the size of an image by *merging* two layers into one using Layer→Merge Down. (For more information on merging, see Step 22 of the section "Importing and Transforming Layers" on page 299.)

- To merge all layers in a composition and return to a flat image, choose **Layer→Flatten Image**. But be aware, this is a radical step. I usually flatten an image only as a preamble to importing it into another program, such as QuarkXPress or InDesign. And even then, I make sure to save the flattened image under a different name so as to maintain my original layered file.

Finally, when in doubt, err on the side of too many layers as opposed to too few. This may sound like strange advice, but it's better to push the limits and occasionally top out than unnecessarily constrain yourself and hobble your file. After all, you can always upgrade your computer to better accommodate your massive compositions. But you can never recover an unsaved layer (that is, one that you merged or flattened before saving and closing the file).

NO, THANKS. ALREADY GOT ONE.
(I FLY AIR SUPREME.)

**Bringing you the world on a string.**\*

≡**AIR**supreme  *We fly everywhere. All the time.*

\* Some strings attached.

**Additional layers, various sizes**
34.4MB in memory, 26.2MB on disk (saved in native PSD format)

Figure 9-4.

# Arranging and Modifying Layers

The most basic use for layers is to keep objects separated from each other so you can modify their horizontal and vertical position as well as their front-to-back arrangement. Photoshop also permits you to transform layers by scaling, rotating, or even distorting them, as you'll see in the second half of the upcoming exercise.

By way of demonstration, we'll take a cue from the classical artist I believe would have benefited most from layers, 16th-century imperial court painter Giuseppe Arcimboldo. Regaled in his time as a master of the "composite portrait," Arcimboldo rendered his subjects as fanciful collections of fruits, vegetables, flowers, meats, animals, trees, and even fish (see Figure 9-5). Naturally, we'll embark on something infinitely simpler—Giuseppe had to thrill and delight Emperor Maximilian II; we don't—but even so, you'll get an ample sense of just how much pure imaging flexibility layers afford.

Figure 9-5.

In the following exercise, you'll begin the process of assembling a layered piece of artwork. You'll establish the content and order of the key layers in the composition, and in the process, learn how to select layers, modify their contents, change their order, and even rotate them.

1. ***Open a composition and some images to add to it.*** We'll be looking at three files altogether, *Composite cowboy.psd*, *Cowboy hat.tif*, and *Eight ball.tif*, all included in the *Lesson 09* folder inside *Lesson Files-PScs 1on1*. At first glance, the layered image (shown on the left in Figure 9-6) looks like a football with flippers standing on a pile of towels. But as we'll see, there's so much more.

Figure 9-6.

2. *Bring up the Layers palette.* If it's already on screen, fabulous. If not, choose **Window→Layers** or press the F7 key. The **Layers** palette shows thumbnails of every layer in the document, from the front layer at the top of the palette to the rearmost layer at the bottom. This arrangement of layers from front to back is called the *stacking order.*

3. *Make the layered composition active.* Click the *Composite cowboy.psd* title bar to make that image active. If you take a peek at the Layers palette, you'll see the file contains ten layers in all. And yet we can see just four items in the image window—football, flippers, towels, and background. (In case you're curious, the flippers are found on the Collar layer.) The other layers are turned off or hidden by the football.

4. *Send the football layer backward.* Click the **Football** layer to make it active. Then drag it down the stack in the Layers palette to just between the **Teeth** and **Collar** layers. This reveals all visible layers from the Teeth upward, as illustrated in Figure 9-7. Of course, things don't look at all right so far, but they will.

Figure 9-7.

5. *Switch to the Paths palette.* Click the **Paths** tab in the Layers palette, or choose **Window→Paths**. You'll find one path that I drew in advance, Face Outline.

6. *Load the path as a selection.* Press the Ctrl key (⌘ on the Mac) and click the **Face Outline** item in the Paths palette. Photoshop selects the cowboy's face.

7. *Choose Select→Inverse.* Or press the shortcut Ctrl+Shift+I (⌘-Shift-I) to reverse the selection and select the area outside the cowboy's face.

8. *Delete the selected pixels.* Make sure the Football layer is active (confirmed in the title bar by the word *Football* in parentheses). Then press Backspace or Delete to erase the selected pixels. Only the cowboy's silhouette remains, as shown in Figure 9-8.

Figure 9-8.

9. *Deselect the image.* We're finished with the selection, so press Ctrl+D (⌘-D).

10. *Click the path in the Paths palette.* Paths are good for more than loading selections. You can use them to paint as well. Any paint, edit, or heal tool can be made to trace the outline of a path. To begin, click the **Face Outline** path to select it.

11. *Select the brush tool in the toolbox.* Press the B key. The selected tool becomes the tracing tool.

12. *Specify the brush attributes.* Click the round **Brush** icon in the options bar to display the pop-up brush palette, and then select the fifth preset in the scrolling list. This gets you a 13-pixel hard brush. Also, make sure the **Mode** is **Normal** and the **Opacity** is 100 percent.

13. *Select a color.* Go to the **Color** palette. (Press F6 if it's not available.) Then set the values to **R** 255, **G** 240, and **B** 180. The result is a pale yellow.

14. *Create a new layer.* No need to switch out of the Paths palette; the Layers palette doesn't have to be visible to make a new layer. Just choose **Layer→New→Layer**, or press Ctrl+Shift+N (⌘-Shift-N on the Mac). Then name the layer "Cowboy Outline" and click **OK**.

15. *Stroke the path.* Click the second icon (○) at the bottom of the Paths palette. Or just press the Enter key on the keypad. Either way, Photoshop traces a 13-pixel hard yellow brushstroke around all parts of the path, as shown in Figure 9-9.

Figure 9-9.

16. *Deactivate the path.* Click in the empty area of the Paths palette, below **Face Outline**, to hide the path and turn it off. This is an important step. An active path outline can distract Photoshop's attention from selection outlines and other elements.

17. *Click the Scruff layer.* Press F7 to return to the **Layers** palette, and then click the item called **Scruff**. It looks like badly rendered sandpaper, but it's actually our fellow's stubbly beard.

18. *Set the blend mode to Multiply.* Click the word **Normal** at the top of the Layers palette to display a list of blend modes. Then choose **Multiply** from the list. Or press the keyboard shortcut Shift+Alt+M (Shift-Option-M on the Mac). Multiply drops out the whites and preserves the dark colors, thus burning the stubble into the cowboy's football flesh, as in Figure 9-10.

19. *Turn on the Hayseed layer.* This time, I want you to click not directly on the **Hayseed** layer but rather in front of it, in the column of 👁 icons. This shows the layer without activating it. The layer in question turns out to be a sliver of barley clasped tightly in the cowboy's teeth (the latter of which are actually seams in a baseball, for what it's worth). Shown in Figure 9-10, the look is inconsistent. The face outline should be in front of

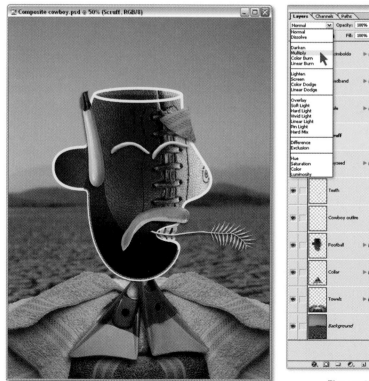

Figure 9-10.

the teeth, hayseed, and scruff. The football flesh needs to be nudged up a couple of notches as well.

20. *Select the Cowboy Outline layer.* You may find it simplest to just click the layer name. But I would be remiss in my duties if I didn't tell you how to do it from the keyboard.

---

You can cycle from one layer to the next by pressing Alt (or Option) with a bracket key. Alt+[ selects down the layer stack; Alt+] selects up. In this case, pressing Alt+[ three times cycles from the Scruff layer down to Cowboy Outline.

---

21. *Bring the Cowboy Outline layer in front of Scruff.* You can accomplish this by choosing **Layer→Arrange→Bring Forward** three times in a row. But isn't life short enough without choosing inconveniently located commands multiple times in a row? Yes it is. Better to learn the shortcut.

---

To move a selected layer up or down the stack, press Ctrl (or ⌘) with a bracket key. Ctrl+[ moves the layer back one notch; Ctrl+] moves it forward. To properly arrange the Cowboy Outline layer, press Ctrl+] three times in a row.

---

22. *Select the Football layer.* Again, you can just click the layer name. But I have another technique for you to try.

---

Press and hold the Ctrl key (⌘ on the Mac) to temporarily invoke the move tool. Then right-click in the image window to display a shortcut menu of layers directly below your cursor. (If you use a one-button mouse on the Mac, press ⌘ and Control and click to see the shortcut menu.) For example, if I Ctrl-right-click the bottom left tip of the hombre's mustache, the shortcut menu lists four layers (see Figure 9-11), all of which contain opaque pixels at the point I clicked. Choose **Football** to go to that layer.

---

23. *Bring the Football layer in front of Hayseed.* Press Ctrl+] (or ⌘-] on the Mac) twice to make it happen. The properly arranged layer elements appear in Figure 9-11.

24. *Click the Collar layer in the Layers palette.* This selects the layer with the flippers on it. Now you might think, "Flippers? On the Collar layer? What in the name of Eric 'Hoss' Cartwright is going on here?" Well, the reason those flippers look more like a dandy kerchief than a rugged collar is that they're upside-down. Let's remedy that, shall we?

25. *Choose the Free Transform command.* Choose **Edit→Free Transform**, or press Ctrl+T (⌘-T), to enter the *free transform mode*, which is where you perform all varieties of transformation—scale, rotate, flip, skew, or distort—in Photoshop.

Figure 9-11.

26. *Rotate the flippers 180 degrees.* Right-click in the image window (or Control-click if you have no right mouse button) to display a shortcut menu of common transformation options, as shown in Figure 9-12 on the next page. Then choose **Rotate 180°** to spin the collar upside-down.

27. *Nudge the flippers upward.* Press Shift+↑ seven times in a row. Each press of Shift+↑ nudges the layer up 10 pixels, so in all, you will have moved it 70 pixels. Or, if you prefer to move the layer manually, you can drag inside the transform boundary. Then press Enter or Return to accept the transformation and exit the free transform mode.

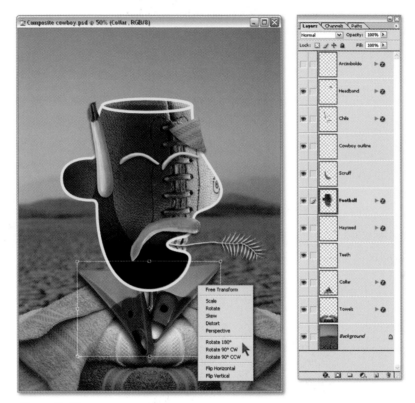

Figure 9-12.

28. *Save your changes thus far.* Choose **File→Save** to update the existing *Composite cowboy.psd* document on disk. Or if you prefer to save versions as you go along—always a splendid idea because it means you can come back and recover elements from your original image later—choose **File→Save As** and give your file a new name. Make sure the **Layers** check box is on and the **Format** option is set to **Photoshop** (*.PSD) or just plain **Photoshop** on the Mac. Photoshop also lets you save layers to the TIFF and PDF formats, but where multilayer compositions are concerned, the native PSD format enjoys wider support among other imaging applications (not to mention, older versions of Photoshop itself).

# Importing and Transforming Layers

Now that you've successfully arranged the layers in the composition, it's time to bring the rest of the elements into the mix, namely the eyes and the hat. In this exercise, you'll introduce portions of the *Cowboy hat.tif* and *Eight ball.tif* images into the composition that you've created so far (and saved in Step 28 of the previous exercise). Then you'll scale and otherwise transform the layers so they fit into place. The result will be a fanciful cowboy face made of objects that you don't often see on cowboys—especially *that* hat.

1. *Bring the eight ball image to front.* Make sure all documents from the previous exercise remain open (namely *Composite cowboy.psd*, *Cowboy hat.tif*, and *Eight ball.tif*). Then click the title bar for *Eight ball.tif*.

2. *Select a central portion of the pool ball.* Use the elliptical marquee tool to select the circular area shown in Figure 9-13. Or, to guarantee your circle exactly matches mine, load the **Circle** mask that I've included in the **Channels** palette. You can do this by Ctrl-clicking (or ⌘-clicking) the alpha channel. Or press Ctrl+Alt+4 (⌘-Option-4).

Figure 9-13.

3. *Drag the eight ball into the cowboy composition.* Press and hold the Ctrl key (⌘ on the Mac) to get the move tool and drag the selection from *Eight ball.tif* into the *Composite cowboy.psd* image window. Drop it near where one of the eyes should go and notice that it lands in an undesirable position, behind the head, as shown in Figure 9-14 on the next page. This is because Photoshop is putting the object in front of the previously selected layer, Collar. Looks like we'll need to rearrange.

4. *Rename the new layer.* Double-click the current layer name, **Layer 1**, to highlight the letters. Then change the name to the more descriptive "Eyes."

5. *Bring the Eyes layer in front of Cowboy Outline.* Either drag the layer up the stack or press Ctrl+] or ⌘-] five times.

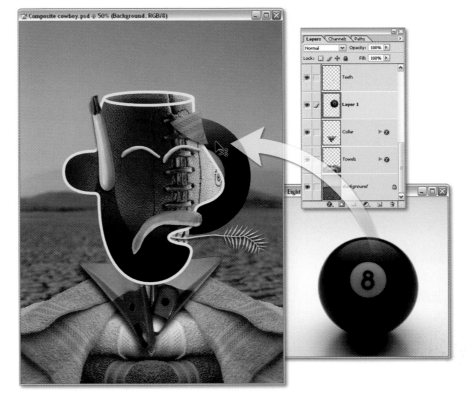

Figure 9-14.

6. *Choose the Auto Contrast command.* The eight ball is dimly lit with respect to its new surroundings. So choose **Image→Adjustments→Auto Contrast** or press Ctrl+Shift+Alt+L (⌘-Shift-Option-L on the Mac) to correct the brightness without upsetting the color balance.

7. *Choose Edit→Free Transform.* The pool ball is too big, so naturally we need to scale it. Press Ctrl+T (⌘-T on the Mac) to enter the free transform mode.

8. ***Scale the layer to 32 percent proportionally.*** You can pull this off two different ways:

- Press the Shift key while dragging a corner handle to constrain the proportions of the ball. Keep an eye on the scale values in the options bar, circled in Figure 9-15. When they reach 32 percent (or thereabouts), release the mouse button, then release Shift.

- Click the 🔗 icon between the W and H scale values in the options bar to constrain the proportions. Enter 32 for either one of them (both values will change), and then press the Enter or Return key to accept the new values.

To accept the scaled image and exit the free transform mode, press the Enter or Return key (yes, again).

Figure 9-15.

All transformations *except* flips and 90- or 180-degree rotations change the number of pixels in a layer. As discussed in the "The Order in Which We Work" section of Lesson 5 (page 136), this means the transformations require interpolation. Photoshop uses the interpolation method selected in the Preferences dialog box. If you notice jagged transitions inside your scaled eight ball *after* pressing Enter or Return for the final time, here's how you fix it: First, undo the transformation. Press Ctrl+K (⌘-K on the Mac) to display the **Preferences** dialog box and change the **Image Interpolation** option to its default setting, **Bicubic**. Then apply the 32 percent scaling.

9. *Move the eye into position.* This eight ball is designed to serve as the left eye (which, to be fair to this fictitious person, is the cowboy's right). Press Ctrl (or ⌘) to get the move tool and drag the eye into the position shown in Figure 9-16.

Figure 9-16.

10. *Set the blend mode to Screen.* Return to the **Layers** palette and change **Normal** to **Screen**. You may also use the keyboard shortcut Shift+Alt+S (Shift-Option-S on the Mac). The opposite of Multiply, Screen drops out the blacks and preserves the light colors, creating the appearance of a glass eyeball against the football background, as in Figure 9-17.

Figure 9-17.

11. *Add a drop shadow.* The eyeball does indeed look glassy now, but it lacks definition. To give it more depth, we'll assign a couple of shadows. First, choose **Drop Shadow** from the ƒ icon at the bottom of the Layers palette. Then enter the settings shown in Figure 9-18 on the next page, by which I mean:

- Set the **Opacity** value to 100 percent.

- Increase the **Distance** value to 10 pixels.

- Change the **Size** value to 25 pixels.

- Make sure **Layer Knocks Out Drop Shadow** is turned on. This prevents the shadows from appearing inside the translucent portions of the eye. (Turn it off if you want to see the difference.)

12. **Add an inner shadow.** Still inside the **Layer Style** dialog box, click the **Inner Shadow** item in the left-hand list. Then enter the same values that you entered in the preceding step, once again as shown in Figure 9-18. (There is no Layer Knocks Out Drop Shadow check box, so don't worry about it.) When you finish, click **OK** to exit the dialog box and accept your changes.

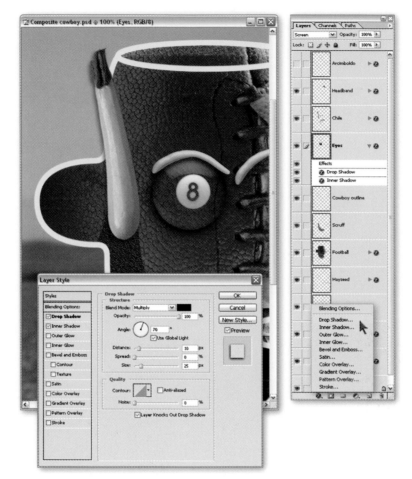

Figure 9-18.

13. **Return to the eight ball image.** The cowboy needs two eyes. You could just duplicate the existing eye, but that's not the best approach. Imagine that the circle with the 8 inside it is the cowboy's iris. Those irises should really point slightly in toward each other so that the cowboy's focus is on the viewer. This means we need to make a new eye. Click the title bar for *Eight ball.tif* to bring the window to the front.

14. **Nudge the selection outline to the right.** The circular selection should still be intact. (If not, press Ctrl+Alt+4 or ⌘-Option-4

to bring it back.) The iris needs to shift left, so the selection should shift right. Press Shift+→ four times to nudge the selection outline 400 pixels.

15. *Drag the eight ball into the cowboy composition.* Press and hold Ctrl (⌘ on the Mac) and drag the selection from *Eight ball.tif* into the *Composite cowboy.psd* image window. Photoshop imports the eight ball in front of the previously active layer, in this case, Eyes. (There's no need to name this new layer because we'll be merging it with the underlying Eyes layer in Step 22.)

16. *Choose Image→Adjustments→Auto Contrast.* Again press Ctrl+Shift+Alt+L (or ⌘-Shift-Option-L) to bump up the brightness of the pool ball.

17. *Repeat the last transformation.* Choose **Edit→Transform→Again** or press Ctrl+Shift+T (⌘-Shift-T) to reapply the last transformation, which in our case happens to be the 32 percent proportional scaling. Just like that, both eyeballs appear the same size, as pictured in Figure 9-19.

Figure 9-19.

18. *Nudge the eye into position.* Although the new eye is sized properly, it's hardly positioned properly. Start by Ctrl-dragging (or ⌘-dragging) the right eye into the horizontal position shown at top in Figure 9-20. Don't worry about the vertical position quite yet; we'll solve that with alignment.

19. *Link the two eye layers.* Click the **Eyes** layer in the **Layers** palette to make it active. Then click to the left of the new layer, **Layer 1**, to display a 🔗 icon (circled in red in Figure 9-20). This links the two layers together.

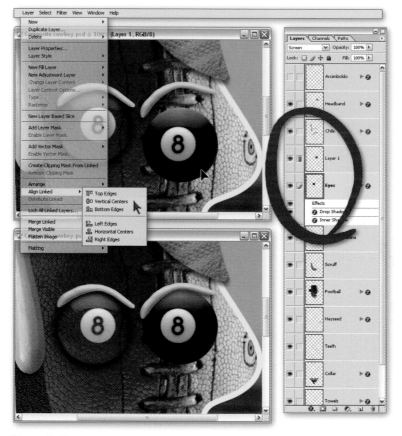

Figure 9-20.

Photoshop does not let you select more than one layer at a time. But you can *link* multiple layers, which is Photoshop's way of binding their relative size and placement. You can move or transform linked layers together. You can also align linked layers, as in the next step.

20. *Choose Layer→Align Linked→Vertical Centers.* Photoshop locks the position of the active layer, Eyes, and moves the linked Layer 1 into alignment with it. The result is two eyes on a level plane, as in the bottom image in Figure 9-20.

21. *Unlink the layers.* Now that the eyes are aligned, there's no need for them to be linked. Besides, the next step won't work properly if they are. So unlink them in either of these two ways:

- Click the 🔗 icon to the left of **Layer 1** to hide the 🔗 and break the link.

- Press Alt (or Option) and click the brush icon (🖌) to the left of **Eyes** to break any and all links with that layer.

22. *Merge the right eye with the left.* Click **Layer 1** in the Layers palette and then choose **Layer→Merge Down** or press Ctrl+E (⌘-E on the Mac). Photoshop combines the two pool ball layers into one. But that's not all it does. As shown in Figure 9-21, the program retains all attributes of the lower layer, including:

- The layer name, Eyes.

- The blend mode, Screen.

- The two layer styles, Drop Shadow and Inner Shadow.

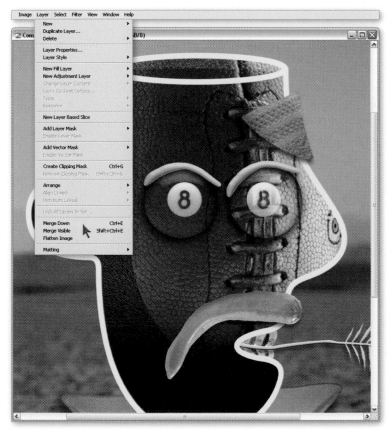

Figure 9-21.

The result shown in Figure 9-21 is amazing. In fact, it may appear more amazing than it really is. The right eye looks as if it's distorting the laces of the football just as a piece of rounded glass really would. But that's an illusion—Photoshop is doing no such thing. The fact that the effect reads like a glass distortion is pure bonus.

The only thing missing is the hat. Let's go get it.

23. ***Bring the cowboy hat image to the front.*** Click the title bar for *Cowboy hat.tif.*

24. ***Select the hat.*** Given that the hat is shot against a white background, this is a pretty easy image to mask. And should you care to test your skills, I wholeheartedly encourage you to make that mask on your own. But in the name of expediency, it is already in the oven. Ctrl- or ⌘-click the **Hat Outline** mask included in the **Channels** palette, as shown in Figure 9-22. Or press Ctrl+Alt+4 (⌘-Option-4 on the Mac).

Figure 9-22.

An interesting thing to note: I did not create this particular mask. The image vendor, PhotoSpin, included this channel with the image. PhotoSpin provides alpha channels and path outlines with many of its "object" photographs, as do many other stock companies.

25. *Drag the hat into the cowboy composition.* Press and hold the Ctrl or ⌘ key and drag the selection from *Cowboy hat.tif* into the *Composite cowboy.psd* image window. Drop the hat near the top of the head. Naturally, it comes in all wrong. The hat is too low on the head, too far down the stack, and *way* too big, as in Figure 9-23. Such are the ways of the layered composition, and the reasons for the remaining steps.

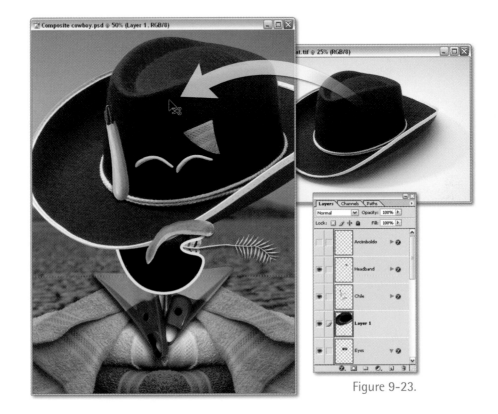

Figure 9-23.

26. *Rename the new layer.* Double-click the current layer name (as always, **Layer 1**) and change its name to "Hat."

27. *Bring the hat to the front of the composition.* Choose **Layer→Arrange→Bring to Front** or press Ctrl+Shift+] (⌘-Shift-] on the Mac). The layer pops to the top of the stack, where it rightly belongs.

28. *Lower the Opacity value to 50 percent.* Assuming a selection tool is active, press the 5 key.

---

We'll want the final hat to be fully opaque. So why lower its opacity? By making the hat translucent in the short term, you can more easily align it with elements underneath. Note that it's essential that you perform this step now; you cannot modify the opacity or blend mode when inside the free transform mode.

---

29. ***Choose Edit→Free Transform.*** Or press Ctrl+T (⌘-T).

30. ***Scale and rotate the layer.*** Circled in red in Figure 9-24, the ideal settings are as follows:

- Scale the hat proportionally to 62 percent, either by Shift-dragging a corner handle or by clicking the 🔒 icon between the W and H values in the options bar and changing either **W** or **H** to 62.

- Move the cursor outside the transform boundary and drag to rotate the hat until the rotate value in the options bar (just right of H) reads 3.5 degrees. Or just enter 3.5 into the rotate option box.

- Drag inside the boundary to move the hat as needed.

Don't press Enter or Return yet—we want to remain in the free transform mode for the next step.

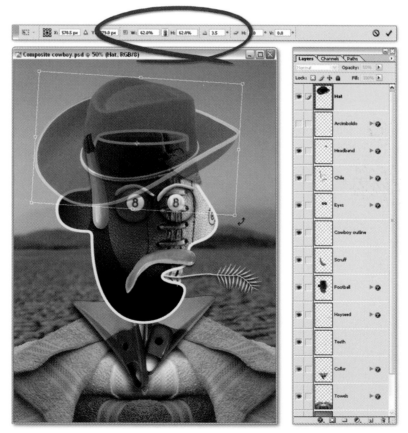

Figure 9-24.

31. *Distort the hat.* The one kind of transformation you can't perform entirely numerically is distortion. Press the Ctrl key (⌘ on the Mac) and drag a corner handle. The handle moves independently of the other handles, stretching the hat in that one direction. I ended up Ctrl-dragging all four corner handles to taper the top of the hat as shown in Figure 9-25.

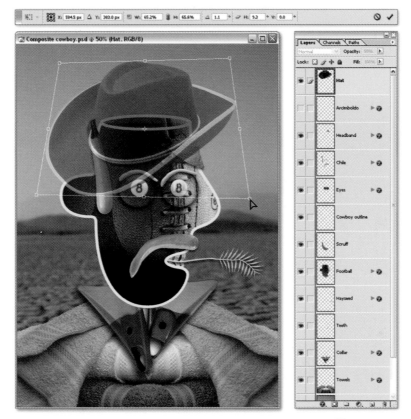

Figure 9-25.

32. *Accept the transformation.* Click the check mark in the options bar. Or press the Enter or Return key. Photoshop applies the various transformations and exits the free transform mode.

PEARL OF WISDOM

Notice that we applied several operations inside one free transform session. This is how you should work when creating your own projects as well. Each session rewrites the pixels in the image, so each is potentially destructive. By applying all changes inside a single session, you rewrite pixels just once, minimizing the damage caused by multiple interpolations.

33. *Restore the opacity to 100 percent.* Press the 0 key (that's zero, not O) or change the **Opacity** value in the Layers palette.

Everything looks pretty good. But in my opinion, the Hat and Cowboy Outline layers are just begging for drop shadows. If you don't share that opinion, skip ahead to the next exercise, "Masks, Knockouts, and Luminance Blending," on page 306. But then you'll miss yet another new technique. For rather than create the shadows from scratch, as you did back in Step 11 (see page 295), we'll repurpose them from other layers.

34. *Copy the Collar layer's drop shadow.* Right-click (or Control-click) on the **Collar** layer in the Layers palette and choose **Copy Layer Style**, as shown in Figure 9-26.

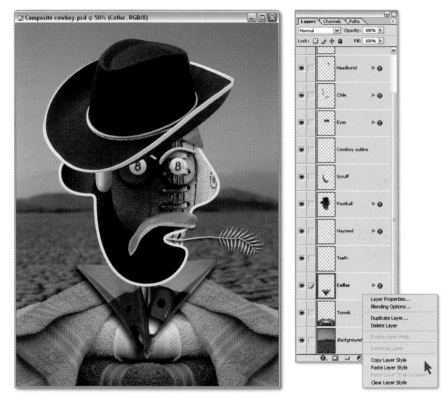

Figure 9-26.

35. *Link the Hat and Cowboy Outline layers.* Click the **Hat** layer to make it active. Then click in the empty box to the left of the **Cowboy Outline** layer to link it to the hat.

36. *Paste the drop shadow on the linked layers.* Right-click the **Hat** layer and choose **Paste Layer Style to Linked**. Both the cowboy hat and the yellow outline receive drop shadows that exactly match the one applied to the flippers, as you can see in Figure 9-27 on the facing page.

37. *Modify the Cowboy Outline drop shadow.* Pasting a layer style can affect multiple linked layers at a time, but editing a layer style cannot. Double-click the **Drop Shadow** item under the Cowboy Outline layer in the Layers palette. This displays the **Layer Style** dialog box. Change the **Opacity** value to 35 percent. Then change both **Distance** and **Size** to 5 pixels. Click the **OK** button to accept your changes. Only the Cowboy Outline layer is affected, as shown in Figure 9-28 on the next page.

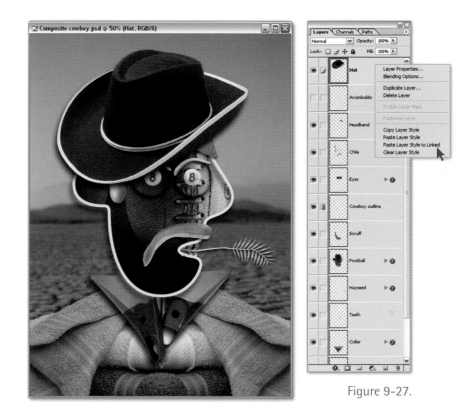

Figure 9-27.

38. *Turn on the Arcimboldo layer.* Click the eyeball in front of the one hidden layer to display a line of frivolous text I drew by hand with a Wacom tablet. Why hand-drawn? Well, Pilgrim, I reckon I jes' like the way it looks.

39. *Save your composition.* So ends another jam-packed exercise. Choose **File→Save** to update the file on disk or choose **File→ Save As** to save an independent version.

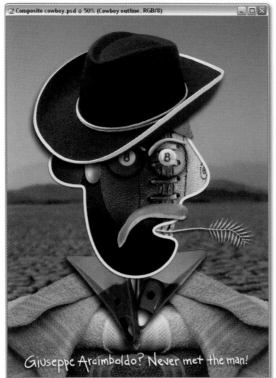

Figure 9-28.

## Masks, Knockouts, and Luminance Blending

Another advantage to layers is that they permit you to blend multiple images while keeping them entirely independent of each other. For example, changing the mode setting or Opacity value in the Layers palette blends the active layer with all layers below it. Such operations are said to be *parametric* because they rely on numerical entries and mathematical parameters that Photoshop calculates and applies on the fly. The benefits of parametric effects are threefold:

- You can't make a mistake. If you select a blend mode and you don't like it, no big deal, just choose another one. This gives you unlimited opportunities to experiment.

- Parametric data is forever editable. As long as you save the composition with all layers intact, you can modify those layers to your heart's content days, months, and years into the future.

- Thanks to their mathematical nature, parametric effects take less time to apply and consume less memory and disk space than traditional pixel-level modifications. In other words, parametric effects are as fast as they are flexible.

Parametric effects aren't the only way to blend layers. You can also apply one of three varieties of layer-specific masks:

- A *layer mask* creates holes in a layer without erasing pixels.

- A *clipping mask* uses the boundaries of the active layer to crop the contents of one or more layers above it.

- A *knockout* uses the contents of the active layer to cut holes in the layers below it.

Plus, you can temporarily drop out luminosity levels and a whole lot more. The only downside to Photoshop's parametric effects and layer-specific masks is that you may be unacquainted with them. Fortunately, that's something we'll remedy in this very exercise, as we use these wonderful functions to create the latest installment in the exciting Dinosaur Planet saga (begun in Lesson 7).

1. *Open a layered composition.* This time, there's just one file to open, *The escape.psd*, which you'll find in the *Lesson 09* folder inside *Lesson Files-PScs 1on1.* Initially, the image looks like nothing more than a snapshot of South Dakota's breathtaking Badlands (see Figure 9-29), which I shot with an Olympus C-3030. But there's much more to it.

Figure 9-29.

Figure 9-30.

Figure 9-31.

2. *Select the Badlands layer in the Layers palette.* Go to the **Layers** palette and make sure the **Badlands** layer is active, as in Figure 9-30. Note that there are several other layers and folders of layers (called *layer sets*), most of which are currently hidden. We'll turn these layers on in future steps.

3. *Scoot the layer down 200 pixels.* You can do this in a couple of ways:

   • Press Shift+↓ 20 times in a row. Sounds ridiculous, but it's pretty routine.

   • Press Ctrl+T (or ⌘-T) to enter the free transform mode. Then click the triangle in the left half of the options bar (circled in Figure 9-31) to turn on relative positioning. Change the **Y** value to 200 pixels and press the Enter or Return key.

   This reveals 200 pixels of sky from the Thin Sky layer behind Badlands. The sky is dramatic, but the transition between the two layers leaves something to be desired, so let's blend them together with a layer mask.

4. *Load the Planet Arc mask as a selection.* Go to the **Channels** palette and Ctrl- or ⌘-click the **Planet Arc** channel. Or just press Ctrl+Alt+4 (⌘-Option-4 on the Mac). A curved selection appears along the horizon of our emerging world.

5. *Click the layer mask icon.* Return to the **Layers** palette and click the tiny ▢ icon at the bottom, indicated by the arrow cursor in Figure 9-32. This converts the selection to a layer mask, creating a smoother transition between Earth and sky.

PEARL OF WISDOM

The mask appears as a thumbnail in the Layers palette, identical to how it appears in the Channels palette. In fact, for all intents and purposes, you just duplicated the mask from one location to another. Where the mask is white, the layer is opaque; where the mask is black, the layer is transparent.

6. *Click the brush tool in the toolbox.* The problem with the curved mask is that it scalps away too much of the rocky cliffs in the central and right-hand portions of the image. But because it's a mask, you can paint the cliffs back. Press B to select the brush tool and then press D to make the foreground color white, the default setting when working in a mask.

7. *Paint inside the mask.* Select a small, hard brush, about 20 pixels in diameter, and paint along the rim of the mountaintops in the image window. Assuming that the layer mask is active (as it should be), you'll reveal the tops of the ridges.

   - If you reveal too much of a ridge, press the X key to switch the foreground color to black and paint inside the image window to erase pixels.

   - If you erase too much, press X again to restore white as the foreground color and then paint.

   - You don't have to limit yourself to brush work. You can select an area with the lasso tool and fill it with white to reveal an area or black to erase it.

Keep painting until you achieve more or less the effect pictured in Figure 9-33. And don't fret too much if you end up with a few stray sky pixels from the Badlands layer. We'll cover them up in a few moments. In other words, be as precise as you want to be.

Figure 9-32.

Figure 9-33.

Masks, Knockouts, and Luminance Blending **309**

If you find yourself adding white or black brushstrokes to your image, it's because you accidentally activated the image instead of the mask. (Inspect the icon to the right of the 👁 for the Badlands layer. A ✏ indicates that the image is active, which is not what we want. A ▢ icon tells you that the mask is active and all is well.) If you encounter this problem, undo any damage and then click the black-and-white layer mask thumbnail directly to the left of the word **Badlands** in the Layers palette. This returns Photoshop's attention to the layer mask, as the ▢ makes clear.

---

Alternatively, you can switch between the image and layer mask from the keyboard. Press Ctrl+\ (⌘-\ on the Mac) to activate the layer mask. Press Ctrl+~ (⌘-~) to switch back to the image. The ▢ and ✏ icons monitor your status.

---

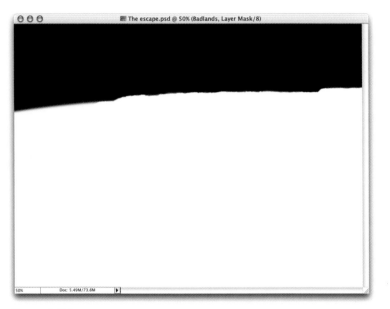

The escape.psd @ 50% (Badlands, Layer Mask/8)

50%    Doc: 5.49M/73.6M

Figure 9-34.

8. *View the mask independently of the image.* To see the layer mask by itself, press the Alt key (Option on the Mac) and click the black-and-white layer mask thumbnail in the Layers palette. You should see a mask like the one pictured in Figure 9-34. Paint or otherwise modify it if you like. To return to the composite image, Alt-click the mask thumbnail again.

---

To view the mask as a rubylith overlay—thus permitting you to see both mask and image—press the backslash key, \. To hide the image and view just the mask, press the tilde key, ~. To display the image, press ~ again. To hide the mask, press \. Throughout, the layer mask remains active.

---

9. **Click the Gradient layer in the Layers palette.** This displays a previously hidden layer that contains a combination of black and brown gradient patterns.

10. *Change the blend mode and opacity.* Choose **Multiply** from the **Layers** palette menu. (You can also use the shortcut Shift+Alt+M or Shift-Option-M, but only *after* you switch from the brush tool to a selection tool.) Photoshop burns in the

blacks and browns and drops out the whites, as shown in Figure 9-35. To temper the effect a little, reduce the **Opacity** value to 80 percent.

11. *Choose Layer→Create Clipping Mask.* This tells Photoshop to clip the Gradient layer to the boundaries of the layer below it, Badlands. As a result, the gradient fits entirely inside the horizon you established in Step 7 (see Figure 9-36). In the Layers palette, the Gradient layer appears inset; the Badlands layer appears underlined to show that it's the base of the clipping mask.

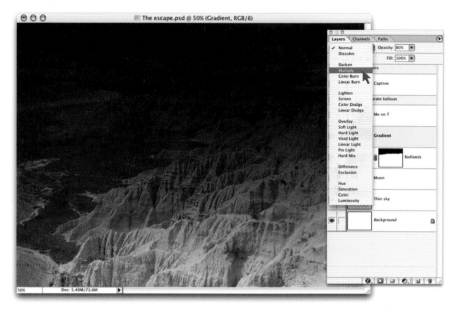

You can use two shortcuts when creating a clipping mask. Press Ctrl+G (or ⌘-G) to invoke the **Create Clipping Mask** command. (Clipping masks used to be called clipping *groups*, hence the G key.) Or press Alt (or Option) and click the horizontal line between the Gradient and Badlands layers in the Layers palette. To release a layer from a clipping mask, press Ctrl+Shift+G (⌘-Shift-G).

Figure 9-35.

Figure 9-36.

12. ***Click the Moon layer in the Layers palette.*** The moon hovers bright and enormous over the horizon, as pictured in Figure 9-37. How did it get so big? Because it's actually the dread Dinosaur Planet in disguise! (Don't be frightened; it's just an exercise.)

Figure 9-37.

13. ***Set the blend mode to Screen.*** Assuming a selection tool is active, you can press Shift+Alt+S (or Shift-Option-S). As I mentioned earlier, Screen drops out the blacks and preserves the light colors. In this case, however, it seems to add brightness even in the black areas (see Figure 9-38).

Figure 9-38.

Well, not quite. Admittedly, the area behind the moon is quite dark, but it isn't altogether black. And unless it's absolutely pitch black, Screen makes it brighter. That means you'll have to drop out the dark colors manually using luminance blending.

14. *Double-click the Moon thumbnail in the Layers palette.* Or right-click the **Moon** layer and choose **Blending Options**. Photoshop displays the Blending Options panel of the **Layer Style** dialog box, which contains a vast array of parametric effect options.

15. *Drag the black This Layer slider triangle.* Make sure the **Preview** check box is on so you can see the results of your changes. Then turn your attention to the two slider bars near the bottom of the dialog box:

    - The first slider bar, **This Layer**, lets you drop out the darkest or lightest colors in a layer.

    - The second slider, **Underlying Layer**, causes the darkest or lightest colors from all layers below to shine through the active layer. (The option name should really be plural, but now I'm nitpicking.)

Drag the black triangle associated with **This Layer** to the right until the space around the moon turns invisible, as shown in Figure 9-39. I find this happens when the first numerical value reads 50, meaning that any color with a luminosity level of 50 or darker is hidden.

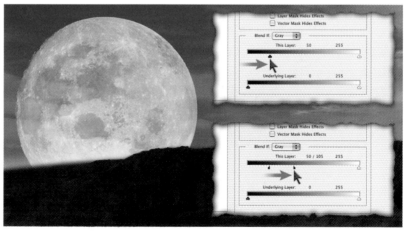

16. *Add some fuzziness.* The problem with the current solution is that it results in a very abrupt transition between visible and invisible pixels. (Zoom in on the left side of the

Figure 9-39.

moon to see what I mean.) To soften the drop off, you need to add some "fuzziness." Press the Alt key (Option on the Mac) and drag the right side of the black triangle to split the triangle in half. Then drag to the right until the first **This Layer** values read 50/105, as shown in Figure 9-39.

Here's what the 50/105 values mean:

- Any color with a level of 50 or darker is invisible.

- Any color with a level of 105 or lighter is visible.

- The colors with luminosity levels between 105 and 50 taper gradually from visible to invisible, respectively. This is the fuzziness range.

The effect looks slick, but not very realistic. The moon appears to be sitting on the sky instead of sunken into it. Part of the problem is that the moon is in front of the clouds. Fortunately, the Underlying Layer slider lets us push the clouds forward.

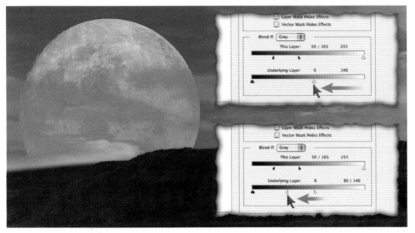

Figure 9-40.

17. *Drag the white Underlying Layer slider triangle.* Drag the white triangle to the left until the second value reads 140, when about half the clouds start to obscure the moon. This uncovers any color with a luminosity level of 140 or lighter.

18. *Again, add some fuzziness.* This time, we have some wicked jagged edges. Press Alt (or Option) and drag the left side of the white triangle until the value reads 80/140. The clouds fade in and out of visibility, blending smoothly with the moon, as shown in Figure 9-40.

19. *Reduce the opacity to 40 percent.* The **Opacity** value at the top of the dialog box is identical to the one in the Layers palette. Click **OK** to accept your changes. The resulting moon appears in Figure 9-41.

20. *Click the Me on T layer in the Layers palette.* This layer sports an off-center picture of me with one of Rapid City's world-famous poorly rendered plaster dinosaurs. This one is supposed to be a tyrannosaur! The

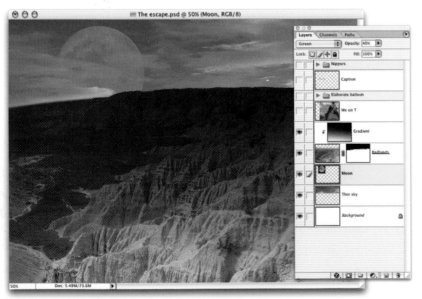

Figure 9-41.

plaster T. Rex really exists and I am really sitting on it. The only change I made to the image was to add the red mittens. The poor thing looked kind of chilly.

21. *Load the Dino Outline path as a selection.* Go to the **Paths** palette. Press Ctrl (or ⌘) and click the **Dino Outline** path to convert it to the selection outline shown in Figure 9-42.

22. *Click the layer mask icon.* Press F7 and click the ⬚ icon at the bottom of the **Layers** palette. This converts the path selection to a layer mask, eliminating my previous background and placing me squarely in the action.

23. *Click the Nippers folder in the Layers palette.* This displays a set of layers that include two little dinosaurs nipping at my heels, as in Figure 9-43.

Figure 9-42.

Figure 9-43.

The only thing missing in this action-packed composition is dialog. After all, you'd think a guy sitting on one dinosaur and running away from others would have something to say. If you'd prefer that I remain mute, you have my blessing to move on to the next exercise, "Working with Layer Comps," which begins on page 319. If you want to stayed tuned for the final dramatic steps, not to mention learn a thing or two about knockouts, keep reading.

24. ***Click the Elaborate Balloon folder, then click Caption.*** The Elaborate Balloon set contains the talk balloon as well as several layers of patriotic falderal required to frame the commanding urgency of the caption. The Caption layer contains more of my hand-drawn text (which appeals to the dinosaur I'm riding to get a move on). Everything we're about to do works just as well with the sort of live typeset text that we discuss in the next lesson; the hand-drawn text just happens to better suit my graphic novel composition.

As shown in Figure 9-44, the text is currently green. But that's just a placeholder color. I ultimately want the letters to cut holes through all the layers in the Elaborate Balloon set and reveal the dark shadows of the Badlands background. I can approach this vexing conundrum in one of two ways:

- Layer masks can be applied to individual layers or entire sets of layers. So I could create a mask for the Elaborate Balloon set in which the text was black (invisible) and the area around the text white (visible). But it would take extra work and it might limit my options in the future.

- I could establish the Caption layer as a knockout, thereby cutting holes in the layers in back of it. Not much work + very flexible = preferred solution.

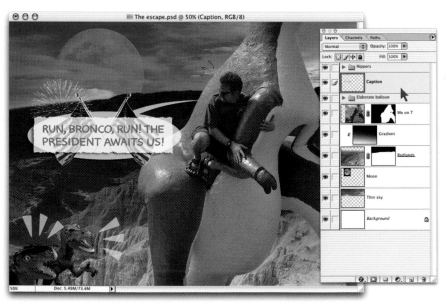

Figure 9-44.

The big question when creating a knockout is, how deep does it drill? Knockouts are either "deep," going all the way to the **Background** layer, or "shallow," ending at the base layer of a group. We just want to burrow through the Elaborate Balloon layers, so a group is needed. And the best kind of group for this purpose is another layer set.

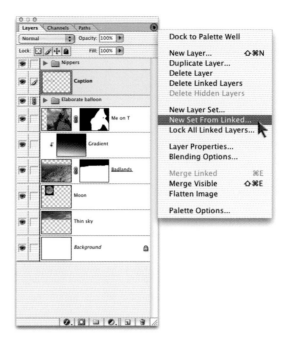

25. *Link the Caption layer and Elaborate Balloon set.* To create a set and put layers inside it in one operation, you have to first link the layers. With the Captions layer active, click the 🖉 icon in front of the Elaborate Balloon folder to bind layer and set together.

26. *Place the linked layers inside a new layer set.* Click the ⊙ arrow at the top of the Layers palette and choose **New Set From Linked**, as in Figure 9-45. (Surprisingly, there is no shortcut for this; you have to choose the command.) Name the new set "Knockout Text" and click **OK**.

27. *Twirl open the new layer set.* Click the ▶ in front of the Knockout Text set to reveal its contents.

28. *Double-click the Caption layer thumbnail.* Photoshop once again displays the always fascinating **Blending Options** panel of the **Layer Style** dialog box.

29. *Choose Shallow from the Knockout pop-up menu.* The **Knockout** option appears circled in red in Figure 9-46. Contrary to what you might reasonably expect, this option has no immediate effect. Instead, it merely establishes the layer as a potential knockout. To put the knockout in play, see the next step.

30. *Reduce the fill opacity to 0 percent.* Identical to the Fill value in the Layers palette, Fill Opacity changes the translucency of pixels in a layer independently of drop shadows and other styles. (See Lesson 11 for more info.) But it also has a symbiotic relationship with the Knockout option.

Figure 9-45.

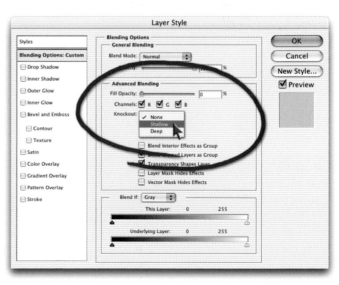

Figure 9-46.

Drag the **Fill Opacity** slider triangle and watch the text fade into the background art. At 0 percent, all you see is background.

31. *Move the Me on T layer into the set.* If you look closely at the text, you'll see that the word "US!" is bisected by the green back of the plaster dinosaur. To make the text bore through the dinosaur as well, just move it into the set. In the **Layers** palette, drag the **Me on T** layer onto the **Knockout Text** folder icon (see Figure 9-47). When you release the mouse button, Photoshop places Me on T at the back of the set and knocks the letterforms out of the dino's hip, just as it should be.

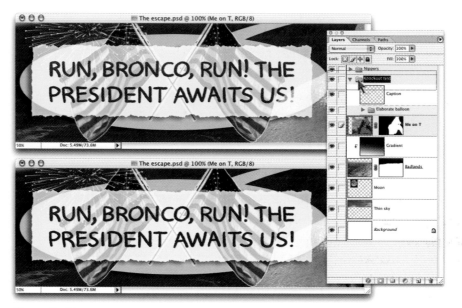

Figure 9-47.

32. *Save your composition.* Choose **File→Save** to update the file on disk. After all, why bother with File→Save As when everything is either a mask or a parametric effect?

The beauty of this exercise is that every single one of the changes you've made is reversible. You can delete the layer masks that you added in Steps 5 and 22, ungroup the clipping mask from Step 11, modify the blending options applied in Steps 15 through 19, and bust up the knockout from Step 29. And the reason the composition is so exceedingly, wonderfully, downright obscenely flexible is because you never changed a single pixel on any of the core layers. If only everything in Photoshop were this flexible—well, the world would be a happier place, wouldn't it?

# Working with Layer Comps

As you increase the complexity of your layered documents, you'll find yourself experimenting with different compositional arrangements. What if you moved this layer over here? What if that layer were hidden? What if you gave this other layer a drop shadow? Sometimes the answer is obvious the moment you give it a try. Other times, the answer eludes you until several steps or even sessions later.

Photoshop CS's new Layer Comps palette lets you save the current state of a document before you venture down an unclear road. As long as you don't delete or merge any of the layers in the saved *layer comp*, you can restore the saved state in its entirety at a later point in time. Layer Comp states are actually saved as part of the PSD file on disk, just like layers, channels, paths, and other specialized data.

To learn which layer attributes the Layer Comps palette can track, see the upcoming sidebar "What Layer Comps Can and Can't Save." To learn how to use layer comps, immerse yourself in the following steps.

1. *Open a layered composition.* Open the next image in our gripping drama, *The capture.psd*, included in  the *Lesson 09* folder inside *Lesson Files-PScs 1on1*. As before, we see the Badlands photo and nothing more. But this time we won't have to build up the layers manually. The work was all done for us ahead of time and saved as comps.

2. *Combine the Layer Comps palette with History.* By default, the Layer Comps tab resides in the docking well on the right side of the options bar. (If it's not there, choose **Window→Layer Comps** to bring it up.) The palette is too useful to be hidden away. So drag the **Layer Comps** tab from the well and drop it into the **History** palette cluster, as shown in Figure 9-48.

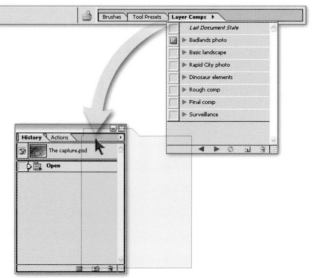

Figure 9-48.

3. *Click in front of a comp name to switch to it.* Clicking in the column on the left side of the Layer Comps palette displays a tiny manuscript icon and shows the layers and effects saved with the corresponding comp. In Figure 9-49, I clicked in front of the third comp, **Rapid City Photo**. Notice that the photo is centered and fully visible. Click in front of **Dinosaur Elements** to see the photo offset and masked. This is the amazing power of layer comps.

Figure 9-49.

4. *Examine a layer comp's settings.* Any comp that has a triangle next to it includes a description. To view the description, click the ► to twirl open the comp, or double-click to the right of the comp name (not directly on the name) to display the **Layer Comp Options** dialog box shown in Figure 9-50. The dialog box lets you view the complete description, as well as which

Figure 9-50.

As shown in the dialog box on the right, a layer comp can save any of the following three attributes:

- **Visibility:** This includes which layers and layer masks are turned on and off. (You turn a mask off and on by Shift-clicking its thumbnail in the Layers palette.)

- **Position:** Remarkably, a layer comp can track the horizontal and vertical position of a layered object. This means you can move layers around between saved comps.

- **Appearance (Layer Style):** Photoshop saves the Opacity setting and blend mode assigned to each layer, as well as knockouts, luminance blending, drop shadows, and all other parametric effects. This one check box is worth the price of admission.

That's all very well and good, but three attributes represents a fairly small collection of saved attributes, especially when you consider all the things that the Layer Comps palette *can't* track, as follows:

- **Arrangement:** If you move a layer up or down the stack, it changes inside all saved comps. This goes for moving layers into or out of sets as well. Frankly, I regard these oversights as enormous gaffs, but it is the way it is.

- **Clipping masks:** Group a layer with the layer below it, and it'll be grouped inside all saved comps. Again, a big oversight; again, nothing we can do.

- **Scale and orientation:** Transformations are pixel-level modifications. So if you scale or rotate a layer, it changes inside all comps.

- **Pixel-level changes:** The same goes for cropping, image size, brushstrokes, color adjustments, and filters.

- **Adjustment layer settings:** As you'll see in Lesson 11, "Layer Styles and Adjustments," adjustment layers are parametric versions of Levels, Curves, and other common adjustment commands. Rather bizarrely, layer comps can't track their settings. Maybe next upgrade.

- **Additions:** If you add a layer, all existing layer comps treat it as off unless otherwise instructed.

- **Deletions:** If you delete a layer, merge a couple of layers, or delete a set, the Layer Comps palette fills with yellow ⚠ icons. In all likelihood, the comps will work as well as can be expected. But you'll have to update the comps (see Step 8 on page 326) to make the warning icons go away.

layer attributes are saved with the comp. To learn more about the check boxes, read the sidebar "What Layer Comps Can and Can't Save." When you're through poking around, press the Esc key to exit the dialog box.

5. ***Click the arrow buttons to cycle between comps.*** The small ◄ and ► buttons at the bottom of the Layer Comps palette let you switch to the previous or next saved state. I clicked the ► button a few times to advance to the final comp, **Surveillance**. Shown in Figure 9-51, this comp features a few layers that we haven't seen before. If the comp is to be believed, it would seem my movements are being monitored.

6. ***Go to the Layers palette.*** If you're ever curious to see how a comp was created, just refer to the **Layers** palette. There you'll find several new layers and sets, some of which are turned on to create the green TV effect. Feel free to explore the layers as you see fit.

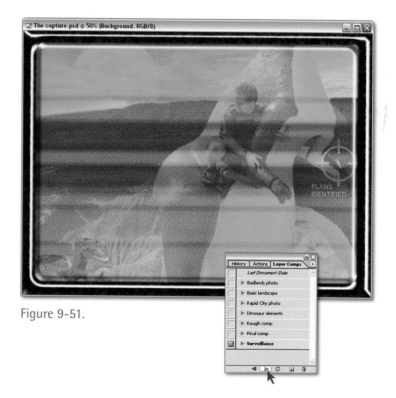

Figure 9-51.

7. *Delete the Plans Identified layer.* Click on the layer called **Plans Identified**. This is an editable text layer (not hand-drawn) that labels the target around the rolled-up paper so deftly hidden in Bronco the dinosaur's mitten, as seen in Figure 9-52 below. The idea is fine, but I ultimately decided that it ruins the subtlety of the piece. (Yes, the piece has subtlety—loads of it.) To delete the layer, click the trash can icon at the bottom of the Layers palette. Then click **Yes** to confirm the deletion.

---

To bypass the confirmation and delete the layer without any guff from Photoshop, press the Alt key (Option on the Mac) when clicking the trash can.

---

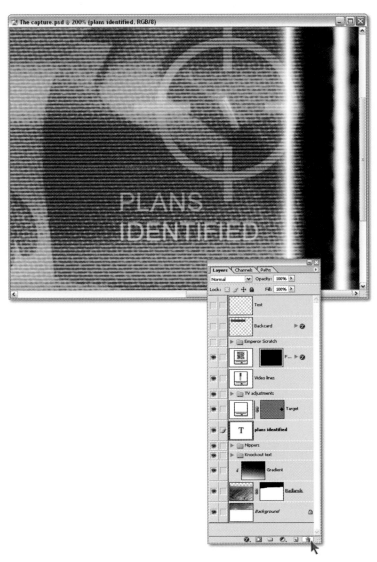

Figure 9-52.

Deleting the Plans Identified layer upsets two layer comps, Surveillance and Rough Comp, which are now marked with yellow ⚠ warning icons. Although only one of the comps actually displayed the layer, both comps were created or updated since the Plans layer was introduced. Therefore, they both knew of the layer's existence; the other comps did not. To get rid of the ⚠ icons, you must update the comps as explained in the next step.

8. *Update the affected layer comps.* You update the two comps in slightly different ways:

   • Because the Surveillance comp represents the current state, you don't need to reload it. Just click the word **Surveillance** in the **Layer Comps** palette to make sure it's active. Then click the ↺ update icon at the bottom of the palette, identified by the cursor in Figure 9-53.

   • To update **Rough Comp**, first click to the left of it to restore the comp's layer settings. (It's very important that you load the comp before updating it so you don't wreck it.) Then click the ↺ icon as before.

Figure 9-53.

9. *Restore the Surveillance comp.* Now we'll create our own comp by basing it on the last comp, **Surveillance**. Click in front of the comp name to restore its layer settings.

10. *Turn on the three hidden layer items.* Go to the **Layers** palette and turn on the hidden set, **Emperor Scratch**, as well as the top two layers, **Text** and **Backcard**. (The quickest way to display all three 👁s is to click in the left column in front of Emperor Scratch and drag up.) The result is the malevolent duckbill skeleton from Lesson 7—augmented with a spiffy row

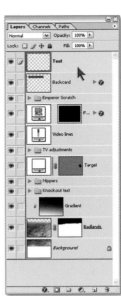

of suspiciously unduckbillish carnivore teeth—along with a fiendish new caption, all of which appear in Figure 9-54. Sounds like he's talking about me, but he's really after Bronco. They're stepbrothers or something, I forget.

Figure 9-54.

11. *Create a new layer comp.* Click the 🖾 icon at the bottom of the **Layer Comps** palette to display the New Layer Comp dialog box. Name the comp "The Menacing Observer" and turn on all three check boxes. If you want to annotate the comp, enter a comment like the one shown in Figure 9-55. Click the **OK** button to add the new state to the Layer Comps palette.

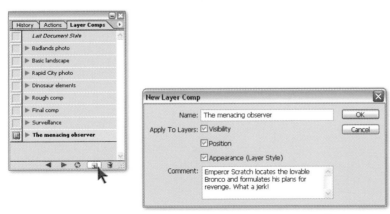

Figure 9-55.

Badlands photo

Rough comp

The menacing observer

Figure 9-56.

12. *Cycle through the comps as desired.* In Figure 9-56, we see details from three of the eight comps. Given that these are views of a single file, and that every one of them relies on the very same collection of 27 layers and 5 sets, it's amazing just how unique each comp is.

13. *Save your changes.* Because we deleted a layer (Step 7, page 323), I recommend you choose **File→ Save As**. Give the image a new name, but keep it in the Photoshop (PSD) format. Photoshop saves all layers and comps with the file. The comp that was active when you saved the file will be in effect the next time you open it.

The results of your toils are eight independent pieces of artwork saved inside one layered composition. This file consumes much less room on disk than it would if each comp was saved as a separate PSD file. And as an added convenience, you can edit the various comps together inside a single file.

# WHAT DID YOU LEARN?

Match the key concept in the numbered list below with the letter
of the phrase that best describes it. Answers appear upside-down
at the bottom of the page.

## Key Concepts

1. Flat
2. Layered composition
3. Stacking order
4. Free Transform
5. Photoshop (PSD) format
6. Merge Down
7. Layer mask
8. Layer set
9. Clipping mask
10. Luminance blending
11. Knockout
12. Layer comp

## Descriptions

A. The name given to a pair of slider bars in the Layer Style dialog box that let you hide or reveal colors based on their luminosity levels.

B. The state of a layered composition at a certain point in time, replete with visibility, vertical and horizontal positioning, blending options, and layer styles.

C. A collection of layers that appears as a small folder icon in the Layers palette.

D. The arrangement of layers in a composition, from front to back, which you can adjust by pressing Ctrl or ⌘ with the bracket keys, [ and ].

E. The ideal file format for saving all layers, masks, and parametric effects in a layered composition.

F. The original single-layer state of a digital photograph or scanned image.

G. An option that uses the contents of the active layer to cut holes in the layers below it.

H. When working with this function, painting with black temporarily erases the pixels on a layer; painting with white makes the pixels visible again.

I. A means for cropping the contents of a group of layers to the boundaries of a layer below them.

J. Choose this command to combine the contents of the active layer with the layer below it.

K. The one command that enables you to scale, rotate, flip, skew, or distort one or more linked layers.

L. A Photoshop document that contains two or more images on independent layers.

## Answers

1F, 2L, 3D, 4K, 5E, 6J, 7H, 8C, 9I, 10A, 11G, 12B

LESSON

10

# TEXT AND SHAPES

**AS YOU'VE NO** doubt discerned by now, Photoshop's primary mission is to correct and manipulate digital photographs and scanned artwork. (If this comes as a shock, I'm afraid you're going to have to go back and re-read *the entire book!*) But there are two exceptions. The culprits are text and shapes, two features that have nothing whatsoever to do with correcting or manipulating digital photographs, scanned artwork, or pixels in general.

Where text and shapes are concerned, Photoshop is more illustration program than image editor. You can create single lines of type or set type inside columns. You can edit typos and check spelling. You have access to all varieties of formatting attributes, from those as common as typeface to those as obscure as fractional character widths. You can even attach type to a path. In addition to type, you can augment your designs with rectangles, polygons, and custom predrawn symbols—the kinds of geometric shapes that you take for granted in a drawing program but rarely see in an image editor.

All this may seem like overkill, the sort of off-topic falderal that tends to burden every piece of consumer software these days. But while you may not need text and shapes for *all* your work, they're incredibly useful on those occasions when you do. Whether you're looking to prepare a bit of specialty type, mock up a commercial message (see Figure 10-1), or design a Web page, Photoshop's text and shape functions are precisely the tools you need.

Figure 10-1.

329

# ABOUT THIS LESSON

## Project Files

Before beginning the exercises, make sure that you've installed the lesson files from the CD, as explained in Step 5 on page xv the Preface. This should result in a folder called *Lesson Files-PScs 1on1* on your desktop. We'll be working with the files inside the *Lesson 10* subfolder.

In this lesson, I show you how to use Photoshop's text and shape tools, as well as ways to edit text and shapes by applying formatting attributes and transformations. You'll learn how to:

- Create a text layer and modify its appearance using formatting attributes, layer styles, and filters . . . . . . . . . . . . . . . page 332

- Adjust common formatting attributes using mouse clicks and keyboard shortcuts . . . . . page 346

- Draw vector-based shapes, convert text to shapes, and repeat a shape using series duplication . . . . . page 351

- Force text to follow the contours of a path and warp text by bending and distorting it . . . . . . . . page 364

## Video Lesson 10: Vector-Based Objects

Text and shapes are treated as special kinds of layers in Photoshop. As long as these layers remain intact, you can edit them to your heart's content. And because they're vector-based layers, you can scale or otherwise transform them without degrading their quality in the slightest.

To learn more about the incredible world of scalable vector art inside Photoshop, watch the tenth video lesson on the CD. Insert the CD, click the **Start Training** button, click the Set **4** button in the top-right corner of your screen, and then select **10, Vector-Based Objects** from the Lessons list. Lasting a mere 7 minutes and 54 seconds, this video introduces you to the following tools and shortcuts:

| Tool or operation | Windows shortcut | Macintosh shortcut |
|---|---|---|
| Type tool | T | T |
| Accept changes to a text layer | Enter on keypad (or Ctrl+Enter) | Enter on keypad (or ⌘-Return) |
| Reject changes to a text layer | Esc | Esc |
| Fill text or shape with background color | Ctrl+Backspace | ⌘-Delete |
| Move text or shape layer | Ctrl-drag layer | ⌘-drag layer |
| Shape tools | U (or Shift+U) | U (or Shift-U) |
| Cycle through custom shapes | [ or ] | [ or ] |
| Constrain proportions of custom shape | Shift-drag | Shift-drag |

# The Vector-Based Duo

Generally speaking, Photoshop brokers in pixels, or so-called *raster art*. But the subjects of this lesson are something altogether different. Photoshop treats both text and shapes as *vector-based objects* (or just plain *vectors*), meaning that they rely on mathematically defined outlines that can be scaled or otherwise transformed without any degradation in quality.

For a demonstration of how vectors work in Photoshop, consider the composition shown in Figure 10-2. The Q is a text layer with a drop shadow. The black crown and the orange fire are shapes. The background is a pixel-based gradient. The reason the artwork appears so jagged is because it contains very few pixels. The image measures a scant 50 by 55 pixels (less than 2,800 pixels in all) and is printed at just 15 pixels per inch!

Clearly, you'd never create such low-resolution artwork in real life. I do it here to demonstrate a point: If this were an entirely pixel-based image, we'd be stuck forevermore with jagged, indistinct artwork. But because the Q, crown, and fire are vectors, they are scalable. And unlike pixel art, making the vectors bigger also makes them smoother.

One way to scale the vectors is to print them to a PostScript-compatible printer, which automatically scales the artwork to the full resolution of the device. The result is a breathtaking transformation. Believe it or not, the low-resolution, jagged artwork from Figure 10-2 prints to a PostScript output device as shown in Figure 10-3. All pixel-based portions of the composition—namely, the gradient and drop shadow—print just as they look on screen. But Photoshop conveys the text and shapes as true PostScript vectors; therefore, they render at the full resolution of the printer.

Few people own PostScript printers; most of us are stuck with standard raster printers. (Your everyday average inkjet device prints just the pixels you see on screen, as in

An incredibly low-res composition (50 x 55 pixels), rendered at 15ppi

Figure 10-2.

The very same low-res file, output from a PostScript printer

Figure 10-3.

The same image, this time scaled
to 480ppi (3200%) using Image Size

Figure 10-4.

Figure 10-2.) So fortunately, there's a second, arguably better way to scale vectors—the Image Size command. To achieve the result pictured in Figure 10-4, I chose Image→ Image Size and turned on the Resample Image check box. (Scale Styles and Constrain Proportions were also turned on.) Then I increased the Resolution value to a whopping 480 pixels per inch. The result looks every bit as good as the PostScript output, except for the drop shadow, which looks even better. (The Image Size command can scale drop shadows, whereas PostScript printing can't.) Now I can print this artwork to any printer—PostScript, ink-jet, or otherwise—and it'll look every bit as good as it does in Figure 10-4.

The upshot is that vectors are a world apart from anything else inside Photoshop, always rendering at the full resolution of the image. To see more on this topic, watch Video Lesson 10, "Vector-Based Objects" (introduced on page 330).

## Creating and Formatting Text

Generally speaking, text inside Photoshop works like it does inside every major publishing application. You can apply typefaces, scale characters, adjust line spacing, and so on. However, because Photoshop isn't well suited to routine typesetting, we won't spend much time on the routine functions. Instead, we'll take a look at some text treatments to which Photoshop is very well suited, as well as a few functions that are exceptional or even unique to the program.

In this exercise, we'll add text to an image and format the text to fit its background. We'll also apply a few effects to the text that go well beyond anything you can accomplish outside Photoshop.

1. *Open an image.* Not every image welcomes the addition of text. After all, text needs room to breathe. So your image should have ample dead space, the kind of empty background you might normally crop away. Such is the case with *Pumpkin light.psd* (see Figure 10-5 on the facing page). Found in the *Lesson 10* folder inside *Lesson Files-PScs 1on1*, this digital photo—which I shot with the ever flexible Olympus E-20N—includes two strong foreground elements with lots of empty space below and above. These are perfect places for some relevant text.

When you open this document, you may see the following alert message: "Some text layers might need to be updated before they can be used for vector based output." If you do, click the **Update** button. This makes the one live text layer in this document editable, as it will need to be.

Figure 10-5.

2. *Make sure the guidelines are visible.* You should see two cyan *guidelines*—one horizontal and one vertical—in the image window. If not, choose **View→Show→Guides** to make them visible. Also make sure a check mark appears in front of **View→Snap**, which makes layers snap into alignment with the guides.

Guidelines are non-printing elements that ensure precise alignment in Photoshop. They are especially useful for positioning text layers, as we'll see in the upcoming steps.

3. *Click the type tool in the toolbox.* Or press the T key. Photoshop provides four type tools in all, but the horizontal type tool—the one that looks like an unadorned T (see Figure 10-6)—is the only one you need.

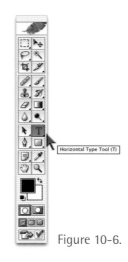

Horizontal Type Tool (T)

Figure 10-6.

4. *Establish a few formatting attributes in the options bar.* The options bar provides access to a few of the most common *formatting attributes*, which are ways to modify the appearance of live text. Labeled in Figure 10-7, they include the following:

- Click the second-from-left ▾ arrow to see a list of typefaces available to your system. I prefer the term *font families* (or just plain *font*) because, technically speaking, most typefaces include multiple stylistic alternatives, including bold, italic, and so on.

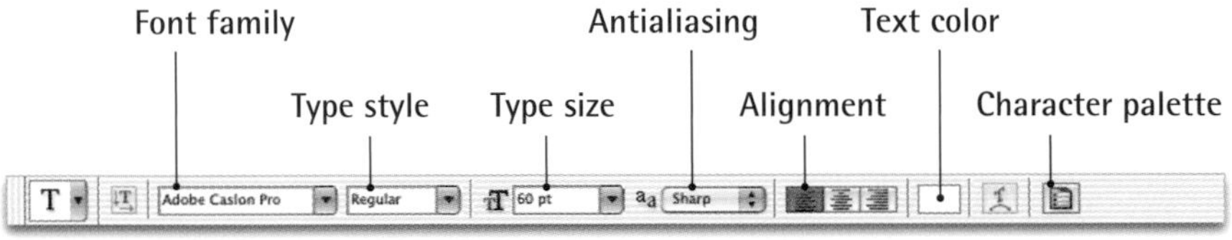

Font family      Antialiasing      Text color

Type style     Type size     Alignment     Character palette

Figure 10-7.

If you purchased the full Adobe Creative Suite, select **Adobe Caslon Pro** (look under the **C**'s). If you purchased a standalone copy of Photoshop CS, select **Times**, **Times New Roman**, or a similar font.

- The type style pop-up menu lists all stylistic alternatives available for the selected font. Change the style to read **Regular** or **Roman**.

- If using Caslon Pro, set the type size to 60 points. If using Times or Times New Roman, set the value to 68 points.

- The next menu determines the flavor of antialiasing (edge softening) applied to the text. We'll examine this option a bit more in Step 19 (page 341), but for now, either **Crisp** or **Sharp** will suffice.

- The alignment options let you align rows of type to the left, center, or right. Click the first icon (▤) to create *flush left* text.

- The color swatch determines the color of the type. By default, it matches the foreground color. For the moment, press the D key and then the X key to make the swatch white.

- Click the far right icon to display the **Character** palette, which contains several more formatting attributes. We'll need this palette later.

You can change every single one of these formatting attributes after you create your text. Getting a few settings established up front merely saves a little time later.

5. *Click in the image window.* Click somewhere in the lower-left portion of the image. For now, don't bother trying to align your cursor with the guidelines. Better to get the text on the page and align it later.

6. *Enter "fright lights."* Lowercase letters are fine. You should see white type across the bottom of your image, as in Figure 10-8. If the **Layers** palette is visible, you'll also notice the appearance of a new layer marked by a **T** icon. This **T** indicates that the layer contains live text.

Figure 10-8.

7. *Select all the text.* Press Ctrl+A (⌘-A on the Mac) to highlight the two words. Now you can modify the type.

8. *Click the all caps icon in the Character palette.* Click the ⊞ icon in the **Character** palette, as in Figure 10-9 on the next page. This switches the lowercase letters to capitals using a temporary style option. This way, if you decide later to revert to lowercase letters, you simply turn the ⊞ icon off.

9. **Accept your changes.** Press the Enter key on the keypad (not the Enter key directly above the Shift key) to exit the type mode and accept the new text layer. You can also press Ctrl+Enter (or ⌘-Return). But don't press the standard Enter or Return key on its own—doing so will wipe out your text and replace it with a carriage return.

Figure 10-9.

At this point, Photoshop changes the name of the new text layer in the Layers palette to **fright lights**. The program will even update the layer name if you make changes to the type. If you like, you can rename the layer just as you would any other layer (especially helpful when the layer name becomes too long), but doing so will prevent Photoshop from automatically updating the layer name later.

10. **Drag the text into alignment with the guides.** Press the Ctrl key (or ⌘) and drag the text until the lower-left corner of the letter F snaps into alignment with both guidelines. When you snap to either guide, the cursor will turn white, as in Figure 10-10 on the opposite page.

11. **Click the Body Copy layer in the Layers palette.** This activates the Body Copy layer, which contains a paragraph of type set in the world's ugliest font, Courier New. (For you, it may appear in some other Courier derivative, but rest assured, they're all

dreadful.) The only reason the layer is here is to spare you the tedium of having to enter the type from scratch on your own. But that doesn't mean there's nothing for you to do. Much formatting is in order.

---

This particular variety of text layer is called *area text*. To create such a text layer, you drag with the type tool to define the boundaries of the column, or "block." As you enter text from the keyboard, Photoshop automatically wraps words down to the next line as needed to fit within the confines of the block.

---

Figure 10-10.

12. *Assign a better font.* As long as a text layer is active, you can format all type on the layer by adjusting settings in the options bar. For starters, click the word **Courier** in the font box. This highlights the font name and provides you with a couple of options:

- Press the ↑ or ↓ key to cycle to a previous or subsequent font in alphabetical order. This permits you to preview the various fonts installed on your system, handy if you have no idea what fonts like *Giddyup* or *Greymantle* look like. (Those are just examples; your strange fonts will vary.)

- Enter the first few letters of the name of a font you'd like to use.

For example, type V-e-r, which should switch you to the commonly available Verdana (included on all personal computer systems). Then press Enter or Return to apply the font and see how it looks. Figure 10-11 shows the text in Verdana.

Figure 10-11.

13. *Make the first two words of the paragraph bold.* Zoom in on the words *Happy Jacks* at the beginning of the paragraph to better see what you're doing, either by pressing Ctrl+plus (⌘-plus on the Mac) or by switching to the zoom tool. Then select the type tool again, if necessary, and follow these instructions:

    • Select both words by double-clicking **Happy** and dragging over **Jacks**.

    • Choose **Bold** from the type style menu in the options bar, as shown in Figure 10-12. You can do the same from the keyboard by pressing Ctrl+Shift+B (⌘-Shift-B on the Mac).

14. *Make the word "clowns" italic.* Find the third-to-last word in the paragraph, **clowns**, and double-click it. Then choose **Italic** from the type style menu in the options bar or press Ctrl+Shift+I (⌘-Shift-I on the Mac).

15. ***Show the rulers and the Info palette.*** The Body Copy text is looking better, but its placement is for the birds. Before we size and position the text block, it helps to lay down a few guidelines. And before we can do that, we have to do the following:

    - Guidelines come from the rulers, so choose **View→Rulers** or press Ctrl+R (⌘-R) to display them.

    - To track the coordinate position of your guides, choose **Window→Info** to display the **Info** palette.

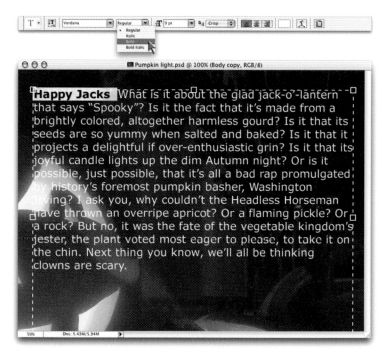

Figure 10-12.

16. ***Add three guidelines.*** Drag from the left-hand ruler to create vertical guides and drag from the top ruler to create horizontal guides. As you do, you can track the location of the guidelines by watching the X: and Y: values in the Info palette. With that in mind, create the following guides:

    - Drag a vertical guide to the coordinate position **X:** 1000.

    - Drag another vertical guide very close to the right edge of the document to the coordinate position **X:** 1540.

    - Drag a horizontal guide to **Y:** 50.

The screen shot in Figure 10-13 shows me in the process of creating the last guide. Note that these values assume your rulers are set to pixels (as established by the installation of the preference settings in Step 7 of "One-on-One Installation and Setup," page xv). If your rulers are set to some other unit of measurement, right-click either ruler and choose **Pixels**.

As you drag, press the Shift key to snap the guideline to the tiny "tick marks" in the ruler (also known as *ruler increments*). If you drop a guideline at the wrong location, you can move it by pressing Ctrl (or ⌘) to get the move tool and then dragging the guide. To delete a guide, Ctrl-drag (or ⌘-drag) it back into the ruler.

Figure 10-13.

17. *Scale the text block to fit within the guides.* We're finished with the rulers, so press Ctrl+R (⌘-R on the Mac) to hide them. With the type tool selected and some portion of the body text block still active (if the word *clowns* is still highlighted, that's fine), move the cursor over the upper-left corner handle. The cursor should change to a bidirectional arrow, indicating that it's ready to scale. Drag the handle until it snaps to the nearest guide intersection. Similarly, drag the lower-right corner handle until it snaps to the rightmost guideline, as shown in Figure 10-14 on the opposite page.

18. **Hide the guides.** At this point, you're done with the guidelines. To hide them so you can focus on your composition, choose **View**→**Show**→**Guides**. Or better yet, press Ctrl+; or ⌘-; (the semicolon key, to the right of the L). The guidelines will no longer be visible, nor will they snap.

Figure 10-14.

19. **Change the antialiasing to Strong.** Now comes one of the sub-tlest formatting changes you can apply in Photoshop. Located in the center of the options bar (as labeled back in Figure 10-7 on page 334), the antialiasing setting controls the way the edges of individual characters blend with their backgrounds. Here are your options:

- Sharp manages to antialias the type while maintaining sharp corners. This preserves the best character definition, especially when applied to small, serifed letters.

- Crisp rounds off the corners slightly.

- Strong shores up small type by expanding the edges very slightly outward, thus resulting in bolder characters.

- In theory, Smooth rounds off corners even more than Crisp. In practice, the two settings are virtually identical.

- The first setting, None, turns antialiasing off and leaves the jagged transitions. For Web work, this is a terrible setting. But for high-resolution print work, it helps reduce some of the blur that can result from antialiasing.

Figure 10-15 shows each setting applied to a magnified detail from the Body Copy layer. The differences verge on trivial, but for this particular layer, I would argue that **Strong** helps thicken the characters and boost legibility.

Figure 10-15.

20. ***Turn on Fractional Widths.*** This next option is likewise subtle but, in my estimation, much more important. By default, Photoshop spaces characters by whole numbers of pixels. This is essential when working with jagged type (as when antialiasing is set to None), but otherwise results in inconsistent letter spacing. To better space one letter from its neighbor, click the ⊙ arrow in the top-right corner of the **Character** palette and choose **Fractional Widths**. This calculates the text spacing for the entire layer in the same way other design programs do, in precise fractions of a pixel. You'll see the text tighten up slightly; you may even see one or two words shift up to different lines.

21. ***Turn on the every-line composer.*** Flush left type is sometimes said to be "ragged right," and the body text in this example is indeed very ragged. To even out the raggedness a bit, switch to the **Paragraph** palette by clicking on its tab in the Character palette. Then click the ⊙ arrow to bring up the palette menu and choose **Adobe Every-line Composer**. Photoshop better aligns the right edges of type, as shown in Figure 10-16.

22. ***Justify the type.*** Less ragged text is great, but let's say you want both the left and right edges to be absolutely flush. To achieve this, click the fourth icon (▤) in the top row of the Paragraph palette to justify the paragraph and leave the last line flush left, as shown in Figure 10-17. You can also press the keyboard shortcut Ctrl+Shift+J (⌘-Shift-J on the Mac).

Jacks What is it about the glad
antern that says "Spooky"? Is it
that it's made from a brightly
altogether harmless gourd? Is it
seeds are so yummy when salted
ed? Is it that it projects a delight-
er-enthusiastic grin? Is it that its
andle lights up the dim Autumn
Dr is it possible, just possible, that
bad rap promulgated by history's
t pumpkin basher, Washington
I ask you, why couldn't the
s Horseman have thrown an
apricot? Or a flaming pickle? Or a
ut no, it was the fate of the veg-
ingdom's jester, the plant voted
ger to please, to take it on the
xt thing you know, we'll all be
clowns are scary.
Jacks What is it about the glad
antern that says "Spooky"? Is
ct that it's made from a brightly
altogether harmless gourd? Is it
seeds are so yummy when salted
ed? Is it that it projects a delightful
enthusiastic grin? Is it that its joyful
ghts up the dim Autumn night? Or
sible, just possible, that it's all a
promulgated by history's foremost
n basher, Washington Irving? I ask
y couldn't the Headless Horseman
rown an overripe apricot? Or a
pickle? Or a rock? But no, it was
of the vegetable kingdom's jester,
t voted most eager to please, to
on the chin. Next thing you know,
be thinking clowns are scary.


Single-line composer

Every-line composer

Figure 10-16.

**PEARL OF WISDOM**

The *single-line composer* (active prior to Step 21) analyzes each line of type in a vacuum. The *every-line composer* (Step 21, Figure 10-16) examines the entire text layer as a whole and spaces the text to give it the most even appearance possible.

Pumpkin light.psd @ 100% (Body copy, RGB/8)
Character
Paragraph
Justify last left
Hyphenate
Happy Jacks What is it a
jack-o'-lantern that says "S
the fact that it's made from a brightly
colored, altogether harmless gourd? Is it
that its seeds are so yummy when salted
and baked? Is it that it projects a delightful
if over-enthusiastic grin? Is it that its joyful
candle lights up the dim Autumn night? Or
is it possible, just possible, that it's all a
bad rap promulgated by history's foremost
pumpkin basher, Washington Irving? I ask
you, why couldn't the Headless Horseman
have thrown an overripe apricot? Or a
flaming pickle? Or a rock? But no, it was
the fate of the vegetable kingdom's jester,
the plant voted most eager to please, to
take it on the chin. Next thing you know,
we'll all be thinking clowns are scary.
50%
Doc: 5.43M/5.94M


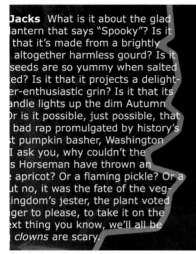

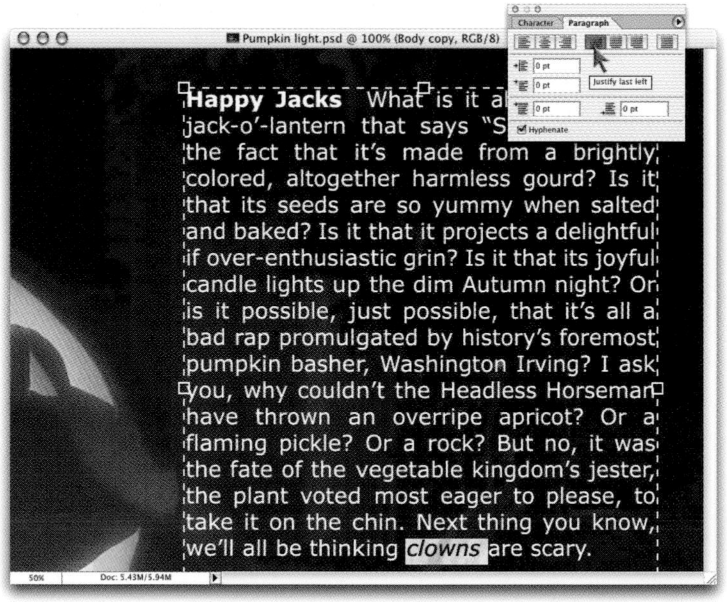

Figure 10-17.

Even after justifying the paragraph, the every-line composer remains in effect, thus ensuring more evenly spaced words from one line of type to the next.

23. ***Select the entire paragraph, except the first two words.*** Let's change all but the first two words, the bold Happy Jacks, to a yellowish orange to match the pumpkin. Start by double-clicking the third word, **What**. Then press Ctrl+Shift+↓ (⌘-Shift-↓ on the Mac) to extend the selection to the end of the paragraph.

24. ***Change the color to a yellowish orange.*** Click the white color swatch in the options bar to display the **Color Picker** dialog box. Then move the cursor into the image window and click in one of the fleshy areas inside the big pumpkin's nose, as shown in Figure 10-18. You should end up with a color in the approximate vicinity of H: 40, S: 50, B: 90. When you do, click the **OK** button to recolor the text.

Figure 10-18.

25. ***Accept your changes.*** Press the Enter key on the keypad or press Ctrl+Enter (⌘-Return) to exit the type mode and accept the changes to the Body Copy layer.

All this editing and formatting is fine and dandy, but it's the kind of thing that you could accomplish in a vector-based program (such as Illustrator or InDesign), which is better designed for composing and printing high-resolution text. For the remainder of this exercise, we'll apply the sort of text treatment that's possible only in Photoshop. Due to the length of this exercise, I've marked these steps as Extra Credit. But between you and me, you won't want to miss them.

26. ***Turn on the Style Holder layer in the Layers palette.*** A tiny brown pumpkin appears above the big pumpkin's head. This layer holds some of the attributes we'll be applying to the large Fright Lights text.

27. ***Eyedrop the brown pumpkin.*** Press the I key to select the eyedropper tool and then click the little pumpkin to make its brown the foreground color.

28. ***Fill the Fright Lights layer with the sampled brown.*** Click the **Fright Lights** layer in the **Layers** palette to make it active. Then press Alt+Backspace (Option-Delete on the Mac) to fill the text with brown, as shown in Figure 10-19. When filling an entire text layer, this handy shortcut lets you recolor text without visiting the Color Picker dialog box.

Figure 10-19.

# A Dozen More Ways to Edit Text

I couldn't begin to convey in a single exercise, even a long one, all the wonderful ways Photoshop permits you to edit and format text. So here are a few truly terrific tips and techniques to bear in mind when working on your own projects:

- Double-click a T thumbnail in the Layers palette to switch to the type tool and select all the text in the corresponding layer.

- Armed with the type tool, you can double-click a word to select it. Drag on the second click to select multiple words. Triple-click to select an entire line; quadruple-click to select a paragraph.

- To increase the size of selected characters in 2-point increments, press Ctrl+Shift+>. To reduce the type size, press Ctrl+Shift+<. (That's ⌘-Shift-> and ⌘-Shift-< on the Mac.)

- In the design world, line spacing is called leading. By default, the leading in Photoshop is set to Auto, which is 120 percent of the prevailing type size. To override this, click the $\frac{A}{|A}$ icon in the Character palette to highlight the leading value (Auto), and then replace the value with a number. In the figure below, I changed the leading to 16 points. Note that the new leading value affects the distance between the selected text and the text above it.

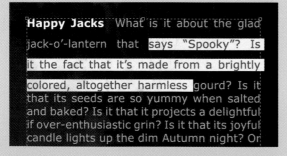

- After you enter a manual leading value (something other than Auto) in the Character palette, you can increase or decrease the leading using keyboard shortcuts. Press Alt+↓ (or Option-↓) to increase the leading; press Alt+↑ (Option-↑) to tighten it.

- Click between two characters and press Alt+← to move them together or Alt+→ to move them apart (Option-← or Option-→ on the Mac). This is called *pair kerning*.

- You can apply those same keystrokes to multiple characters at a time. For example, in the figure below, I triple-clicked to select a line of type. Then I pressed Alt+← to move the characters together and permit another word to wrap onto that line. Photoshop calls this *tracking*.

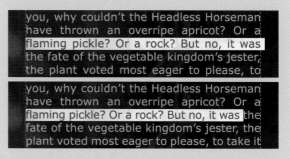

- When text is active, press Ctrl (or ⌘) and drag inside the text to move it.

- Also when text is active, press Ctrl+T (⌘-T) to display or hide the Character palette. Press Ctrl+M (⌘-M) to do the same with the Paragraph palette.

- The Color palette does not always reflect the color of highlighted text. But if you change the Color palette settings, any highlighted text changes as well.

- To change the formatting of multiple text layers at a time, first link the layers. Then press the Shift key when choosing a typeface, style, size, or other formatting setting. When Shift is down, all linked text layers change at once.

- When editing text, you have one undo, which you can exercise by pressing Ctrl+Z (or ⌘-Z). If you need more undos, press the Esc key to abandon *all* changes made since you entered the text editing mode. But be careful when using this technique. If you press the Esc key in the midst of creating a new text layer, you forfeit the entire layer. And because Esc can't be undone, there's no way to retrieve the layer.

29. *Expand the image window.* The next trick is to add a *cast shadow*—that is, a shadow cast by the letters in the direction opposite the light source. In this case, the light source is the pumpkin, so a cast shadow would extend toward the viewer in the area below the letters. To do this, you'll need a bit of extra room at the bottom of the image. So drag the lower-right of the image window to enlarge the window and reveal an inch or so of empty gray pasteboard.

30. *Transform and duplicate the text layer.* Press Ctrl+Alt+T (⌘-Option-T on the Mac). This does two things: It duplicates the layer and enters the free transform mode. But for the moment, you'll have to take this on faith; the Layers palette doesn't show you the new layer until you begin editing it.

31. *Flip and scale the duplicate layer.* I have a few instructions for you here:

    • Drag the top handle downward, beyond the bottom of the canvas and into the gray pasteboard. The text will flip upside down, hinging at its base, much like a reflection.

    • Press Shift+↓ to scoot the text 10 pixels down from the bottom of the original, upright text.

    • Again, drag what is now the bottom handle until the crossbar of either H comes close to, but does not touch, the edge of the canvas.

    I'd love to give you an exact percentage value to note in the options bar, but Photoshop does not track flipped images properly. The final position is illustrated in Figure 10-20 on the next page. When you get it more or less right, press Enter or Return to accept the transformation.

    ---
    PEARL OF  WISDOM

    A couple of special benefits when transforming a text layer: The type remains live and editable, so you can add text or fix typos. And because Photoshop is working from vectors, the transformation does not stretch pixels or otherwise reduce the quality of the graphic. This means you can transform the text in multiple sessions without fear of degrading the quality.

    ---

32. *Rename the layer.* Double-click the name of the new layer in the **Layers** palette and change it to "Cast Shadow." Then press Ctrl+[ or ⌘-[ to move it behind the Fright Lights layer.

33. *Set the blend mode to Multiply and reduce the opacity.* This is a shadow, so it must darken its background. Choose **Multiply** from the blend mode menu at the top of the Layers palette, or press Shift+Alt+M (Shift-Option-M on the Mac). Also press the 9 key to reduce the **Opacity** to 90 percent.

Figure 10-20.

Figure 10-21.

34. *Choose Filter→Blur→Gaussian Blur.* To create a soft shadow, you need to apply the Gaussian Blur filter. But Photoshop's filters are exclusively applicable to pixels; none of them can change live type. So when you choose **Gaussian Blur**, the program alerts you that continuing requires you to *rasterize* the type—that is, convert it to pixels. Click **OK** to confirm (see Figure 10-21). From here on, you can no longer edit this particular layer with the type tool.

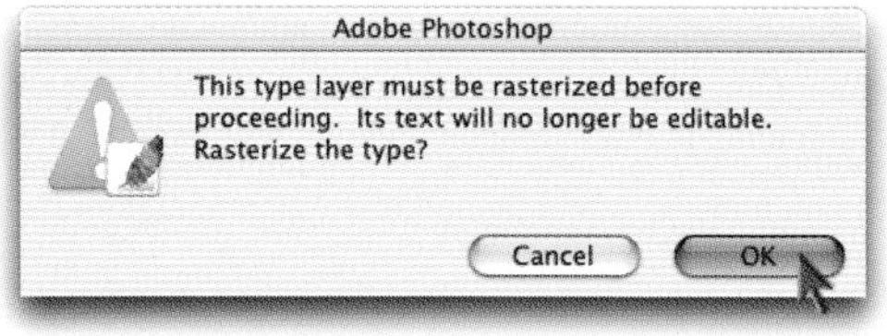

35. *Enter a Radius value of 6 pixels.* Then click the **OK** button. The blurred shadow type appears in Figure 10-22.

36. *Again enter the free transform mode.* Now let's give the shadow some directional perspective so it looks like it extends out toward the viewer. Press Ctrl+T (or ⌘-T) to enter the free transform mode, this time without creating a duplicate.

37. **Distort the shadow type.** The image in Figure 10-23 illustrates the two distortions I want you to apply, the first highlighted in red and the second in blue:

- Press both Shift and Ctrl (or Shift and ⌘) and drag the handle in the lower-right corner directly to the right. The Ctrl key distorts the type; the Shift key constrains the angle of the distortion. Keep dragging until the rightmost **H:** value in the options bar, which indicates the horizontal angle of the slant, reads 50 degrees (red in Figure 10-23).

- Still pressing Ctrl and Shift, drag the handle in the lower-left corner to the left, this time until the **W:** value reads 120 percent (blue in Figure 10-23).

When you're satisfied that your shadow looks like mine—or, if you prefer, more to your liking than mine—press the Enter or Return key to apply the perspective distortion.

It may occur to you to wonder why one distortion is tracked by a slant value and the other only by a scale value. Although I'm confident that some deep recess of Photoshop's code provides a reason, I know of none that sheds light on the program's performance. It is, simply put, a byproduct of Photoshop's fundamental inability to track distortions numerically.

Figure 10-22.

Figure 10-23.

You may also wonder why I had you wait until now to apply this distortion. Why didn't we do it at the same time we were flipping and stretching the text back in Step 31? Because while Photoshop lets you scale, rotate, and slant live type, you can't distort it. Therefore, this step had to wait until after the rasterization that took place in Step 34.

Figure 10-24.

38. *Copy the effect from the Style holder layer.* Finally, let's make the Fright Lights letters appear backlit. Click the ▶ to the right of the **Style Holder** layer to twirl it open and reveal a single layer style. Then drag that style, **Bevel and Emboss**, and drop it onto the bottom half of the **Fright Lights** layer, as shown in Figure 10-24. If the new style is hidden, click the eyeball (👁) in front of the word **Effects** to turn it on.

39. *Delete the Style Holder layer.* Drag the **Style Holder** layer to the trash icon at the bottom of the Layers palette. The finished artwork appears in Figure 10-25.

40. *Choose File→Save As.* Give the file a different filename, such as "Happy Jacks.psd," and click **Save**. If you decide to revisit this file in the future, the live text layers will remain editable with the type tool. Other layers (the shadow and background) will remain independently editable as pixels.

Figure 10-25.

# Drawing and Editing Shapes

Photoshop's shape tools allow you to draw rectangles, ellipses, polygons, and an assortment of prefab dingbats and symbols. On the surface, they're a pretty straightforward bunch. But when you delve into them a little more deeply, you quickly discover that the applications for shapes are every bit as wide-ranging and diverse as those for text.

You got a sense of how to draw rectangles and ellipses back in the "Using the Marquee Tools" section of Lesson 4 (see page 108). Those same rules apply to the rectangle and ellipse shape tools as well. So in the following exercise, we'll focus on those shapes we haven't yet seen—polygons, lines, and custom shapes—as well as ways to blend vectors and images inside a single composition.

1. *Open an image.* For simplicity's sake, we'll start with a more or less neutral background. Open the file *Election.psd* located in the *Lesson 10* folder inside 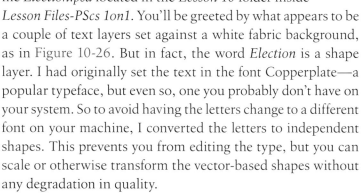 *Lesson Files-PScs 1on1*. You'll be greeted by what appears to be a couple of text layers set against a white fabric background, as in Figure 10-26. But in fact, the word *Election* is a shape layer. I had originally set the text in the font Copperplate—a popular typeface, but even so, one you probably don't have on your system. So to avoid having the letters change to a different font on your machine, I converted the letters to independent shapes. This prevents you from editing the type, but you can scale or otherwise transform the vector-based shapes without any degradation in quality.

Figure 10-26.

2. ***Convert the 2008 layer to shapes.*** Let's say we want to similarly prevent the text *2008* from changing on another system. Click the **2008** layer in the **Layers** palette. Then choose **Layer→Type→Convert to Shape**. Photoshop converts the characters to shape outlines, which will easily survive the journey from one system to another.

**PEARL OF WISDOM**

Note that the numbers *2008* are now surrounded by path outlines, like those we learned about in the section "Drawing Precise Curves" in Lesson 4 (page 122). The Layers palette shows a mostly gray *vector mask* thumbnail, as shown in Figure 10-27. The area inside the mask (indicated by white in the thumbnail) is opaque; the area outside the mask (indicated by gray) is transparent.

3. ***Display the guidelines.*** This image contains a total of eight guides—four vertical and four horizontal. If you can't see the guides, choose **View→Show→Guides** or press Ctrl+; (⌘-; on the Mac). The guides will aid us in the creation of our shapes.

4. ***Select the polygon tool in the toolbox.*** Click and hold the rectangle tool icon below the type tool to display the flyout menu pictured in Figure 10-28. Then choose the polygon tool, which lets you draw regular polygons—things like pentagons and hexagons—as well as stars.

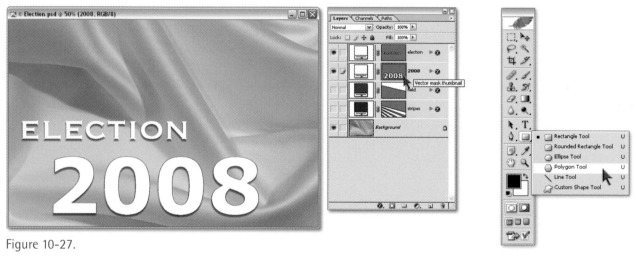

Figure 10-27.

Figure 10-28.

5. ***Click the Shape Layers icon in the options bar.*** Highlighted on the far left in Figure 10-29, this icon tells the polygon tool to draw an independent shape layer.

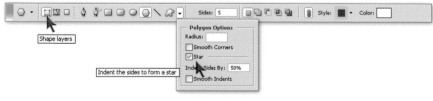

Figure 10-29.

6. *Set the Polygon Options to Star.* Our image is an election graphic, so naturally one feels compelled to wrap the composition in stars and stripes. Click the ▾ arrow to the left of the **Sides** value in the options bar. This displays the **Polygon Options** pop-up menu pictured in Figure 10-29:

- Turn on the **Star** check box to instruct the polygon tool to draw stars.

- Make sure both **Smooth** check boxes are off so the corners are nice and sharp.

- Set the **Indent Sides By** value to 50 percent. This ensures that opposite points align with each other, as is the rule for a 5-pointed star.

7. *Set the Sides value to 5.* This is the default value, so it's unlikely you'll have to make a change. But if you do, here's a trick:

---

To raise the Sides value in increments of 1, press the ] key. To lower the value, press the [ key. Add the Shift key to raise or lower the value by 10. This tip likewise holds true for any other value that may occupy this space in the options bar.

---

8. *Draw the first star.* The polygon tool draws shapes from the center out. To draw the star shown in Figure 10-30, drag from the guideline intersection highlighted by the yellow ⊕ to the one highlighted by the dark green ⊕. (Make sure you end your drag on the second guide from the left and the closest to the bottom, just above the left half of the 8.) Photoshop automatically matches the attributes of the 2008 layer, giving the star a white fill and a drop shadow.

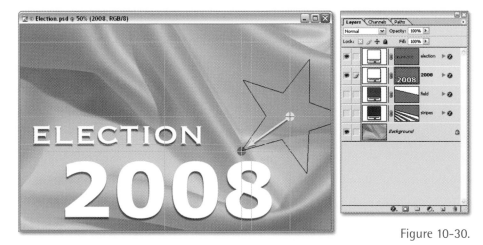

Figure 10-30.

9. *Carve a second star out of the first.* Press the Alt key (or Option on the Mac) and draw another star from the same starting point (marked by the yellow ⊕ in Figure 10-31) to the next guideline intersection (the dark green ⬤ in Figure 10-31). Because the Alt or Option key is down, Photoshop subtracts the new shape from the previous one. The result is a star-shaped white stroke.

Figure 10-31.

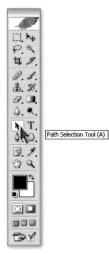

Figure 10-32.

10. *Click the arrow tool in the toolbox.* Or press the A key to select the black arrow, which Photoshop calls the path selection tool (see Figure 10-32). As we'll see, it permits you to select and modify path outlines in a shape layer.

11. *Select both inner and outer star paths.* Click one of the star paths to select it. Then press the Shift key and click the other star. Photoshop selects both paths.

12. *Transform and duplicate the star.* Press Ctrl+Alt+T (⌘-Option-T on the Mac) to duplicate the selected star paths and enter the free transform mode. As usual, you have to take on faith that you've duplicated the star because, for the moment, the cloned paths exactly overlap the originals.

13. ***Scale, rotate, and move the duplicate star.*** At this point, I need you to make some rather precise adjustments:

- Click the 🔗 icon between the W: and H: values to scale the star paths proportionally. Then change either the **W:** or **H:** value to 80 percent.

- Tab to the rotate value and change it to −16 degrees. This tilts the star counterclockwise.

- Drag the star until what used to be the upper-left handle clicks into alignment with the intersection of the topmost and leftmost guidelines, as shown in Figure 10-33.

When the new star appears in the proper position, press the Enter or Return key to confirm the transformation.

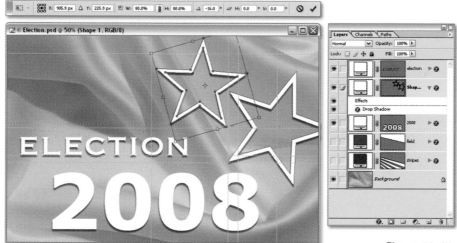

Figure 10-33.

14. ***Repeat the above transformation three more times.*** Press Ctrl+Shift+Alt+T (⌘-Shift-Option-T on the Mac) to repeat all the operations performed in the preceding step. This means Photoshop duplicates the second star group, scales it proportionally to 80 percent, rotates it −16 degrees, and moves it to the left. Press Ctrl+Shift+Alt+T (⌘-Shift-Option-T) twice more to further repeat the operations. The result is the arcing sequence of five stars shown in Figure 10-34 on the next page.

This succession of duplicate, transform, and repeat is known as *series duplication*. In Photoshop, it invariably begins with the keyboard shortcut Ctrl+Alt+T (⌘-Option-T) and ends with several repetitions of Ctrl+Shift+Alt+T (⌘-Shift-Option-T). Set up properly, series duplication helps automate the creation of derivative paths and shape patterns.

15. *Name the new layer.* By default, the layer full of stars is called Shape 1. Double-click the layer name in the **Layers** palette and enter the new name "Stars."

---

If you find that the names of some of your layers are getting truncated, it's because the Layers palette is too narrow to display them. Move the palette away from the right edge of your screen. Then drag the lower-right corner of the palette to expand it.

---

Figure 10-34.

16. *Turn on the Field layer.* Click the **Field** layer in the Layers palette to display a slanted blue shape layer. I created this layer by drawing a plain old rectangle with the rectangle tool and then distorting it in the free transform mode.

17. *Set the Field layer to Hard Light.* Choose the **Hard Light** mode or press Shift+Alt+H (Shift-Option-H on the Mac). On the PC, press the Esc key to deactivate the blend mode setting. Then press 8 to lower the **Opacity** value to 80 percent. Even though Field is a vector shape layer, it's subject to the same blend modes and transparency options that are available elsewhere throughout Photoshop.

18. **Turn on the Stripes layer.** Click the **Stripes** layer to turn on a sequence of red stripes. I created the top stripe by distorting a rectangle. Then I used series duplication to make the other four.

19. **Set the Stripes layer to Multiply.** Press Shift+Alt+M (or Shift-Option-M) to burn the stripes into the background image. The result appears in Figure 10-35.

---

By now, you may have noticed Photoshop's penchant for showing you the outlines of your paths whenever you view a shape layer. To hide the paths, click the vector mask thumbnail to the right of the color swatch in the Layers palette. Alternatively, if the arrow tool or one of the shape tools is active, you can press Enter or Return.

---

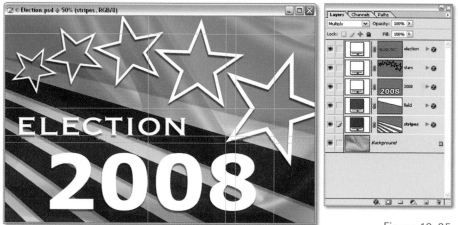

Figure 10-35.

Now suppose we want the stripes to vary in opacity, from nearly transparent on the left to opaque on the right. One solution is to fill the layer with a transparent-to-red gradient (Layer→ Change Layer Content→Gradient). But the more flexible solution is to add a layer mask. This may seem like an odd notion, given that the layer already has a vector mask. But any kind of layer in Photoshop—even a text layer—can include one vector mask *and* one pixel-based layer mask, thus permitting you to blend the best of both worlds.

If adding a layer mask to a vector shape doesn't sound like a regular barrel of monkeys to you, skip to the "Bending and Warping Type" exercise, which begins on page 364. Then again, if it sounds like more fun than you've had in years, enjoy the remaining steps.

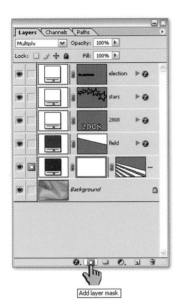

Figure 10-36.

20. *Add a layer mask.* With the Stripes layer still active, click the small ▢ icon at the bottom of the Layers palette. Photoshop adds another mask thumbnail, as shown in Figure 10-36.

21. *Click the gradient tool in the toolbox.* Or press the G key. (If this selects the paint bucket, press the G key again.) Also, confirm the following settings:

  • Press the D key to set the foreground color to white and the background to black (the masking defaults).

  • Make sure the gradient bar on the left side of the options bar displays a white-to-black gradient. If it does not, press Shift+, (that's Shift+comma) to reset it.

  • Select the first style icon in the options bar (the one labeled Linear Gradient in Figure 10-37).

  • The other options should be set to their defaults: **Mode**: **Normal**, **Opacity**: 100 percent, **Reverse** off, and the last two check boxes on.

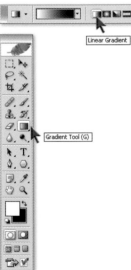

Figure 10-37.

22. *Draw the gradient mask.* Drag in the image window from inside the top hole in the 8 to just beyond the left edge of the image window, matching the angle of the neighboring stripe, as illustrated in Figure 10-38 atop the facing page. The result is that the stripes fade as they progress from right to left.

If you don't like the result of the gradient mask, just redraw it. Because the gradient is opaque, it completely replaces any previous gradient you've drawn; no undo needed.

Figure 10-38.

23. **Select the line tool.** The next step is to draw a rule under the word *Election*. The best tool for this job is the line tool. You can select it in any of the following ways:

- Select the line tool from the shape tool flyout menu, just as you chose the polygon tool back in Step 4.

- Click the current occupant of the shape tool slot. Then click the line tool icon in the options bar, as shown in Figure 10-39.

Figure 10-39.

- Press the U key twice. The first keystroke selects the last used shape tool, the polygon tool; the second advances to the line tool. (If you skipped the preference settings recommended in Step 7 on page xv of the Preface, press U and then Shift+U.)

24. **Increase the Weight value to 12 pixels.** The Weight value determines the thickness of lines drawn with the line tool. You can modify the value directly in the options bar, or press Shift+] to raise the value by 10 and ] to raise it another 1.

25. **Click the Stars layer in the Layers palette.** By selecting this layer, you do two things: First, you tell Photoshop to create the next shape layer in front of the Stars layer. Second, you tell it to match the Stars layer's color and style attributes.

26. ***Draw a line under the word Election.*** Because we want the rule to extend beyond the left edge of the canvas, it's easiest to draw from right to left. So begin your drag just to the right of the N in *Election* and between the two horizontal guides, as demonstrated in Figure 10-40. (If you find yourself snapping to one guide or the other, zoom in and try again.) *After* you begin dragging, press and hold the Shift key to constrain the rule to precisely horizontal. (If you press Shift before starting to drag, you'll add the line to the existing star layer.) Drag beyond the edge of the canvas before releasing the mouse, then release Shift.

Figure 10-40.

---

You can adjust the position of the line as you draw it or after you finish. To move the line as you draw it, press and hold the spacebar. To move the line after you draw it, press Ctrl (or ⌘), click the path outline to select it, and press the appropriate arrow key (↑, ↓, ←, or →).

---

27. ***Name the new layer.*** Again, the layer is called Shape 1. Double-click the layer name and enter the new name "Underscore."

28. ***Select the custom shape tool.*** Now to draw the final shape, which will be a crown over the letter T. Photoshop permits you to draw prefab graphics using the custom shape tool. To select this tool, click the ✿ icon, the one to the right of the line tool in the options bar. Or press the U key.

29. **Load all custom shapes included with Photoshop.** Photoshop CS ships with a large custom shape library, but only a few are loaded by default. To load them all:

- Click the ⚏ arrow to the right of the word **Shape** in the options bar.

- Click the ⊙ arrow in the pop-up palette to display a long menu of options, and then choose **All**.

- As shown in Figure 10-41, Photoshop asks whether you want to append the shapes from the All library or replace the current shapes. As its name implies, the All library includes *all* of Photoshop's custom shapes, so click the **OK** button to avoid duplicates.

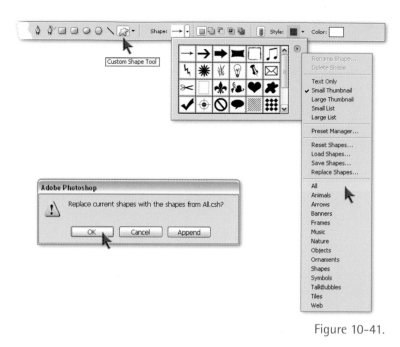

Figure 10-41.

30. **Select the Crown 2 shape.** To better see the shapes, choose **Large Thumbnail** from the pop-up palette's menu. Photoshop's shape collection includes five crowns. Select the second one (♛), which I've outlined in red in Figure 10-42.

31. **Draw the crown shape.** Draw the crown above the letter T, as shown in Figure 10-43 on the following page. As you do, press and hold the Shift key to constrain the crown to its original aspect ratio, so it appears neither stretched nor squished. (Again, be sure to press Shift *after* you begin dragging, not before.) Don't forget that you can press the spacebar to position the crown on the fly.

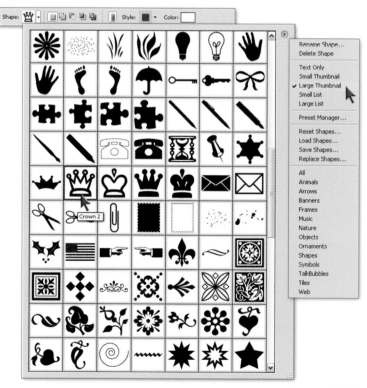

Figure 10-42.

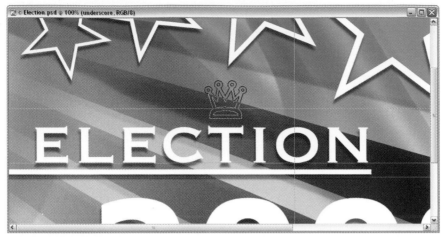

Figure 10-43.

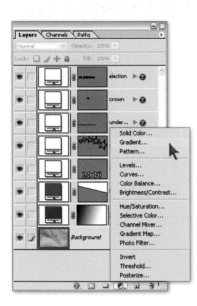

Figure 10-44.

32. *Name the new layer.* Double-click the newest layer's name in the **Layers** palette and enter "Crown" instead.

33. *Switch to the Background layer.* That takes care of all the shapes. My remaining concern with the design is that the word *Election* is too near in color to its background. So I'd like to add a gradient just above the Background layer to create more contrast. Press Shift+Alt+[ (Shift-Option-[ on the Mac) to make the Background layer active.

34. *Change the foreground color to black.* Press D to call up the default foreground and background colors. The active foreground color influences the gradient we're about to create.

35. *Add a gradient layer.* Press the Alt key (Option on the Mac) and click the ⊘ icon at the bottom of the Layers palette. Then choose the **Gradient** command. This forces the display of the **New Layer** dialog box. Enter the settings shown in Figure 10-44 and described below:

- Name the new layer "Shading."

- Set the **Mode** option to **Multiply**. You can always change this later directly inside the Layers palette, but we might as well set it up properly in advance.

- Lower the **Opacity** value to 50 percent.

Then click the **OK** button.

36. *Set the angle to 50 degrees.* Photoshop next displays the **Gradient Fill** dialog box (see Figure 10-45), which shows a black-to-transparent gradient, perfect for our needs. (The black comes from the foreground color.) Change the **Angle** value to 50 degrees and click **OK**. The result is an independent gradient layer that you can adjust later by double-clicking its thumbnail in the Layers palette.

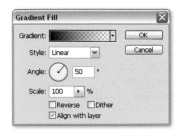

Figure 10-45.

37. *Hide the guides.* Choose **View**→**Show**→**Guides** or press Ctrl+; (⌘-; on the Mac). The final artwork appears in Figure 10-46.

Figure 10-46.

The beauty of this design is that virtually everything about it is scalable. For example, to turn this into a piece of tabloid-sized poster art, choose **Image**→**Image Size** and change the **Width** value in the **Document Size** area to 17 inches. Make sure all three check boxes at the bottom of the dialog box are selected and then click **OK**. Every single shape, drop shadow, and gradient scales to fit the new document size, as shown in Figure 10-47. The background image gets interpolated, of course, but given the dominance of the foreground elements, it's not something anyone's going notice.

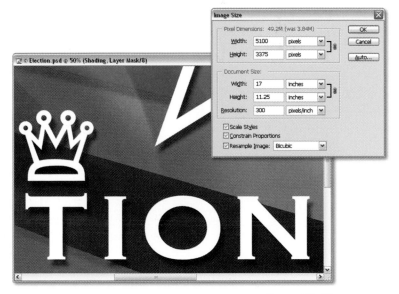

Figure 10-47.

## Bending and Warping Type

Back in Step 37 of the "Creating and Formatting Text" exercise (see page 349), I mentioned that you can't distort live type in the free transform mode. But that doesn't mean distortions are entirely out of the question. In fact, Photoshop CS offers two ways to distort live text layers:

- The first allows you to combine a text layer with a shape outline to create a line of type that flows along a curve, commonly known as *text on a path*.

- The second is a text-specific distortion function called Warp Text. It's so fantastic and easy to use, I very much lament that it can't be applied to shapes and images.

This exercise shows you how the two features work. First, we'll wrap text around the perimeter of a circle. Then we'll stretch and distort letters inside the contours of a text warp shape. All the while, our text layers will remain live and fully editable.

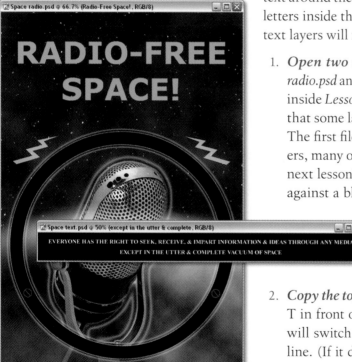

Figure 10-48.

1. *Open two images.* The files in question are *Space radio.psd* and *Space text.psd*, both in the *Lesson 10* folder  inside *Lesson Files-PScs 1on1*. If Photoshop complains that some layers need to be updated, click the **Update** button. The first file contains a handful of text, shape, and image layers, many of which I've assigned layer styles (the subject of the next lesson). The second file contains two lines of white type against a black background. Our first task is to take the text from the second file and flow it around the black circle in the first file. So click the title bar for *Space text.psd* to bring it to the front, as shown in Figure 10-48.

2. *Copy the top text layer.* In the **Layers** palette, double-click the T in front of the layer named **Everyone (top line)**. Photoshop will switch to the type tool and select all the type in the top line. (If it does not, it's probably because you double-clicked the layer name instead of the T. Try again.) Then choose **Edit→ Copy** or press Ctrl+C (⌘-C on the Mac).

3. *Switch back to the Space radio.psd composition.* Press the Esc key to exit the text editing mode. Then click the title bar for the image with the microphone in it.

4. *Display the guidelines.* If you can already see the guidelines, super. If not, choose **View→Show→Guides** or press Ctrl+; (⌘-; on the Mac).

5. *Select the ellipse tool in the toolbox.* To create text around a circle, we need to draw a circle for the text to follow. Click and hold the shape tool icon and choose the ellipse tool, as shown in Figure 10-49.

6. *Click the Paths icon in the options bar.* You can set text around any kind of path outline, whether it's part of a shape layer or stored separately in the Paths palette. But given the number of circles in this document, it'll be easier to see what's going on if we work with the Paths palette. So click the icon highlighted in Figure 10-50.

Figure 10-49.

Figure 10-50.

7. *Draw a big circle.* Drag from one guide intersection to the opposite intersection. Figure 10-51 illustrates the correct and proper left-hander's view. Those of you cursed with the popular blight of right-handedness can drag from left to right instead.

   Speaking of Figure 10-51, the cyan lines are the guides, the black circle is the new path. The beginning of my drag appears as an orange ⊕; the end appears as a violet ⬤. The actual image is dimmed so you can better see what's going on.

8. *Name the new path.* Strictly speaking, you don't *have* to name the path. But you might as well be organized and save your work as you go along. So with that in mind, switch to the **Paths** palette, either by clicking the Paths tab or by choosing **Window→Paths**. Then double-click the **Work Path** item and rename it "Big Circle."

9. *Hide the guidelines.* The sole purpose of the guides was to help you draw the big circle. Now that we're finished with that, choose **View→Show→Guides** or press Ctrl+; (or ⌘-;) to make them go away.

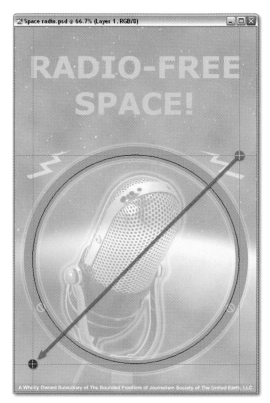

Figure 10-51.

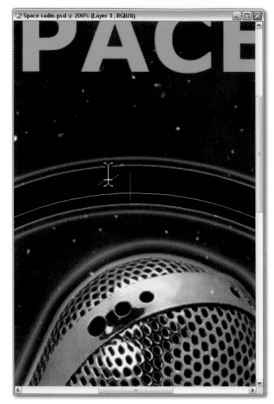

Figure 10-52.

10. **Click the type tool in the toolbox.** Or press the T key. As I mentioned earlier, the horizontal type tool is the one and only text tool you ever need. It creates point text, area text, and now, text on a path.

11. **Click at the top of the big circle.** When you move your cursor over the circular path, the cursor changes slightly to include a little swash through its center. This indicates you're about to append text to the path. Click at the center topmost point in the path to set the blinking insertion marker on the path, as shown in Figure 10-52.

12. **Paste the text.** Choose **Edit→Paste** or press Ctrl+V (⌘-V on the Mac). Photoshop pastes the text you copied back in Step 2 along the circumference of the path. The copied text was centered, and so the pasted text is centered as well, exactly at the point at which you clicked in the preceding step. The result is a string of characters that rest evenly along the top of the circle, centered between the red ⊘s, as shown in Figure 10-53.

Figure 10-53.

If your text is not quite so evenly centered as in Figure 10-53, you may need to reposition it slightly. Press the Ctrl key (or ⌘ on the Mac) and move the cursor over the letters to get an I-beam with two arrows beside it. Then drag the text to move it around the circle until the first E and the last A are equidistant from the two red ∅s. Small drags usually produce the best results.

When you have the type where you want it, press the Enter key on the keypad (or Ctrl+Enter or ⌘-Return) to accept the new text layer and move on.

13. *Copy the second line of type.* Now to create the text along the bottom of the circle. Switch to the *Space text.psd* window. Double-click the T in front of the layer named **Except (bottom line)** in the **Layers** palette to select the text. Then choose **Edit**→ **Copy** or press Ctrl+C (⌘-C).

14. *Select the next layer down in the composition.* Press Esc to deactivate the text. Then return to the *Space radio.psd* composition. Press Alt+[ or Option-[ to select the **Radio-Free Space!** layer. We're doing this for two reasons: First, I want the next layer you create to appear in front of this one. Second, it'll allow us to start with a fresh circle path instead of repurposing the one used in the top layer.

15. *Click at the bottom of the big circle.* Go to the **Paths** palette and click the **Big Circle** item to once again display the circle in the image window. Still armed with the type tool, click at the center of the bottom of the circular path. Again, Photoshop displays a blinking insertion marker, this time emanating down from the circle.

16. *Paste the text.* Choose **Edit**→**Paste** or press Ctrl+V (⌘-V). As before, Photoshop pastes the text along the perimeter of the circle. But this time, the text comes in upside-down, as shown in Figure 10-54.

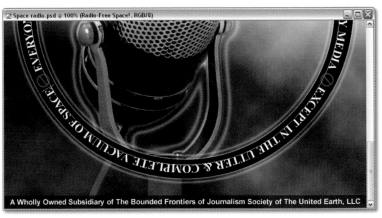

Figure 10-54.

17. ***Flip the text to the other side of the path.*** Press and hold the Ctrl key (⌘ on the Mac) and hover the cursor over the bottom of the text (roughly the *O* in *COMPLETE*) to get the I-beam with the double arrow. Then drag upward. Photoshop flips the text to the other side of the path, turning it right-side-up as shown in Figure 10-55.

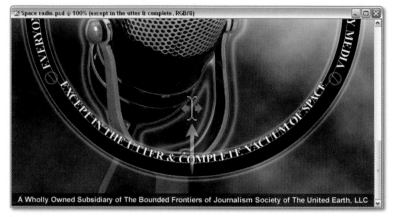

Figure 10-55.

18. ***Select all of the type.*** Next we need to nudge the type down using a function called *baseline shift*, which raises or lowers selected characters with respect to their natural resting position, the so-called *baseline*. Press Ctrl+A (or ⌘-A) to select all the characters in the new text layer.

19. ***Bring up the Character palette.*** Click its tab if it's already on screen. Otherwise, choose **Window**→**Character** or press Ctrl+T (⌘-T on the Mac).

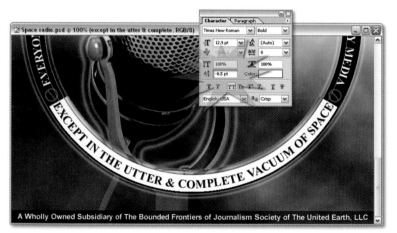

Figure 10-56.

20. ***Set the baseline shift value to −8.5.*** In the **Character** palette, click the icon that looks like a capital letter paired with a superscript one (**A**<u>**a**</u>) to select the baseline shift value, highlighted in Figure 10-56. Then enter −8.5 to shift the letters down 8.5 points, which translates to about 18 pixels inside this 150 ppi image.

---

You can also nudge the baseline shift value incrementally from the keyboard. Press Shift+Alt+↓ (or Shift-Option-↓) to lower the characters 2 points at a time. Shift+Alt+↑ (or Shift-Option-↑) raises the characters.

---

Press Enter on the keypad to accept your changes. (If the baseline shift value is selected, you may have to press Enter twice.) This completes the text on the circle. Now let's move on to warping some text.

21. *Select the Radio-Free Space! Layer.* Press Alt+[ or Option-[ to drop down to the layer. Right now, the text treatment is almost comically bad. Cyan letters, wide leading, Verdana—how much worse could it get? We'll start by spicing up the text with some layer styles, and then we'll warp the text for a classic pulp fiction look.

22. *Turn on the layer styles.* In the **Layers** palette, click the ▶ to the right of the **Radio-Free Space!** layer name to twirl open the layer and reveal a list of three styles I applied in advance: Outer Glow, Bevel and Emboss, and Stroke. Click in front of the word **Effects** to display the three styles.

23. *Set the blend mode to Overlay.* Select **Overlay** from the pop-up menu at the top of the Layers palette. Or press Shift+Alt+O (Shift-Option-O on the Mac). The result appears in Figure 10-57.

24. *Click the warp icon in the options bar.* The type tool should still be active. Assuming that it is, look to the right side of the options bar for an icon featuring a skewed T above a tiny path (highlighted in Figure 10-58). Click this icon to bring up the **Warp Text** dialog box.

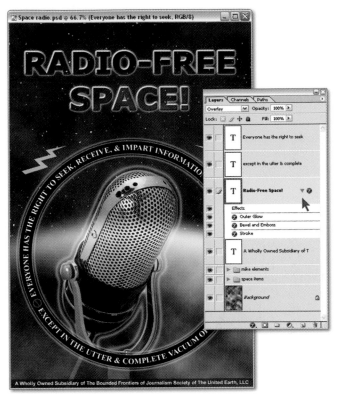

Figure 10-57.

Figure 10-58.

25. *Apply the Arc Lower style.* The Warp Text dialog box features the following options:

    - Select the shape inside which the text bends from the **Style** menu. The icons provide hints as to what the effect will look like. But if in doubt, choose an option and watch the preview in the image window.

    - Change the angle of the warp by selecting the **Horizontal** or **Vertical** radio button. Assuming Western-world text like we're working with here, Horizontal bends the baselines and Vertical warps the individual letters.

- Use the **Bend** value to determine the amount of warp and the direction in which the text bends. You can enter any value from –100 to 100 percent.

- The two **Distortion** sliders add perspective-style distortion to the warp effect.

For example, Figure 10-59 shows four variations on the Arc Lower style. The icon next to the style name shows the effect is flat on top and bent at the bottom. Assuming Horizontal is active, this means the warp is applied exclusively to the bottom of the text. A positive Bend value tugs the bottom of the text downward (first image); a negative value pushes it upward (second).

---

To achieve a strict perspective-style distortion, choose any Style option and set the Bend value to 0 percent. Examples of purely horizontal and vertical distortions appear in the last two images in Figure 10-59.

---

For this exercise, choose **Arc Lower** from the **Style** pop-up menu. Then set the **Bend** value to –40 percent. The resulting effect looks awful—easily the worst of those shown in Figure 10-59—but that's temporary. Have faith that we'll fix things in future steps and click **OK**.

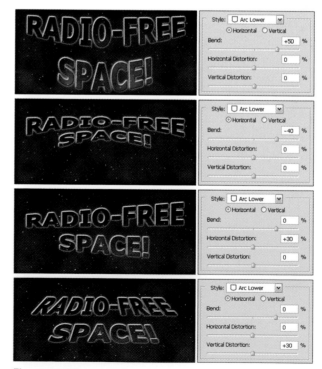

Figure 10-59.

26. ***Increase the size of the word SPACE!*** Triple-click on the word *SPACE!* with the type tool to select both it and its exclamation point. Press Ctrl+Shift+> (or ⌘-Shift->) to increase the type size incrementally until the width of the selected text matches that of the text above it. (To resize faster, press Ctrl+Shift+Alt+> or ⌘-Shift-Option->.) Or just click the ⇅T icon and change the type size value to 88 points, as in Figure 10-60.

Figure 10-60.

27. ***Increase the vertical scale of all characters.*** One of the byproducts of warping is that it stretches or squishes characters, thus requiring you to scale them back to more visually appealing proportions. In our case, the text is *really* squished, so some vertical scaling is in order. In the **Character** palette, click the ⇅T icon to select the vertical scale value, highlighted in Figure 10-61. Then enter 167 percent and press the Enter or Return key to make the letters taller without making them wider.

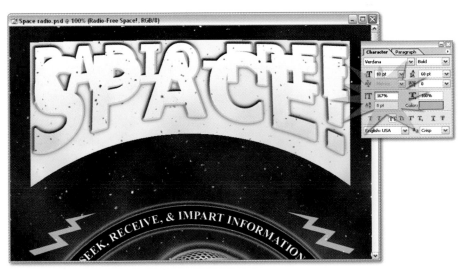

Figure 10-61.

Figure 10-62.

28. ***Increase the leading.*** Press Alt+↓ (on the Mac, Option-↓) to incrementally increase the leading. Press Ctrl+Alt+↓ (or ⌘-Option-↓) to increase the leading more quickly. I eventually arrived at a leading value of 126 points (see Figure 10-62).

29. ***Press Enter to accept the warped text.*** Remember to press Enter on the keypad. The final composition appears in Figure 10-63.

It's important to note that throughout all these adjustments, every single text layer remains fully editable. For example, to change the text from *RADIO-FREE SPACE* (indicating a space free of radio) to *RADIO FREE SPACE* (which implies that the radio in space is free to all), simply replace the hyphen with a space character. The layer effects are likewise live. To change the style of warp, simply select the text layer and click the text warp icon in the options bar.

Figure 10-63.

# WHAT DID YOU LEARN?

Match the key concept in the numbered list below with the letter
of the phrase that best describes it. Answers appear upside-down
at the bottom of the page.

## Key Concepts

1. Raster art
2. Vector-based objects
3. Formatting attributes
4. Point text
5. Area text
6. Fractional character widths
7. Every-line composer
8. Pair kerning
9. Indent Sides By
10. Series duplication
11. Text on a path
12. Warp Text

## Descriptions

A. Font family, type style, size, leading, alignment, and a wealth of other options for modifying the appearance of live text.

B. This numerical value lets you adjust the sharpness of points in a star drawn with the polygon tool.

C. A column of type created by dragging with the type tool, useful for setting long sentences or entire paragraphs.

D. Digital photographs and scanned artwork composed exclusively of colored pixels.

E. A special kind of text layer in which text is attached to a path outline to create a line of type that flows along a curve.

F. The best means for calculating text spacing, which permits Photoshop to move a character by a fraction of a pixel.

G. A succession of duplicated objects, scaled, rotated, and otherwise transformed in equal increments.

H. Mathematically defined text and shapes that can be scaled or otherwise transformed without any degradation in quality.

I. An option that spaces all lines of type in a selected layer by similar amounts to give the layer a more even, aesthetically pleasing appearance.

J. A text layer that has no maximum column width and aligns to the point at which you clicked with the type tool.

K. This dialog box bends and distorts live text to create wavy, bulging, and perspective effects.

L. The adjusted amount of horizontal space between two neighboring characters of type.

## Answers

LESSON

**11**

# LAYER STYLES AND ADJUSTMENTS

I LONG FOR the day when everything in Photoshop is a live effect. Just imagine if hours after applying the Unsharp Mask command, you elected to revisit the filter and tweak its settings. But instead of applying the new settings on top of the old ones, as happens now, you were able to apply them *in place of* the old ones. In other words, just imagine if the filter was dynamic. And not just Unsharp Mask, but every single function in the entire program. It would be impossible to make a mistake, impossible to harm an image, impossible to go wrong.

Alas, that glad day continues to elude us. But that's not to say the present is entirely bleak in this particular regard. Today's Photoshop provides us with a small glimpse of its future dynamic self in the form of layer effects and adjustment layers. Both are parametric, forever editable, and wonderfully flexible. In fact, if everything in Photoshop were this well implemented, I'd learn how to play a happy instrument like the banjo just so I could sing the program's praises. As it is, we are still left with considerable (if not banjoworthy) cause for joy.

## The Amazing World of Live Effects

*Layer effects* are a collection of dynamic color and contour attributes that let you add dimension, lighting, and texture to otherwise flat, drab objects. *Adjustment layers* are collections of dialog box settings, modeled after the color adjustment commands we examined in Lessons 2 and 3, that correct or modify the colors of the layers behind them.

# ABOUT THIS LESSON

## Project Files

Before beginning the exercises, make sure that you've installed the lesson files from the CD, as explained in Step 5 on page xv of the Preface. This should result in a folder called *Lesson Files-PScs 1on1* on your desktop. We'll be working with the files inside the *Lesson 11* subfolder.

In this lesson, you'll explore the worlds of layer effects and adjustment layers. Specifically, you'll learn how to:

## Video Lesson 11: Introducing Effects

Many folks regard layer effects as little more than a means for adding drop shadows. But that's only the beginning. Used properly, layer effects are automated painting tools that let you not only enhance photographic layers, but also turn hand-drawn elements, text layers, or vector shapes into fully realized objects with dimension and depth.

For a firsthand introduction to layer effects, as well as the predefined styles Photoshop includes in its Styles palette, watch the eleventh video lesson on the CD. Insert the CD, click the **Start Training** button, click the Set **4** button, and then select **11, Introducing Effects** from the Lessons list. In this 9 minute 34 second movie, I tell you about the following operations and shortcuts:

| Operation | Windows shortcut | Macintosh shortcut |
| --- | --- | --- |
| Show or hide the Styles palette | F6, then click Styles tab | F6, then click Styles tab |
| Display the Layer Style dialog box | Double-click layer effect | Double-click layer effect |
| Duplicate an entire image | Ctrl+Shift+Alt+D* | ⌘-Shift-Option-D* |
| Append one layer style to another | Shift-click item in Styles palette | Shift-click item in Styles palette |
| Save layer style for later use | Click inside Styles palette | Click inside Styles palette |

* Works only if you loaded the Deke Keys keyboard shortcuts (as directed on page xvii of Preface).

As their names imply, both layer effects and adjustment layers depend on layers to work their magic. So I've assembled a simple layered document to show you how both features work:

- Figure 11-1 shows a composition with two floating layers—an image and a strip of torn paper—set against a beige background. Each layer has one of the most common kinds of layer effects applied to it, a *drop shadow*, which is nothing more than a silhouette of the layer that is offset and blurred. The shadow implies a gap in depth between the layers. And because they drop downward, the shadows suggest a light source that shines from above.

- Drop shadows are handy, but they are just one of several different kinds of layer effects. In Figure 11-2, I created a new layer. Using two separate layer effects, I traced a dark outline around the outside of the layer and a light outline around the inside. This results in a slight "toasting" effect, which helps separate the layer from its environment even more.

Figure 11-1.

Figure 11-2.

Figure 11-3.

• The lower-right corner of Figure 11-3 sports an adjustment layer. Based on the Gradient Map command (see the "Colorizing a Grayscale Image" exercise, which begins on page 75 of Lesson 3), this adjustment layer inverts and colorizes the paper, photograph, and background layers below it.

• Figure 11-4 illustrates another adjustment layer modeled after the Gradient Map command. But this one doesn't invert colors; it just changes them, including the layer of blue from the previous figure. I even managed to assign an effect to the adjustment layer, one that sculpts the perimeter of the layer.

The upshot is that layer effects and adjustment layers possess an amazing capacity for interaction. One layer effect can mix with another, one adjustment layer can modify another, and layer effects can be applied directly to adjustment layers. You'll see examples of these interactions—and get a sense of just how useful they can be—in the upcoming exercises.

Figure 11-4.

# Layer Attributes Versus Layers

Layer effects and adjustment layers share many things in common. Both are parametric, take up very little room in memory, are accessible from the Layers palette, and remain editable as long as you save them in the native Photoshop PSD or TIFF format.

But layer effects and adjustment layers are ultimately unique functions, implemented in different ways:

- You assign a layer effect to an existing layer. An adjustment layer exists as a layer all its own. Figure 11-5 shows examples of each.

- A layer effect controls the appearance of just one layer at a time. An adjustment layer affects the color and luminosity of all layers below it.

- You can duplicate layer effects by dragging them from one layer to another. To duplicate an adjustment layer, you clone it by pressing Ctrl+J (or ⌘-J) or by dragging it from one image window and dropping it into another.

- You can store a collection of layer effects as a custom *layer style* in the Styles palette. To save the settings for an adjustment layer, click the Save button in the layer's color adjustment dialog box.

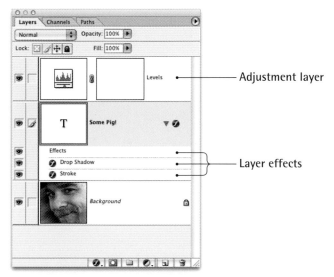

Figure 11-5.

The first four exercises in this lesson are devoted to the myriad applications for layer effects. Adjustment layers are every bit as useful. But because we already looked at the core color adjustment commands in Lessons 2 and 3, we cover them in a single exercise, beginning on page 405.

# Adding Layer Effects

Layer effects serve two opposing, highly practical purposes: to set layers apart and to bring them together. For example, a layer effect that casts a shadow suggests that the layer is raised above the surface of its surroundings. This calls attention to the perimeter of the layer and adds depth to the image, both of which help to distinguish the layered element from a busy composition. Meanwhile, a layer effect can also blend the interior or perimeter of a layer with its background. The independent layers appear not as disparate elements of a composition, but as seamless portions of a cohesive whole.

The following exercise demonstrates both capacities of layer effects using Photoshop's most venerable effects, Drop Shadow and Inner Shadow. Both are *directional effects*, meaning that they cast colors by a specified distance at a specified angle. The effects may occur either outside or inside the layer and, as you'll see, they can just as easily result in highlights as in shadows. The exercise will end with the Color Overlay effect, which is most useful for overriding the colors in a layer.

1. **Open a couple of images.** Go to the *Lesson 11* folder inside *Lesson Files-PScs 1on1* and open the files *Happy Juice.psd* and *Max in kitchen.tif*, both of which appear in Figure 11-6. The former is a half-finished advertisement for a snappy fruit-like beverage; the latter is a picture of my son, Max, enjoying his first carbonated beverage.

2. **Display the guidelines.** Bring the *Happy Juice.psd* image to the front. You should see three guides—one horizontal and two vertical. If not, choose **View→Show→Guides** or press Ctrl+; (⌘-; on the Mac) to make them visible. You will use these to position the imported image of Max.

3. **Load Max's mask as a selection.** After reading the former aloud three times fast, click the *Max in kitchen.tif* title bar to bring that image window to the front. Then open the **Channels** palette and Ctrl-click (or ⌘-click) on the **Mask** item or press Ctrl+Alt+4 (⌘-Option-4 on the Mac) to load the selection outline.

4. **Drag the selection into the ad composition.** Press and hold the Ctrl key (⌘ on the Mac) to get the move tool and then drag Max from *Max in kitchen.tif* into the *Happy Juice.psd* image window. Drop him any old place for now. Max should land directly in front of the Background layer, as in Figure 11-7 on the facing page.

Figure 11-6.

5. ***Move Max into alignment with the guides.*** Again press Ctrl (or ⌘) and drag Max inside his new home until he exactly aligns with *all three* of the guidelines. Figure 11-7 uses red arrowheads to highlight the three points of contact.

6. ***Hide the guides and rename the new layer.*** We're done with the guides, so press Ctrl+; (or ⌘-;) to make them go away. In the **Layers** palette, double-click the new layer name, **Layer 1**, and rename it "Spokesboy."

   The mask around Max is pretty darn good, if I do say so myself. (Heaven knows, I spent enough time on it!) But the transitions are still a bit iffy in places. Also, given the extreme nature of this ad, I want Max to pop off the page, as if he's a cartoon character pasted into a different environment. Thankfully, you can smooth out transitions and add a bit of cartoon depth using layer effects.

7. ***Choose the Drop Shadow layer effect.*** We'll start with the most popular and arguably the most useful layer effect, the drop shadow. Click the florin-in-a-circle icon (*ƒ*) at the bottom of the Layers palette to bring up a menu of ten layer effects. Then choose **Drop Shadow** (see Figure 11-8).

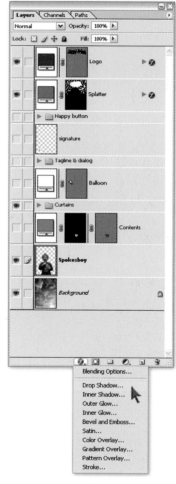

Figure 11-7.

Figure 11-8.

8. ***Turn on the Preview check box.*** You'll be working inside the **Layer Style** dialog box for several long steps, so naturally you'll want to be able to see what you're doing to the image.

9. ***Adjust the Drop Shadow settings.*** The Layer Style dialog box is notorious for the sheer number of options it offers. But every one of them serves a purpose, so it's worth taking a moment to understand them. Here's a quick rundown of the options that currently confront you, along with the settings I want you to enter (pictured in Figure 11-9):

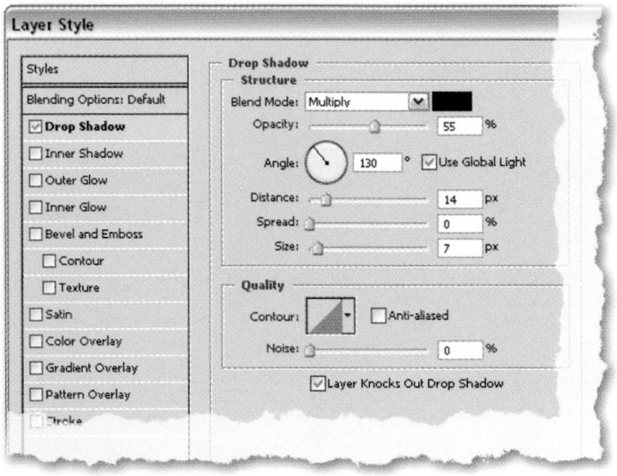

Figure 11-9.

- Leave the **Blend Mode** set to **Multiply**. Although it has no effect on black (black doesn't get any darker), Multiply is the one blend mode that ensures that any color, black or otherwise, darkens its background in the same manner as a bona fide shadow.

- Leave the color swatch set to black. Other colors can serve as shadows, but since black does the job just fine, why change it?

- At 100 percent **Opacity**, the black shadow would be fully opaque, subject to the softness specified by the Size value. For my son, reduce this value to 55 percent.

- Set the **Angle** value to 130 degrees, which puts the light source, or "sun," above and to the left of the layer. This casts a shadow in the opposite direction, –50 degrees, or down and to the right.

- Turn on **Use Global Light**. This locks in the sun at 130 degrees for all directional layer effects, including Drop Shadow, Inner Shadow, and Bevel and Emboss.

- Enter a **Distance** of 14 pixels, so that the shadow is offset down and to the right 14 pixels from the original.

For the record, modifying values isn't the only way to change the angle and distance of a drop shadow. You can also move your cursor into the image window and drag the shadow directly. If the Use Global Light check box is on, Photoshop moves all other directional effects linked to this option as well.

- The **Spread** value defines the sharpness of the shadow. Leave it set to 0 percent for a soft, blurry effect.

- The **Size** value blurs the shadow. It's a lot like the Radius value in the Feather or Gaussian Blur dialog box, except that it's calculated as a linear function instead of Gaussian (see "Gaussian Blur and Median," Step 5, page 259). In other words, the shadow drops off evenly like a gradient, and the Size value defines the size of that gradient. However you care to think about it, change the value to 7 pixels.

- The **Contour** option lets you change how the shadow drops off. For example, if you want a Gaussian distribution, choose the hill-shaped Gaussian icon, as in Figure 11-10. But in our case, the default Linear setting (the straight slope) works just fine.

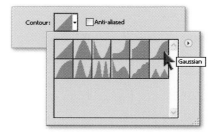

Figure 11-10.

- The **Anti-aliased** check box smoothes out rough spots in the event you select a spiky Contour setting. We did not, so leave it off.

- The **Noise** value lets you add random flecks to an image to mimic the look of film grain. In this case, it's unnecessary. Leave the value set to 0 percent.

- Leave the **Layer Knocks Out Drop Shadow** check box turned on. This ensures that the drop shadow appears exclusively around the edges of a layer and not inside. Turn the option off only if you want to see through a layer to its shadow (as when the layer is translucent or includes a blend mode).

The result of all these settings is a small but relatively focused shadow that darkens everything behind it. And because it's parametric, you can modify it on the fly. It also takes up just a few K in memory and on disk.

10. ***Add an Inner Shadow effect.*** Click the **Inner Shadow** item on the left-hand side of the dialog box to turn on the default Inner Shadow effect and display its settings in the Layer Style dialog box.

11. ***Adjust the Inner Shadow settings.*** Most of the options available when defining an Inner Shadow are the same as those we saw when defining the Drop Shadow. So I'll focus strictly on those options that are different, or whose values I want you to change (as shown in Figure 11-11):

- The left side of Max's hair is too dark compared with its background, so let's lighten it. That's no problem—the Inner Shadow effect can lighten just as easily as it can darken. All you have to do is set the **Blend Mode** option to **Screen** and select a light color.

- Click the black color swatch to bring up the **Color Picker** dialog box. Then click in a light portion of the image background to bring some of the blue sky into Max's hair. For my part, I got H, S, and B values of 210, 55, and 95, respectively. Click the **OK** button to return to the **Layer Style** dialog box.

- Change the **Opacity** value to 75 percent (unless it's that way already, in which case, leave it).

- As long as **Use Global Light** is turned on, the **Angle** value is 130 degrees, as before. The difference is that the shadow now extends down and to the right from the upper-left inside edge—that is, inside Max's hair. Perfect, move on.

- You want the effect to be as subtle as possible—to fix the problem, but no more. The best way to accomplish that is to combine a small Distance value with a larger Size value. Set the **Distance** value to 6 pixels.

- **Choke** is the equivalent of Spread in the Drop Shadow panel; that is, it sharpens the effect. You want blurry, so leave it set to 0.

- Enter a **Size** value of 11 pixels. This results in a soft, diffused highlight.

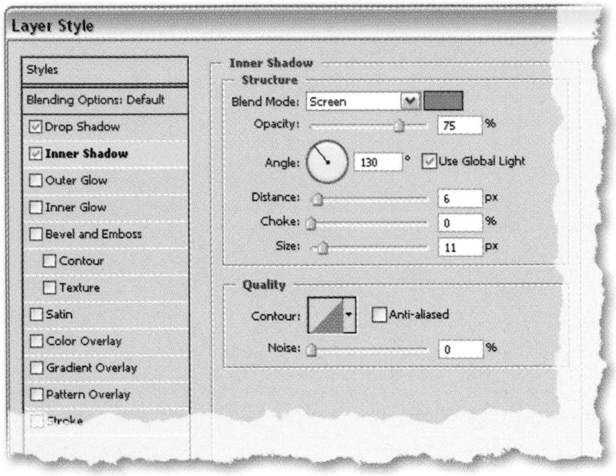

Figure 11-12 compares Max before and after the drop and inner shadow effects. The drop shadow is consistent with the shadows on his face; the inner shadow highlights the dark edges of his hair.

Figure 11-11.

12. **Add a Color Overlay effect.** Still inside the Layer Style dialog box, click the **Color Overlay** item on the left-hand side. Photoshop covers Max with an opaque shellacking of red. Why would anyone want to coat a layer with red? Clearly, no one would, which is why you'll modify the settings in the very next step.

13. **Adjust the Color Overlay settings.** For once, Photoshop graces us with very few options, and for this we are glad. Set them as shown in Figure 11-13 and as outlined below:

   - Reduce the **Opacity** value to 30 percent. Now you can see Max through the red.

   - Click the red color swatch and change the **H** value in the **Color Picker** dialog box to 30 degrees, or orange. Then click **OK**.

   - Back in the Layer Srtyle dialog box, set the blend mode to **Color**. Photoshop restores the original luminosity values and blends them with the orange skin tones.

The new coat of orange serves two purposes. First, it evens out some of the variations in Max's skin tones. (Hey, he's my kid, so it stands to reason we share the same pale, pinkish skin.) Second, it matches him to the product color, as if he's chock full of Happy Juice.

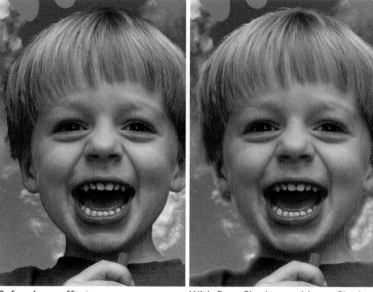

Before layer effects      With Drop Shadow and Inner Shadow

Figure 11-12.

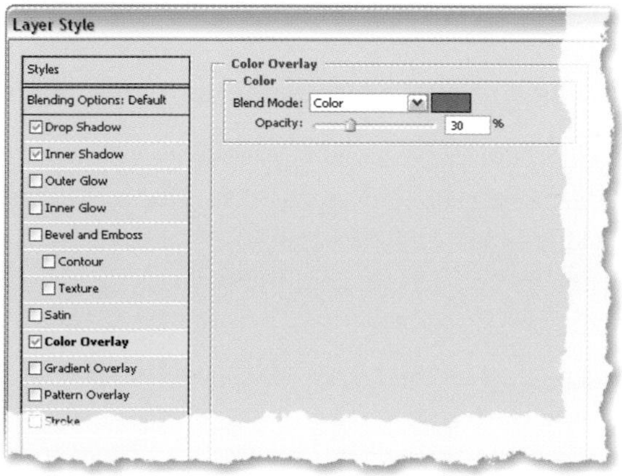

Figure 11-13.

Figure 11-14.

14. ***Click the OK button.*** Photoshop closes the Layer Style dialog box and accepts your changes. Three new effects appear below the Spokesboy layer in the Layers palette—Drop Shadow, Inner Shadow, and Color Overlay—as in Figure 11-14.

---

If after applying a layer effect, you decide you don't want it, don't throw it away. Just click its eyeball (👁) to turn it off. This gets rid of the effect without trashing its settings. This way, you can re-establish the effect later, along with your previous settings.

---

15. ***Save your composition.*** Choose **File→ Save As**. Name your modified composition "Happy Juice edit-1.psd" and save it in the same *Lesson 11* folder inside *Lesson Files-PScs 1on1*. Be very certain you've saved this file because it will serve as the starting point for the next exercise.

## Applying Strokes and Glows

So far, you've seen three of the ten layer effects available to Photoshop. While we won't be looking at every single one of them, we owe it to ourselves to experiment with a few more.

And so it is we proceed to the next category of effects, strokes and glows, which trace colors uniformly around the perimeter of a layer. A *stroke* traces the layer with an outline of a specified thickness. The two *glows*, Outer Glow and Inner Glow, heap on additional attributes such as blur, noise, and contour. As with shadows, a stroke or glow may produce a light or dark effect depending on the blend mode and color you select.

In this exercise, you'll use strokes and glows to outline a few elements in our ongoing Happy Juice composition. As you'll see, these effects can be used to delineate objects and improve the legibility of large display type.

1. ***Open the image you saved in the last exercise.*** If you're following on the heels of the last exercise, the file may still be open. If not, open the file *Happy Juice edit-1.psd* in the *Lesson 11* folder inside *Lesson Files-PScs 1on1*. The file and its layers should appear as in Figure 11-14. (Note that this is a file you created and saved in the last exercise. If you cannot locate the file, you can create it by following the steps in the preceding section.)

2. ***Turn on the Balloon layer.*** Three levels up from Spokesboy is a layer called **Balloon**. Click its gray vector mask thumbnail in the **Layers** palette to display the layer, make it active, and prevent the path outline from displaying on screen. (You have to move your cursor away from the thumbnail for the outline to go away.) If the path outline persists, click the vector mask thumbnail again. Your composition should now contain a talk balloon.

3. ***Choose the Stroke layer effect.*** Click the ⊘ icon at the bottom of the Layers palette and choose the **Stroke** option. Photoshop displays the **Layer Style** dialog box.

4. ***Adjust the Stroke settings.*** Shown in Figure 11-15, the options for the Stroke effect are a relatively simple bunch, so I'll run through them quickly:

   - The **Size** value determines the thickness of the stroke. Set it to 2 pixels.

   - Use the **Position** option to define how the stroke traces the perimeter of the layer. It may be fully inside the layer, fully outside, or half in, half out (Center). Select **Outside** to create the smoothest corners.

   - Set the **Blend Mode** to **Normal** and the **Opacity** to 100 percent for a solid, opaque stroke.

   - The **Fill Type** may be a solid color, a gradient, or a predefined pattern. For this image, leave the option set to **Color**.

   - Click the **Color** swatch. Inside the **Color Picker** dialog box, change the **S** and **B** values to 0 percent to get black. Then click **OK**.

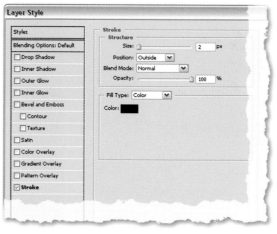

Figure 11-15.

Figure 11-16.

When you're finished, click **OK** to close the Layer Style dialog box and apply the black stroke. The stroked talk balloon appears in Figure 11-16.

---

Notice that in the figure the stroke appears antialiased, with soft transitions around the curves. This is a function of the stroke tracing a shape layer. If you applied the stroke effect to a pixel-based image layer, however, it would appear jagged. When stroking pixel-based images, it is better to use the Outer Glow effect with the Spread value set between 70 and 80 percent.

---

5. *Lower the fill opacity.* Reduce the **Fill** value in the **Layers** palette to 70 percent. This reduces the so-called *fill opacity*, which is the opacity of the interior of the layer. In this case, it makes the white talk balloon translucent without affecting the black stroke one iota, as in Figure 11-17. (The standard Opacity value would reduce the opacity of both the balloon and the stroke.) The Fill value gives you the option of controlling the opacity of a layer and its effects independently.

---

To change the Fill value from the keyboard, first make sure one of the selection tools is active, and then press Shift with a number key. In this example, you'd press Shift+7.

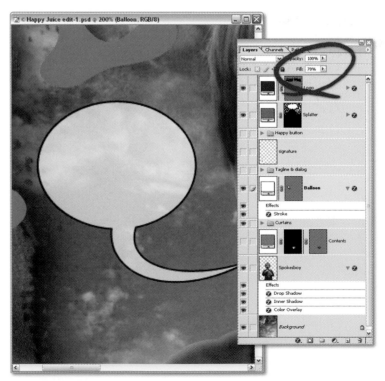

Figure 11-17.

Note that the Fill value in the Layers palette is identical to the Fill Opacity value in the Blending Options section of the Layer Style dialog box. Although they have slightly different names, they serve the same purpose; moreover, changing one value likewise changes the other.

6. **_Turn on the Tagline and Dialog layer set._** Click this folder in the Layers palette to make the layers inside the set visible. The set includes several text layers, including the contents of the talk balloon, as pictured in Figure 11-18.

7. **_Turn on the effects for the Logo layer._** Click the vector mask thumbnail for the **Logo** layer to make it active and hide the path outlines. Then click the ▶ to the right of the layer name to twirl open the layer. Click in front of the word **Effects** to turn on two layer effects, Drop Shadow and Bevel and Emboss.

Unfortunately, the introduction of the layer effects makes the text less legible than before. But as luck would have it, the official Happy Juice logo includes a couple of strokes around it, one light and one dark, which will help it stand out. The Stroke effect can't accommodate concentric rings of color, but an Outer Glow can.

8. **_Turn on the Outer Glow effect._** Double-click either **Drop Shadow** or **Bevel and Emboss** to display the **Layer Style** dialog box. Then click **Outer Glow** in the left-hand list to turn on the effect and display its settings.

Figure 11-18.

9. **Adjust the Outer Glow settings.** I often see artists use the Outer Glow effect to add bright, happy highlights behind a layer. But it's most useful for creating controlled stroke effects, as I've established in Figure 11-19. Here's how it works:

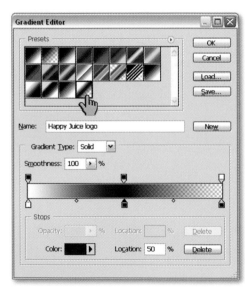

Figure 11-19.

• As when applying the Stroke effect a moment ago, you want a fully opaque outline. So set the **Blend Mode** to **Normal** and the **Opacity** to 100 percent.

• The **Noise** option randomizes the display of pixels inside the Outer Glow effect. Leave it set to 0 percent.

• For the moment, skip the color swatch and move on to the **Technique** setting. The Softer option rounds off corners in a layer; the Precise option exactly traces them. Choose **Softer** for the smoothest, most consistent strokes.

• As when setting a Drop Shadow, the **Spread** value sharpens the effect, precisely what you need when creating strokes. Raise the value to 40 percent.

• To increase the thickness of the stroke, raise the **Size** value to 10 pixels.

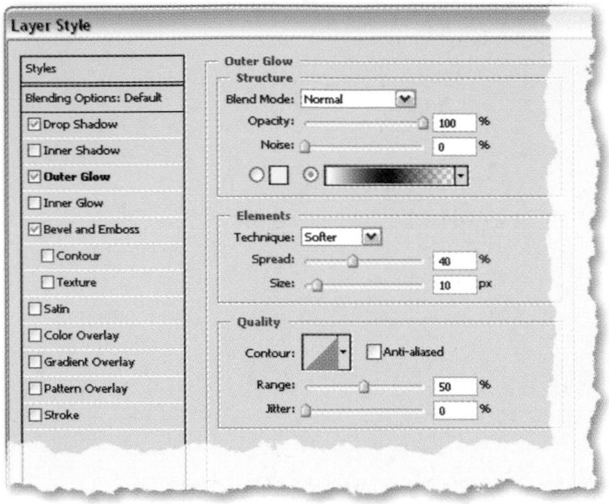

The Quality settings allow you to create variations in the opacity of a stroke by selecting a Contour setting. You can also move the variations toward and away from the perimeter of the layer with the Range value. We have no need to do either, so leave these options set to their defaults.

10. **Assign a gradient.** Here's where things get interesting. The Outer Glow effect lets you outline a layer with a flat color or a gradient. The latter results in concentric rings of color, necessary for creating multicolored strokes. Click the gradient bar to open the **Gradient Editor** dialog box, pictured in Figure 11-20.

11. **Load and assign a custom gradient.** Click the **Load**  button on the right side of the dialog box and then find the *Lesson 11* folder inside the *Lesson Files-PScs 1on1* folder. Open the file called *Logo gradient.grd*. A new white-to-blue swatch appears inside the Gradient Editor dialog box. Click the new gradient swatch. The Name option now reads Happy Juice Logo, as in Figure 11-20. Click **OK** to apply the gradient to the Outer Glow effect.

Figure 11-20.

12. **Click the OK button.** Clicking **OK** closes the Layer Style dialog box and accepts your changes. Photoshop now displays a double-stroke effect around the type, increasing its legibility as witnessed in Figure 11-21. (If the white portion of your stroke appears a bit bluer, don't worry; it's entirely a function of your screen display. Press Ctrl+Alt+0 or ⌘-Option-0 to zoom in to the 100 percent zoom ratio for a more accurate look.)

13. **Save your composition.** Again choose **File→Save As**. Name this newest eye-catching piece of commercial art "Happy Juice edit-2.psd" and save it to the *Lesson 11* folder inside *Lesson Files-PScs 1on1*. This step is not optional; the file you save will serve as the starting point for the very next exercise.

Figure 11-21.

## Simulating Reflections with Bevel and Emboss

So far you've used layer effects to augment layers in a composition and trace shape outlines. But you can also use layer effects to transform flat, dull layers into photorealistic, three-dimensional ones. And the best effect for this purpose is the most complex one, Bevel and Emboss. Another of Photoshop's directional effects, Bevel and Emboss traces highlights along one side of a layer and shadows along the opposite side.

The goal of this exercise is to employ the Bevel and Emboss effect to turn the layer of orange spots into deliciously plausible liquid. Whether it'll really fool viewers of your artwork is highly unlikely. But it'll make them *want* to believe—and in the realm of special effects, that's the greatest trick of all.

1. **Open the image you saved in the last exercise.** If it's already open, fantastic. If not, open the *Happy Juice edit-2.psd* file that you saved in Step 13 of the previous exercise, which should be in the *Lesson 11* folder inside *Lesson Files-PScs 1on1*. The image should appear as in Figure 11-21. (If you can't locate the file, you'll need to follow the steps in the previous two sections.)

2. ***Turn on the effects for the Splatter layer.*** Click the **Splatter** layer to make it active. Then twirl open the layer and click in front of the word **Effects** to turn on two layer effects, our dear friends Drop Shadow and Inner Shadow. Both are set to make authentic shadows, as shown in Figure 11-22. The effect is slightly slimy, but hardly liquid.

Figure 11-22.

3. ***Open the Bevel and Emboss effect.*** Double-click either **Drop Shadow** or **Inner Shadow** to display the **Layer Style** dialog box. Then click **Bevel and Emboss** in the left-hand list to turn on the effect and display its settings. Even using the default settings, Bevel and Emboss gives the Splatter layer a sense of depth, as in Figure 11-23. But we can do better.

4. ***Adjust the Bevel and Emboss settings.*** The settings you're about to enter all appear in Figure 11-24. But because this effect is more complicated than the others, we're going to take it more slowly, starting with the **Structure** options:

   • The **Style** setting decides whether the beveled edges appear inside or outside the boundaries of the layer. Inner Bevel is in, Outer Bevel is out, Emboss is both, Pillow Emboss inverts the outer

Figure 11-23.

bevel with respect to the inner, and Stroke Emboss applies a beveled edge to an outline defined using the Stroke layer effect. Choose **Inner Bevel**.

- The **Technique** option controls just how "edgy" the beveled edges are. The two Chisel options result in different variations on serrated effects. If you don't want your layer to look as if it were cut with a bread knife—as you clearly do not when illuminating liquid—select **Smooth**.

- Use the **Depth** value to modify the degree of contrast and speed of transition between highlights and shadows. For this image, I recommend a Depth of 120 percent.

- Change the **Direction** option to invert the beveled edges, so the layer appears to recede away from you rather than swell toward you. In this case, we want the latter effect, so leave the Direction option set to **Up**.

- To increase the thickness of highlights and shadows, raise the **Size** value to 20 pixels.

- The **Soften** value smoothes over rough spots produced when Technique is set to one of the Chisel settings. Leave it set to 0 pixels.

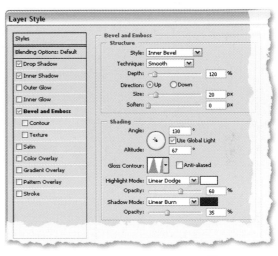

Figure 11-24.

At this point, the Splatter layer appears as depicted in Figure 11-25. Dimensional? Yes. Plastic? Most certainly. Molten? Maybe. But yummy, juicy liquid? No. There is more work to be done.

Figure 11-25.

5. **Set the Angle and Altitude values to 130 and 67, respectively.** As with other directional effects, the **Angle** value determines the angle of the light source or sun with respect to the layer. Turn on **Use Global Light** to set this value to 130 degrees, thus matching the other directional effects. Meanwhile, **Altitude** describes the angle of the sun along the horizon—90 degrees for noon, 0 degrees for sunset. Figure 11-26 shows a few variations. Notice that modifying this value affects the Splatter and Logo layers in unison, both of which are tied to Use Global Light. Feel free to experiment, but return the Altitude value to 67 degrees for the best results.

Altitude: 10°

Altitude: 40°

Altitude: 60°

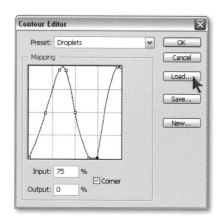
Altitude: 75°

Figure 11-26.

6. **Assign a contour.** The Gloss Contour option adjusts the way shadows and highlights play off the surface of the layer. Click the **Gloss Contour** icon to display the **Contour Editor** dialog box pictured in Figure 11-27. The problem with all of Photoshop's default contours is that they're either too soft or too pointy to represent sharp water reflections. Which is why we must design our own.

7. **Load and assign a custom contour.** Click the **Load** button.  Then find the *Lesson 11* folder inside the *Lesson Files-PScs 1on1* folder, and open the file called *Liquid shine.shc*. A radical zigzag of lines appear inside the central brightness graph, as pictured in Figure 11-27. You can click a point and move it if you like. But if you do, take heed to retain the sharp plateaus along the bottom and the top of the brightness graph. These ensure the sudden contrasts between lights and darks that appear regularly in water and other liquids. Click **OK** to accept the new contour and return to the Layer Style dialog box.

Figure 11-27.

8. ***Turn Anti-aliased off.*** This check box is designed to smooth over precisely the sort of sharp-edged contour that you just loaded. But unless the transitions turned jagged, you really don't need it. To achieve the effect shown in Figure 11-28, leave the check box turned off.

Figure 11-28.

So far, so good. But I'm not quite satisfied by the level of contrast between the highlights and shadows. What we need is bright flashes of light—known as *specular highlights*—to provide glimmering sheen, complemented by translucent patches of color to suggest shadows refracted through water. This you can accomplish with blend modes.

9. ***Set the Highlight Mode to Linear Dodge.*** Currently, the Highlight Mode is set to Screen, which lightens universally. To amplify the highlights, change this setting to **Linear Dodge** and reduce the **Opacity** to 60 percent. The result is vivid, yellowish highlights.

10. ***Change the color and the Shadow Mode.*** Click the black swatch and set the **H**, **S**, and **B** values to 30, 100, and 35, respectively, to create a deep, highly saturated orange. Click **OK** to return to the **Layer Style** dialog box. Then amplify the shadows by switching the **Shadow Mode** setting to **Linear Burn** and reduce the **Opacity** to 35 percent.

11. ***Click the OK button.*** And with that, Photoshop closes the Layer Style dialog box and applies your changes. You might regard the new effect, pictured in Figure 11-29, as less liquid than garish. But that's because we have one last change to make.

Figure 11-29.

12. ***Change the blend mode and fill opacity.*** Choose the **Screen** blend mode from the top of the **Layers** palette. Then change the **Fill** value to 85 percent. Or press Shift+Alt+S (Shift-Option-S on the Mac), and then hold Shift and press 8-5. The happy, juicy result appears in Figure 11-30.

Figure 11-30.

13. **Save a new layer style.** After spending this much time on such a nifty effect, you might as well save the result as a layer style. Display the **Styles** palette by clicking its tab or choosing **Window→Styles**.

- Click the ⬛ icon at the bottom of the palette. Or move your cursor over an empty spot in the palette and click, as in Figure 11-31.

- Name your style "Orange Liquid."

- Check **Include Layer Effects**, which saves all layer effects applied to the Splatter layer—namely Drop Shadow, Inner Shadow, and Bevel and Emboss.

Figure 11-31.

- Also check **Include Layer Blending Options** to save the 85 percent fill opacity and Screen blend mode.

- Click the **OK** button to create the style.

Your new layer style appears as a small orange jewel in the Styles palette. It will be available to all other open documents. To apply it to a layer in the future, just click it.

PEARL OF ⬤ WISDOM

Unlike styles in other programs, there is no dynamic link between a layer style and a layer. And there's no way to update a style either. So if you decide to make changes, your only option is to save a new style. I agree, it's an oversight—but as your humble messenger, I feel compelled to let you know.

14. **Save your composition.** By now, you probably know the drill. But if not, here's the skinny: Choose **File→Save As**, name the file "Happy Juice edit-3.psd," and save it to the same *Lesson 11* folder inside *Lesson Files-PScs 1on1* that we used in the preceding lessons. As before, this step is not optional; the file you save will serve as the starting point for the next exercise. The composition thus far, with all layers and effects, appears in Figure 11-32.

Figure 11-32.

# Fixing Problem Effects

As you gain more familiarity with layer effects, you'll discover how powerful and flexible they really are. But you'll also discover the occasional odd interaction between the effect, its layer, and the layers around it. The good news is that Photoshop permits you to address these interactions using a collection of check boxes. The bad news is, the check boxes are so strangely named and oddly placed that you'd never find them on your own. Hence the following exercise.

In all, Photoshop provides five check boxes for fixing problem effects. They appear smack dab in the middle of the Blending Options panel of the Layer Style dialog box:

- The first check box, Blend Interior Effects as Group, constrains effects that fall entirely inside a layer (specifically Inner Glow and the three Overlay effects). With the option off, Photoshop permits interior effects to blend through the active layer to the layers below. With the option on, interior effects are relegated to the active layer only. You'll see this option in action in Steps 7 and 12 (pages 403 and 404).

- The next check box, Blend Clipped Layers as Group, applies the blend mode assigned to a clipping mask to all masked layers above it. Leave it on; there's rarely any need to change it.

- On by default, Transparency Shapes Layer makes sure a layer effect traces around the edge of a layer. About the only reason to turn this option off is to fill an entire image with one of the Overlay effects. But even then, there are better solutions. Leave this option turned on.

- Turn on Layer Mask Hides Effects to use a layer mask to clip the edges of a drop shadow, stroke, or other effect that falls outside the perimeter of a layer. To discover just how useful this option can be, see Step 19 (page 404).

- Vector Mask Hides Effects is the same as above, but it clips exterior effects with the vector mask instead. In theory, the option seems like a good idea, but I have yet to apply it in practice.

To recap, out of the five options: the second and third are on by default and should be left that way, the fifth is of questionable merit, and the first and fourth are absolutely essential. In fact, you'll use the first and fourth options to solve a few problems that arise in this very exercise.

1. ***Open the image you saved in the last exercise.*** If the file is already open, fine. If not, open the file you saved in Step 14 of the preceding exercise, which ought to be *Happy Juice edit-3.psd* in the *Lesson 11* folder inside *Lesson Files-PScs 1on1*. The composition should look like the one pictured in Figure 11-32 back on page 397.

   From a marketing perspective, our advertisement's biggest shortcoming is that Max holds an empty glass. The beverage may near completion, but it can never actually be gone. Luckily, I have a layer of juice ready and waiting.

2. ***Turn on the Contents layer.*** Click the vector mask for the **Contents** layer to display the layer, make it active, and hide the path outlines. Solid orange with feathered edges, the layer should align precisely with Max's juice glass, as in Figure 11-33.

---

PEARL OF WISDOM

If the layers don't align, you may not have properly snapped Max to his guidelines way back in Step 5 of the first exercise (see page 381). At this late stage in the game, it's up to you how you solve the problem. You can reposition either Max's Spokesboy layer or the Contents layer, whatever looks best to you.

---

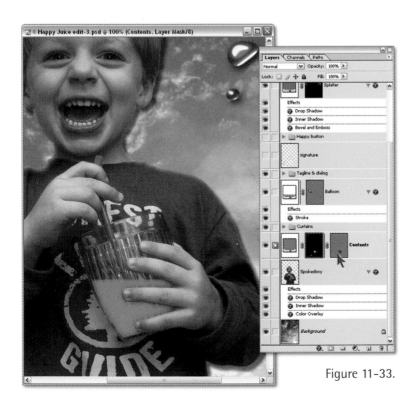

Figure 11-33.

3. ***Change the blend mode to Overlay.*** Choose **Overlay** from the blend mode pop-up menu at the top of the Layers palette or press Shift+Alt+O (Shift-Option-O on the Mac). This merges the juice and background so the former appears to be inside the glass. But I also want to add a bit of radioactive froth at the top. So it's time to add another layer effect.

4. ***Choose the Gradient Overlay effect.*** Click the ❷ icon at the bottom of the Layers palette and choose **Gradient Overlay** to see Photoshop's small array of gradient selection functions.

5. ***Adjust the Gradient Overlay settings.*** The default Gradient Overlay settings are mostly fine. The Gradient strip should show black-to-white, Reverse is off, Style is Linear, and the Angle is 90 degrees. Here's what you need to change:

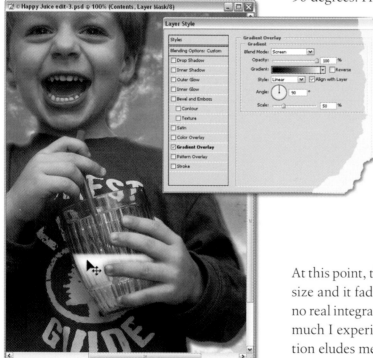

- Change the **Blend Mode** setting to **Screen**. This drops out the blacks and leaves only the whites.

- Reduce the **Scale** value to 50 percent to decrease the size of the gradient by half.

- Move your cursor into the image window to get the move tool. Then drag the gradient upward about the width of one of Max's fingers, as demonstrated in Figure 11-34. This wonderful technique lets you position a gradient inside the image window while the Layer Style dialog box is open.

At this point, the white froth at the top of the drink is the proper size and it fades nicely. But it doesn't look right at all. There's no real integration between froth and drink, and no matter how much I experiment with the opacity or blend mode, the solution eludes me. Good thing I have my check boxes.

Figure 11-34.

6. ***Switch to the Blending Options.*** Click **Blending Options** in the upper-left corner of the dialog box. This displays the various knockout and luminance blending features you learned about in Lesson 9, as well as the strange but cool check boxes that are the subject of this exercise.

7. **Turn on Blend Interior Effects as Group.** The moment you do, Photoshop blends the gradient froth into the glass and beverage, as in Figure 11-35. It's as if the white and orange of the Contents layer were merged before mixing the Contents and Spokesboy layers using the Overlay blend mode. More to the point, it looks great.

8. **Click the OK button.** Goodbye Layer Style dialog box, hello incandescent Happy Juice. Yum yum.

   The Blend Interior Effects as Group check box is an essential tool for integrating a layer effect into the surrounding image. But you can also use it to hide portions of a layer effect, as you'll see in the following steps.

9. **Turn on the Signature layer.** This displays and activates a scanned version of my signature (unsuited to checks and credit card receipts!) in the lower-left corner of the image. As seen in Figure 11-36, the signature is black against a white background, typical of scanned art and logos. Alas, you can't scan a signature or logo set against transparency, but you can do the next best thing: With the help of a blend mode, you can drop out the white background and leave only the black.

10. **Change the blend mode to Multiply.** Choose **Multiply** from the pop-up menu at the top of the **Layers** palette or press Shift+Alt+M (or Shift-Option-M). The Multiply mode treats white as neutral, meaning that all traces of white drop away entirely, as in Figure 11-37 on the very next page.

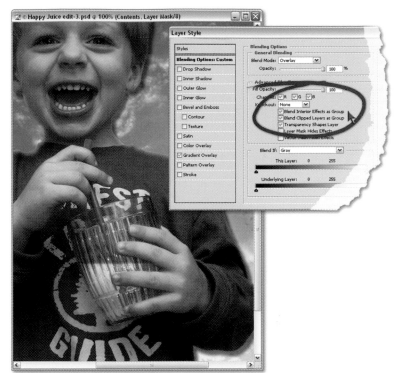

Figure 11-35.

Figure 11-36.

Figure 11-37.

Figure 11-38.

Figure 11-39.

Now let's say you want to color the signature so that it appears red, more or less matching the fabric border. The problem is, how do you go about colorizing the black of the signature without upsetting the white? With the help of a Color Overlay effect, that's how.

11. **Apply a Color Overlay effect.** Click the ⊘ icon at the bottom of the Layers palette to display the list of layer effects, and then choose **Color Overlay**.

- Leave the color swatch set to red and the **Opacity** at 100 percent.

- Change the **Blend Mode** to **Lighten**.

By all accounts, the Lighten mode should color the black script and leave the white unchanged. After all, when using Lighten, the lightest color wins, end of story. And yet, as Figure 11-38 shows, the white area is every bit as red as the black signature. The reason is that, by default, Photoshop permits an interior effect to mix with all layers in back of it. In other words, Photoshop blends the Signature layer with those behind it and *then* heaps on the Color Overlay effect. So the Lighten mode never sees white; it sees and lightens the composite colors.

12. **Turn on Blend Interior Effects as Group.** Click **Blending Options** in the upper-left corner of the **Layer Style** dialog box. Then check **Blend Interior Effects as Group**. Now the order changes. First, Photoshop mixes the Color Overlay effect with the blacks and whites of the Signature layer. Then it mixes the results with the underlying layers. Click the **OK** button to achieve the effect shown in Figure 11-39.

PEARL OF ⬤ WISDOM

Now you might say, if Blend Interior Effects as Group is so great, why isn't it on by default? For the simple reason that most of the time, you don't want it on. For example, when the option is off, the Fill value in the Layers palette (as well as Fill Opacity in the Layer Style dialog box) changes the opacity of a layer but leaves the effects alone. Turn the check box on, and Fill affects layer and effects as one, just like the Opacity value. So except in special cases, it's best to leave Blend Interior Effects as Group turned off.

13. **Turn on and twirl open the Happy Button layer set.** Click the **Happy Button** folder to make the layers inside the set visible, as in Figure 11-40. Then click the ▶ to the left of the folder to reveal its contents, the 0% Juice text layer and the green Circle shape layer. Twirl open the **Circle** layer and you'll see that it includes a sharp Outer Glow.

PEARL OF WISDOM

Suppose you want to tuck the green circle behind Max's shoulder. You could drag the Circle layer down the stack, but to get it behind Max, you'd have to move it behind every other layer except Background, as in Figure 11-41. Obviously that's no good. (Don't do it yourself, in other words, as the red ⃠ over the cursor indicates.) Instead, you'll have to resort to a layer mask.

14. **Add a layer mask to the Circle layer.** Click its gray vector mask thumbnail to activate the layer and hide the path outline. Then click the ▢ icon at the bottom of the Layers palette. Photoshop adds a white thumbnail to the layer.

15. **Load the selection outline for the Spokesboy layer.** Press Ctrl (⌘ on the Mac) and click on any portion of the **Spokesboy** layer in the Layers palette—even one of the effects. The result is a series of marching ants that exactly traces the boundaries of Max.

16. **Fill the selection with black.** Press the D key to establish the default masking colors, white for the foreground and black for the background. Take a moment to make sure the layer mask for the Circle layer is active. (The white thumbnail should have a double outline.) Then press Ctrl+Backspace (⌘-Delete on the Mac) to fill the selection with black.

Figure 11-40.

Figure 11-41.

Figure 11-42.

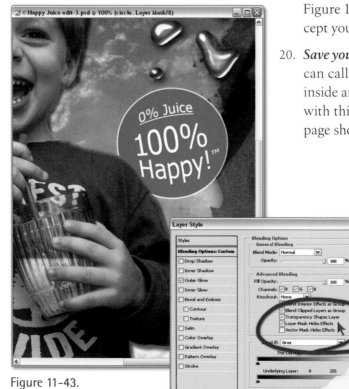

Figure 11-43.

17. **Dismiss the selection.** Press Ctrl+D (or ⌘-D) to make the selection outline go away. This not only clips the green circle but also forces Photoshop to trace around the perimeter of the clipped circle, as in Figure 11-42. You may also notice a couple of white dots on Max's shoulder, the result of Outer Glow tracing stray pixels in the mask. Unacceptable; let's fix it.

18. **Open the Blending Options.** Right-click on the green thumbnail in the **Circle** layer and choose **Blending Options** from the shortcut menu. (If you have a one-button mouse on the Mac, press the Control key and click to see the shortcut menu.) Up comes the **Layer Style** dialog box.

19. **Turn on Layer Mask Hides Effects.** Checking this option tells Photoshop to clip Outer Glow and shape alike using the layer mask. The result is a clean edge, free of extra stroke, as in the sublime Figure 11-43. Click the **OK** button to accept your change.

20. **Save your composition.** And for once, you can call it anything you want and toss it inside any old folder, because we're done with this file. Figure 11-44 on the facing page shows the final result.

Figure 11-44.

## Creating and Modifying Adjustment Layers

We now move from layer effects to the realm of adjustment layers. These insanely practical functions permit you to apply most of the commands under the Image→Adjustments submenu. For example, of the commands we discussed in Lessons 2 and 3, the only ones *not* implemented as adjustment layers are Variations and Shadow/Highlight. What's more, an adjustment layer works just like its command counterpart. The Levels adjustment layer shows you the same dialog box—complete with Input Levels values and histogram—as does Image→Adjustments→Levels. However, unlike commands, an adjustment layer affects all layers below it and remains editable far into the future.

Adjustment layers are so flexible, in fact, that many designers use them to correct flat photographs. This way, if you later decide to tweak the colors in an image to meet the demands of a different screen or printing environment, you always have your original photograph on hand, with the last-applied color correction ready and waiting in the wings.

And because adjustment layers are fully functioning layers, you can mix and match them, as well as combine them with blend modes, layer masks, shapes, layer effects, and even clipping masks. Simply put, they permit you to venture into creative territories that static commands simply can't accommodate.

In this exercise, your assignment is to build a book cover for a dime-store novel using a couple of digital photos and a petroglyph silhouette that I stored in an alpha channel. The publisher has asked for something "dark, brooding, and suspenseful." But because this is all the instruction you've received, it seems imprudent to make any permanent changes to the images. So you wisely decide to do everything with adjustment layers.

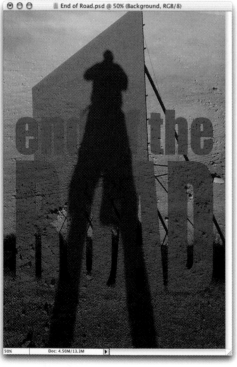

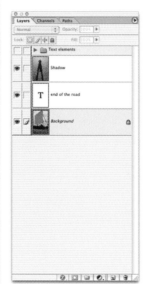

Figure 11-45.

1. **Open a layered image.** This time we're going to work from a single file, *End of Road.psd*, which you'll find in the *Lesson 11* folder inside *Lesson Files-PScs 1on1*. (If Photoshop asks to update the text layers, click the **Update** button.) Pictured in Figure 11-45, this composition contains a text layer sandwiched between two image layers, both shot years ago using a 1.5-megapixel Kodak DC265. The image of my shadow is set to the Multiply blend mode, thus burning into the orange type and drive-in movie screen.

2. **Add an Invert adjustment layer.** What's the easiest, most brain-dead way to make an image look scary? Invert it, of course. And that's exactly what we're going to do with the drive-in screen. Check that

the Background layer is active in the Layers palette. Click the half-black, half-white ◑ icon at the bottom of the palette to display a menu of 15 specialty layers (3 fills followed by 12 adjustments). Then choose **Invert**, as shown in Figure 11-46. Photoshop adds a layer called Invert 1 that creates a negative version of the drive-in movie screen behind it.

3. *Change the blend mode to Luminosity.* Currently, the Invert 1 layer reverses both the luminosity values and the colors in the drive-in image. This means that the blue of the sky turns to orange, and the orange of the ground turns to blue. Fine, but suppose you don't want that; suppose you want to invert only the luminosity values. Then choose **Luminosity** from the blend mode pop-up menu at the top of the Layers palette, or press Shift+Alt+Y (Shift-Option-Y on the Mac). Photoshop restores the blue sky and orange ground, as in Figure 11-47.

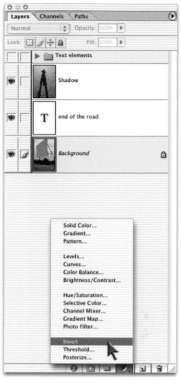

Figure 11-46.

Inverted background image | Inversion set to Luminosity mode

Figure 11-47.

4. *Add a Levels adjustment layer.* Inverting the background made the image overly dark, and the best way to lighten it is with the Levels command. But you can't apply Levels to the Invert 1 layer, and if you lighten the Background layer directly, you'll darken the inverted image because the luminosity values are reversed.

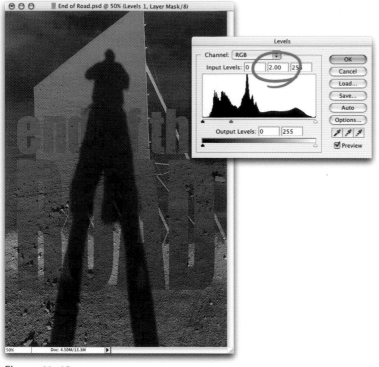

Figure 11-48.

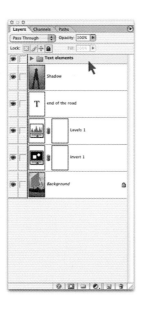

Figure 11-49.

Solution: Click the ⬭ icon at the bottom of the Layers palette and choose **Levels**. Inside the **Levels** dialog box, advance to the second **Input Levels** value and change the gamma to 2.00, as demonstrated in Figure 11-48. Then click the **OK** button to apply the adjustment.

5. ***Turn on the Text Elements layer set.*** Click the **Text Elements** folder at the top of the **Layers** palette to display text layers at the top and bottom of the cover. The publisher provided these layers to you with the directive, "Keep the quote and author's name in blue, and make them leap off the page." But because blue is one of the most pervasive colors in the image, the text gets a little lost (see Figure 11-49). Obviously, another adjustment layer is warranted.

PEARL OF WISDOM

Incidentally, all the blue text is housed on editable text layers. So you might wonder how I applied those round corners to the quote and author letters. Answer: I added an Inner Glow effect to each layer and lowered the fill opacity to 0 percent. Want to know more? Just twirl open the **Text Elements** set and its layers and then double-click the **Inner Glow** items. Just like that, you'll see the exact settings I used. Yet another marvel of parametric effects—you can always conjure up what you've done as well as check out other people's work.

6. ***Add a Hue/Saturation adjustment layer.*** Click the **Levels 1** layer in the Layers palette to specify where you want to insert the next layer. Then press the Alt key (or Option key) as you choose **Hue/Saturation** from the ⬭ icon at the bottom of the palette. This allows you to name the new layer as you create it. Call it "Color Spin" and click the **OK** button to display the **Hue/Saturation** dialog box.

7. **Rotate the hues 180 degrees.** Change the **Hue** value to 180 degrees to invert all colors in the image. Then boost the **Saturation** value to +50 percent and reduce the **Lightness** value to –50 percent. Click **OK** to accept the changes, pictured in Figure 11-50 below.

At this point, you might quite naturally wonder why in the world we just inverted the colors when we were so careful *not* to invert the colors in Step 3. The reason is that for the moment, all we're concerned about is making the blue text "leap off the page." Once that's accomplished, we'll restore the appearance of the central portion of the image using a layer mask (see Step 9). But first...

8. **Change the blend mode to Multiply.** As far as the blue text is concerned, the background art remains too light. To make it darker, choose **Multiply** from the blend mode pop-up menu at the top of the **Layers** palette, or press Shift+Alt+M (Shift-Option-M on the Mac).

9. **Click the gradient tool in the toolbox.** If you look at the Layers palette, you'll see that each one of the three adjustment layers that you've created so far includes a white thumbnail to the right of it. This white thumbnail is a potential layer mask. Painting black inside the mask will hide that portion of the color adjustment. We'll paint inside the Color Spin layer mask using the gradient tool. Click the tool's icon or press the G key to select it.

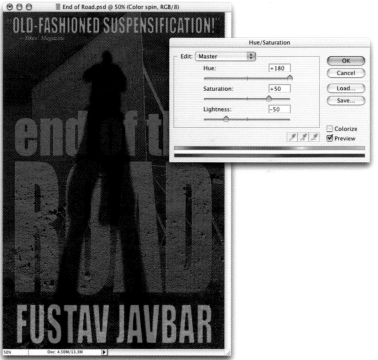

Figure 11-50.

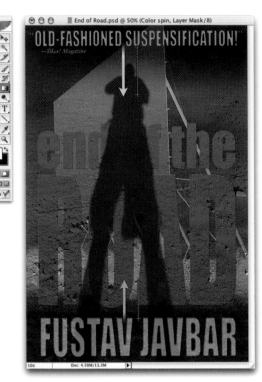

Figure 11-51.

10. ***Paint gradients at the top and bottom of the image.*** The aim is to relegate the effects of the Color Spin layer to the areas immediately behind the blue text at the top and the bottom of the image. That means painting the central portion of the layer mask black. It's a tricky proposition, so I'll break it into pieces:

- Press the D key to make the foreground color white and the background color black.

- Press Shift+comma (Shift+,) to set the gradient tool to draw gradients from the foreground color to the background color, or white to black.

- Press the Shift key and drag from directly below the top text to the chest in the shadow, as indicated by the yellow arrow at the top of Figure 11-51. This should lighten all but the topmost portion of the image.

- Now to reinstate some darkness at the bottom of the image. Start by pressing the period key (.), which changes the style of gradient to Foreground-to-Transparent.

- In the image window, Shift-drag from directly above the author name (the esteemed Fustav Javbar) to about an inch or so up, as indicated by the orange arrow at the bottom of Figure 11-51. Both the top and bottom of the image should now appear dark.

11. ***Duplicate the End of the Road layer.*** Now we're ready to address the book's title. The publisher has informed us that as long as we make Fustav Javbar's name prominent, we can do anything we want with the title. So let's have some fun. For starters, create a backup copy of the title in case you need to revisit it later. Here's how:

- Click the **End of the Road** item in the **Layers** palette.

- Press Ctrl+J (⌘-J) to clone the text to a new layer.

- Click the **End of the Road** layer again.

- Press Ctrl+Shift+] (or ⌘-Shift-]) to pop the layer to the top of the stack, as in Figure 11-52.

- Click the eyeball in front of the **End of the Road** layer to hide the layer.

- Click **End of the Road Copy** (the duplicate layer) to make it active. This is the layer you'll be working on.

- Double-click the layer name and rename it "Title Invert."

If this all seems like a lot of busy work, take heart: It prepares you for the upcoming steps and gets a few important house-keeping chores out of the way.

PEARL OF WISDOM

For those wondering why we renamed the duplicate layer Title Invert, it's because I want to use the letters to invert the portion of the image below them. The only problem is that Photoshop doesn't let you fill live text with an adjustment layer. So we first have to convert the text to a shape layer.

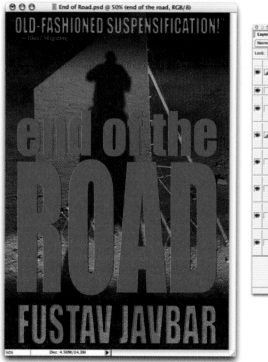

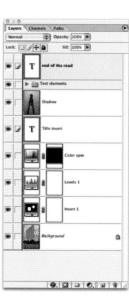

Figure 11-52.

12. ***Convert the character outlines to shapes.*** With the Title Invert layer active, Choose **Layer→Type→Convert to Shape**. Photoshop traces the letters with path outlines, indicating that you now have a shape layer. An orange color swatch and a gray vector mask thumbnail also appear inside the Layers palette. The orange swatch shows that this is a solid color layer, which is a kind of specialty fill layer. And as it just so happens, you can convert a fill layer to an adjustment layer as easily as choosing a command.

13. ***Replace the orange fill with an Invert layer.*** Choose **Layer→Change Layer Content→Invert**. The orange color of the letters is replaced with an Invert adjustment layer, which affects all layers below it. Shown in Figure 11-53, the effect is high in drama but low in legibility, particularly if we were to turn off the non-printing path outlines. One solution is to increase the contrast of the inversion effect, as in the next step.

14. ***Add a Threshold adjustment layer.*** Press the Alt key (Option on the Mac) and choose **Threshold** from the ⬤ icon at the bottom of the Layers palette. This displays the **New Layer** dialog box. Enter the name "Black or White" because the Threshold command changes all colors to either black or white. Then turn on the check box **Use Previous Layer to Create Clipping Mask** (see Figure 11-54) to clip the new adjustment layer inside the letters of the Title Invert shape layer.

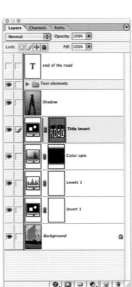

Figure 11-53.

Figure 11-54.

15. *Accept the default Threshold value.* Click the **OK** button to display the **Threshold** dialog box. Shown in Figure 11-55, this dialog box changes all luminosity values darker than the Threshold Level to black and all values lighter to white. A **Threshold Level** of 128 splits the colors right down the middle. Click **OK** to apply this setting.

   Notice that rather than making the text layer black and white, the Threshold adjustment seems to have made it black and gravelly. The text is actually black and white; the Shadow layer above it is responsible for burning the gravel into the white areas.

16. *Add a Color Overlay layer effect.* Let's say you want the black portions of the text to appear in color. The easiest way to do this is to apply a Color Overlay effect. Make sure the **Black or White** layer is active. Then click the ✿ icon at the bottom of the **Layers** palette and choose **Color Overlay** to display the **Layer Style** dialog box.

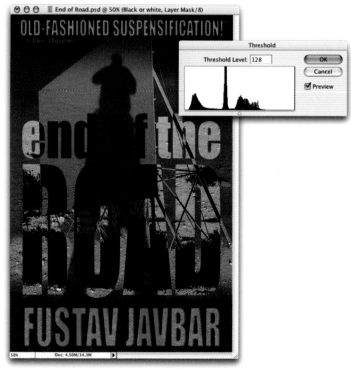

Figure 11-55.

17. **Set the color to pink and the blend mode to Lighten.** Click the red color swatch to display the **Color Picker** dialog box. Change the **S** value to 30 percent for a pale pink and click the **OK** button. Back inside the **Layer Style** dialog box, set the **Blend Mode** option to **Lighten** (so the pink fills just the black areas). Leave the **Opacity** set to 100 percent. Click the **OK** button to accept your changes, shown in Figure 11-56.

Figure 11-56.

18. **Switch back to the Title Invert layer.** The text could use a little extra definition in the form of a drop shadow. However, you can't apply the drop shadow to the Threshold layer (Black or White) because it has no edge; the layer is as big as the entire canvas. Instead, click the gray vector mask for the **Title Invert** layer to activate that layer and hide its path outlines.

19. ***Add a Drop Shadow layer effect.*** Click the ❼ icon at the bottom of the Layers palette and choose **Drop Shadow** to display the **Layer Style** dialog box. Then enter these settings:

- The **Blend Mode** and color are fine as is (**Multiply** and black, respectively).

- Change the **Opacity** value to 100 percent.

- Change the **Angle** value to –90 degrees so that the sun is shining from below and the shadow is straight up.

- Change both the **Distance** and **Size** values to 10 pixels.

- Click the **OK** button to accept your spine-tingling drop shadow, shown in Figure 11-57.

PEARL OF ⬤ WISDOM

If you ask me, the title text looks really cool, especially if you're right on top of it. It's the kind of book cover that looks really great when you hold it in your hands. But most people never get that close to a book. They see the cover on a crowded Web page or in a bookstore window across the aisle at an airport. And from any distance, this title is illegible. Although the original orange type was less interesting, it was entirely legible (see Figure 11-52 on page 411). A compromise seems to be in order.

Figure 11-57.

20. ***Turn on the top layer and set the blend mode to Screen.*** Click the **End of the Road** layer at the top of the **Layers** palette to make it active. Then choose **Screen** from the blend mode pop-up menu, or press Shift+Alt+S (Shift-Option-S on the Mac). In this one simple operation, we manage to maintain the interesting texture and detail from the Title Invert layer and at the same time increase its legibility several times over, as witnessed in Figure 11-58.

The next and final task is to add a ghost to the book cover. The publisher has provided the ghost to us in the form of an alpha channel. (For what it's worth, it actually hails from a several hundred-year-old Native American petroglyph.) We'll use this alpha channel to create one last adjustment layer.

21. ***Click the Color Spin layer in the Layers palette.*** The ghost needs to sit between the various title layers and any other adjustment layers that might otherwise modify it. In other words, it belongs in front of the Color Spin layer.

Figure 11–58.

22. ***Load the Petroglyph channel as a selection outline.*** Go to the **Channels** palette. There you'll see two alpha channels; one being the layer mask for the Color Spin layer and another called Petroglyph. Press the Ctrl key (⌘ on the Mac) and click on the **Petroglyph** item (see Figure 11-59) to invoke the ghostly selection outline.

23. ***Add a Hue/Saturation adjustment layer.*** To name the layer as you make it, press Alt (or Option) as you choose **Hue/Saturation** from the ⊘ icon at the bottom of the **Layers** palette. Name the layer "Blue Man" and click the **OK** button. Then adjust the settings in the **Hue/Saturation** dialog box as outlined below and shown in Figure 11-60:

    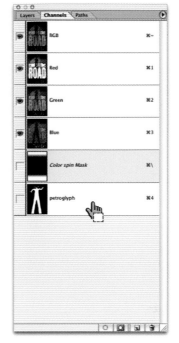

    Figure 11-59.

    - Turn on the **Colorize** check box.

    - Change the **Hue** value to 220 degrees, a cobalt-blue that matches the color of the text layers.

    - Increase the **Saturation** to 100 percent.

    - Raise the **Lightness** value to 80 percent. Normally, I recommend against using this option because it's such an indelicate tool. But in this case, we're using Lightness not to correct colors, but to create an effect. And in that regard, it works just dandy.

    - Click the **OK** button to apply your settings.

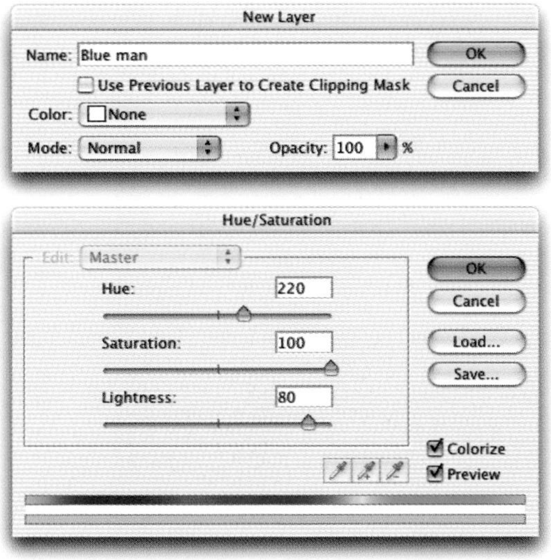

Figure 11-60.

24. *Save your composition.* Choose **File**→**Save As** and name the file "Bestseller in Blue.psd." Figure 11-61 shows the finished composition. Notice that the Hue/Saturation adjustment layer exactly filled the confines of the Petroglyph selection outline. Photoshop managed this by converting the selection into a layer mask, as you can see in the Layers palette. And in fact, this is always the way it works. If a selection outline is present when you create a new adjustment layer, Photoshop converts the selection to a layer mask.

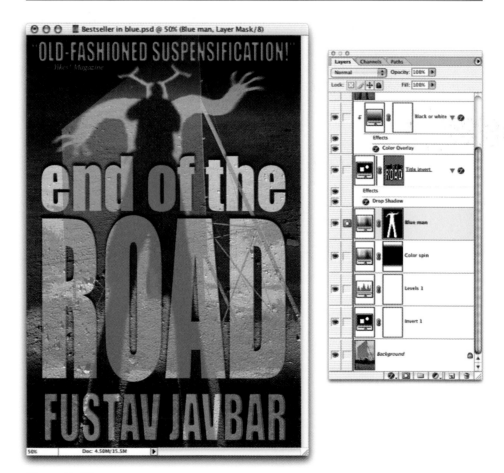

Figure 11-61.

# WHAT DID YOU LEARN?

Match the key concept in the numbered list below with the letter of the phrase that best describes it. Answers appear upside-down at the bottom of the page.

## Key Concepts

1. Layer effects
2. Drop shadow
3. Layer style
4. Directional effects
5. Use Global Light
6. Color Overlay
7. Strokes and glows
8. Bevel and Emboss
9. Specular highlights
10. Blend Interior Effects as Group
11. Adjustment layer
12. A few K

## Descriptions

A. A group of layer effects that trace one or more colors uniformly around the perimeter of a layer.

B. A layer effect that casts colors both by a specified distance and at a specified angle.

C. When turned on, this check box blends a Glow or Overlay effect with the active layer before blending the layer with its neighbors.

D. This check box locks down the light source so that all directional effects cast highlights and shadows at a consistent angle.

E. The size of a layer effect or adjustment layer, both in memory and when saved to disk.

F. A collection of drop shadows, bevels, and other layer effects stored in the Styles palette.

G. This layer effect coats the active layer with a selected color, useful for colorizing the layer or replacing one color with another.

H. Useful for creating both shadows and highlights, this layer effect offsets and blurs a silhouette of the active layer.

I. This most powerful of layer effects lets you add both highlights and shadows to a layer in accordance with a specified light source.

J. A series of dynamic color and contour attributes that let you assign dimension, lighting, and texture to a layer.

K. Bright flashes of light that accompany a highly reflective surface, such as metal, glass, or liquid.

L. A group of color adjustment settings that correct or modify the colors of the layers below them.

## Answers

LESSON

12

# PRINTING AND OUTPUT

**PRINTING FROM** Photoshop is at once a primitive and a sophisticated experience. On the primitive side, the program is designed to print one image per page. There's no way to print multipage documents. Even if you open multiple files, you can't print them all in one fell swoop; you must print each image in turn. You can't even print independent layers; the program always prints all visible layers. And you can print just one copy of a file per page. So if you want to double up images, you have to repeat the image inside the file before choosing Print.

In fact, you could argue that Photoshop isn't a printing program at all. Rather, it's designed to prepare images that you plan to import into programs that are specifically designed to amass and print pages, such as Adobe InDesign or QuarkXPress. In Figure 12-1, for example, the scanned images on the left were corrected and modified in Photoshop; the page on the right was assembled and printed in Quark.

So what's the sophisticated part? Well, what Photoshop lacks in page control, it makes up for in real-world acumen. First, it realizes that you have different output destinations. Sometimes you want to print a full-color page to a printer in your home or office. Other times, you want to print several hundred or even thousand copies of your artwork for mass distribution. Second,

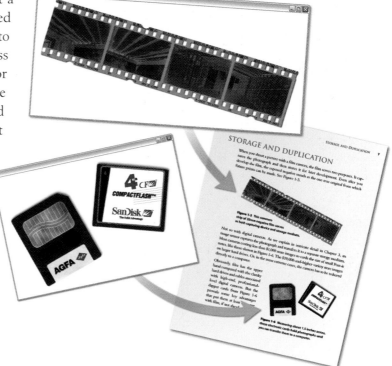

Figure 12-1.

# ABOUT THIS LESSON

## Project Files

Before beginning the exercises, make sure that you've installed the lesson files from the CD, as explained in Step 5 on page xv of the Preface. This should result in a folder called *Lesson Files-PScs 1on1* on your desktop. We'll be working with the files inside the *Lesson 12* subfolder.

This final lesson covers topics related to inkjet printing, professional output, and CMYK color conversion. You'll learn how to:

## Video Lesson 12: From Screen to Print

When printing images to paper, your foremost concern is color accuracy. At some stage in the process, Photoshop must convert the image from RGB to the radically different world of CMYK. Every pixel in every color channel must undergo a change, and it's easier to make accurate changes if you understand how the conversion works.

Because color theory is at the heart of the printing process, I take you on a guided tour of both the theory and reality of color in the twelfth video lesson on the CD. Insert the CD, click the **Start Training** button, click Set **4** in the top-right corner of your screen, and then select **12, From Print to Screen** from the Lessons list. The 11-minute, 54-second movie (which includes a closing message from yours truly) explains the following functions and shortcuts:

| Operation | Windows shortcut | Macintosh shortcut |
| --- | --- | --- |
| Display Preferences dialog box | Ctrl+K | ⌘-K |
| Show Channels palette | F7, then click Channels tab | F7, then click Channels tab |
| Switch between RGB color channels | Ctrl+1, 2, or 3 | ⌘-1, 2, or 3 |
| Fill image with white | Ctrl+Backspace | ⌘-Delete |
| Hide or show toolbox and all palettes | Tab | Tab |
| Switch between CMYK color channels | Ctrl+1, 2, 3, or 4 | ⌘-1, 2, 3, or 4 |

Photoshop understands that regardless of your destination, you want the colors that you see on screen to translate accurately onto the printed page. Most programs don't give either of these very important aspects of printing much attention. Yet for Photoshop, these are the only printing issues that matter. And as you'll discover in this lesson, Photoshop happens to be right.

## Local Printing Versus Commercial Reproduction

Technically speaking, "print" and "output" are different names for the same thing: the act of getting something you see on screen onto a piece of paper. But in the workaday world of computer imaging, the words tend to be used to imply different things:

- To *print* an image is to turn on your printer, choose the Print command from Photoshop's File menu, and wait for the page to come out.

- To *output* an image is a more deliberate operation. You might be rendering the image to a high-end film recorder or a PostScript-equipped imagesetter. Or more likely, you're preparing an image for inclusion in a newsletter or other widely distributed document. Output requires a greater investment of time and money, as well as more attention to detail.

The irony is that printing from a modern inkjet printer can produce better results than professional, commercial output. In fact, an inkjet print can look every bit as good as a photographic print from a film developer. But it's simply not affordable for large-scale reproduction. For example, printing a single copy of a 100-page glossy magazine would cost $50 to $100 in ink and paper. Commercially outputting the magazine requires you to lay down more cash up front, but the per-issue costs are pennies per page.

So when you just want to make a few copies, printing offers the advantages of convenience and quality. But if you're planning a big print run, commercial output is the way to go.

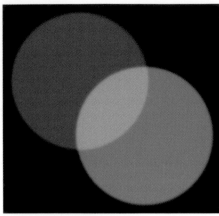

Lights intersect to make lighter colors

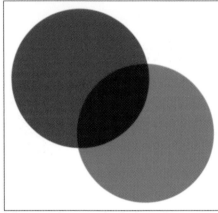

Inks overprint to make darker colors

Figure 12-2.

# RGB Versus CMYK

Whether an image is bound for inkjet or imagesetter, it must make the transition from one color space to another. And that presents a problem because monitors and printers use opposite methods of conveying colors. Whereas images on a monitor are created by mixing colored lights, print images are created by mixing inks or other pigments. As illustrated in Figure 12-2, lights mix to form lighter colors, inks mix to form darker colors. Moreover, the absence of light is black, while the absence of ink is the paper color, usually white. Just how much more different could these methods be?

PEARL OF WISDOM

Given that monitors and printers are so different, it's not surprising they begin with different sets of primary colors. Monitors rely on the *additive primaries* red, green, and blue, which make up the familiar RGB color space. Printers use the *subtractive primaries* cyan, magenta, and yellow, known collectively as CMY. The two groups are theoretical complements, meaning that red, green, and blue mix to form cyan, magenta, and yellow—and vice versa—as illustrated in Figure 12-3. (For more information on this intriguing topic, watch Video Lesson 12, "From Screen to Print," introduced on page 422.) The intersection of all three additive primaries is white; the intersection of the subtractive primaries is a very dark gray that is nearly but not quite black. Therefore, a fourth primary ink, black, is added to create rich, lustrous shadows. Hence, the acronym CMYK for cyan, magenta, yellow, and the "key" color black.

Fortunately, Adobe and most printer vendors are aware of the vast disparities between RGB and CMYK. They are equally aware that you expect your printed output to match your screen image. So they've come up with a two-tiered solution:

- When printing an image directly to an inkjet printer or another personal device, leave the image in the RGB mode and let the printer make the conversion to its native color space automatically.

- When preparing an image for commercial *color separation*— in which the cyan, magenta, yellow, and black inks are each printed to separate pages—you should convert the image to the CMYK color space inside Photoshop. Then save it to disk with a different filename to protect the original RGB image.

I provide detailed discussions of both approaches in the following exercises. And I'll provide insights for getting great looking prints with accurate colors along the way.

# Printing to an Inkjet Printer

When it comes to printing full-color photographic images, your best, most affordable solution is an inkjet printer. Available from Epson, Hewlett-Packard, and a cadre of others, a typical inkjet printer cost just a few hundred dollars. In return, it's capable of delivering outstanding color and definition (see the sidebar "Quality Comes at a Price" on page 432), better than you can achieve from your local commercial print house. But you can't reproduce artwork for mass distribution from a color inkjet printout. Inkjet printers are strictly for personal use.

In the following exercise, you'll learn how to get the best results from your inkjet device. If you don't have a color inkjet printer, don't fret. You won't be able to follow along with every step of the exercise, but you'll get an idea of how the process works.

Assuming you have an inkjet device at your disposal, please load it with the best paper you have on hand, ideally a few sheets of glossy or matte-finish photo paper, readily available at any office supply store (again see "Quality Comes at a Price" for more information). If you don't have such paper, or if you simply don't feel like parting with the good stuff for this exercise, go ahead and load what you have. Just remember what kind of paper you loaded so you can address it properly in Steps 15 and 16 on page 430.

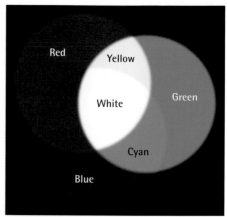

**The primary colors of light, RGB**

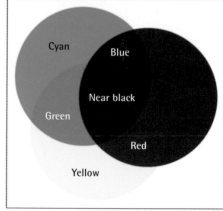

**The primary colors of pigment, CMY**

Figure 12-3.

Obviously, I have no idea what printer you're using, so your experience may diverge from mine starting at Step 14, as I explain in the exercise. And I must leave it up to you to make sure your printer is set up properly and in working order. This means that the power is turned on, the printer is connected to your computer, print drivers and other software are installed, the printer is loaded with plenty of paper and ink, and the print head nozzles are clean. For more information on any of these issues, see the documentation that came with your printer.

1. *Open the test image.* Look in the *Lesson 12* folder inside *Lesson Files-PScs 1on1* and you'll find a file called *Y2K+10 invite.psd*. Pictured in Figure 12-4 on the next  page, this file hails from a wildly successful Y2K party some friends and I threw a few years back. In addition to making some adjustments for time—who knows what Y2010 has in store?— I expanded the range of hues and luminosity values to make it easier to judge the accuracy of our color prints. The image is sized at 4 by 5 inches with a resolution of 300 pixels per inch. But as you'll see, that can be changed to fit the medium.

Figure 12-4.

2. *Choose the Flatten Image command.* This file contains a handful of pixel-based layers, a bit of rasterized text, and a shape layer. As you may recall from Lesson 10, text and shape layers can be output at the maximum resolution of a PostScript-compatible printer, but very few inkjet devices include PostScript processors (and those that do are *very* expensive). So the layers won't help the image's print quality. Layers also require more computation and thus slow down the print process. Best solution: Get rid of them by choosing **Layer→Flatten Image**.

3. *Save the image under a new name.* Naturally, you don't want to run the risk of harming the original layered image, so choose **File→Save As**. As long as you save the image under a different name, you're safe. But here are the settings I recommend:

   • In the Save As dialog box, choose **TIFF** from the **Format** pop-up menu.

   • Make sure the **ICC Profile** check box is on (that's **Embed Color Profile** on the Mac).

   • Click the **Save** button.

   • In the **TIFF Options** dialog box, turn on the **LZW** option to minimize the file size without changing any pixels.

   • From **Byte Order**, select the platform that you're working on, PC or Mac.

   • Click the **OK** button to save the file.

   The original layered file is safe as houses and the flat file is ready to print.

4. ***Choose the Print with Preview command.*** Choose **File→Print with Preview** or press Ctrl+Alt+P (⌘-Option-P on the Mac). Print with Preview is preferable to the plain vanilla Print command because it lets you see how the image sits on the page, as in Figure 12-5.

5. ***Click the Page Setup button.*** Before going any further, it's important to specify the size and orientation of the paper that you'll be printing to. Click the **Page Setup** button to display the Page Setup dialog box.

6. ***Select your printer model.*** As illustrated in Figure 12-6, the method for doing this varies on the PC and the Mac:

   • If you're using Windows 2000 or XP, click the **Printer** button to display yet another dialog box, still called Page Setup. Then choose the model of printer you want to use from the **Name** pop-up menu and click the **OK** button to return to the first Page Setup dialog box.

   • On the Mac, choose the printer model from the **Format For** pop-up menu.

7. ***Choose the desired paper size.*** If you're using special photo paper, consult the paper's packaging to find out the physical page dimensions. In the case of my so-called Premium Glossy Photo Paper, each piece of paper measures 8 by 10 inches, slightly smaller than the letter-size format.

   • Under Windows, choose the page size from the **Size** pop-up menu in the **Paper** section of the Page Setup dialog box.

   • On the Mac, choose the page size from the **Paper Size** pop-up menu.

   Then click the **OK** button to close the Page Setup dialog box and return to the print preview window.

8. ***Turn on the Scale to Fit Media check box.*** Located to the right of the image preview, this option expands the image to fill the maximum printable portion of the page. Note that Photoshop does not resample the image; it merely lowers the resolution value so that the pixels print larger. This way, you don't waste any of your expensive paper by, say, printing a tiny image smack dab in the middle of the page.

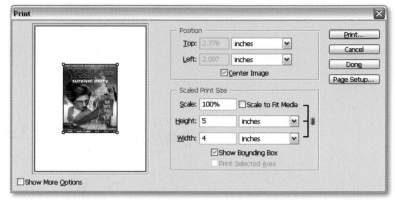

Figure 12-5.

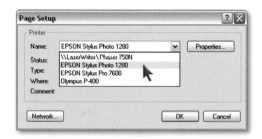

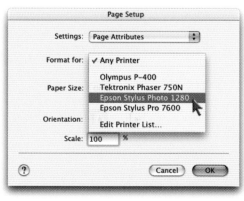

Figure 12-6.

As I mentioned earlier, Photoshop's Print commands print just one image file per page. If you want to print multiple images at a time, you must first combine the images into a single file using File→Automate→Picture Package, discussed in the "Packing Multiple Pictures onto a Single Page" exercise on page 447.

9. ***Turn on the Show More Options check box.*** The bulk of the options in the Print dialog box are devoted to helping you position and scale the image on the page. But even more important is a hidden option that can be displayed only by selecting **Show More Options** below the image preview.

10. ***Choose the Color Management option.*** Photoshop greets you with one of two groups of options: Output, which includes a bunch of PostScript printing functions specifically applicable to commercial reproduction, or Color Management, which is what we want. If you see a bunch of buttons marked Background, Border, Bleed, and the like, you're in the wrong area. Choose **Color Management** from the pop-up menu directly below the Show More Options check box to see the options pictured at the bottom of Figure 12-7 on the facing page.

11. ***Confirm the source and printer spaces.*** To print the colors in an image as accurately as possible, you must identify the *source space*—the color space used by the image itself—and the *destination space* employed by the printer software.

    - In the **Source Space** area, select **Document: Adobe RGB (1998)**. This is the variety of RGB employed by the *Y2K+10 invite* image file.

    - I have yet to encounter an inkjet printer that is calibrated to use a color space other than *sRGB*, the standard RGB space embraced by all varieties of consumer-level hardware. To accommodate this popular trend, click the **Profile** pop-up menu in the **Print Space** area and choose the lengthy **sRGB IEC61966-2.1**.

    - Set the **Intent** option to **Perceptual**, which maintains the smoothest transitions when converting colors—the best solution for photographic images.

    - Turn on **Use Black Point Compensation**. This redefines black in the image to match the definition of black according to the printer, thus maintaining rich, colorful shadows.

Figure 12-7 shows the dialog box as it should appear up to this point. Only the dimmed Scale Print Size values may read differently, to reflect the different dimensions of your paper.

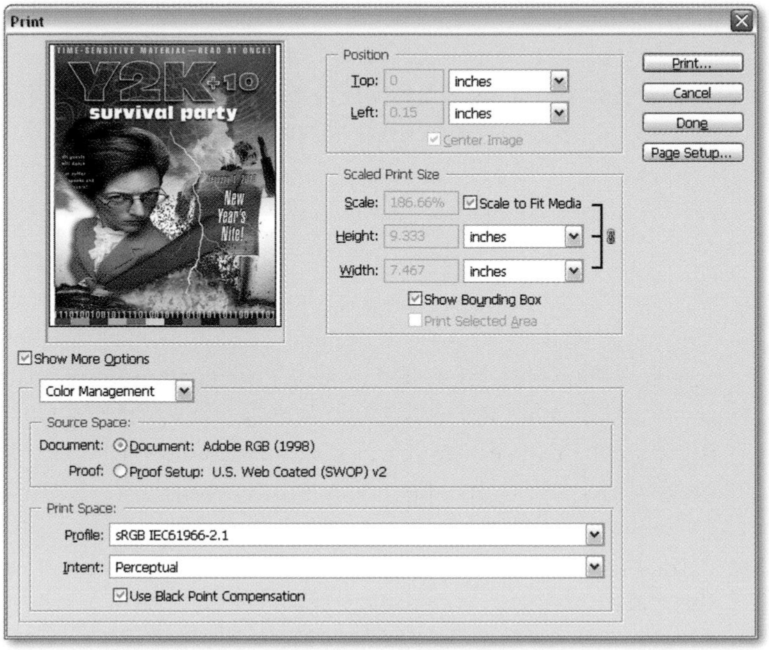

Figure 12-7.

12. ***Click the Print button.*** This closes the print preview window and sends you on to the main **Print** dialog box.

13. ***Verify that the right printer is selected.*** This is mostly a problem on the Mac, but it's worth confirming on the PC, too. Under Windows, check the **Name** option. On the Mac, check the **Printer** option. Both appear in Figure 12-8.

14. ***Display the specific properties for your printer.*** From here on, things vary fairly significantly between the PC and the Mac, as well as from one model of printer to another:

   • Under Windows, click the **Properties** button to display the options defined by the printer's driver software.

   • On the Mac, choose **Print Settings** from the third pop-up menu from the top of the dialog box (the one that initially reads **Copies & Pages**).

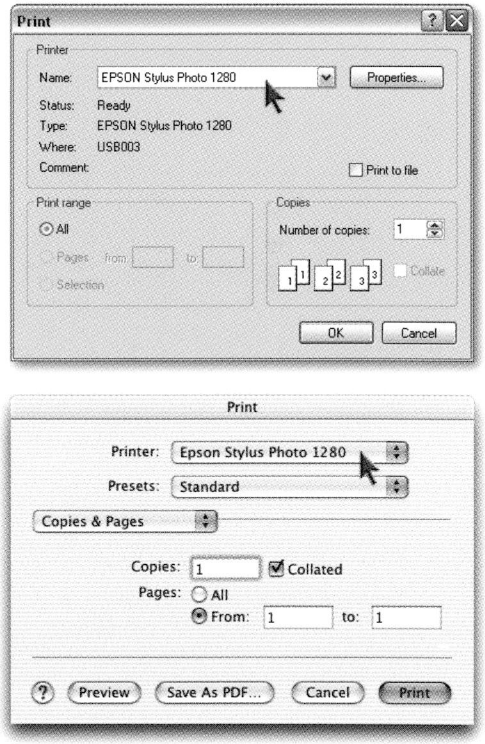

Figure 12-8.

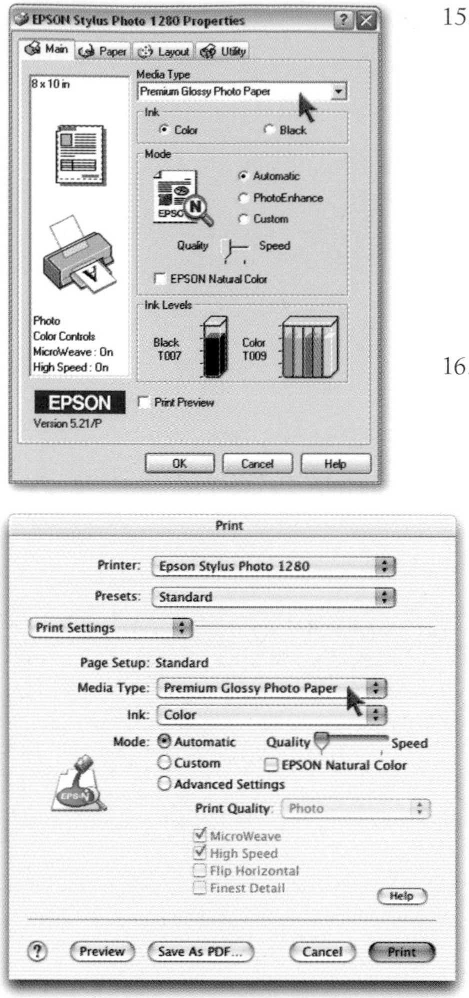

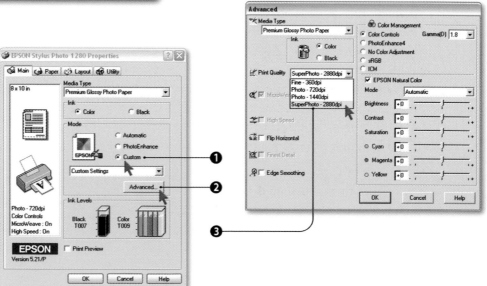

Figure 12-9.

15. *Indicate the kind of paper you have loaded into your printer.* Look for an option called **Media Type** or the like. In my case, I changed Media Type to **Premium Glossy Photo Paper** (see the arrow cursors in the PC and Mac interfaces in Figure 12-9), which happens to be a literal match of the name listed on the paper's original packaging (see the second figure on page 432). If possible, try to find a literal match for your brand of paper as well.

16. *Select the highest print quality for your printer.* This assumes you're printing to photo-grade paper. If not, choose a lower setting. The quality setting can be hard to find, so you may have to do a bit of digging. For example, on the PC, I have to forage through the following options, illustrated by the numbered items in Figure 12-10:

- I first select **Custom** from the **Mode** options (labeled ❶ in Figure 12-10). This gives me access to a more sophisticated set of options.

- Then I click the **Advanced** button (❷) to enter yet another dialog box.

- There, I find the option that I'm looking for, **Print Quality**. I set it to the printer's maximum, **Super-Photo – 2880dpi** (❸ in the figure).

Figure 12-10.

On the Macintosh, I switch from **Automatic** to **Advanced Settings** (labeled ❶ in Figure 12-11). Then I change the **Print Quality** option to **Photo – 2880dpi** (❷).

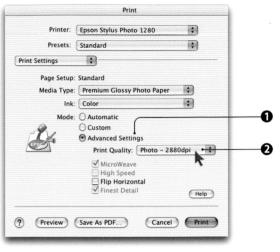

Figure 12-11.

> **PEARL OF WISDOM**
>
> If you have problems finding the print quality option (or its equivalent), consult the documentation that came with your printer. Remember: Choose the highest setting *only* if you're using photo-grade paper. Standard photocopier-grade bond cannot handle that much ink; the high-quality setting will produce a damp, smeared page, thereby resulting in a ruined print and wasted ink.

Once you've selected the right paper and the correct print resolution, all that's left is to select the most accurate means of reproducing the colors.

17. ***Select the best color management method.*** In Step 11, you told Photoshop how to convert the RGB colors in the image to the color space used by the printer. Now you're presented with the trickier proposition of explaining to the printer's software how it should convert colors from the RGB space to CMYK.

Not all printer manufacturers permit you to modify the color management method. And those that do often offer paltry controls. As it turns out, Epson's printer drivers do about the best job of it, as illustrated in Figure 12-12.

• In the **Advanced** dialog box on the PC, I find a series of **Color Management** radio buttons. Most require you to mess with imprecise slider bars and image comparisons. But by selecting **sRGB**, I'm able to identify sRGB as the source space for the color once it leaves Photoshop. From there, it's up to the printing software to do the work. (A second-best solution is to select **ICM**, which uses the color matching software built into the Windows operating system.)

• On the Mac, I chose **Color Management** from the third pop-up menu (labeled ❶ in Figure 12-12), the one that used to say Print Settings. Then I selected the second radio button, **ColorSync** (❷). This enabled Apple's ColorSync color matching software, which is built into OS X and just so happens to be one of the best color management solutions on the planet. If ColorSync isn't available, pick sRGB.

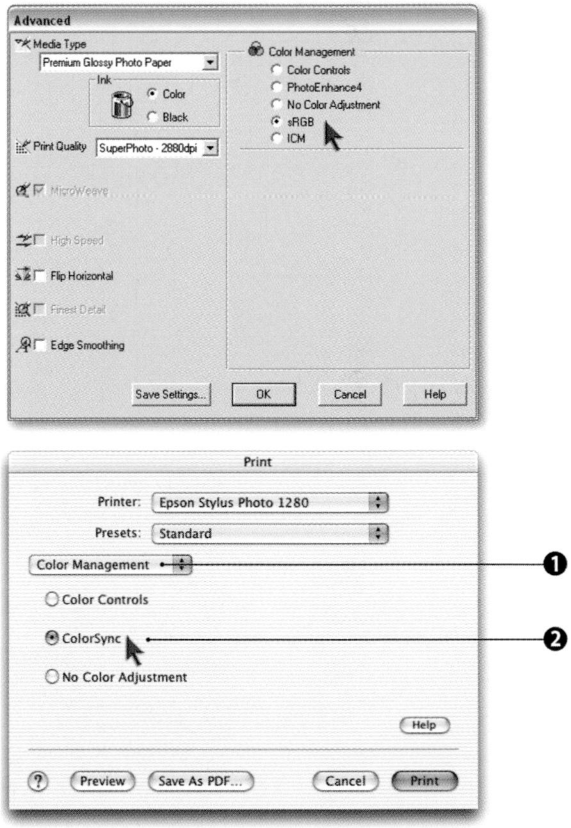

Figure 12-12.

# Quality Comes at a Price

Inkjet printers are cheap, often sold at or below cost. But the *consumables*—the paper and the ink—are expensive, easily outpacing the cost of the hardware after a few hundred prints. Unfortunately, this is one area where it doesn't pay to pinch pennies. Simply put, the consumables dictate the quality of your inkjet output. Throwing money at consumables doesn't necessarily ensure great output, but scrimping guarantees bad output.

Consider the following scenario:

- Of the handful of inkjet devices I own, my current favorite under $1,000 is the Epson Stylus Photo 1280. As I write this, the printer retails for about $400. Given that it can print as many as 2880 dots per inch, that's a heck of a deal.

- The Stylus Photo 1280 requires two ink cartridges, pictured below. The first cartridge holds black ink; the second contains five colors, including two shades of cyan, two shades of magenta, and yellow. (As the reasoning goes, the lighter cyan and magenta better accommodate deep blues, greens, and flesh tones.) Together, the cartridges cost about $60 and last for 45 to 120 letter-sized prints, depending on the quality setting you choose. The higher the setting, the more ink the printer consumes. So the ink alone costs 50¢ to $1.33 per page.

- You can print to regular photocopier-grade paper. But while such paper is inexpensive, it's also porous, sopping up ink like a paper towel. To avoid over-inking, you have to print at low resolutions, so the output tends to look substandard—about as good as a color photo printed in a newspaper.

- To achieve true photo-quality prints that rival those from a commercial film processor, you need to use *photo-grade paper* (or simply *photo paper*), which increases your costs even further. For example, 20 sheets of the stuff in the packet below costs $13.50, or about 67¢ a sheet.

The upshot: a low-quality plain paper print costs about 50 cents; a high-quality photo paper print costs about 2 bucks. Although the latter is roughly four times as expensive, the difference in quality is staggering. The figure below compares details from the two kinds of output magnified to 6 times their printed size. The plain paper image is coarse, riddled with thick printer dots and occasional horizontal scrapes where the paper couldn't hold the ink. Meanwhile, the photo paper image is so smooth, you can clearly make out the image pixels. Where inkjet printing is concerned, paper quality and ink expenditure are the great determining factors.

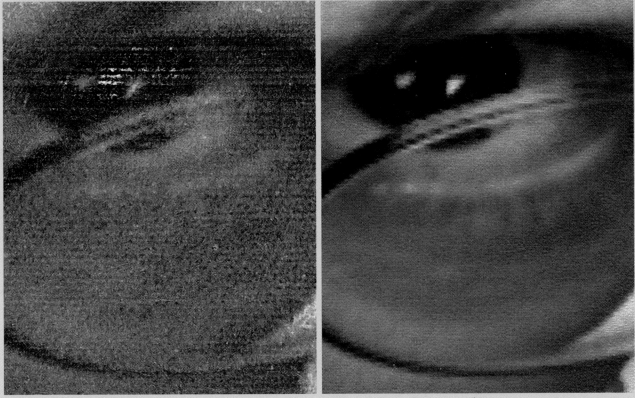

360 dots per inch, plain paper, 50¢                2880 dpi, glossy photo paper, $2⁰⁰

Thanks to the large number of printer vendors, your options may vary significantly in this area. You may even encounter additional options. For example, on the PC, Hewlett-Packard includes an **ICM Method** option (best set to **Host**) and an **ICM Intent** (best set to **Picture**). If none of the options I've mentioned so far is available on your screen, you'll need to experiment to find the settings that work best.

18. ***Save your settings.*** Whether you can save a collection of print settings on the PC depends on your printer software. In the case of my Epson device, I can click a **Save Settings** button in the Advanced dialog box and give the settings a name, such as "Premium hi-res."

    On the Mac, choose **Save As** from the **Presets** pop-up menu near the top of the Print dialog box. The named settings then appear as an option in the Presets pop-up menu.

19. ***Send the print job on its way.*** On the PC, you may have to exit a few dialog boxes to apply your changes. I had to click two **OK** buttons to dig my way back up to the Print dialog box, and then click **OK** again to start the job printing. On the Mac, click the **Print** button.

    If you see a warning about "PostScript specific printing settings," like the one in Figure 12-13, click the **Don't Show Again** check box and then click the **OK** button. Obviously, PostScript options aren't going to work with a non-PostScript printer, which is why we so wisely avoided them.

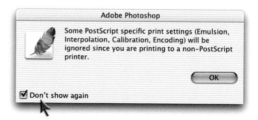

Figure 12-13.

20. ***Wait and compare.*** It takes a long time to print a high-quality image from an inkjet printer, usually several minutes. But thanks to the miracle of background printing, you can continue to use Photoshop and even get a head start on the next exercise. When the print job finishes, compare it to the image on screen. Assuming that your printer is functioning properly (no missing lines, no paper flaws, all inks intact), the colors in the printout should bear a close resemblance to those in the screen image.

But there are always variations. Figure 12-14 shows three versions of the same image printed to photo-grade paper from a Stylus Photo 1280. The only differences are the computer and the method of color management used to print the image.

- While a bit more yellow than the others, the ColorSync image is a very close match to what I saw on my Macintosh screen and most in keeping with what I hoped to achieve with the composition.

- The image printed from Windows using the sRGB setting (pictured second in Figure 12-14) is darker and bluer than the other two. But it also bears the closest resemblance to the image I saw on my PC screen. Therefore, the result is a rousing success.

- I printed the third image using Microsoft's ICM color matching. Although it more closely matches the Macintosh ouput, it strays from its appearance on the PC monitor. Therefore, I would characterize it as the least successful print.

PEARL OF ⬤ WISDOM

If the output doesn't match the screen image to your satisfaction, try experimenting with your printer-specific options (those covered in Steps 14 through 17) until you arrive at a better result. Once you do, write the settings down and use them in the future.

Mac output, ColorSync (yellow)    Windows output, sRGB (dark, blue)  Windows output, ICM (cyan, blue)

Figure 12-14.

# Preparing a CMYK File for Commercial Reproduction

We now move from the realm of personal printers into the larger world of commercial prepress. The *prepress* process involves outputting film that is burned to metal *plates* (or output directly from computer to plates), which are then loaded onto a high-capacity printing press for mass reproduction. (Hence the *pre* in *pre*press.) Each page of a full-color document must be separated onto four plates, one for each of the four *process colors*: cyan, magenta, yellow, and black. By converting an image to CMYK in advance, you perform the separation in advance. All the page-layout or other print application has to do is send each color channel to a different plate, and the image is ready to output.

Converting an image from RGB to CMYK in Photoshop is as simple as choosing Image→Mode→CMYK Color. This one command separates a three-channel image into the four process colors. (For insight into how this happens, read the sidebar "Why (and How) Three Channels Become Four" on page 444.) Converting the image properly, however, is another matter. If you don't take time to *characterize* the output device—that is, explain to Photoshop how the prepress device renders cyan, magenta, yellow, and black inks—the colors you see on screen will not match those in the final output.

Photoshop gives you two ways to characterize a CMYK device:

- Ask your commercial print shop if they have a ColorSync or ICM *profile* for the press they'll be using to output your document. (They might also call it an ICC profile—same diff for our purposes.) Such profiles are entirely cross-platform, so the same file will work on either the PC or the Mac. Just make sure that the filename ends with the three-letter extension ICC or ICM. You can then load the profile into Photoshop.

- Wing it. Every print house should be able to profile its presses. But you'd be surprised how many won't have the vaguest idea what you're talking about when you request a profile, or will proffer an excuse about why profiling isn't an option. In this case, you'll have to create a profile on your own through trial and error. It's not the optimal solution, but I've done it more often than not and I generally manage to arrive at moderately predictable output.

The following exercise explores both options. You'll learn how to load a CMYK profile, should you be so lucky as to procure one. I'll also show you how to edit the CMYK options to create your own profile. And finally, you'll see how to convert the image to CMYK and save it in a format that either QuarkXPress or Adobe InDesign can read.

1. **Open the test image.** For consistency's sake, we'll be using the same composition we used in the previous exercise. So open *Y2K+10 invite.psd* from the *Lesson 12* folder in *Lesson Files-PScs 1on1*. Make sure to open the original PSD file, not the TIFF file that you saved in Step 3 on page 426.

2. **Choose the Color Settings command.** On the PC, choose **Edit→Color Settings**. On the Mac, choose the **Color Settings** command from the **Photoshop** menu. Or press Ctrl+Shift+K (⌘-Shift-K on the Mac). Photoshop displays the Color Settings dialog box, pictured in all its gruesomeness in Figure 12-15.

3. **Turn off the Advanced Mode option.** If the **Advanced Mode** check box in the top-left corner of the dialog box is turned on, then click it to turn it off. Although not an essential step, this will help to simplify things a bit by reducing the number of options shown inside the dialog box.

4. **Load the CMYK profile provided by your commercial print house.** In this exercise, your print house happens to be the highly esteemed and completely fictional Prints-R-Us. Click the words **U.S. Web Coated (SWOP) v2** to the right of the first **CMYK** option to display a pop-up menu of CMYK profiles. As in Figure 12-16, choose **Load CMYK** to load an ICC profile from disk. Locate the file called *Prints-R-Us profile.icc* in the *Lesson 12* folder in *Lesson Files-PScs 1on1*. Then click the **Load** button to make the profile part of Photoshop's color settings.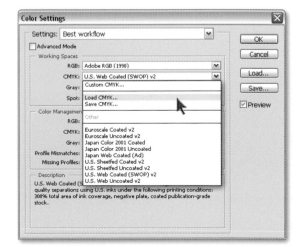

5. **Click the OK button.** Photoshop closes the Color Settings dialog box and accepts your new CMYK settings.

6. **Turn off the Text Elements layer set.** Go to the **Layers** palette and click the 👁 icon in front of the **Text Elements** folder to hide the text layers. You'll have an easier time judging this image if the distracting text layers are out of the way.

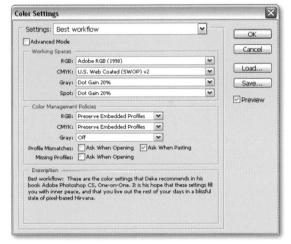

Figure 12-15.

Figure 12-16.

7. ***Choose the CMYK Color command.*** Choose **Image→Mode→ CMYK Color**. When Photoshop asks you if you want to flatten the image, as in Figure 12-17, click the **Flatten** button to reduce the image to a single layer. Blend modes are calculated differently in CMYK than in RGB, so retaining layers can result in severe color shifts. Flattening isn't always the ideal solution, but in this case, there's no harm, so we might as well.

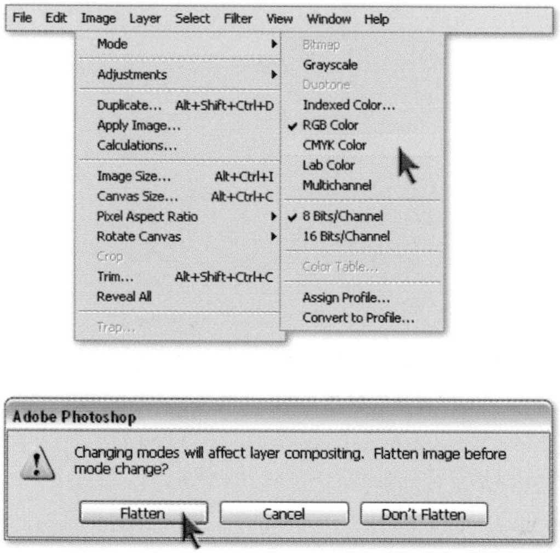

Figure 12-17.

8. ***Save the image under a new name.*** You should never save over your original layered image, and you should never *ever* save a CMYK image over the original RGB. CMYK is a more limited color space than RGB, less suited to general image editing. So choose **File→Save As** and do the following:

   • In the Save As dialog box, choose **TIFF** from the **Format** pop-up menu. TIFF is a wonderful format to use when handing off CMYK files because it enjoys wide support and prints without incident.

   • Name the image **Y2K+10 CMYK.tif**.

   • Turn on **ICC Profile: Prints-R-Us profile**. (On the Mac, the check box reads **Embed Color Profile: Prints-R-Us profile**).

   • Click the **Save** button.

   • Inside the **TIFF Options** dialog box, turn on **LZW** under **Image Compression**. Every once in a while, a print house will balk at this setting, but it's rare. And they can always open the file and resave it with this option off.

- Select the platform that your print house will be using from the **Byte Order** options.

- Click the **OK** button to save the file.

9. ***Hand off the TIFF file to your commercial print house.*** The only way to judge the success of the profile supplied to you by the print house is to actually put it to use. When you get the printed output back, you can decide whether changes are in order or not. For purposes of this exercise, we'll imagine that the overly light Figure 12-18 represents the final output provided to us by Prints-R-Us.

10. ***Compare the output to the CMYK file on screen.*** To see how the two images compare for me, look at Figure 12-19. Fortunately, the colors in the printed image do not differ radically from those in the screen version. However, there is a big difference in brightness. The printed image is significantly lighter and the shadows are weak. We're also missing some of the richness in the reds of the flesh tones and the lava. In fact, the warm colors in the output suffer from a slightly yellow cast. These must all be resolved.

Figure 12-18.

The CMYK output          The CMYK image as it looks on screen

Figure 12-19.

To fix the CMYK image, you need to modify the Prints-R-Us CMYK profile. The best way to judge the results of our modifications is to apply them on the fly to the open image and compare the resulting screen image to the output. This means releasing the image from the grips of the existing CMYK profile. Admittedly, it's not a particularly intuitive step, but it's a necessary one. So here we go.

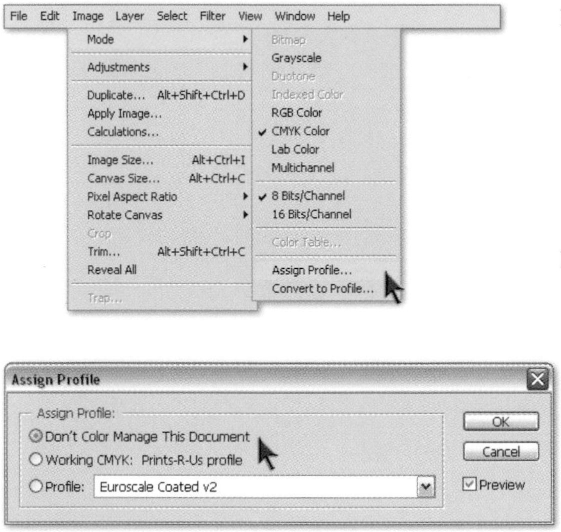

Figure 12-20.

11. ***Disable color management for the current document.*** Choose **Image→Mode→Assign Profile**. Then select the **Don't Color Manage This Document** option, as in Figure 12-20, and click the **OK** button. From now on, the open image, *Y2K+10 CMYK.tif*, will respond dynamically to the changes you make to the CMYK color profile.

12. ***Again choose the Color Settings command.*** Remember, the command is under the **Edit** menu on the PC and under the **Photoshop** menu on the Mac. Or simplify your life and press Ctrl+Shift+K (⌘-Shift-K). Photoshop redisplays the **Color Settings** dialog box.

Be sure that the dialog box doesn't entirely block your view of the image window. If that means dragging the dialog box off screen so only the Working Spaces options are visible, so be it. You can also zoom out from the image by pressing Ctrl-minus (⌘-minus on the Mac) to view more of your image at a time.

13. ***Confirm that the Preview check box is turned on.*** Your job will be to make the screen image look like the CMYK output. After all, the CMYK output is the accurate representation of the printer's CMYK space; if the screen image doesn't match, then Photoshop's CMYK display space must be wrong. Only with the **Preview** check box on can you judge the effects of the changes you're about to make.

Note that I'm *not* suggesting that you somehow adjust the brightness and contrast of your monitor to make it match the CMYK output. That would alter everything you see on screen, inside Photoshop and out, and it wouldn't solve your problem. An incorrect adjustment to your monitor would inform your impression of future RGB images and thus further compound your problems. The aim here is to make sure Photoshop's understanding of the CMYK space matches that of the printer, and nothing more.

14. *Choose the Custom CMYK option.* Click the words **Prints-R-Us profile** to the right of the first **CMYK** option and choose **Custom CMYK**, as in Figure 12-21. Photoshop displays the little-known **Custom CMYK** dialog box, which allows you to change how the program converts colors to CMYK and displays them on screen.

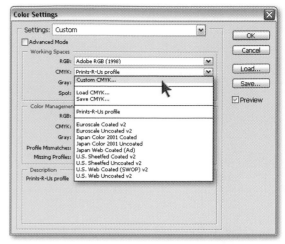

Figure 12-21.

Although I don't want to engender fear of this dialog box, I caution you to regard most of its controls as off limits. This is especially true of the **Separation Options** at the bottom of the dialog box, which are based on attributes of the printing press that you could not possibly know unless you were to use it yourself or interview someone who does. (For those who are curious, I discuss a couple of these options, **GCR** and **Total Ink Limit**, in the sidebar "Why (and How) Three Channels Become Four" on page 444.) In fact, with the exception of **Name**, there's really only one subjective option in the dialog box: **Dot Gain**.

15. *Adjust the Dot Gain value.* With very few exceptions, commercial presses use small circles of colored ink, called *halftone dots,* to impart different shades of color. Dark areas get big dots, light areas get small dots. Illustrated in Figure 12-22, the term *dot gain* refers to how much the halftone dots grow when they're absorbed into the paper.

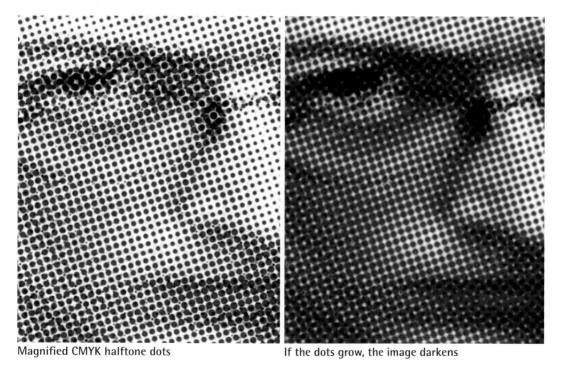

Magnified CMYK halftone dots          If the dots grow, the image darkens

Figure 12-22.

The Prints-R-Us profile includes a **Dot Gain** value of 35 percent, which means the print house anticipates that its halftone dots will grow 35 percent in size when printed on a specific grade of paper. Obviously, there's a mistake here; if the dot gain was really 35 percent, the image would tend to print dark, not overly light, as it did for us. So the current Dot Gain value is overcompensating.

The rules of thumb for adjusting the Dot Gain:

- If the printed image looks lighter than your screen display, as in this example, nudge the Dot Gain value down by pressing the ↓ key.

- If the printed image appears darker, raise the value by pressing the ↑ key.

Small changes result in significant adjustments, so give the screen time to refresh between each press of the ↑ or ↓ key. I find that a value of 22 percent provides a pretty close match.

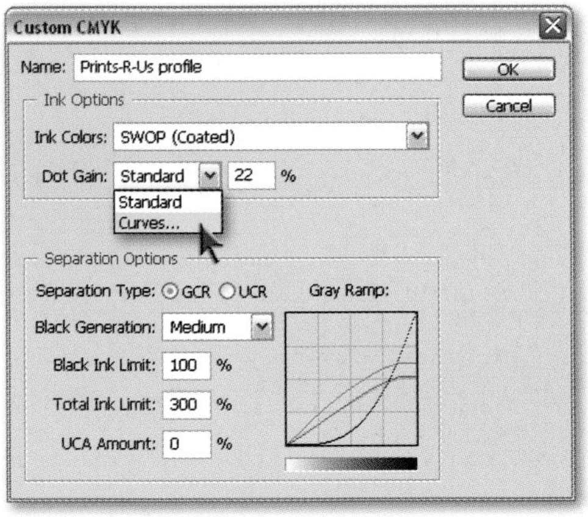

16. ***Choose Curves from the Dot Gain pop-up menu.*** The problem with adjusting the Dot Gain value is that it lightens or darkens all color channels at once. So while the brightness of the screen image roughly matches the output in Figure 12-18, the reds don't appear washed out enough. To adjust each channel independently, choose the **Curves** option from the **Dot Gain** pop-up menu (see Figure 12-23). Photoshop responds with the **Dot Gain Curves** dialog box.

17. ***Adjust the Dot Gain Curves values for each channel.*** If the **All Same** option on the right side of the Dot Gain Curves dialog box is checked, turn it off. Use the **Cyan**, **Magenta**, **Yellow**, and **Black** options to switch between the four color channels and modify their luminosity values independently. This lets you effectively correct the colors of the CMYK screen display one ink at a time.

To keep things as simple as possible—and by my reckoning, we could dearly use a bit of simplicity right about now—I modified only the **50%** value for each channel. As shown in Figure 12-24 on the facing page, I lowered the values for the Cyan, Magenta, Yellow, and Black channels to 70, 66, 70, and 72.

Figure 12-23.

You may well ask how I arrived at these values. To which I would answer— as I so often do—trial and error. But to shed some light on my reasoning: Lower values lighten the screen image to bring it more in line with the CMYK output. Pressing ↓ lowers a value in increments of 0.1 percent; more useful, Shift+↓ lowers a value by a full 1 percent. Using Shift+↓, I lowered the Cyan and Magenta values by roughly equal amounts (18 and 19 percent, respectively). I lowered the Yellow and Black values by smaller amounts (15 and 13, respectively) to keep more yellows and blacks in the image, which I found necessary to match the color balance of the output.

18. **Click the OK button three times in a row.** This exits the Dot Gain Curves, Custom CMYK, and Color Settings dialog boxes and updates the definition of the Prints-R-Us CMYK profile.

19. **Undo the last two operations.** Before you can apply the new color profile, you must first undo the effects of the previous one. So press Ctrl+Alt+Z (⌘-Option-Z on the Mac) twice in a row to undo the operations performed in Steps 11 and 7, respectively, first reinstating CMYK color management and then restoring the layered RGB image.

Be sure to press Ctrl+Alt+Z (⌘-Option-7), and *not* Ctrl+Z (⌘-Z)! The latter will undo all the work that you've achieved in the Color Settings dialog box, everything from Step 12 through and including Step 18. If you do accidentally press Ctrl+Z, press Ctrl+Z again to restore the color settings, and *then* press Ctrl+Alt+Z twice.

20. **Again choose the CMYK Color command.** Choose **Image→ Mode→CMYK Color** and click the **Flatten** button when asked to do so. The result doesn't look all that different than the CMYK image we created in Step 7. But now that you've improved the accuracy of the CMYK color space, you can trust what you see on screen a bit more.

21. **Save the improved CMYK image.** Because you renamed the image *Y2K+10 CMYK.tif* back in Step 8, there's no harm in saving over it. Choose **File→Save** or press Ctrl+S (or ⌘-S) to update the file on disk.

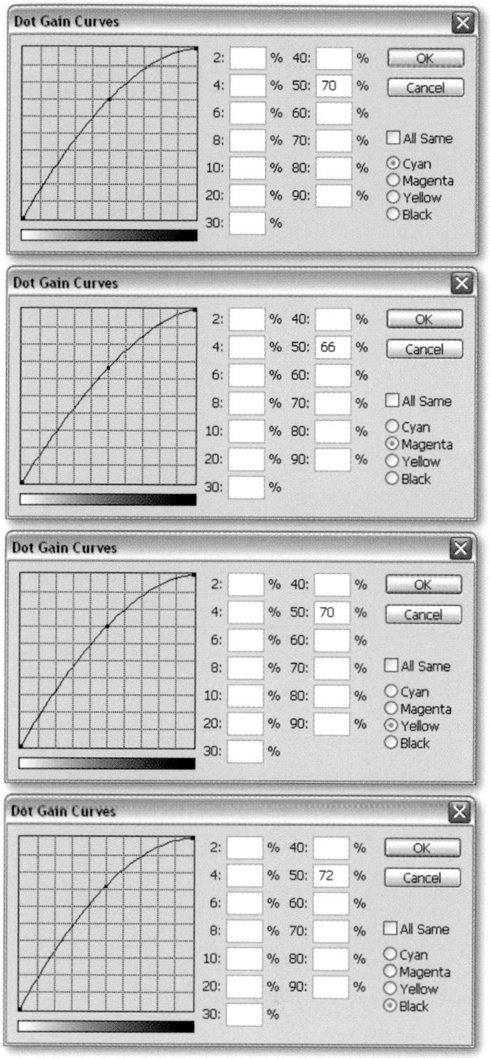

Figure 12-24.

# Why (and How) Three Channels Become Four

If this were a perfect world, cyan, magenta, and yellow would be all the colors you need to print an RGB image. But alas, the world is perfect only in its lack of perfection. Thus, it's the job of the key color, black, to set the world straight. In fact, you could argue that the fourth channel, Black, is the most important ink in CMYK output.

In the world of RGB, black exists naturally; in CMYK, it has to be generated. Let's start with RGB. Here, black is the default color, the one that appears if no other color is present. As pixels are turned on, the black goes away. As illustrated in the figure directly below, light pixels in the Red channel add red, those in the Green channel add green, and those in the Blue channel add blue. Any one channel is very dark on its own; only by combining can they overcome the darkness, as the middle and bottom rows of the figure show.

By contrast, color printing is about overcoming the lightness. In the collection of images below this column, we see the results of converting the RGB channels from the previous figure into cyan, magenta, yellow, and black using the very same conversion table that you created in "Preparing a CMYK File for Commercial Reproduction" (page 438). Assuming you output to white paper, the default color of printing is white, and therefore it's the job of the inks to make the white go away. The channels start out very light, as in the top row of the figure; but as one layer of ink mixes with another, the photograph becomes progressively darker, as in the middle and bottom rows. (To help you navigate through the figure, samples with three or more inks include a black outline.)

The CMY channels are derived in large part from their RGB complements. But because every printer subscribes to

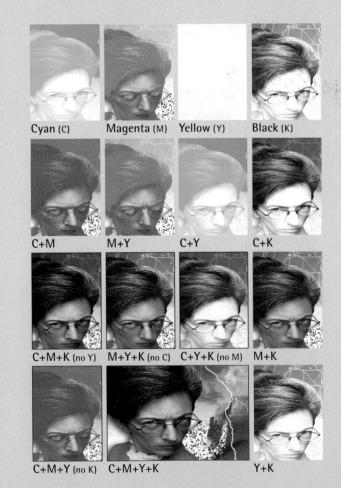

Red

Green

Blue

Red + Green

Green + Blue

Blue + Red

Red + Green + Blue

Cyan (C)

Magenta (M)

Yellow (Y)

Black (K)

C+M

M+Y

C+Y

C+K

C+M+K (no Y)

M+Y+K (no C)

C+Y+K (no M)

M+K

C+M+Y (no K)

C+M+Y+K

Y+K

different standards, there is no one hard-and-fast formula. Rather, channels are mixed together in varying degrees according to the recipe outlined in the conversion table. So for example, the Cyan channel is mostly a duplicate of the Red channel, but it also mixes in bits of the Green and Blue channels to account for the idiosyncrasies of a given press.

Looking at the figure below, however, you might find this hard to believe. The top row shows grayscale versions of the RGB channels; the middle row shows their CMY complements. The CMY channels bear passing resemblance to the ones above them, but it's as if the darkest levels have been replaced with light gray. And that's precisely what has happened. Photoshop generates the contents of the Black channel by leeching shadows from the Cyan, Magenta, and Yellow channels. When we add the Black channel, as in the bottom row of the figure, the

CMY channels more closely match the brightness of the RGB channels in the top row. (Yellow + Black appears lighter than Blue only because yellow is such a light ink.)

The most popular method for transferring dark pixels to the Black channel is called *gray component replacement*, or *GCR*. The idea is that paper can absorb only so much ink, after which point the ink begins to smear. Most presses subscribe to a *total ink limit* of around 300 percent, meaning that the percentages of cyan, magenta, yellow, and black ink can add up to no more than 300. GCR makes sure the total ink limit never goes higher, even in the darkest shadows in the image. Photoshop steals the shadows from the CMY channels, puts them in the Black channel, and then darkens the old CMY shadows until the total ink limit is met. And so it is that black restores the darkness that is at the heart of the RGB image.

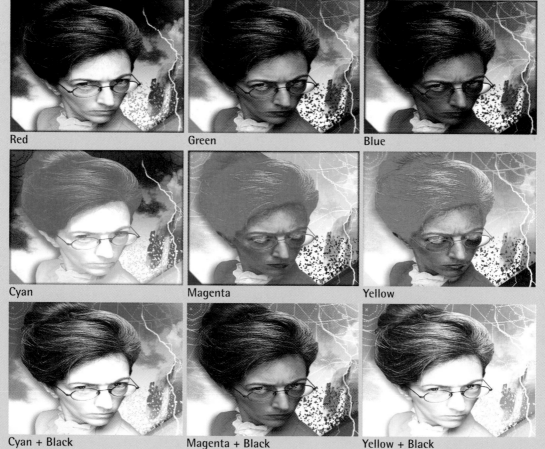

Red

Green

Blue

Cyan

Magenta

Yellow

Cyan + Black

Magenta + Black

Yellow + Black

22. ***Hand off the revised file to your commercial print house.*** This time, the image prints much more accurately. In fact, as demonstrated in Figure 12-25, it's difficult to tell the CMYK output from the CMYK image we see on screen. The reds are still a tad weaker than I'd like, but the output is close enough to qualify as a successful conversion. (For proof beyond a shadow of a doubt, compare Figure 12-25 to Figure 12-19 on page 439.)

The new & improved CMYK output…           better matches the image on screen

Figure 12-25.

Mind you, it's not always possible to create such accurate color conversions by winging it with Photoshop's Dot Gain controls. But given the uniformity of process inks and the fact that most domestic presses are calibrated to relatively common standards, it's worth a try. And there's nothing so empowering as successfully tweaking Photoshop's color settings so that your images output reliably to a commercial printing press.

# Packing Multiple Pictures onto a Single Page

Our final exercise is a cakewalk compared to the others in this lesson. It shows you how to combine multiple copies of one or more images onto a single page using File→Automate→Picture Package. This command was originally designed to accommodate portrait photographers who routinely need to print common picture sizes onto cut sheets that they can sell to their clients. But over the past few years, the command has increased in functionality to the point that I for one use it habitually. Whether you want to assemble quick-and-dirty proof sheets or make the most of expensive inkjet paper, Picture Package does a superb job of fitting differently sized images onto a page—which is precisely what we'll do in the following exercise.

1. **Open a photographic image.** For this, our swan song exercise, we'll create a proof sheet of my various children starting with the mirthful Sammy. Enter the folder called *All My Children* inside the *Lesson 12* folder inside *Lesson Files-PScs 1on1*. Then open the photograph *Youngest son.jpg*, pictured in Figure 12-26. The image has been cropped and sized to 3 by 4 inches at 300 pixels per inch. But as you'll see, Picture Package doesn't give a darn about the size of the original photograph; it resamples the image to whatever size you specify in the following steps.

Figure 12-26.

2. **Choose the Picture Package command.** Choose **File→Automate→ Picture Package**. The job of the Picture Package command is to import multiple copies of an image into a new document. In fact, if you watch closely, you can see Photoshop create that new document before displaying the **Picture Package** dialog box. The command then offers to arrange two 5 by 7-inch copies of the photograph, as in Figure 12-27.

Figure 12-27.

3. *Specify the Page Size.* At first, Picture Package lets you select from three **Page Size** options, including letter and tabloid formats. (You can create others by clicking the Edit Layout button.) Assuming you'll be printing to a letter-sized page, select **8.0 x 10.0 in**.

4. *Select a Layout option.* Select the number of photos you want to print and the size of those photos from the **Layout** menu. I chose **(1)5x7 (2)3.5x5** to get a total of three photos, as in Figure 12-28. Notice that Photoshop automatically orients the images to fit as many on a page as possible. The assumption is that you'll slice apart the photos and turn them any which way you want after the page is printed.

5. *Raise the Resolution value.* By default, the **Resolution** value is set to 72 pixels per inch, which is so ludicrously low as to verge on bizarre. I suggest raising the value to 300 ppi.

6. *Set the color mode to RGB.* Assuming that you'll be printing to an inkjet printer or some other personal color output device, leave the **Mode** option set to **RGB Color**.

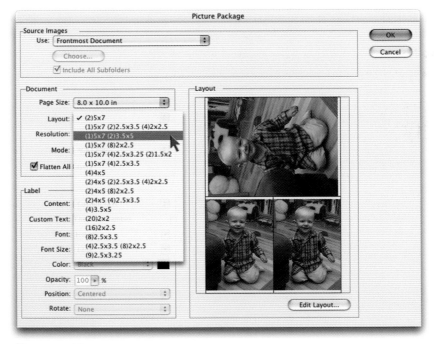

Figure 12-28.

7. *Set the Label options.* Featured in Figure 12-29, the **Label** options in the bottom left quadrant of the dialog box permit you to add captions or copyright statements to your images.

- Start by selecting an option from the **Content** pop-up menu. The **Custom Text** setting adds whatever text you enter into the option below. **Filename** lists the name of the file on disk. The others reference metadata entries created using **File→File Info** (see Lesson 1, "Using Metadata," page 17). In Figure 12-29, I selected **Title**, which grabs the Document Title text from the File Info dialog box. But you can select any option you want.

- To streamline the command's performance, Picture Package permits you just three **Font** choices. For legibility's sake, I'd choose **Arial** on the PC or **Helvetica** on the Mac.

- Leave the **Font Size**, **Color**, and **Opacity** options set to their defaults (12 point, black, and 100 percent).

- Set the **Position** to **Bottom Left** and leave **Rotate** set to **None**. As you'll see, this makes it easier to reposition the text so that it doesn't overlap the images.

Note that Photoshop makes no attempt to preview your labels on the right side of the dialog box. But not to worry; the labels will appear when you click the OK button.

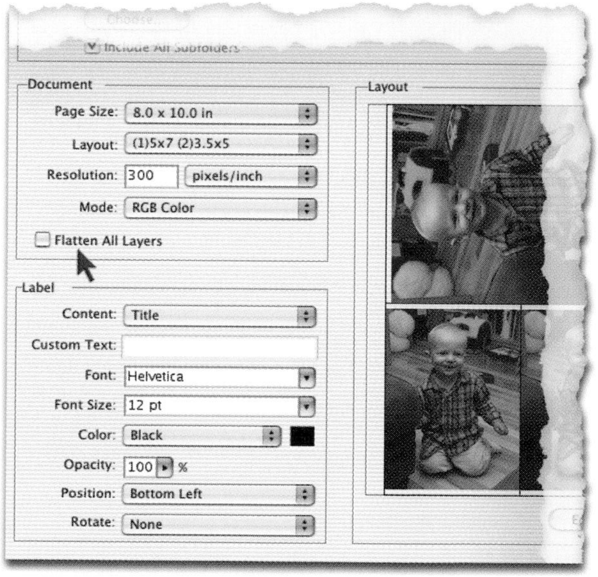

Figure 12-29.

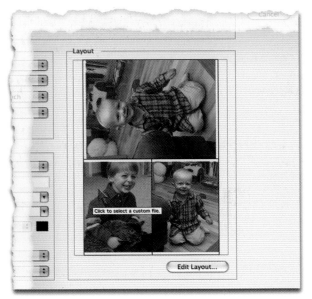

Figure 12-30.

8. ***Turn off the Flatten All Layers check box.*** If you ask me, labels are a wonderful idea with a very odd implementation. Regardless of which Position option you select, Photoshop places the labels directly in front of the images, thus obscuring some portion of the photograph. (The labels aren't intended as captions but as copy protection.) If you want to be able to move the text off the images, you must keep all the text layers intact by turning off **Flatten All Layers**.

9. ***Load a second photograph.*** By default, the Picture Package command repeats a single photograph multiple times. But you can switch out a photo if you prefer. Click the lower-left image in the preview area, as indicated by the position of the arrow cursor in Figure 12-30. An open dialog box will appear. Navigate to the *All My Children* folder inside *Lesson 12* inside *Lesson Files-PScs 1on1*. Then open the file named *Eldest son.jpg* to load a picture of Max.

10. ***Load a third photo.*** Just to round things out, let's load a picture of the newest addition to the household. Click the lower-right picture of Sammy. Then open the image named *The baby.jpg* from the same *All My Children* folder. Honestly, have you ever seen anything so adorable in all your life?

11. ***Click the OK button.*** Photoshop begins the automated process of opening files, scaling them, rotating them if necessary, and pasting them into the layered composition. Whatever you do, don't click anything as these operations are happening or you're liable to interrupt the process. Just wait until you see Photoshop add the final image—the silver G5 Mac—to the composition, as in Figure 12-31.

12. ***Link the text layers and modify them.*** At first, you may think your text layers didn't make it. But if you look closely, you'll see that they overlap the lower-left corners of their photos. Fortunately, because the text is housed on independent layers, you can move and edit them.

- To adjust all text layers at once, link them together. Click one of the text layers in the **Layers** palette to make it active. Unlink it's image layer by clicking the 🔗 icon in front of the image layer name. Then link the other two text layers by clicking in the boxes just to the left of each of them, thus adding 🔗 icons.

- Press the Ctrl key (⌘ on the Mac) and drag inside the image window to move the linked layers.

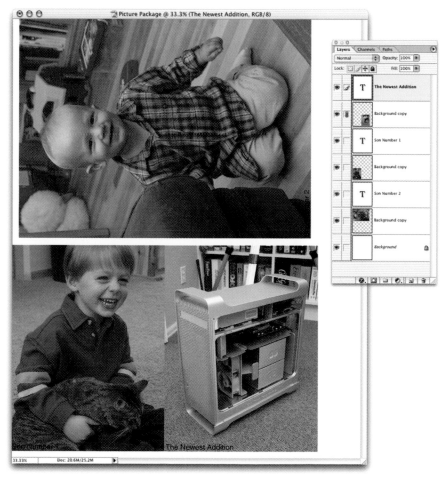

Figure 12-31.

- To change the font and size of the text layers as I've done in Figure 12-32, press T to switch to the type tool. Then press Shift and choose the desired formatting attribute from the options bar at the top of the screen.

You may have to adjust the position of one or two text layers by themselves as well. To do so, unlink the layer you want to move by Alt-clicking (or Option-clicking) its ✍ icon in the Layers palette. Then Ctrl-drag (or ⌘-drag) the text to a different location. I also moved the images apart from each other to give them a little breathing room, again by Ctrl-dragging (or ⌘-dragging) them.

13. ***Save the composition.*** Press Ctrl+S (⌘-S on the Mac) or choose **File→Save**. Because the composition hasn't been saved before, Photoshop displays the Save As dialog box. Choose **Photoshop** from the **Format** pop-up menu. Name the image "The New Generation. psd" and click the **Save** button.

The composition is now ready for you to print to an inkjet printer or other device as outlined in the exercise "Printing to an Inkjet Printer," which begins on page 425.

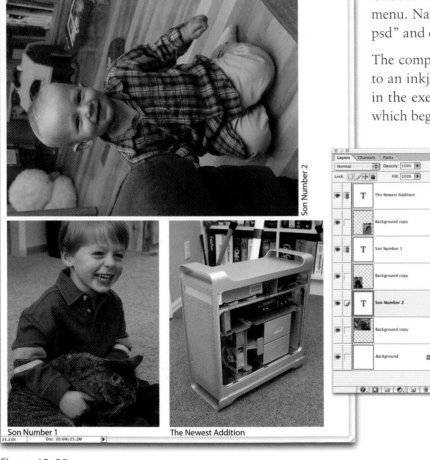

Figure 12-32.

# WHAT DID YOU LEARN?

Match the key concept in the numbered list below with the letter
of the phrase that best describes it. Answers appear upside-down
at the bottom of the page.

## Key Concepts

1. Output
2. Subtractive primaries
3. Color separation
4. Print with Preview
5. Photo-grade paper
6. sRGB
7. Commercial prepress
8. Color profile
9. Color Settings
10. Dot gain
11. Gray component replacement
12. Picture Package

## Descriptions

A. A bit of code that describes a specific flavor of RGB or CMYK that is uniquely applicable to a display or print environment.

B. The most popular method for transferring dark pixels from the Cyan, Magenta, and Yellow channels to the Black channel, thus producing rich, volumetric shadows.

C. The best way to print images from Photoshop, this command lets you scale an image on the page and adjust the color management.

D. The output that occurs before a document is loaded onto a professional printing press for mass reproduction.

E. The act of preparing an image for mass reproduction, usually as a CMYK document.

F. This command combines multiple copies of one or more images into a single document so you can print them to a single sheet of paper.

G. The command that defines the RGB and CMYK color spaces employed by Photoshop.

H. A printing process that outputs each of the CMYK color channels to independent plates so that they can be loaded with different inks.

I. The degree to which professionally output halftone dots grow when they are absorbed by a sheet of printed paper.

J. A standardized color space embraced by consumer-level hardware, including nearly all brands of inkjet printers.

K. Cyan, magenta, and yellow, each of which absorb light when printed on paper and mix to form progressively darker colors.

L. A variety of glossy or matte-finished paper that holds lots of ink, allowing you to print extremely high-resolution images.

## Answers

1E, 2K, 3H, 4C, 5L, 6J, 7D, 8A, 9G, 10I, 11B, 12F

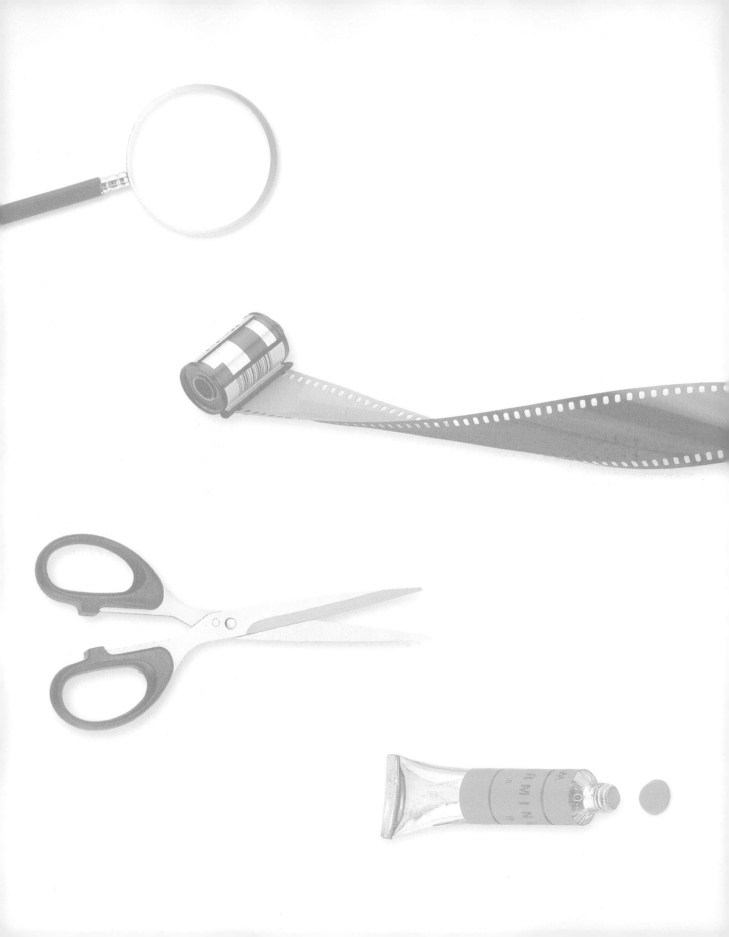

# INDEX

# C

## W

wand tool (*see* magic wand tool)
Warp Text command,  369
white arrow tool,  125
white balance,  83
    (*see also* Video Lesson 3 on the CD)
White Balance option (camera raw
        files),  83
window controls,  9
windows, arranging,  38
Wood burn gradient,  80
workspace, creating and saving,  10

## X

X-ray invert gradient,  80

## Z

zooming in/out,  4
    with magnifying glass,  4
    (*see also* Video Lesson 1 on the CD)

# Master the techniques behind the art

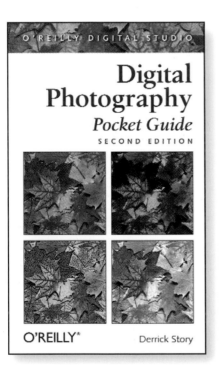